British Social
Attitudes
the
7th report

British Social Attitudes
the
7th report

Edited by
Roger Jowell
Sharon Witherspoon
& Lindsay Brook
with Bridget Taylor

Gower

SOCIAL & COMMUNITY
SCPR
PLANNING RESEARCH

Published by
Gower Publishing Company Limited,
Gower House,
Croft Road,
Aldershot,
Hants GU11 3HR
England

Gower Publishing Company,
Old Post Road,
Brookfield,
Vermont 05036,
USA

British Library Cataloguing in Publication Data

British social attitudes: the 7th report
  1. Public opinion — Great Britain   2. Great Britain — Social conditions
  —1945–
  I. Jowell, Roger   II. Witherspoon, Sharon   III. Brook, Lindsay
  IV. Taylor, Bridget
  941.085′8   HD400.P8

ISSN 0267 6869
ISBN 0566 05840 5
ISBN 0566 05844 8 (Pbk)

Typeset in Great Britain by ATSS Ltd, Stowmarket, Suffolk.
Printed in Great Britain by Woolnough Bookbinding, Irthlingborough, Northants.

Contents

CHAPTER 3. WOMEN AND THE FAMILY
by Jacqueline Scott **51**

CHAPTER 4. LIVING UNDER THREAT
by Ken Young **77**

CHAPTER 5. AIDS AND THE MORAL CLIMATE
by Kaye Wellings and Jane Wadsworth **109**

CHAPTER 6. SELF-EMPLOYMENT AND
THE ENTERPRISE CULTURE
by David G. Blanchflower and Andrew J. Oswald **127**

CHAPTER 7. RECIPES FOR HEALTH
by Aubrey Sheiham, Michael Marmot, Bridget Taylor
and Andrew Brown **145**

CHAPTER 8. INDIVIDUALISM
by John Rentoul **167**

CHAPTER 9. THE NORTHERN IRISH DIMENSION
by John Curtice and Tony Gallagher **183**

Introduction

The longevity of this series – started in 1983 and still thriving – owes much to the steadfast support it has received from its principal funders, the Sainsbury Family Charitable Trusts. Since they took over the lion's share of its funding in 1984, they have been generous both with their financial support and, above all, with their time, consideration and guidance. We are extremely grateful to the trustees and the directorate for their continued confidence.

A good deal of funding for the series now comes from other sources too, principally central government. But there is no doubt that *core funding* from a 'disinterested' source such as the Trusts remains an important element in the success and influence of the series. It enables the investigators (not the funders) to determine the coverage, the questions and the interpretation of results without fear or favour, helping to ensure not only that the series continues to be independent and impartial, but also that it is *seen* to be so among all shades of opinion.

The aim of this volume, like that of its six annual predecessors, is to chart the territory covered by the latest survey and to take a first look at selected findings. We do not attempt here to undertake comprehensive or definitive analyses, leaving those tasks to be performed (in less haste) by the wider social science community. The primary role we set for ourselves each year is to bring out the report and deposit a well-documented dataset (at the ESRC Data Archive) in good enough time for others to peruse or use it as they wish. Once again we are fortunate as editors in having such an impressive group of commentators this year to describe and interpret a fascinating set of findings.

Through SCPR's links with Nuffield College Oxford, dating back to 1982, the *British Social Attitudes* series continues to have close associations with the *British General Election Study* series (see Heath *et al*, forthcoming). Now a new Joint Unit for the Study of Social Trends (JUSST) has been set up by SCPR and Nuffield College to strengthen these links. The Joint Unit has been granted long-term funds by the Economic and Social Research Council and has been awarded the status of an ESRC Research Centre. One of its primary aims is to improve and help to standardise key measures of social and political attitudes in Britain. Work has already started on a series of methodological experiments which will, we hope, feed into future studies.

In addition, links between this series and other similar series abroad continue to be fostered: the number of national teams in the *International Social Survey Programme* (ISSP) has now risen to 14. We reported on some of the early findings from this series in our *Special International Report* last year. Since then a new volume (Becker *et al*, 1990) has appeared, covering further ground. With 14 annual national surveys (in Australia, Austria, Hungary, Republic of Ireland, Israel, Italy, Netherlands, New Zealand, Norway, Philippines, Soviet Union, UK, USA and West Germany), each containing an agreed module of questions on a rotating set of topics, the dataset produced each year is immensely rich and interesting. Our continued participation in this series is now assured, thanks to ESRC funding.

Nearer home, this is the first volume to contain findings from Northern Ireland (see Chapter 9). Although part of the UK, of course, Northern Ireland is routinely excluded from most supposedly 'national' survey series, including – until 1989 – this one. The omission was rectified through joint funding for a linked *Northern Ireland Social Attitudes* survey (of around 900 respondents) for three years from the Nuffield Foundation and the Central Community Relations Unit in Northern Ireland. In collaboration with colleagues at the Policy Research Institute (at Queen's and Ulster universities) and at the Policy Planning and Research Unit (PPRU, Stormont), we developed a separate but overlapping questionnaire which was administered, under SCPR's guidance, by PPRU interviewers at the same time as the British survey was in the field. The result is a unique study of differences in outlook and values between UK citizens on either side of the Irish Sea. A more comprehensive investigation of the findings than this chapter is able to give is to be published in a separate volume next year (Stringer and Robinson, forthcoming).

Next year too will see at last the appearance (scheduled by Gower for the spring) of *British Social Attitudes: Cumulative Sourcebook 1983–1989*. Arranged and indexed within detailed subject categories, this comprehensive directory will contain the questions asked, together with year-by-year distributions of answers (numbers and percentages) from 1983 to 1989. Part-funded by Shell UK Ltd, the *Sourcebook* is intended both as a ready reference guide for those who wish just to follow broad trends in attitudes to one or two subjects, *and* as a detailed codebook for those who wish to dissect and analyse the ever-larger dataset. It will be updated at intervals.

Followers of the series will know that it attempts to blend continuity with change, replicating most questions and modules regularly in the hope of capturing changes in attitude, while also introducing fresh questions and new modules in an attempt to cover more areas and to respond to emerging issues. This year, for instance, we report for the first time not only on Northern Ireland (Chapter 9), but also on attitudes to trade unions (Chapter 2). In addition, we include two chapters (Chapter 6 and Chapter 8) which for the first time use data from 1983 to 1989 to examine by different routes whether Britain's national psyche has, after all, been transformed during that period from the condition of 'nanny state' to that of 'enterprise culture'. The other five chapters in this volume bring us up to date on subjects we have touched on before.

Next year's book will, we hope, bear the fruits of further refreshment of the series which is now taking place. First we have devised and fielded a module on attitudes to civil liberties. Funded by a grant from the Nuffield Foundation, the module has been formulated in consultation with the Home Office, academic specialists and lobbyists. A subset of its questions will also be asked in most of the 14 ISSP countries. Second, via funding from the Health Education Authority, we have devised a new module on attitudes to smoking and health. Third, we have introduced a number of new questions to our existing module on environmental issues and 'green' concerns, designed to tap changes in behaviour as well as attitudes.

From now on the Home Office and the Department of Health will join two other government departments, Employment and Environment, together with the Health Education Authority and the Countryside Commission, as co-funders of the series. In each case these public funds are directed at particular modules of questions rather than at the study as a whole. We are extremely grateful for this support not only because it helps to fund and reinforce the series, but also because it focuses at least part of the questionnaire directly on policy concerns. The advice and guidance we receive from colleagues in government, together with the admirable absence of pressure, are greatly appreciated.

Once again we wish to pay tribute to our colleagues at SCPR who have to absorb the pressure placed on them by this demanding annual survey. In particular, the field controllers, interviewers, coding supervisors, coders and programmers bear the brunt of the work, but at the time of going to press we are, as always, conscious of our indebtedness to SCPR's excellent secretarial team for converting numerous messy drafts of chapters into final text. We also wish to welcome and thank our new research colleague in the *British Social Attitudes* team, Gillian Prior, for plunging into the intricacies of this volume and helping us get it to press so soon after her arrival.

But our most heartfelt vote of thanks is reserved, as usual, for the 4,000 or so respondents in Britain and Northern Ireland who agreed to provide the raw material for this volume.

RMJ
SFW
LLB
BJT

References

BECKER, J., DAVIS, J., ESTER, P. and MOHLER, P. (eds) *Attitudes to Social Inequality and the Role of Government*, Sociaal en Cultureel Planbureau, Rijswijk (1990).
HEATH, A., JOWELL, R., CURTICE, J., EVANS, G., FIELD, J. and WITHER-SPOON, S., *Understanding Political Change: The British Voter 1966–1987* Pergamon, Oxford (forthcoming).
STRINGER, P. and ROBINSON, G., *Social Attitudes in Northern Ireland, 1989* Avebury, Aldershot (forthcoming).

1 Social welfare: the unkindest cuts

Peter Taylor-Gooby*

The British welfare settlement at the close of the Second World War established a wide range of services at adequate minimum standards. Health care, social security benefits, state pensions and education were made available to all citizens regardless of income and according to need. This basic structure of society-wide core provision, supported by a broad cross-party consensus until only a decade or so ago, has recently been challenged from two directions. First, the successive Conservative governments of the 1980s have embarked on a series of radical reforms in every area of welfare provision. These changes have been designed to constrain state spending, reduce direct taxation, encourage the growth of the private sector in the health and other social services, and target state benefits more precisely on the poor. The family has been exhorted to take greater responsibility for meeting the needs of its members. The effect of government provision as of right is assumed to undermine self-reliance and to encourage what has popularly been called 'the nanny state'.

The second challenge to the notion of welfare citizenship has come from some academics and policy analysts: demographic, economic and social changes, they claim, are making it increasingly difficult for governments of any persuasion to provide adequate levels of welfare within the traditional universalist framework. An ageing population intensifies pressure on social provision. Government is finding it increasingly difficult to pay for improvements in welfare. Growing inequalities in income threaten support for collective provision.

Both the performance of the economy and people's sense of their own relative prosperity are likely to play an important role in the debate over welfare provision. Average living standards are rising, but at the same time inequality between the comfortable majority and those left behind by their progress is becoming more marked (House of Commons Select Committee on Social Services, 1990). This increasing disparity might gradually serve to undermine support for common

---

* Reader in Social Policy, University of Kent.

services, since the better off might increasingly opt to pay for private provision. If so, they may also become less inclined to pay taxes which do not directly benefit them.

This chapter uses data collected since 1983 in the *British Social Attitudes* series to examine how far these challenges to citizenship welfare correspond to the pattern of public opinion. Is there growing public support for a restructuring of state welfare along the lines proposed in recent policy innovations? And does income inequality tend to erode support for universal welfare services by widening the gap between the attitudes of rich and poor people?

Welfare reform

There are four main elements in the present government's welfare reform programme: tax and spending cuts (the one implied by the other); the expansion of private welfare provision; a shift towards greater selectivity, with benefits directed at defined groups of the poor; and an attempt to replace state services by individual responsibility. Alongside the stated policy to reduce government intervention is a desire – no less strong for being less clearly defined – to change the moral basis of state welfare provision.

Spending constraints and tax cuts

First we consider the central plank of government domestic policy – holding back state spending to make room for tax cuts, and relying on economic growth to make up the difference. Since welfare accounts for nearly two-thirds of total state spending, a determination to restrain public expenditure (especially against the background of a less buoyant economy) is bound to have a serious impact on the welfare state, at least in the short term.

Throughout the 1980s, data from the *British Social Attitudes* series have shown a substantial and rising level of public support for increases in state welfare, and an apparent readiness to pay increased taxes to provide them. The 1989 survey shows clearly how far the centre of public opinion has shifted decisively against cuts and towards the expansion of state welfare. Each year we have asked:

*Suppose the government had to choose between the three options on this card Which do you think it should choose?**

	1983 %	1986 %	1989 %
Reduce taxes and spend less on health, education and social benefits	9	5	3
Keep taxes and spending on these services at the same level as now	54	44	37
Increase taxes and spend more on health, education and social benefits	32	46	56

*Figures for three years only are shown but the trend is consistent over the six readings.

In 1983, around a third of respondents opted for extra social spending; by 1989 the proportion had risen to well over half. Moreover, not only has the overall level of support for welfare gone up substantially during a period of insistent government demands for spending cuts, but it has gone up most steeply among the professional and managerial classes (Social Classes I and II), who were in 1983 the least enthusiastic about increased social spending. Of course, the better off have recently benefited from a substantial reduction in their tax burden, and this may have something to do with the change.

% supporting higher taxes to pay for more social spending	1983	1989	% Difference
Social Class:			
I/II	28%	57%	+29
III Non-manual	35%	53%	+18
III Manual	32%	58%	+26
IV/V	33%	56%	+24

Detailed figures are given in **Table 1.1**.

Two further features in the pattern of answers show how *political* attitudes have shifted. First, all previous surveys in this series have shown a majority of Conservative identifiers in favour of the *status quo* on this issue – hardly surprising among supporters of the party of government. By 1989, however, the highest proportion – by a small margin – even of this group endorsed higher taxes and more welfare spending. Secondly, the political centre has shifted decisively towards welfare statism. In 1983 Alliance identifiers stood roughly midway between Conservative and Labour Party supporters. In 1989 Liberal Democrat and SDP identifiers were much closer to their Labour counterparts:

	Conservative		SLD/SDP		Labour	
	1983	1989	1983	1989	1983	1989
	%	%	%	%	%	%
Reduce taxes and social spending	10	3	6	2	8	3
Keep both the same as now	63	46	54	29	46	25
Increase taxes and social spending	24	48	36	65	42	68

We shall continue to follow these trends in response to further political developments over the next year or two. But the persuasive evidence from the last six surveys is of a growing consensus among supporters of all parties for a switch to welfarist, rather than individualist, taxation and social spending policies.

More evidence about attitudes to the level of state spending emerges from responses to another series of questions that explore *priorities* for state spending. These show that it is the universal welfare state services that command by far the strongest support, and that this support also increasingly transcends class and political boundaries. The National Health Service receives overwhelming support as the service most urgently in need of extra resources. Education comes a poor second, followed by housing and social security (see **Table 1.2** for further details).

Priorities for extra government spending*

	First priority		Second priority	
	1983	1989	1983	1989
	%	%	%	%
Health	37	61	26	23
Education	24	19	26	36
Help for industry	16	2	13	5
Housing	7	7	13	15
Social security benefits	6	5	6	9

*Defence, public transport, roads, police and prisons and overseas aid attracted no more than four per cent support in any year and so are omitted from this table.

Since 1983, actual state spending on the NHS has increased by 17 per cent (taking general price inflation into account*) and actual education spending by nine per cent (Treasury, 1989, p. 75). Yet the public appears to take the view that these levels of expenditure are inadequate. This view is, of course, supported both by the House of Commons Select Committee on Social Services (1988), which concluded that NHS spending falls substantially below that required to maintain standards at a time of increasing demands upon its services, and by Her Majesty's Inspectorate of Education (1987), who blamed spending cuts for the unsatisfactory state of many school buildings.

But generalised calls for more spending are not all that informative. We find that the proposed targets of extra spending tend to shift as the years go by. We always ask respondents to choose their first and second priorities for extra state spending on social security benefits. As the table below shows, the needs of the unemployed, never a top priority anyway, nowadays command even less public sympathy than they did in the early 1980s (see **Table 1.3** for further details).

Priorities for extra government spending on social security benefits

	First priority		Second priority	
	1983	1989	1983	1989
	%	%	%	%
Retirement pensions	41	43	23	24
Benefits for disabled people	24	26	33	34
Benefits for the unemployed	18	11	15	14
Child benefits	8	14	13	16
Benefits for single parents	8	6	13	11

The universalist state retirement pension still attracts the greatest support. There is, however, more support than before for extra spending on child benefits, caused perhaps by the freeze in child benefit rates since 1987 which has effectively cut their real value by just over 11 per cent. Similarly, the decoupling of the state retirement pension from rises in average earnings has resulted in a fall in its relative value of just over 20 per cent since 1979.

So the policy of spending cuts allied to cuts in direct taxation has still not attracted public support on anything like the scale the present government would

---

* The NHS specific index of pay and prices, which takes into account the changes in the prices of goods and services it uses, is generally reckoned to be substantially higher than RPI (Bosanquet, 1988, p.94).

doubtless wish. Indeed attitudes have shifted decisively, even among supporters of the party of government, in the opposite direction. Even in those areas where spending *has* risen, respondents are inclined to doubt the adequacy of increases.

Privatisation and the welfare state

A second aspect of policy reform is the growing emphasis placed on expanding the private sector. The *British Social Attitudes* surveys have addressed welfare privatisation mainly in relation to the National Health Service, often regarded as the flagship of the welfare state. In recent years the NHS has generated fiercer political dispute than has any other service. While, as we have seen, it has consistently been top public priority for extra spending, Government policy through the 1980s has been to strengthen the role of the private sector. New legislation has now been passed by Parliament with provisions to increase tax subsidies to private medicine, introduce spending limits for GPs, set up an internal market within the NHS, and encourage Health Authorities to include private sector institutions in that market. These reforms, it is argued, will help increase the efficiency of the NHS, offer patients a wider choice as to where they are treated, cut waiting lists and curb costs. Critics have expressed concern that the changes will pave the way for wholesale privatisation and lead to a two-tier health service: basic state medicine for the poor, and a superior subsidised private sector for those who can afford it.

Successive *British Social Attitudes* surveys have shown strong support for the principle that the state should be dominant in the provision of medical care. Despite the expansion through the 1980s in private medical insurance, in the number of private hospital beds and in the level of private medical treatment, there is even less support nowadays than in 1983 for the policy of targeting the NHS on low-income groups. We put this proposition to respondents:

It has been suggested that the NHS should be available only to those with lower incomes. This would mean that contributions and taxes would be lower and most people would then take out medical insurance or pay for health care. Do you support or oppose this idea?

	1983	1986	1989
	%	%	%
Support	29	27	22
Oppose	64	67	74
Don't know	7	6	4

So by 1989 almost three quarters of respondents opposed a two-tier approach to medical services. Interestingly, in 1983 those who were most likely to be excluded were the ones most strongly opposed to a two-tier NHS: 73 per cent of those in the highest income group were against the idea compared with 64 per cent of the population at large. After all, it is the better off who would lose their right to free treatment under these proposals. However, in 1989, opposition was not only more determined but also more united. Concern about low spending on the NHS, added perhaps to worries about a stronger emphasis on the role of market forces, appears to have been accompanied by a greater homogeneity in public attitudes in opposition to the reforms.

Opinion has also shifted against private medicine in general, or at least against its expansion within the NHS. Under the 'internal market' system, health authorities will be encouraged to purchase medical services from both state and private hospitals and clinics for NHS patients. The White Paper on the future of the NHS states: "there is already a growing partnership between the NHS and the independent sector" (Department of Health, 1989, p.68). The 1984 survey tackled this issue by asking respondents whether they thought "the existence of private medical treatment in hospitals was a good or a bad thing for the NHS?" The question was repeated in 1986 and 1989.

	1984	1986	1989
	%	%	%
Private medical treatment in NHS hospitals:			
Is good for the NHS	23	27	24
Is bad for the NHS	42	40	47
Makes no difference	30	28	24

A further question asks directly whether private medicine should be abolished, confined to private hospitals, or allowed throughout the system.

	1984	1986	1989
	%	%	%
Private medical treatment should be:			
Abolished in all hospitals	9	11	12
Allowed in private hospitals only	48	46	50
Allowed in all hospitals	39	41	35

On this issue there has been rather less movement during the last few years. There is still a conspicuous lack of support for the banning of private medical treatment, but there is also even less support nowadays (especially compared with 1986) for allowing private medicine *within the NHS*. Nearly half of all respondents think that private practice damages the NHS, and fewer respondents than in 1986 see its effect as neutral.

The small decline in support for private medicine between 1986 and 1989 is a reversal of the trend over the two earlier years. The intense political debate about the future of the NHS started about the time of the 1987 General Election and came to a head with the publication of the government's plans in January 1989, shortly before fieldwork on this survey began. At that stage anyway, public opinion was less in favour of closer cooperation (or increased competition) between the state and private sectors than it had been three years earlier.

We have noted the marked shift between 1983 and 1989 among Liberal and SDP identifiers in favour of higher state spending, and found that Conservative identifiers too (by a small majority) had opted for increased spending rather than the *status quo*. A similar (but rather less pronounced) pattern is evident in attitudes to private medicine, although on this issue the shift appears to have taken place only after 1986:

	Conservative		SLD/SDP		Labour	
	1986	**1989**	**1986**	**1989**	**1986**	**1989**
	%	%	%	%	%	%
Private medical treatment						
should be:						
Abolished in all hospitals	3	4	9	12	19	22
Allowed in private						
hospitals only	38	43	48	62	53	54
Allowed in all hospitals	58	51	40	25	26	21

So in 1989 the policies embodied in the new health service legislation seemed to kindle little enthusiasm, even among Conservative identifiers. Further work is needed to explore public attitudes towards policies designed to increase the role of the private sector in other areas such as local government services and rented housing. As far as the NHS is concerned, however, it appears that popular sentiment may be responding to the continuing debate over its future shape. We shall keep on monitoring changes in attitudes, as the reforms embodied in the new legislation begin to take effect.

Poverty, inequality and selectivity

The third aspect of policy reform is a growing emphasis on targeting social security benefits. Income inequality in Britain has grown more marked over the period covered by the *British Social Attitudes* series. Between 1983 and 1988 the ratio between the top and bottom quartiles of income distribution shifted from 3.44:1 to 4.37:1 (Central Statistical Office, 1983 and 1988, Table 24). Some commentators fear the re-emergence of an 'underclass' in British cities, as has happened recently in the United States (see for example, Field, 1989). A European Community survey has shown that the proportion of people in Britain living in poverty has almost doubled in recent years – from 6.6 per cent of the population in 1975 to 12 per cent by 1985 (O'Higgins and Jenkins, 1989).

Our 1989 survey repeated a series of questions about attitudes to poverty first asked in 1986. The answers show that public perception of the extent of poverty in Britain has grown over this period: in 1986, 55 per cent thought that "there is quite a lot of real poverty in Britain today"; in 1989, 63 per cent agreed. It is, perhaps, the growth in large cities of beggars and of homeless people, (particularly 16–18 year olds, most of whom since 1988 no longer get Income Support) that has helped to increase public awareness of poverty.

We also asked respondents about the perceived causes of poverty in Britain, presenting them with four possible explanations and asking them to choose one. The distribution of answers in 1986 and 1989 is similar but a slightly higher proportion nowadays attributes poverty to "injustice in society" (a rise from 25 per cent to 29 per cent), and correspondingly fewer adopt the fatalistic explanation, that poverty is just "an inevitable part of modern life".[1]

Not surprisingly, party political divisions continue to be marked on both the extent of poverty in Britain today and the reasons for it. What is perhaps surprising is the size of these divisions:

Agreeing that:	All	Conservative	SLD/SDP	Labour
There is quite a lot of real poverty in Britain today	63%	47%	62%	81%
There are people who live in need:	%	%	%	%
Because it's an inevitable part of modern life	34	39	38	30
Because of injustice in our society	29	12	33	46
Because of laziness or lack of willpower	19	30	10	9
Because they have been unlucky	11	12	11	8

Almost four times as many Labour as Conservative identifiers attribute poverty to injustice in society, and three times as many Conservative as Labour supporters attribute poverty to laziness. These attitudes should be seen in the context that Conservative identifiers are much less likely than their Liberal, SDP and (especially) Labour counterparts to concede the existence of much real poverty anyway. These ideological divisions are all the more interesting when we see (in **Table 1.4**) that attitudes vary little according to income level. In other words, working-class Conservatives are similar to middle-class Conservatives in their view of the extent of poverty in Britain and its causes.

How do people define the emotive word 'poverty'? We asked respondents whether or not they agreed with three different definitions: the *relative* notion ("enough to buy the things they really needed, but not enough to buy the things most people take for granted"); the *breadline* definition ("enough to eat and live, but not enough to buy other things that they needed") and a *sub-minimal* conception ("not enough to eat and live without getting into debt"). As in 1986, the most popular notion of poverty is the most meagre, although a majority endorses the 'breadline' definition too.

% agreeing with each definition of poverty:	1986	1989
Relative	25%	25%
Breadline	55%	60%
Below minimum subsistence	95%	95%

Even the least advantaged – members of the 'core' of manual working class, unemployed people and those on low incomes – are hardly more likely than others to view poverty as merely *relative* deprivation.

Attitudes to poverty (and consequently evaluations of policies needed to tackle the problem) are inevitably influenced by popular imagery of the groups who are most vulnerable, as well as by common notions of need.[2] We tried to explore popular conceptions of groups at risk from poverty by asking respondents (in both 1986 and 1989) about their impressions of the living standards of two hypothetical couples receiving benefit – one on the state pension and the other on unemployment benefit. We discovered that there is a much greater likelihood for people on state pensions than those on unemployment benefit to be regarded as really poor. And when we went on to confront respondents with the *actual* benefits received by the two groups, they shifted away from conventional imagery and changed their assessments – radically in the case of unemployed people:

| | Unemployed couple | | Pensioner couple | |
	On benefit %	On £53[+] a week %	On state pension %	On £66[+] a week %
Really poor	12	42	22	30
Hard up	49	49	55	52
Enough to live on	27	6	19	16
More than enough	2	*	*	*

[+] These figures exclude housing benefit which, since the amounts received vary so widely, we decided (reluctantly) to discount.

This pattern of responses may help to explain why pensioners are seen as the highest priority group for extra social security spending. In reality, however, unemployed people apparently run a greater risk of poverty than do pensioners. In 1987, 86 per cent of unemployed people were poor enough to qualify for income support, as against 33 per cent of pensioners (House of Commons Select Committee on the Social Services, 1990, pp. x–xi). On the other hand, pensioners may well be regarded as somehow more 'deserving' than the unemployed.

So the majority view of poverty is that it implies only the direst need; yet many people (nearly two out of three) believe nonetheless that poverty in Britain is widespread. How then do they think poverty should be tackled? Government policy, as summed up in the social security review (Department of Health and Social Security, 1985) is firmly committed to the notion of 'targeting' – directing resources selectively to the most needy, and abandoning the structure of universal benefit provisions.

The *British Social Attitudes* series has not addressed the issue of targeting specifically, but it has included some regular questions addressing redistribution from the better off to the worse off as a means of promoting greater social equality. The answers in 1989, as in earlier years, show firm support for the view that the goals of the welfare state should embrace at least a measure of redistribution, in addition to direct provision for the needs of the poor:

Redistribution and equality

% agreeing that:

Ordinary people do not get their fair share of the nation's wealth	65%
The government should spend more money on welfare benefits for the poor, even if it leads to higher taxes	61%
Government should redistribute income from the better off to those who are less well off	50%

These answers reinforce other evidence that the concept of a generous welfare state still appears to have wide public support.

The moral impact of welfare

Another aspect of the new welfare policies concerns the balance between state provision and self-help. Does the 'nanny state' engender "the sullen apathy of dependence" as the then Secretary of State for Social Services claimed in a widely-reported speech (Moore, 1987)? The survey has addressed this issue in two ways. First, respondents are invited to respond to a series of statements about the impact of state welfare on self-help, citizenship and mutual aid. These have been a feature of the survey since 1983. Secondly, the questionnaire has carried several questions designed to gauge beliefs about so-called 'welfare scrounging', again since 1983.

Answers to the first series of questions show that the current of opinion continues to run towards the welfare state. Moreover, far from being blamed widely for encouraging selfishness, dependency and a lack of self-reliance, the welfare state is criticised rather more strongly for inducing stigma than for undermining self-reliance. On all four measures, state welfare emerges at the end of the 1980s as enjoying more public confidence than it did in 1983, although the trend is by no means linear.

Images of the welfare state

% agreeing that:	1983	1989
The welfare state makes people nowadays less willing to look after themselves	52%	39%
The welfare state encourages people to stop helping each other	37%	32%
People receiving social security are made to feel like second class citizens	48%	53%
Social workers have too much power to interfere with people's lives	47%	36%

On these questions, as on earlier ones, the political divisions run deep. Conservative identifiers are much more likely than Labour identifiers to think that welfare makes people unwilling to help themselves and others, and much less likely to think welfare stigmatic. The idea of a 'dependency culture', nourished by overgenerous state welfare, receives majority support solely among this group.

Images of the welfare state by party political identification

% agreeing that:	Conservative	SLD/SDP	Labour
The welfare state makes people nowadays less willing to look after themselves	51%	36%	25%
The welfare state encourages people to stop helping each other	38%	32%	24%
People receiving social security are made to feel like second class citizens	36%	59%	69%

Table 1.5 gives further details and analyses the attitudes of other subgroups.

Responses to the second cluster of questions indicate support for the view that social security claimants deserve help. Nonetheless opinions are divided on whether claimants 'fiddle', and a majority feel that the ranks of the unemployed contain a large number of people who are simply workshy.

Attitudes to social security claimants

		Agree	Neither	Disagree
Many people who get social security don't really deserve any help	%	28	27	45
Most people on the dole are fiddling one way or another	%	31	31	37
Around here, most unemployed people could find a job if they really wanted one	%	52	19	28

On the first two measures, opinion has scarcely moved in recent years, but on the third we have noted a sharp rise since 1987 in the proportion of people who blame unemployment, at least to some extent, on the unemployed themselves. This may well be in response to the steady fall in the unemployment figures over that period. In contrast, responses since 1983 to another set of questions – on the propensity to claim benefits – have been remarkably stable. Majorities feel both that "large numbers of people these days falsely claim benefits" and that "large numbers of people who are eligible for benefits fail to claim them", but the latter proportion exceeds the former one.

	1983	1989
% agreeing that:		
Large numbers claim falsely	65%	65%
Large numbers fail to claim	81%	84%

Associations with party and income are weak (see **Table 1.6**)

Thus there is evidence that large numbers of people think that the social security system is failing in one way or another. It is both too lax and too stringent. The rhetoric of punishing scroungers while targeting on the truly needy chimes in with this pattern of ideas.

In summary, large majorities want more state welfare spending on 'core' services and benefits and say they are prepared to pay the taxes required to finance them; the expansion of private medicine within the NHS is viewed with much disquiet; equality through redistribution as a policy aim is endorsed (again by a substantial proportion of the population) and there is little support for restricting the role of the state to the provision of highly selective benefits for the poor; the claim that state provision in itself has a debilitating effect on work and civic responsibility is not widely endorsed. On the other hand, substantial majorities of the population also suspect that there is widespread welfare scrounging and a core of workshy unemployed people: government measures to tackle these abuses are therefore likely to receive considerable approval. What must be worrying for the present government, however, is not merely that the tide of public opinion continues on the whole to move against its core welfare policies, but that even its own supporters appear increasingly to have moved with that tide.

We now turn to the question of whether widening income inequality in Britain has itself begun to challenge the very concept of citizenship welfare.

Polarisation and support for the welfare state

The polarisation thesis which we now examine suggests that the post-war welfare settlement is under threat not so much from short-term shifts in political ideology, but from longer-term social and economic changes that undermine support for mass services. There are two main arguments advanced by those who claim that growing income inequality at a time of rising real living standards for the majority threatens support for the welfare state. First they suggest that the better off will prefer to choose from the *à la carte* range of services provided by the private sector rather than subject themselves to the *table d'hôte* offered by the welfare state. Secondly they suggest that 'comfortable Britain' will feel less and less inclined to pay taxes to fund welfare benefits and services for groups with whom it has little contact or common feeling.

Responses to two sets of questions asked in *British Social Attitudes* surveys contain information on the extent to which better-off people prefer choice in the private sector to standard provision in the state sector.*

Choice and private medicine

Our discussion of attitudes to the creation of the two-tier health service has already indicated that support for a universal NHS is as strong or stronger among the better off than among the population at large. 'Comfortable Britain' is well aware of the advantages it can gain from common access to tax-financed welfare. However, this does not imply that it wishes to turn down the opportunity to gain preferential access to additional, or speedier, services from the private sector. Indeed, the wealthiest quarter of our 1989 sample – those with an income of over £20,000 a year – is rather keener than average on the introduction of private medicine into NHS hospitals. This opens up (for them, and perhaps for others too) the possibility of enjoying privileges such as choice of consultant and by-passing the waiting list. In any case they are inclined to see private practice as "good for the NHS". But the differences are not marked:

	All	Household income	
		Under £6,000pa	Over £20,000pa
Oppose 'two-tier' NHS	74%	69%	74%
Believe that private medical treat-			
ment should be:	%	%	%
Abolished in all hospitals	12	15	11
Allowed in private hospitals only	50	47	48
Allowed in all hospitals	35	34	41
Believe that private medical treat-			
ment in NHS hospitals:	%	%	%
Is good for the NHS	24	19	31
Is bad for the NHS	47	47	45
Makes no difference	24	28	21

---

* We also looked at social class patterns; but since they tended to mirror income level patterns, we have chosen to show the latter only.

Almost the same proportion (around one half) of the most affluent and of the poorest in our sample believes that private medicine in NHS hospitals harms the NHS. So far, then, strong evidence to support the polarisation thesis is lacking. This impression is reinforced by responses to a series of questions which ask whether the better off should be able to purchase superior provision in other spheres of the welfare state.

Privilege and private welfare

We asked three parallel questions to explore attitudes in those contexts where the policies of the 1980s have encouraged the better off to take advantage of various forms of private welfare. Private health care, education and pensions have all expanded as a result of rising average real incomes (enabling more people to afford them) and of extra government subsidies (through new forms of tax relief and through specific grants). Moreover, perceived and real reductions in the standards of state services, caused by teacher shortages, hospital budgeting difficulties, changes in the state earnings-related pension scheme and so on, have presumably acted as a spur to those who could afford them to make arrangements of their own. Questions on these issues were first introduced in 1986, so comparisons can be made over only a comparatively brief period.

	1986	1989
% agreeing that those who can afford it should be able to pay for better:		
Health care	53%	49%
Education	52%	46%
Pensions	61%	63%

For education and health care, there is slightly less support for differential access than there was in 1986; for pensions there is no significant difference. Variation by income group is once again small and more or less constant across the two surveys, so we show results for 1989 only.

	All	Household income	
		Under £6,000pa	Over £20,000pa
% agreeing that those who can afford it should be able to pay for better:			
Health care	49%	45%	49%
Education	46%	42%	47%
Pensions	63%	54%	74%

On the basis of these questions therefore (and the evidence so far is admittedly thin) there is little support for the belief that income inequalities undermine support for mass welfare services, as the better off transfer to the private sector. However, there is a strong current of support for allowing people to choose between the state and private market, and this support is expressed rather more forcibly by those in the best position to benefit from such arrangements. The better off value state provision, but they wish to be able to complement it from the private sector.

Priorities for welfare spending

While growing income inequality does not lead the better off to believe that the state should reduce its role in the provision of welfare services, it may nonetheless lead to demands for a *redirection* of state spending; and this is what our analysis of attitudes to welfare spending suggests. Those on higher incomes are just as keen on more welfare spending as is the population as a whole, but when we examine *priorities* for spending, substantial differences appear. Better-off people are noticeably more enthusiastic than average about increased spending on education and on child benefit (and a little more likely to give priority to benefits for disabled people).

Of course state education funded from general taxation is a service from which the better off especially benefit. Many policy analysts have pointed out that sixth-form to university education is not only almost entirely a middle-class preserve but that it is also the most costly part of the service (see, for example; Le Grand, 1982, p.58). And child benefit, of course, is not related to income. By the same token, as the table below shows, those in the lowest income group tend to give higher priority to social security benefits (especially pensions) – which are most likely to benefit *them* disproportionately.

First priority for extra government spending*

	All	Household income	
		Under £6,000pa	Over £20,000pa
	%	%	%
Health	61	59	56
Education	19	15	26
Housing	7	9	6
Social security benefits	5	11	2
	%	%	%
Retirement pensions	43	52	41
Benefits for disabled people	26	24	27
Child benefits	14	8	14

* This table is selective. Not all the items presented to respondents are included.

Analysis of spending priorities by class shows that working-class people tend to give the NHS and housing greater priority than does the population as a whole (see **Tables 1.2 and 1.3**).

In general then, our data lend little support to those who claim that the demands of advantaged groups for greater choice in welfare undermine their willingness to pay for improved services. There are strong indications, however, that income (and social class) have a bearing upon the strength of support for different *kinds* of welfare provision.

Polarisation and welfare for the poor

Redistribution, equality and poverty

Alongside considerable support for the main bastions of the welfare state, our findings also suggest a certain lack of sympathy among the better off for recipients of means-tested benefits. This is evident in responses to a series of questions about the role of government in targeting and in redistribution, equality before the law, the moral impact of social security, and the extent and definition of poverty. Not surprisingly, for instance, we find that people on high incomes are less likely than those on low incomes to view the current distribution of wealth as unfair, to support a more generous welfare system, and to see the system as inequitable. On the other hand, sizeable proportions even within the best-off quartile support all three propositions.

	All	Household income	
		Under £6,000pa	Over £20,000pa
% agreeing that:			
Ordinary people do not get their fair share of the nation's wealth	65%	76%	48%
The government should spend more on welfare benefits for the poor, even if it leads to higher taxes	61%	75%	54%
There is one law for the rich and one for the poor	69%	78%	55%

Although people's views on the principles of redistribution and equality differ quite markedly by class and income, much less division is evident when we ask about the more tangible issues of welfare dependency and scrounging. Only on the matter of the stigma associated with social security do the views of the better off diverge noticeably from those of the poorest in our sample.

For the polarisation thesis to be valid, sympathy for the poor should decline with income, and indeed this is the case to some extent. Those with household incomes of over £20,000 a year are much more likely to deny that poverty in Britain is widespread, and to take a sanguine view about whether it is increasing. They are also noticeably more likely to see poverty as inevitable, rather than as the result of either social injustice or fecklessness.

	All	Household income	
		Under £6,000pa	Over £20,000pa
% agreeing that:			
There is a lot of real poverty in Britain today	63%	66%	58%
Poverty has increased over the last ten years	50%	57%	40%
Poverty will increase over the next ten years	44%	45%	38%
There are people who live in need:	%	%	%
Because it is an inevitable part of modern life	34	29	42
Because of injustice in our society	29	33	21
Because of laziness or lack of willpower	19	20	19
Because they have been unlucky	11	12	11

The better off are also slightly more likely to adopt a 'minimum subsistence' definition of poverty, and rather more likely to see those on state benefits or low incomes as "hard up" rather than "really poor". All these patterns do not differ greatly from those we found in 1986.

In summary, our data do not confirm the view that state welfare is becoming less popular (on the contrary); nor do they provide much evidence that income polarisation is eroding support for the welfare state. Since much state welfare spending distributes benefits across a wide range of income groups, and since some state spending helps the better off out of proportion to their numbers, the exclusive welfare territory of the poor is comparatively small (see, for example, Taylor-Gooby, 1989, p.219). While polarisation may threaten this preserve to some extent, it does not appear to be much more threatening now than it used to be.

'Comfortable Britain' versus 'miserable Britain'

Our examination of the possible effects of polarisation has focused so far largely on the 1989 data. But since polarisation implies a process of social change over time, the central question is whether there is a *widening* gap between different groups in their attitudes to collective provision. As before, we limit our analysis to the highest and lowest income groups and look for evidence of movements between 1983 and 1989 in their attitudes towards a range of benefits, services and policies. During this period radical new policies in social security, education, housing and the NHS were either enacted or proposed. An analysis of trends should thus give an indication of the way in which the relatively well off and the relatively poor have responded to the new welfare agenda. The income groups chosen could be said to correspond roughly to the division between 'comfortable Britain' and 'miserable Britain' made in the much-publicised report (*Faith in the City*, 1985) on urban deprivation (see Halsey, 1988, pp.26-33 for a summary).

Two main conclusions emerge from this analysis. First, there is virtually no area under scrutiny in which the attitudes of comfortable and miserable Britain have grown markedly further apart: instead, across a wide range of issues they have come closer or converged. Indeed on some, notably those concerning the level of public spending, access to the NHS, and private treatment in NHS hospitals, a former substantial gap in the position adopted by the wealthiest and poorest parts of the population has now narrowed dramatically or almost vanished:

	1983		1989	
	Poorest quartile	Wealthiest quartile	Poorest quartile	Wealthiest quartile
Keep taxes and social spending at the same level as now	44%	61%	34%	36%
Oppose idea of two-tier NHS	57%	73%	69%	74%

	1984		1989	
	Poorest quartile	Wealthiest quartile	Poorest quartile	Wealthiest quartile
Private medicine should be:				
Allowed in private hospitals only	54%	40%	47%	48%
Allowed in all hospitals	32%	52%	34%	41%

There is only one issue on which the attitudes of the two contrasting income groups have diverged since 1983, and that is on their perception of the power of social workers. On our first reading, 48 per cent of both groups agreed that "social workers have too much power over people's lives". Our latest survey suggest both groups are nowadays less inclined to support that proposition, but the wealthiest are *much* less so (34 per cent, as opposed to 43 per cent of the least well off). It appears then that those most likely to have direct or indirect contact with the social services are conspicuously more suspicious of their powers.

The second point to stress about these findings is that, in some respects, the attitudes of the two income groups have stayed stubbornly divergent over time. For instance, the wealthiest were in 1983 inclined to give higher priority to education and are no less keen on it nowadays. And the poorest quartile gave and still gives considerably greater priority to social security (especially to the state retirement pension). But such issues are small in number, and the overall conclusion must be that growing income inequality has simply not led to the expected polarisation of attitudes towards state welfare. To an extent the reverse is true. High income groups still have an interest in preserving the welfare state, especially in fostering a symbiosis between exclusive private services and common-access state provision. Society at large therefore has an interest in efficient and effective health and welfare services. In the last part of this chapter, we examine our data to see whether this widespread demand appears to be being met.

Dissatisfaction with welfare provision

Public anxiety about the efficiency and effectiveness of certain aspects of the welfare state has increased sharply, most strikingly over the National Health Service. Overall dissatisfaction with the way the NHS is run has been steadily mounting. In 1983 only 26 per cent of the public expressed dissatisfaction; by 1986 this proportion had risen to 39 per cent, and by 1989 to 46 per cent. Overall satisfaction has accordingly dropped from 55 per cent in 1983 to 37 per cent in 1989.

The source of dissatisfaction is more or less confined to hospital services which have been cash-limited over the past few years. Attitudes to primary health care services (especially to GPs who have received the biggest increases in spending) have been stable and largely uncritical over the period.

	1983	1989
% expressing dissatisfaction with:		
Local doctors/GPs	13%	12%
Being in hospital as an in-patient	7%	15%
Attending hospital as an out-patient	21%	30%

Plans for the NHS include introducing GP budgets, allowing hospitals to opt out of the service, increasing subsidies to private medicine, introducing internal markets and encouraging the private sector to operate within the service – all with the aim of increasing efficiency and improving organisation and management within the NHS.

According to our findings, any improvement would be welcomed. And it remains to be seen whether more private provision will achieve that aim. As the following figures show, a substantial number of hospital services are seen to be in need of improvement, more so in 1989 than two years earlier. We give responses for 1987 (when these questions were first asked) and 1989, and also analyse responses for 1989 by household income.

Aspects of NHS hospitals in need of improvement*

	1987	1989		
			Household income	
			Under	Over
	All	All	£6,000pa	£20,000pa
% saying in need of a lot or some improvement:				
Hospital waiting lists for *non-emergency* operations	87%	85%	82%	90%
Waiting time before getting appointments with hospital consultants	83%	86%	83%	90%
Staffing level of nurses in hospitals	75%	75%	67%	82%
Staffing level of doctors in hospitals	70%	75%	65%	81%
Hospital casualty departments	54%	59%	45%	68%
Condition of hospital buildings	53%	61%	48%	76%
Quality of medical treatment in hospitals	30%	36%	23%	45%
Quality of nursing care in hospitals	21%	27%	19%	32%

* We also asked about the service provided by GPs, figures for which are shown in Appendix III.

The *pattern* of responses is substantially similar in both years, though public concern has risen noticeably. On every aspect we asked about, better-off people were more aware of deficiencies (or more confident in expressing them). So it may be the perceived inadequacies of state health provision, rather than any ideological objections to it, that propels the better off towards the private sector. As the table above shows, what seems to worry people most is not so much the quality of care (the last two items above), as the basic level of resources devoted to caring: waiting lists and staffing levels (two sides of the same coin), casualty departments and capital spending. The NHS reforms are unlikely in themselves to disperse public misgivings about the resources available for state health care, "rationed by queuing and delivered under great strain" (Bosanquet, 1988, p.101). The radical new policies certainly address some of the pertinent issues that exercise public opinion. However, organisational reform, partnership with the private sector and more stringent welfare targeting are unlikely to reduce public concern over what they see essentially as an inadequate level of provision.

Conclusions

This series has now accumulated a good deal of evidence that attitudes to state welfare throughout the 1980s have become more and more critical of policies which are seen to constrain health and welfare provision. There is also evidence, however, that better-off people would like to retain access to a substantial private sector operating alongside the welfare state. While in the future there may be tension between support for common state provision and for privileged private services, with 'comfortable Britain' then withdrawing support for common services and opting instead for a two-tier welfare state, such a fracture is not yet in sight.

Many of the welfare reforms of the 1980s tackle policy issues about which there is real public concern: for example, the efficiency of the NHS, and the ability of the social security system to provide adequate and timely benefits to those who really need them. However, while the government has identified the right problems, it seems to be offering the wrong remedies; the new policies offer a sophisticated programme of organisational changes, when public opinion clearly favours more public spending on these services. In the immediate future, therefore, these reforms seem very unlikely to satisfy persistent, and increasingly consensual, demands for improvements in the welfare system.

Notes

1. The EC's *Eurobarometer* survey, which has charted changes in attitudes among citizens of European Community countries since 1976, confirms the trend among Britons towards the perception of poverty as either the outcome of injustice or as inevitable in the modern world (Commission of the European Communities, 1990, p.37).

2. Evidence from the 1989 *Eurobarometer* survey carried out in the 12 EC countries, reinforces the impression that British attitudes to poverty are especially stringent. Whereas in answer to a question about whether people have adequate incomes, Britain had the third highest proportion of respondents who felt they 'constantly had to restrict spending', the British were the least likely of citizens of all 12 nations to report awareness of poverty in their own neighbourhoods (Commission of the European Communities, 1990, pp.5 & 25).

References

BOSANQUET, N., 'An ailing state of National Health', in Jowell, R., Witherspoon, S. and Brook, L. (eds), *British Social Attitudes : the 5th Report,* Gower, Aldershot (1988).

CENTRAL STATISTICAL OFFICE, *Family Expenditure Survey*, HMSO, London (1983), p. 70

CENTRAL STATISTICAL OFFICE, *Family Expenditure Survey*, HMSO, London (1988), p. 68

COMMISSION OF THE EUROPEAN COMMUNITIES, *Eurobarometer, Poverty 3*, EC, Brussels (1990).

DEPARTMENT OF HEALTH, *Working for Patients*, HMSO, London (1989).

DEPARTMENT OF HEALTH AND SOCIAL SECURITY, *The Reform of Social Security*, Cmnd 9517, HMSO, London (1985).

Faith in the City: a Call for Action by Church and Nation, Archbishop of Canterbury's Working Party on Urban Priority Areas, Church House Publishing, London (1985).

FIELD, F., *Losing Out*, Basil Blackwell, Oxford (1989).

HALSEY, A.H. (ed), *British Social Trends since 1900*, Macmillan, London (1988).

HER MAJESTY'S INSPECTORATE OF EDUCATION, *The Effect of Spending Policies on Local Authority Education*, [mimeo], HMI, London (1987).

HOUSE OF COMMONS SELECT COMMITTEE ON SOCIAL SERVICES, *Resourcing the NHS – Short-term Issues*, HCP 264–1 (1988).

HOUSE OF COMMONS SELECT COMMITTEE ON SOCIAL SERVICES, *The Income Support system and the Distribution of Income in 1987*, HCP 378-11 (1990).

LE GRAND, J., *The Strategy of Equality*, George Allen and Unwin, London (1982).

MOORE, J., 'Welfare and Dependency', *Speech to Conservative Constituency Parties Association*, (September, 1987).

O'HIGGINS, M., and JENKINS, S., *Poverty in Europe: Estimates for 1975, 1980 and 1985*. Paper given at a seminar on Poverty Statistics in the European Community, sponsored by the Commission of the European Communities (October 1989).

TAYLOR-GOOBY, P., 'Welfare Privatization : the British Experience', *International Journal of Health Studies*, Vol.19, No.2 (1989), pp.209–20.

TREASURY, *The Government's Expenditure Plans, 1989/90 to 1991/92*, Cmnd 621, ch 21, HMSO, London (1989).

1.1 SOCIAL SPENDING AND THE LEVEL OF BENEFITS, 1983 AND 1989 (1989:Q71) by social class, compressed Goldthorpe class schema (1989 only) and age

1983

THE GOVERNMENT SHOULD:	TOTAL	SOCIAL CLASS				AGE		
		I/II	III non-manual	III manual	IV/V	18–34	35–54	55+
	%	%	%	%	%	%	%	%
Reduce taxes, lower social spending	9	9	4	9	13	8	8	10
Keep same as now	54	59	59	56	49	55	54	54
Increase taxes, increase social spending	32	28	35	32	33	33	34	30
None/don't know/not answered	5	4	2	3	5	5	4	6
BASE: ALL RESPONDENTS Weighted	1719	334	268	365	300	532	594	587
Unweighted	1761	343	281	362	316	525	623	607

1989

THE GOVERNMENT SHOULD:	TOTAL	SOCIAL CLASS				COMPRESSED GOLDTHORPE CLASS SCHEMA					AGE		
		I/II	III non-manual	III manual	IV/V	Salariat	Routine non-manual	Petty bourgeoisie	Foremen & technicians	Working class	18–34	35–54	55+
	%	%	%	%	%	%	%	%	%	%	%	%	%
Reduce taxes, lower social spending	3	2	2	4	3	2	2	3	4	3	4	2	2
Keep same as now	37	37	40	35	36	36	41	36	34	36	37	35	38
Increase taxes, increase social spending	56	57	53	58	56	59	52	58	58	56	55	59	55
None/don't know/not answered	4	4	5	3	4	4	5	3	3	4	4	4	5
BASE: ALL RESPONDENTS Weighted	2930	695	637	689	661	688	661	226	176	1015	931	1050	942
Unweighted	3029	725	659	702	686	716	686	234	176	1046	933	1098	988

1.2 PRIORITIES FOR EXTRA GOVERNMENT SPENDING (Q67)
by social class, party identification, age and annual household income

	TOTAL	SOCIAL CLASS				PARTY IDENTIFICATION				AGE			HOUSEHOLD INCOME			
		I/II	III non-manual	III manual	IV/V	Cons.	SLD/ SDP	Labour	Non-aligned	18-34	35-54	55+	Less than £6000	£6000 - £11999	£12000 - £19999	£20000 +
FIRST PRIORITY	%	%	%	%	%	%	%	%	%	%	%	%	%	%	%	%
Health	61	54	64	62	64	56	60	67	55	60	62	60	59	62	62	56
Education	19	25	17	19	15	21	25	14	22	20	23	13	15	16	21	26
Housing	7	6	5	6	9	5	7	7	11	8	5	7	9	8	5	6
Social security benefits	5	3	4	5	8	3	4	8	5	5	2	8	11	5	3	2
Police and prisons	2	2	3	1	1	4	1	1	2	2	2	3	2	2	3	2
Help for industry	2	4	2	2	1	4	1	1	1	2	2	2	2	2	2	2
FIRST OR SECOND PRIORITY	%	%	%	%	%	%	%	%	%	%	%	%	%	%	%	%
Health	83	80	85	83	86	81	85	86	81	83	85	81	81	83	86	82
Education	55	61	53	52	51	54	60	53	53	58	64	41	40	52	64	64
Housing	21	16	20	24	26	16	22	25	29	24	18	23	28	23	17	16
Social security benefits	14	10	11	16	18	9	15	21	13	13	9	21	27	14	9	8
Police and prisons	7	8	9	6	6	12	4	4	4	5	7	9	7	9	7	6
Help for industry	7	9	9	7	5	11	3	4	7	6	6	8	6	7	7	9
BASE: ALL RESPONDENTS																
Weighted	*2930*	*734*	*695*	*637*	*689*	*1157*	*330*	*982*	*208*	*931*	*1050*	*942*	*671*	*645*	*676*	*563*
Unweighted	*3029*	*764*	*725*	*659*	*702*	*1198*	*335*	*1017*	*215*	*933*	*1098*	*988*	*733*	*657*	*680*	*574*

Defence, Public transport, Roads and Overseas aid were chosen by less than 5 per cent of respondents as first or second priority, so figures are not shown here.

1.3 PRIORITIES FOR SPENDING ON SOCIAL BENEFITS (Q68)
by social class, party identification, age and annual household income

	TOTAL	SOCIAL CLASS				PARTY IDENTIFICATION				AGE			HOUSEHOLD INCOME			
		I/II	III non-manual	III manual	IV/V	Cons.	SLD/ SDP	Labour	Non-aligned	18-34	35-54	55+	Less than £6000	£6000 - £11999	£12000 - £19999	£20000 +
FIRST PRIORITY	%	%	%	%	%	%	%	%	%	%	%	%	%	%	%	%
Retirement pensions	43	40	43	50	42	48	40	41	29	25	44	60	52	42	39	41
Disabled benefits	26	30	28	22	24	30	31	21	22	22	27	28	24	25	26	27
Child benefits	14	13	13	13	15	11	13	15	23	25	13	4	8	16	18	14
Unemployment benefits	11	12	10	9	11	6	11	16	13	17	11	6	10	11	12	12
Single parent benefits	5	4	6	5	7	4	5	6	12	11	5	1	6	5	4	5
FIRST OR SECOND PRIORITY	%	%	%	%	%	%	%	%	%	%	%	%	%	%	%	%
Retirement pensions	67	67	67	72	64	74	65	62	55	47	69	83	72	65	68	63
Disabled benefits	60	63	65	58	55	67	65	52	51	47	60	73	65	57	55	61
Child benefits	30	27	28	32	31	25	25	33	39	44	29	16	23	32	35	29
Unemployment benefits	25	24	22	23	28	16	26	33	28	31	24	19	24	28	22	24
Single parent benefits	17	16	17	13	20	15	16	18	23	29	16	7	14	17	16	19
BASE: ALL RESPONDENTS																
Weighted	2930	734	695	637	689	1157	330	982	208	931	1050	942	671	645	676	563
Unweighted	3029	764	725	659	702	1198	335	1017	215	933	1098	988	733	657	680	574

1.4 EXTENT AND EXPLANATIONS OF POVERTY (B89a, B91)
by annual household income and annual household income within party identification

	TOTAL	HOUSEHOLD INCOME				CONSERVATIVE IDENTIFIERS					LABOUR IDENTIFIERS				
						ALL	INCOME				ALL	INCOME			
		Less than £6000	£6000 - £11999	£12000 - £19999	£20000 +		Less than £6000	£6000 - £11999	£12000 - £19999	£20000 +		Less than £6000	£6000 - £11999	£12000 - £19999	£20000 +
HOW MUCH POVERTY IS THERE IN BRITAIN TODAY?	%	%	%	%	%	%	%	%	%	%	%	%	%	%	%
Very little	34	30	32	34	39	49	50	48	49	51	17	18	18	19	7
Quite a lot	63	66	64	64	58	47	43	47	50	46	81	79	80	81	89
Don't know/not answered	4	5	4	2	3	4	8	5	1	3	2	3	2	-	4
WHY ARE THERE PEOPLE WHO LIVE IN NEED?	%	%	%	%	%	%	%	%	%	%	%	%	%	%	%
Inevitable part of modern life	34	29	39	30	42	39	29	52	34	45	30	33	34	24	27
Because of injustice in society	29	33	26	35	21	12	15	8	14	7	46	43	38	60	54
Because of laziness/lack of willpower	19	20	18	20	19	30	39	24	30	26	9	8	14	8	7
Because they have been unlucky	11	12	9	8	11	12	13	8	12	13	8	11	8	4	6
Other answers	2	1	2	3	4	3	-	3	5	6	1	1	1	-	4
None/don't know/not answered	5	5	6	4	3	4	4	5	4	3	5	6	6	4	2
BASE: E RESPONDENTS															
Weighted	1461	342	322	324	282	593	101	112	147	158	463	160	123	81	51
Unweighted	1516	365	325	334	295	626	107	116	154	171	477	171	121	86	48

1.5 IMAGES OF THE WELFARE STATE (A230b,c,d,e) by social class, party identification, age and compressed Goldthorpe class schema

	TOTAL	SOCIAL CLASS				PARTY IDENTIFICATION				AGE			COMPRESSED GOLDTHORPE CLASS SCHEMA				
		I/II	III non-manual	III manual	IV/V	Cons.	SLD/SDP	Labour	Non-aligned	18-34	35-54	55+	Salariat	Routine non-manual	Petty bourgeoisie	Foreman and technicians	Working class
	%	%	%	%	%	%	%	%	%	%	%	%	%	%	%	%	%
PEOPLE RECEIVING SOCIAL SECURITY ARE MADE TO FEEL LIKE SECOND CLASS CITIZENS																	
Agree strongly/agree	53	52	47	55	59	36	59	69	58	58	54	47	51	50	40	57	58
Neither agree nor disagree	22	23	26	18	21	30	24	14	16	20	24	23	25	25	24	20	19
Disagree strongly/disagree	24	24	26	27	19	33	17	17	25	22	21	28	22	25	34	22	22
THE WELFARE STATE MAKES PEOPLE NOWADAYS LESS WILLING TO LOOK AFTER THEMSELVES																	
Agree strongly/agree	39	41	43	39	32	51	36	25	41	30	36	51	40	42	47	42	35
Neither agree nor disagree	23	20	24	23	24	22	21	21	36	29	21	19	22	23	18	20	24
Disagree strongly/disagree	37	39	33	37	42	26	43	53	20	41	41	29	38	34	35	36	39
SOCIAL WORKERS HAVE TOO MUCH POWER TO INTERFERE WITH PEOPLE'S LIVES																	
Agree strongly/agree	36	36	32	42	36	36	39	34	40	33	36	40	34	34	32	46	40
Neither agree nor disagree	35	34	38	31	35	35	31	34	35	37	34	32	38	36	36	26	33
Disagree strongly/disagree	28	29	29	26	27	27	31	31	23	30	30	26	28	29	33	27	26
THE WELFARE STATE ENCOURAGES PEOPLE TO STOP HELPING EACH OTHER																	
Agree strongly/agree	32	36	29	30	32	38	32	24	33	22	33	39	35	30	32	37	30
Neither agree nor disagree	27	22	28	28	27	29	19	24	39	35	23	23	22	28	32	23	28
Disagree strongly/disagree	41	40	42	42	38	33	49	51	28	42	43	36	41	42	36	37	41
BASE: A RESPONDENTS																	
Weighted	1274	321	302	264	308	511	135	444	83	427	430	414	306	286	94	83	437
Unweighted	1307	332	315	272	311	518	141	454	86	421	455	428	318	295	95	78	448

1.6 ATTITUDES TOWARDS STATE BENEFITS (Q69, Q70, Q231q,r) by social class, party identification, age and annual household income

	TOTAL	SOCIAL CLASS				PARTY IDENTIFICATION				AGE			HOUSEHOLD INCOME			
		I/II	III non-manual	III manual	IV/V	Cons	SLD/SDP	Labour	Non-aligned	18-34	35-54	55+	Less than £6000	£6000–£11999	£12000–£19999	£20000+
★MANY PEOPLE FALSELY CLAIM BENEFITS	%	%	%	%	%	%	%	%	%	%	%	%	%	%	%	%
Agree strongly/slightly	65	59	70	70	66	73	58	59	70	66	66	65	63	70	67	61
Disagree strongly/slightly	26	32	23	22	26	19	31	33	19	29	27	23	25	24	26	32
Don't know/not answered	8	9	7	8	8	8	10	8	12	5	8	12	12	6	7	7
★MANY PEOPLE FAIL TO CLAIM BENEFITS																
Agree strongly/slightly	84	84	83	84	85	81	84	86	84	86	88	77	79	84	87	87
Disagree strongly/slightly	10	9	10	9	10	13	8	8	5	11	7	11	10	9	10	8
Don't know/not answered	7	7	7	7	6	6	8	6	11	4	5	11	10	7	3	5
★BENEFITS FOR THE UNEMPLOYED ARE …																
Too low and cause hardship	52	48	46	52	61	33	55	71	47	60	52	44	56	54	51	50
Too high and discourage job finding	27	29	32	26	21	40	21	14	30	21	28	31	24	28	30	26
†MANY PEOPLE WHO GET SOCIAL SECURITY DON'T DESERVE HELP																
Agree strongly/agree	28	25	27	32	29	35	22	20	28	19	28	36	32	28	29	21
Neither agree nor disagree	27	26	28	29	25	32	27	20	30	26	25	29	24	28	25	27
Disagree strongly/disagree	45	48	45	37	45	32	50	58	43	53	46	34	42	43	46	52
†MOST PEOPLE ON THE DOLE ARE FIDDLING																
Agree strongly/agree	31	24	29	36	38	36	25	28	35	31	29	34	35	32	34	24
Neither agree nor disagree	31	30	35	33	26	35	30	25	34	29	29	34	31	31	28	32
Disagree strongly/disagree	37	45	35	30	34	28	43	46	31	39	40	31	33	36	37	44
★BASE: ALL RESPONDENTS Weighted	2930	734	695	637	689	1157	330	982	208	931	1050	942	671	645	676	563
Unweighted	3029	764	725	659	702	1198	335	1017	215	933	1098	988	733	657	680	574
†BASE: SELF-COMPLETION Weighted	2529	654	607	551	574	1033	292	830	169	817	915	791	556	570	606	506
Unweighted	2604	676	633	567	584	1069	302	848	176	813	956	826	606	578	608	517

2 The state of the unions

*Neil Millward**

Trade unions in Britain have been of enduring political, economic and sociological interest since their foundation in the 19th century. For much of this century they have also been a cornerstone of the Labour Party. And until recently they have played a major role in many of the country's national economic institutions. Despite this, the characteristics and attitudes of trade unionists have rarely been the focus of large-scale, systematic survey research. We still know little about the characteristics of union members, or about their reasons for belonging to unions or about any distinctive attitudes they may have.

Some recent studies (see, for instance, Elias, 1990; Gallie, 1989; Stevens, Millward and Smart, 1989) have, however, begun partly to remedy the omission. The *British Social Attitudes* series has gone further in three important respects. First, since its inception in 1983 it has included a small number of basic questions about trade union membership which now provide the start of a valuable time-series through a period of rapid change. Secondly, the series has provided the basis for systematic comparisons across a number of countries on the characteristics of union members and on some of the broader economic effects of trade unions (see the chapter by Blanchflower and Oswald in *The 6th Report*). Thirdly, by including a small module of new questions (designed for repetition), the 1989 survey provides the opportunity to explore in more depth both the attitudes associated with union membership and some of the social and institutional supports for it.

This chapter provides an initial examination of these important new data. It begins by discussing public attitudes towards unions and then goes on to review trends in union membership over recent years. It then moves to the question of compulsory union membership – the closed shop – and the issue of 'free-riders', both from the standpoint of union members and of non-members. Finally the chapter looks at attitudes to work and perceptions of the workplace, and the association between union membership and party identification.

* Senior Fellow, Policy Studies Institute.

Trade unions and popular opinion

The survey series includes several questions – some asked regularly, others intermittently – to tap perceptions of trade unions among the public at large. We briefly discuss the findings of three of these items: on the perceived power of the unions; their efficiency; and their relevance in protecting employees' interests. These questions are asked of all respondents (employees and non-employees) on the self-completion supplement.

Union power

We have asked since 1985: "Do you think that trade unions in this country have too much power or too little power?", and followed this question by two similar questions on the power of business and industry, and of the government. As the table below shows, there have been marked shifts on all three measures:

	Trade unions		Business and industry		Government	
	1985	**1989**	**1985**	**1989**	**1985**	**1989**
%believing each has:	%	%	%	%	%	%
Far too much/too much power	54	40	21	36	48	54
About right amount	28	33	47	42	41	37
Too little/far too little power	11	19	13	8	4	3
Can't choose	7	9	19	14	7	6

As recently as 1985, a majority saw the unions as over-powerful. By 1989, however, although two in five respondents are still suspicious of their power, a significantly higher proportion than before feels either that the balance is about right, or that the unions now have too little power. In contrast, wariness of government and (especially) business and industry has grown.

Among which groups has criticism of union power fallen most steeply? Predictably, perhaps, it is among those who were formerly the most critical: older people (particularly older women), those in the professional and managerial classes and, more surprisingly perhaps, Conservative identifiers. In 1985, 82 per cent of Conservatives thought that the unions had too much power; only 58 per cent believe that nowadays. And the fall has been even sharper among those trade union members in the sample who are Conservative Party supporters. Otherwise the shifts in attitude are common to all economic sectors and are of a similar size among both union members and non-members.

We also asked employees with recognised unions at their workplace if they thought that their union wielded too much power there. Only four per cent thought so. Around half thought that it had about the right amount, and 37 per cent said that it had too little power. Clearly the public image of trade unions is one thing; their role in the workplace is quite another.

How well are the unions run?

In several of the fieldwork rounds we have asked respondents how well various large British institutions are run. The latest data (from 1987) bring the unions little comfort. Trade unions were among a small cluster of institutions (local government, nationalised industries, the NHS and state schools) that were seen by around two-thirds of the public as not well run ("not very" or "not at all"). In fact, unions (at 68 per cent) were the most criticised of 15 national institutions presented. But at least this proportion has remained more or less stable over the years – in contrast to the slump in esteem experienced by the NHS, the press and the police. More details are given in Jowell and Topf in *The 5th Report* (1988, pp. 118–20, 125–6).

Favourable perceptions of the unions decline steeply with age. They are also, as on the issue of trade union power, strongly associated with party politics. In 1987, only 16 per cent of Conservative identifiers thought that the unions were well run, as against 45 per cent of Labour identifiers. The decline between 1983 and 1987 in esteem of trade unions appears to be particularly sharp among skilled manual workers, and among the youngest group in our sample (aged 18–24) – but younger people tend to be more critical than their elders of many other British institutions too.

The relevance of unions

Despite the fact that many people nowadays feel that trade union power has been reduced too much, or at least to the right sort of level, there is also a growing feeling (although still a minority one) that strong unions are not all that necessary.

In 1985 we asked respondents whether they agreed or disagreed that "employees need strong trade unions to protect their interests". The question was repeated in 1989. The figures have moved only a little; more people still agree than disagree, but the gap has narrowed.

	1985		1989	
	All	Employees only	All	Employees only
	%	%	%	%
Employees need strong trade unions to protect their interests:				
Agree stongly/agree	45	43	41	37
Neither	26	29	22	26
Disagree/disagree strongly	27	28	32	34

Predictably enough, unions are seen as less relevant (on this criterion at least) among some population subgroups than among others: for instance, among those in non-manual occupations; among those in the private, non-manufacturing sector; and among women, especially women aged over 35. In 1989, 53 per cent of union members felt that unions were necessary to protect employees' interests, while only 27 per cent of employees who were not union members thought so. It is among non-members that the change in attitudes since our first reading in

1985 has been especially marked: they are even less convinced of the importance of strong unions than they used to be. So far we have sufficient data to give only signals, not firm time-trends. Nonetheless the signals must convey worrying messages to the union movement.

Trends in union membership

Union density

In common with many industrialised countries, Britain has experienced a decline in union membership in the 1980s. The figures in the table below are based on employees only, since they are by far the largest group of people who are members at any one time.[1]

Union density and recognition, 1983–1989

	1983	1984	1985	1986	1987	1989
% of employees:						
Belonging to trade unions*	49%	47%	47%	46%	46%	44%
With recognised unions at their workplace	66%	66%	63%	62%	63%	56%

* Including staff associations

Union density – the percentage of employees who are trade union members – declined from 49 per cent to 44 per cent between 1983 and 1989.[2] This represents a loss of something over a million members. The decline since 1979 has probably been over two and a half million.[3]

The reasons for this fall are a matter of considerable debate. Some analysts, on the basis of the annual figures for union membership, have argued that inflation, or more particularly the threat of a decline in real wages, produces an increase in membership (Carruth and Disney, 1988), as happened in the late 1970s. They also identify a (rather weak) link with the level of unemployment, which they attribute to increased employer resistance to unions when unemployment is high. These aggregate, 'business cycle' explanations have sometimes incorporated a political dimension too, noting relative declines in membership under Conservative governments. This view of the macroeconomic and political determinants of union membership has recently been challenged by one that focuses on the impact of labour relations legislation, attributing virtually all the decline in membership since 1980 to the legal changes affecting unions in particular, and industrial relations generally (Freeman and Pelletier, 1989).

A contrasting body of analysis, using cross-sectional or 'snap-shot' data in the main, links the overall decline in union membership with a reduction in the numbers of jobs in the more heavily unionised sectors of the economy. The decline in large-scale manufacturing employment, in manual and less-skilled jobs, in male full-time employment relative to female part-time employment, and in public sector jobs have all been identified as contributing to falling union membership (Bain and Elias, 1985; Millward and Stevens, 1986; Gallie, 1989). More recently, longitudinal studies have provided data on union membership and job history for the whole of an individual's working life; so a number of additional factors associated with the prospensity to join (and remain in) a union can be identified. These include length of previous membership, proximity to other unionised workplaces and access to reserved internal promotion opportunities (Elias, 1990). Furthermore, these data suggest that "there has been no major collapse of commitment to the unions among trade union members in the 1980s and that structural factors are the most decisive influences on the level of membership" (Gallie, 1989, p.23).

We have examined the *British Social Attitudes* data to try to discover if the fall in union membership has been across the board, or whether the decline has been faster among some groups than others. Our subsamples are not large, so the evidence should be regarded with caution. But it does appear that the drift away from membership has been a little faster among men than among women, and among older employees than among those aged under 35. There are indications too that a smaller proportion of semi- and unskilled workers are members now than was the case in 1983. Profiles of union members in both 1983 and 1989 are shown in **Table 2.1**.

There is also some evidence (from the 1984 and 1989 data) that whereas union membership has remained more or less steady in smaller workplaces (with fewer than 25 employees) and very large ones (with over 500), it may be dropping faster in those of medium size – and also in the public sector.* All these findings are, however, tentative.

Union recognition and 'free-riders'

Whatever the strengths of the competing or sometimes complementary explanations of membership decline, a clear pointer to the reasons for the five percentage point fall in union density comes from the second line in the table above. This shows a fall of eight points since 1983 in the percentage of employees who say that there are trade unions at their place of work which are recognised by the management for negotiating pay and conditions of employment – a very similar *rate* of decline to that in union density. As we shall see later, the reasons people themselves give for being union members are considerably less numerous and less compelling when they are in workplaces where the union has no formal negotiating role in respect of pay; a decline in union recognition – itself arising from a mix of structural and contextual changes – seems a strong candidate as one of the main causes of declining membership.[4]

It is tempting to focus on the difference between the 58 per cent in workplaces with recognised unions and the 44 per cent who belong to a union. At face value this 14 percentage point gap suggests that unions have failed to recruit a substantial minority of employees at workplaces where they are already strongly established. In fact, as many as 16 per cent of all employees – or 28 per cent of those with a recognised union at their workplace – fall into this category. (This 16 per cent reduces to 14 per cent when we subtract those employees who are union members, but have no recognised union at their workplace).

However, not all employees who have a recognised union at their workplace

---

* Economic sector was not coded in 1983; neither did we collect detailed information on workplace size in the first year of the survey series.

are in practice potential recruits for the unions. For instance, unions are unlikely to have much success in recruiting senior managers in the private sector, some of whom they will be negotiating with as employers' representatives. Except in the public sector, union negotiations rarely cover the higher levels of management (Millward and Stevens, 1986). Nonetheless the bulk of non-members in workplaces with recognised unions *are* potential recruits, even if some are in occupations that are not currently covered by union-management negotiations. Because the effects of union activity on, for example, pay levels and grievance handling spill over to other groups of workers at the same workplace, employees who are not members but who have a recognised union at their workplace are commonly referred to in the academic literature as 'free-riders' – people who receive some of the benefits of union activity but who make no contribution to it. In some countries it is common practice for free-riders to make payments to the union in return for the benefits it has negotiated; in others (as in Britain briefly in the 1970s) they make an equivalent donation to charity.* Current legislation discourages such arrangements in Britain, so the issue remains a substantial one for the unions, apparently affecting up to a quarter of employees in workplaces with recognised unions.

Many trade unions in Britain, and indeed elsewhere, have addressed this endemic problem by instituting various forms of compulsory membership, commonly referred to as 'the closed shop'. In some industries and occupations such arrangements have a long history – for example among printers and professional musicians. Periodically the closed shop has been the target of government legislation, notably in the early 1970s and the 1980s. Anticipating a further round of legislation finally to "outlaw the closed shop", a recent government White Paper (Department of Employment, 1989) stressed the economic ill-effects of the practice, and reiterated the moral repugnance of the government to obligatory union membership.

At about the same time, discussions within the European Community were leading towards what has subsequently become the *Community Charter of the Fundamental Social Rights of Workers* (commonly referred to as the 'Social Charter') and its associated Action Programme. These discussions, and the Labour Party's policy review of industrial relations, highlighted the absence of a positive legal right in Britain to belong to a trade union, as well as the issue of a right *not* to belong to a union.

It was in this climate of heightened public interest in trade union membership, and the compulsion associated with the closed shop, that it was decided to include a small module of specific questions on the topic in the *British Social Attitudes* series. The results may be used to estimate the extent of the closed shop in Britain and to explore whether there are significant differences in attitudes between union members in closed shops, other union members, and non-members.

Compulsory union membership

The *British Social Attitudes* question on compulsory union membership is very similar to one included at about the same time in a government-sponsored survey

---

* The legal aspects of the free-rider issue are extensively discussed in Wedderburn (1990).

(see Stevens, Millward and Smart, 1989). It asks employees what would happen if they left their present job and were replaced by someone else. Would their replacement "have to be a union member *before being considered* for the job, *before starting* the job, *after starting* the job, or would they *not* be required to join a union?" The overall results for 1989 are as follows:

Employees in closed shops

	All employees %	All union members %
Trade union membership required:		
Before being considered for the job	2	4
Before starting the job	3	7
After starting the job	10	22
Total membership of closed shops	**15**	**33**

Thus about one in seven employees – one in three of all those who are union members – consider that they work in circumstances where trade union membership is a job requirement. And a third of these closed-shop members (five per cent of employees) are covered by the more rigorous version of the arrangement, the 'pre-entry' closed shop.[5]

The characteristics of workplaces with, and of employees in, closed shops are very much in line with those found in other surveys (Millward and Stevens, 1986; Stevens, Millward and Smart, 1989). Closed-shop members are more likely to be found in larger workplaces, a relationship partly, but not wholly, reflecting the pattern of union membership in general (see **Table 2.2**). The difference between state-owned industries and private sector industry and commerce is particularly striking. In state-owned industries, two-fifths of employees – over a half of union members – say that they are working in a closed shop; in contrast, within the private sector only one-eighth of employees – about a third of union members – are in a closed shop. In the public services union membership is nearly as high as in the state-owned industries, but closed-shop membership is very much lower.

Closed shop membership is even more strongly associated with the employee's age than is union membership as a whole (again see **Table 2.2**); the fact that employees aged 55 and over are substantially more likely to be in closed shops than are younger workers itself suggests a continuing decline in the closed-shop population, irrespective of other influences. However, we should caution against predicting an early demise of the closed shop on the basis of employment trends for men and women. For even though many more male than female full-time employees are closed shop members, *part-time* employees (most of whom are female) are actually more likely to be in closed shops than are full-time female employees. Nearly a half of female union members working part time see themselves as in a closed shop, compared with less than a quarter of female full-time employees who do so. **Table 2.2** gives full details.

British Social Attitudes 1989 is the first national sample survey to give a clear indication of the broad occupational groups in which closed-shop members are concentrated. Not surprisingly, perhaps, manual workers are far more likely to be in a closed shop than non-manual workers. Moreover, not much of the difference is accounted for by the lower rate of union membership among non-manual workers. Among manual workers, fully a quarter of employees and one half of union members are in closed shops. Of all employees who report that they are in a closed shop, 38 per cent are skilled manual workers and 29 per cent are partly skilled manual workers. In all, manual workers account for very nearly three-quarters of closed shop membership (again see **Table 2.2**).

Reasons for union membership

The circumstances in which employees come to join trade unions vary greatly, as do the benefits that membership brings. Eleven per cent of members say they are required to be members to obtain their job in the first place, and 22 per cent have to become members to keep their jobs. A further 63 per cent also gain the direct benefits of collective bargaining by their union, and a small minority (four per cent) does not benefit directly from collective bargaining, but may have other work benefits such as grievance representation. Do these different circumstances affect the reasons people give for being a member?

Those union members who were employees were read a list of eight possible reasons for belonging to a trade union and asked to say how important each one was for them. The answer category of "does not apply to me" was also offered. The responses, summarised in the table below, should be seen as an amalgam of past and current reasons.*

Reasons for belonging to a trade union

		Very/fairly important	Not very/not at all important/does not apply to me
To protect me if problems come up	%	93	6
To get higher pay and better working conditions	%	80	20
To get members' benefits	%	71	29
To help other people I work with	%	76	23
I believe in them in principle	%	67	33
Most of my colleagues are members	%	55	45
It's a tradition in my family	%	15	84
It's a condition of having my job	%	38	62

Mutual protection and higher wages have been the bedrock of trade unionism since its birth. So it should be no surprise that the two most widely endorsed reasons for union membership are "to protect me if problems come up" (rated as important by over 90 per cent of members) and "to get higher pay and better working conditions" (80 per cent). However, higher pay weighs even more heavily with members of closed shops than with other members (see **Table 2.3**). This

---

* The question did not attempt to distinguish people's original reasons for joining a union from their reasons for remaining in one; such distinctions would have needed more elaborate questioning than was possible within the space available.

accords with recent studies which have underlined the effectiveness of unions –
and of those operating closed shops in particular – in achieving higher wages
than in comparable non-union workplaces (Stewart, 1987; Metcalf, 1988; Blanchflower, Oswald and Garrett, 1990).[6] Indeed, as Blanchflower and Oswald have
shown in *The 6th Report*, "British trade unions have much the same impact on
wages as do their counterparts in mainland Western Europe", but rather less so
than in Australia and (especially) the USA (p.26).

Interestingly, 'protection' is the most common of all the reasons given by the
very small number of members in workplaces where their union is not recognised
by management for pay bargaining.[7] Among these members 'protection' is the *only*
instrumental reason endorsed by the majority – an indication, presumably, of the
union's potential role in dealing with *grievances*, but its lack of an established role
in *bargaining*. However, since grievance representation is virtually universal in
workplaces with recognised unions (Millward and Stevens, 1986), it is unsurprising
that almost all members in both closed and open shops also think that the protection
union membership offers is an important reason for joining (and staying a member).

A third instrumental reason – that is, one clearly grounded in self-interest –
is "to get members' benefits like financial or health schemes", and this also
receives widespread support (from 71 per cent). This may in part reflect the
increased emphasis that some unions have put on these benefits in recent years
(Industrial Relations Services, 1990).

Two 'solidaristic' reasons for membership, concerned with mutal assistance or
the pursuit of collective interests, also receive majority endorsement: "to help other
people I work with" (important to just over three-quarters of members) and "I
believe in them in principle" (around two-thirds of members). Helping workmates
or colleagues is particularly widely cited by employees in pre-entry closed shops –
probably reflecting strong occupational loyalties built up through apprenticeships or
similar work socialisation.[8] Belief in trade unionism as a principle is widespread
among members, and hardly varies between the two main types of closed shop or
between the two types of open shop. But closed-shop members *as a whole* cite
principle more frequently than do members not in closed shops. Strikingly, two-
thirds of (the admittedly small number of) unionists who are *not* represented for
pay bargaining in their employment feel that belonging to a union is an important
principle, despite not deriving one of the most demonstrable benefits of unionism.

Other reasons relate to social pressures. The first of these, "most of my
workmates or colleagues are members", is endorsed by a majority of members
and is naturally of much greater prevalence in closed shops than open shops[9]
(see **Table 2.3**). Family tradition, though not seen as important by many (15
per cent overall), is noticeably more widespread as a reason among members in
pre-entry closed shops, perhaps reflecting the greater continuity between generations
in occupations associated with the pre-entry closed shop.

Not surprisingly, nearly 80 per cent of closed-shop members refer to their union
membership as "a condition of having my job". But a sizeable proportion (17
per cent) of members in *open* shops also give this reason for membership. Why
should they believe this? We suspect it is because (as we have noted) our question
did not attempt to distinguish between past and current reasons for being a
member: some respondents may have been referring to their original reasons for
having joined a union, not to their reasons for continuing to be a member. Further
explanations may be that some workers – particularly skilled manual workers –
use their union membership as evidence of an occupational qualification, such as

a trade apprenticeship, and that some workers (such as vehicle drivers) need a union card when visiting the premises of some other, unionised, employers.

It is important to note that closed-shop members do not regard their union membership just as a matter of compulsion. On the contrary, they tend to regard *all* the other reasons offered as important, except for family tradition. This suggests that continued employment in a closed shop may actually strengthen trade union allegiance, as also appears to be the case among union members generally (Gallie, 1989). However, as we shall see later, closed-shop members are more active in union affairs. So the strong endorsement by closed-shop members of both instrumental and solidaristic reasons for belonging, and the reinforcement that this gives to *continued* membership, suggests that, even if their workplace were to change to an open shop, their trade union allegiance would be unlikely to weaken, at least in the short term. Thus, although legislative changes may outlaw the pre-entry closed shop, it appears unlikely that they would diminish this type of union membership in any dramatic way.

The relative strength of workplace union organisation, be it pre-entry closed shop at the one extreme or the lack of basic recognition at the other, clearly has some bearing on members' reasons for belonging to their union. But other factors, such as age and job status, also have an important bearing. Instrumental reasons, particularly "higher pay and better working conditions", are most often cited by members early in their working lives, at an age when family formation is likely to bring economic difficulties. Those lower down the occupational hierarchy, and hence generally the lower paid, also give relatively greater weight to instrumental reasons rather than to principle.

% of members saying each reason is important for belonging to a union	To get higher pay and better working conditions	Belief in unions in principle
Total:	81%	67%
Age:		
18–24	86%	51%
25–34	87%	69%
35–44	75%	68%
45–54	80%	69%
55+	82%	72%
Socio-economic group:		
Higher professional and managerial	69%	64%
Intermediate non-manual	73%	63%
Junior non-manual	80%	59%
Skilled manual	86%	75%
Semi-skilled and unskilled manual	90%	71%

Employees in the youngest age group – and hence least likely to be in positions of authority – particularly stress "protection" (virtually all 18–24 year olds think this important). Solidaristic reasons are more relevant for the older age groups, and particularly for those in skilled manual jobs. Similarly, "family tradition", although rarely seen as *very* important, is markedly more often cited by older men in manual jobs. The association with age is dramatic: only five per cent of members aged under 25 see a family tradition of trade unionism as important, compared with a quarter of members aged 55 and over.

A rather different question, earlier in the interview, asked employees with recognised unions at their workplace what the unions should be trying to achieve there. Respondents were shown 10 possible objectives and asked to rate them as first, second or third in terms of importance. The responses reflect the primacy of economic concerns (pay and job security), already shown when we asked members why they belonged. They also reflect, to a lesser extent, concerns about equity and about lack of control over their work situation:

	Most important reason		Most, second or third most important reason	
	Members	Non-members	Members	Non-members
What should the unions do at your workplace?	%	%	%	%
Protect existing jobs	30	23	68	55
Improve pay	29	25	70	66
Improve working conditions	21	20	61	58
Have more say over management's long-term plans	7	5	32	19
Have more say over how work is done day-to-day	3	3	20	16
Reduce pay differences at the workplace	5	7	19	22
Work for equal opportunities for women	2	5	15	22
Work for equal opportunities for ethnic minorities	*	*	4	7
None of these/don't know/not answered	2	11	n/a	n/a

Improving pay and working conditions, together with job protection, are the objectives that both members and non-members most frequently mention. Between a fifth and a third think these the *most* important aims for the unions to pursue, and between a half and three-quarters gave these goals as one of the three most important. A substantial minority attaches importance to pursuing equal opportunities for women; but only a very small proportion of both members and non-members mention the pursuit of equity for ethnic minorities as an important role for unions at their workplace; this may, in part at least, reflect the fact that fewer workplaces employ people from ethnic minorities than employ women. Minorities also attach importance to the role of the unions in reducing pay differences between different occupational groups, having more say over day-to-day matters and over management's long-term plans.

A rather surprising finding, perhaps, is that the differences between union members and non-members (the so-called 'free-riders') are not very pronounced. True, rather more non-members are undecided about which of the 10 objectives is most important (and significantly fewer of them endorse job protection as the most important issue for the unions to pursue); but in other respects they are hardly distinguishable from members in terms of what they think the unions should be doing. Free-riders, then, are generally in accord with members over what aims the unions should be pursuing at their workplace. Their reasons for not belonging to a union are thus of some interest.

Reasons for non-membership

Non-membership – as with membership – of a union may result from a variety of circumstances. Those who have had experience of union membership in the past might be expected to have rather different reasons for current non-membership from those who have never belonged. More importantly, not being a member is quite different in a workplace where unions negotiate pay (the 'free-rider') from not being one in a workplace where unions are not recognised by management. We use these distinctions later. But first we show the overall reasons that non-members give for not belonging to a union.

Reasons for not belonging to a union

		Very/fairly important	Not very/not at all important/does not apply to me
I can't see any advantage in joining	%	28	70
It costs too much	%	6	92
Management disapproves of them at my workplace	%	13	83
I feel it would damage my job prospects	%	11	87
They would only cause trouble at my workplace	%	17	80
I disagree with them in principle	%	23	75
Don't approve of the one I could join at my workplace	%	5	93
Not appropriate to my work	%	26	71
No-one has ever asked me to join	%	11	88
There is no union at my workplace	%	17	81

As the table above shows, large proportions of non-members are simply indifferent to the question of union membership. Across the range of 10 possible reasons offered for not being a union member, none was chosen by more than a third as being "very" or "fairly" important; on average each reason was endorsed by only 16 per cent of non-members. This compares with an average of 62 per cent of *members* who think each of the eight suggested reasons for being a member is important.

To begin with the instrumental reasons, 28 per cent can see no positive advantage in joining; six per cent say that belonging would cost too much. Both of these reasons are more commonly given by employees in workplaces with recognised unions – broadly speaking, the 'free-riders' (see **Table 2.4**). Indeed nearly a half of free-riders see no benefit in joining – the most frequently endorsed of the 10 reasons offered. This indicates both the scale of the problem facing trade unions in recruitment, and the potential membership gains should free-riders be won over. But the impediments are substantial, as we go on to see.

Employer opposition is clearly an important barrier to union recruitment. Around a tenth of free-riders believe that management disapproves of unions at their place of work, despite the fact that they currently recognise a union for collective bargaining. Again around a tenth of free-riders think that joining a union would damage their job prospects, and a similar number feel union activity would only cause trouble at the workplace. Non-members in workplaces *without* recognised unions are somewhat more likely to cite each of these three reasons as important. Overall, virtually all those employees who cite management disapproval of unions have jobs in private sector industry and services – notably in the engineering industry and in distribution, hotels and catering.* Surprisingly perhaps, management disapproval is more commonly reported in large workplaces than in those with fewer than 500 employees.

Around a quarter of non-members cite disagreement with unions in principle as a very or fairly important reason for them personally. Respondents aged 55 or over and manual workers are particularly likely to give disagreement in principle as an important reason for non-membership. But the most striking difference is between men and women: 34 per cent of female non-members cite "principle" as against only 19 per cent of males. It seems unlikely that occupational differences would account for such a large variation, but the matter merits further investigation. Dissatisfaction with the particular union at their workplace is cited by 14 per cent of free-riders, rather more commonly by those with previous experience of being in a union than those without. Fuller details are shown in **Table 2.4.**

About a quarter of non-members say that unions are inappropriate to their kind of work. This view is rather more common in workplaces with recognised unions and among employees who have never been union members. (About a quarter of these are in professional and managerial occupations and might not be free-riders in the narrow sense.) Among the remaining occupational groups there are no substantial differences.

Finally, around a tenth of non-members say an important reason was that no-one had ever asked them to join; and nearly a quarter of non-members in workplaces without recognised unions cite the lack of a union to join as an important reason (again see **Table 2.4**). Further potential for union recruitment may thus come as much from penetrating a wider range of workplaces as from signing up free-riders in those that are already unionised.

Work attitudes, workplace perceptions and unionism

We have seen something of the reasons for union membership and non-membership. We now look at some of the wider attitudes towards work with which union membership might be associated. For example, are the more 'instrumental' attitudes of closed-shop trade unionists towards their union membership also apparent in their attitudes to their work? Do they seek or expect less intrinsic satisfaction from their jobs than do members in open shops?

Attitudes to work may, of course, be shaped by the characteristics of the job itself and of the circumstances under which the work is done. Particular types of jobs may in themselves engender certain types of attitude. So we make no claim

---

* SIC Divisions 3 and 6 respectively.

that trade union membership and activity has any priority in the complex web of causality that determines attitudes towards work. Indeed, we have examined the associations reported below, to see if they persist when we confine the analysis to particular occupational groups; generally speaking they do *not*. It seems likely, then, that if trade union membership plays any direct role in influencing work attitudes, it is a minor one. Both work attitudes and union membership are likely to be influenced by a range of factors, including job characteristics and general social values. Further analysis is needed to clarify the matter. Nevertheless the association between union membership and work attitudes may be of interest, though this association is likely to be at least partly an artefact of respondents' job characteristics, rather than a result of their union membership.

Attitudes to work

Employees were asked: "If without having to work, you had what you would regard as a reasonable living income, do you think you would still prefer to have a paid job or wouldn't you bother?". A further question (an "agree/disagree" statement) sought to probe employees' commitment to their jobs. As the table below shows, the opinions of closed- and open-shop members seem to be more divided on the latter question than on the former, but the general tendency for closed-shop employees to have more instrumental attitudes is apparent.

Employees' commitment to work

	Union members		Non-members
	Closed shop	Open shop	
Would work even if no financial need	66%	71%	77%
Work is more than just a means of earning a living	56%	74%	70%

We also asked employees about the characteristics they themselves would look for in a new job, and the advice they would give to a young person choosing his or her first job:

Employees' preferred job characteristics

	Union members		Non-members
	Closed shop	Open shop	
Most important job characteristic when choosing a new job:	%	%	%
Interesting work	18	35	30
Job security	27	20	15
Good pay	20	12	13
Most important job characteristic when advising young persons on job choice:	%	%	%
Interesting work	26	35	42
Secure job for the future	57	49	44
Good starting pay	11	5	4

Union members in closed shops appear to be less likely than those in open shops to say that "interesting work" is the most important feature when choosing a new job. Similarly, in advising a young person on a first job, they are rather less likely to emphasise work interest. On both these questions they put greater stress on good pay and job security. Their emphasis on job security is particularly striking, since union members appear to have more of it anyway: union members in pre-entry closed shops are the least likely of the three groups to have been unemployed in the previous five years (and half as likely as all non-members).

However, this emphasis placed by closed-shop members on job security should not necessarily be interpreted as a more general resistance to change at work. As the table below shows, just as many closed-shop members as union members in open shops are willing to be retrained if they have to move jobs. Indeed, it is non-members who are least willing to retrain.

Employees' job flexibility*

| | Union members | | Non-members |
	Closed shop	Open shop	
% saying would be:			
Very willing to retrain if ob-			
liged to take another job	46%	45%	37%
Very/quite willing to move			
area to find another job	24%	30%	29%
Very/quite willing to settle			
for an inferior job	45%	38%	37%

*These questions were asked only of employees who said that, if they lost their job, they would be unlikely to be able to find another job for at least three months.

As the table above shows, members and non-members of unions do not differ in their willingness to move area to get another job or in their willingness to settle for an inferior job if necessary. Nor are there any indications that members in closed shops are less 'flexible' in these respects than trade unionists as a whole.

Perceptions of the workplace

We also sought to discover whether members and non-members of trade unions have different perceptions of their workplaces which help to explain differences in attitude. We can see from the table below that, overall, the great majority of employees, union members as well as non-members, report that their workplace is well managed and that relationships between management and employees are good. However, trade unionists seem rather less inclined than non-unionists to have such favourable views, on these dimensions and on a range of others:

Employees' perceptions of the workplace

	Union members		Non-members
	Closed shop	Open shop	
Well-managed workplace	74%	77%	83%
Good management – employee relations	70%	76%	86%
Pay is reasonable or on the high side	59%	60%	61%
Respondent should have more say in decisions affecting job	60%	55%	35%
Unions at workplace have too little power	46%	41%[†]	29%[*]
Respondent expects workplace to reduce workforce in next year	35%	28%	12%

* Percentage based on non-members in workplaces with recognised trade union(s).
† Percentage based on members in open-shop workplaces with recognised trade union(s).

As we can see, union members are much more likely to expect a decline in employment at their workplace – a realistic view, as we know from other sources (Blanchflower, Millward and Oswald, 1989), though again it should be remembered that there are many other factors related to employment decline, besides unionism, as that analysis shows. Members are also more likely than non-members to say that they personally should have more say in decisions about their work, and to believe that the union at their workplace has too little power.

On all but one of these dimensions – pay levels – closed-shop members contrast most sharply with non-unionists, while open-shop union members are in an intermediate position. Again, we analysed the data by socio-economic group and most of the differences are not statistically significant. Many (but not all) of the differences between closed-shop members, open-shop members and non-members can be 'explained away' by differences between the types of jobs they hold.

Two noteworthy distinctions between union members in closed shops and other employees emerge from these analyses. Union members appear to gain lower intrinsic satisfaction from their work, and they are more dissatisfied with the degree of influence they have over it. This suggests the average trade unionist in a closed shop might look to union activity as a source of satisfaction more commonly than his or her counterparts in open shops. The survey results certainly bear out this hypothesis. On every one of the six trade union activities asked about – including putting motions to union meetings, taking industrial action, picketing and serving as a representative – union members in closed shops report greater participation than other unionists. Moreover, those in pre-entry closed shops were much more likely to be 'activists' than members in post-entry ones were. **Table 2.5** gives full details.

Union membership and party political identification

The association between commitment to trade unionism and allegiance to the Labour Party has been an enduring fact of British political life. In one of the most recent confirmations of this, Gallie (1989) finds "the single most important influence leading to a higher level of favourability to the unions is allegiance to the Labour Party" and that "experience of trade union membership over the work history emerges as the second most important" influence encouraging commitment to trade unionism. We have noted the higher levels of participation in union activities by closed-shop members; so the question arises as to whether closed-shop members show higher identification with the Labour Party than other unionists. The answer seems clear enough: they do, even after discounting their different occupation profiles.

Party identification and union membership*

	Union members		
	Closed shop	Open shop	Non-members
	%	%	%
Conservative	27	36	46
SLD/SDP	11	13	11
Labour	45	33	26

*This analysis is limited to employees only.

Union members in closed shops are much more likely than members in open shops to the Labour Party identifiers and much less likely to be Conservative Party identifiers;[10] even so, fewer than half of closed-shop members identify with the Labour Party. But perhaps the most surprising feature of this table is that over a quarter of closed-shop union members are Conservative identifiers. As far as open shops are concerned, union members are just as likely to be Conservative supporters as Labour supporters.

Of course, there is unlikely to be any simple causality underlying the association between being in a closed shop and identifying with the Labour Party. On the other hand it is plausible that the more active participation in union affairs of the average closed-shop member could reinforce a predisposition to support the Labour Party. If so, and if the closed shop continues its decline of the last decade, for whatever reason, there could be long-term repercussions not only for the industrial and economic map of Britain, but for the political map too.

Notes

1. Throughout the remainder of this chapter, the term 'union' refers to both trade unions and staff associations, although the two types of organisation are distinguished in the survey questions. We have combined them because in most cases staff associations have much the same role *vis-à-vis* employers as do trade unions; moreover our initial analysis revealed very few differences between trade union and staff association members.
2. The main groups excluded from the figures for union members are retired employees, the unemployed and the self-employed. Employees normally working fewer than 10 hours per week are also excluded from the figures throughout this chapter; they account for around six per cent of all employees and are mostly women.
3. The focus here is on trade union membership among employees in Britain. Official figures published in the Employment Department *Gazette* cover the whole of the UK and union membership amongst other groups besides employees. Despite these differences, the rate of decline in the official figures is similar to that revealed in the *British Social Attitudes* series over a similar period: the former give a decline of 10 per cent from the end of 1982 to the end of 1988: the *British Social Attitudes* results for early 1983 to early 1989 also show a 10 per cent fall. The official figures indicate a drop of nearly three million members since 1979; this may be an overstatement, however, since membership figures from some unions in the late 1970s are thought to have been exaggerated.

4. In principle, of course, the causal mechanism could be the reverse of what is suggested here. However, on present evidence it seems unlikely that the withering away of membership within workplaces (causing management to withdraw recognition) will be a major factor in the *overall* decline in recognition.
5. These estimates are broadly comparable with those from a NOP survey given in Stevens, Millward and Smart (1989), and predictably a little higher because employees working less than 10 hours a week are not asked these questions on *British Social Attitudes* surveys. The assumption that none of the six per cent of employees working these short hours were in a closed shop would reduce the estimate from *British Social Attitudes* to 14 per cent of all employees. Even without this, the overall figures of 15 per cent from *British Social Attitudes* and 12 per cent from the NOP survey are within conventional limits of sampling error.
6. However, a specific and separate closed-shop wage premium has not been identified in the 1989 *British Social Attitudes* data. The inclusion of a closed-shop variable, instead of a union recognition variable, in the wage equations reported in Table 2 in Blanchflower (1990) produced no significant closed-shop coefficient. I am grateful to David Blanchflower for allowing me to report this result.
7. Since there were only 26 respondents in this category, these findings are subject to larger than usual sampling errors. However, the findings presented here are generally in agreement with those from a NOP survey for the same category of members (Stevens, Millward and Smart, 1989), where the size of the subsample was somewhat larger.
8. The base for members in pre-entry closed shops is rather small (75 cases). The base for those in post-entry closed shops is 137.
9. The importance of social custom in explaining union membership levels in open shops has recently been highlighted by Naylor and Raaum (1989), following Booth (1985).
10. Respondents were classified as identifying with a political party if they thought of themselves as a supporter of the party, or a little closer to it than to others, or if they said they would vote for it if there were a general election tomorrow.

References

BAIN, G.S. and ELIAS, P., 'Trade union membership in Great Britain: an individual level analysis', *British Journal of Industrial Relations*, vol. 23, no. 1, (1985), pp. 79–92.
BLANCHFLOWER, D.G., *Fear, Unemployment and Pay Flexibility*, National Bureau of Economic Research, Boston. Working Paper No. 3365, (1990).
BLANCHFLOWER, D.G. and OSWALD, A.J., 'International patterns of work', in Jowell, R., Witherspoon, S, and Brook, L., *British Social Attitudes: special international report*, Gower, Aldershot (1989).
BLANCHFLOWER, D.G., MILLWARD, N. and OSWALD, A.J., *Unionization and Employment Behaviour*, Discussion Paper No. 339, Centre for Labour Economics, London (1989).
BLANCHFLOWER, D.G., OSWALD, A.J. and GARRETT, M.D., 'Insider power in wage determination', *Economica*, (1990, forthcoming).
BOOTH A.L., 'The free-rider problem and a social custom model of trade union membership', *Quarterly Journal of Economics*, vol. 100, no. 1, (1985), pp. 253–61.
CARRUTH, A. and DISNEY, R., 'Where have two million trade union members gone?', *Economica*, vol. 55, no. 1 (1988), pp. 1–20.
DEPARTMENT OF EMPLOYMENT, *Removing Barriers to Employment*, Cmnd 655, HMSO, London (1989).
ELIAS, P., *Growth and Decline in Trade Union Membership in Great Britain: Evidence from Work Histories*, Working Paper No. 16, ESRC Social Change and Economic Life Initiative, Oxford, (1990).

FREEMAN, R.B. and PELLETIER, J., *The Impact of Industrial Relations Legislation on British Union Density*, Working Paper No. 3167, National Bureau of Economic Research, Boston, (1989).

GALLIE, D., *Trade Union Allegiance and Decline in British Urban Labour Markets*, Working Paper No. 9, ESRC Social Change and Economic Life Initiative, Oxford, (1989).

INDUSTRIAL RELATIONS SERVICES, 'Union services – the way forward?', *Industrial Relations Review and Report*, No. 457, London, (1990), pp. 6–12.

JOWELL, R. and TOPF, R., 'Trust in the establishment', in Jowell, R., Witherspoon, S. and Brook, L. (eds), *British Social Attitudes: the 5th Report*, Gower, Aldershot (1988).

METCALF, D., *Trade Unions and Economic Performance: the British Evidence*, Discussion Paper No. 320, Centre for Labour Economics, London (1988).

MILLWARD, N. and STEVENS, M., *British Workplace Industrial Relations 1980-1984: The DE/ESRC//PSI/ACAS Surveys*, Gower, Aldershot (1986).

NAYLOR R. and RAAUM O., *The open-shop union, wages and management opposition*, Warwick Economic Research Papers No. 332, Warwick (1989).

STEVENS, M., MILLWARD, N. and SMART D., 'Trade union membership and the closed shop in 1989', *Employment Gazette*, vol. 97, no. 11 (1989), pp. 615–22.

STEWART, M.B., 'Collective bargaining arrangements, closed shops and relative pay', *Economic Journal*, vol. 97, no. 1 (1987), pp. 140–56.

WEDDERBURN, Lord, *The Social Charter: European Company and Employment Rights*, Institute of Employment Rights, London (1990).

Acknowledgement

SCPR is grateful to the Department of Employment whose financial support for the survey series since 1984 has enabled us to continue to ask questions on labour market and workplace issues and to expand the module periodically to cover new topics of mutual interest. Researchers at the Department have also provided valuable guidance on both questionnaire coverage and wording. However, final responsibility for this, and for the interpretation of the findings, lies with SCPR, the editors and the author.

2.1 PROFILE OF UNION MEMBERS, 1983 AND 1989 (1989:Q909a)
by sex, age, social class and party identification

	TOTAL	SEX		AGE			SOCIAL CLASS				PARTY IDENTIFICATION			
		Men	Women	18-34	35-54	55+	I/II	III non-manual	III manual	IV/V	Cons.	Alliance SLD/SDP	Labour	Non-aligned
1983														
Union/staff association member	% 27	% 38	% 18	% 26	% 37	% 17	% 37	% 30	% 37	% 37	% 23	% 27	% 35	% 19
Non-member	68	61	74	68	40	78	62	70	63	62	72	67	60	80
BASE: *ALL RESPONDENTS* *Weighted*	1719	793	926	532	594	586	334	268	365	300	664	252	565	137
Unweighted	1761	807	954	525	623	607	343	281	362	316	676	258	584	139
1989														
Union/staff association member	% 26	% 33	% 19	% 27	% 32	% 17	% 31	% 20	% 34	% 23	% 20	% 28	% 31	% 24
Non-member	74	67	80	73	68	82	69	80	66	77	80	71	69	76
BASE: *ALL RESPONDENTS* *Weighted*	2930	1356	1575	931	1051	943	734	695	637	689	1157	330	982	208
Unweighted	3029	1396	1633	933	1098	988	764	725	659	702	1198	335	1017	215

2.2 CLOSED SHOP MEMBERSHIP (Q40)
by age, social class, hours of work within sex, size of workplace and economic sector

	TOTAL	AGE 18-34	35-54	55+	I/II	III Non-manual	III Manual	IV/V	MEN Full time	MEN Part time	WOMEN Full time	WOMEN Part time	SIZE Less than 25	25-499	500+	Private manuf.	Private non-manuf.	Public service & trans.	Public manuf.
TRADE UNION MEMBERSHIP REQUIRED:	%	%	%	%	%	%	%	%	%	%	%	%	%	%	%	%	%	%	%
Before being considered for the job	2	1	2	3	1	1	5	1	2	(7)	1	1	2	1	4	4	*	1	7
Before starting the job	3	2	3	6	1	1	5	7	5	(-)	1	2	2	3	7	4	2	2	15
After starting the job	10	8	10	17	5	6	16	17	11	(16)	7	11	6	10	16	14	3	14	29
TOTAL WORKING IN CLOSED SHOP	15	12	15	25	8	8	26	25	18	(23)	10	15	10	14	26	22	5	17	52
Union membership not required	83	87	82	70	91	91	71	72	80	(76)	89	80	87	84	73	75	93	80	45
BASE: ALL EMPLOYEES *Weighted*	1432	565	697	169	434	359	308	306	754	(13)	405	259	428	708	272	361	531	407	67
Unweighted	1462	566	719	175	448	373	312	306	767	(14)	413	267	439	719	275	363	545	414	71
UNION MEMBERS	%	%	%	%	%	%	%	%	%	%	%	%	%	%	%	%	%	%	%
Pre-entry closed shop	11	8	11	17	5	5	18	17	15	(27)	5	8	11	8	17	18	10	5	26
Post-entry closed shop	22	19	21	35	12	14	29	34	23	(60)	15	30	22	22	23	33	14	18	35
Open shop	65	71	66	43	82	80	50	47	60	(14)	79	58	64	68	60	47	75	75	36
BASE: EMPLOYEES WHO ARE UNION MEMBERS *Weighted*	624	226	316	81	189	123	162	144	354	(4)	177	90	121	319	178	156	116	276	57
Unweighted	647	230	332	83	197	132	167	145	372	(4)	179	92	123	336	181	160	123	282	61

2.3 REASONS FOR BELONGING TO A TRADE UNION (Q43b-i) by type of membership and union recognition at workplace

	TOTAL	TYPE OF MEMBERSHIP			UNION RECOGNITION		
		Pre-entry closed shop	Post-entry closed shop	Open	Closed shop, recognised	Open, recognised	Not recognised
	%	%	%	%	%	%	%
TO PROTECT ME IF PROBLEMS COME UP							
Very/fairly important	93	94	90	94	92	95	(80)
Not very/not at all important	6	5	7	5	6	5	(14)
Doesn't apply	*	-	-	1	-	*	(6)
TO GET HIGHER PAY AND BETTER WORKING CONDITIONS							
Very/fairly important	80	87	91	76	90	77	(48)
Not very/not at all important	14	8	8	16	8	16	(16)
Doesn't apply	6	6	1	8	2	6	(35)
TO GET MEMBERS' BENEFITS, LIKE FINANCIAL OR HEALTH SCHEMES							
Very/fairly important	70	83	82	65	83	66	(37)
Not very/not at all important	23	10	14	28	13	28	(30)
Doesn't apply	6	4	3	8	4	6	(32)
TO HELP OTHER PEOPLE I WORK WITH							
Very/fairly important	76	90	75	75	80	77	(44)
Not very/not at all important	17	10	17	19	14	19	(20)
Doesn't apply	5	-	6	6	4	4	(35)
I BELIEVE IN THEM IN PRINCIPLE							
Very/fairly important	67	74	72	64	73	64	(64)
Not very/not at all important	29	25	25	31	25	31	(36)
Doesn't apply	4	1	2	4	2	5	(-)
MOST OF MY WORKMATES OR COLLEAGUES ARE MEMBERS							
Very/fairly important	55	75	74	45	75	46	(33)
Not very/not at all important	39	22	22	47	22	48	(33)
Doesn't apply	6	1	3	7	3	6	(33)
IT'S A TRADITION IN MY FAMILY							
Very/fairly important	15	32	21	10	25	10	(9)
Not very/not at all important	51	51	55	50	54	50	(46)
Doesn't apply	33	18	23	40	21	40	(45)
IT'S A CONDITION OF HAVING MY JOB							
Very/fairly important	38	88	73	17	78	18	(6)
Not very/not at all important	24	12	24	25	20	26	(20)
Doesn't apply	38	-	3	58	2	57	(73)
Weighted	624	69	138	405	207	382	(25)
Unweighted	637	75	137	423	212	399	(26)

BASE: EMPLOYEES WHO ARE UNION/STAFF ASSOCIATION MEMBERS

2.4 REASONS FOR NOT BELONGING TO A TRADE UNION (Q44a-j) by sex, age, union recognition at workplace and past union membership

	TOTAL	SEX		AGE			UNION RECOGNITION		PAST UNION MEMBERSHIP	
		Men	Women	18-34	35-54	55+	Recognised	Not recognised	Ever member	Never member
I CAN'T SEE ANY ADVANTAGE IN JOINING	%	%	%	%	%	%	%	%	%	%
Very/fairly important	28	27	30	23	32	29	44	22	26	30
Not very/not at all important	29	31	27	30	30	24	32	28	29	29
Doesn't apply	41	40	42	46	36	44	23	48	43	39
NOT APPROPRIATE TO MY WORK	%	%	%	%	%	%	%	%	%	%
Very/fairly important	26	27	26	27	27	23	32	25	23	29
Not very/not at all important	32	33	32	31	33	35	37	31	33	32
Doesn't apply	38	37	39	39	37	39	29	42	40	36
I DISAGREE WITH THEM IN PRINCIPLE	%	%	%	%	%	%	%	%	%	%
Very/fairly important	23	19	27	21	23	29	26	22	21	24
Not very/not at all important	42	46	37	45	40	36	46	41	42	41
Doesn't apply	33	33	34	33	34	31	26	36	34	33
THEY WOULD ONLY CAUSE TROUBLE AT MY WORKPLACE	%	%	%	%	%	%	%	%	%	%
Very/fairly important	17	18	16	19	16	15	9	20	18	16
Not very/not at all important	31	32	30	31	31	29	45	26	31	31
Doesn't apply	49	48	50	48	50	51	45	51	47	51
THERE IS NO UNION AT MY WORKPLACE	%	%	%	%	%	%	%	%	%	%
Very/fairly important	17	18	16	19	15	19	4	22	15	19
Not very/not at all important	44	45	42	45	44	36	25	51	47	42
Doesn't apply	38	36	40	35	40	42	70	25	28	38
MANAGEMENT DISAPPROVES OF THEM	%	%	%	%	%	%	%	%	%	%
Very/fairly important	13	14	13	16	12	11	8	16	14	13
Not very/not at all important	30	29	32	29	31	35	42	26	33	29
Doesn't apply	53	55	51	51	55	51	48	55	49	55
I FEEL IT WOULD DAMAGE MY JOB PROSPECTS	%	%	%	%	%	%	%	%	%	%
Very/fairly important	11	12	10	12	11	10	9	12	12	10
Not very/not at all important	33	31	34	32	33	36	47	27	32	33
Doesn't apply	54	55	53	55	54	51	42	59	53	55
NO-ONE HAS EVER ASKED ME TO JOIN	%	%	%	%	%	%	%	%	%	%
Very/fairly important	11	10	11	12	10	9	13	10	11	11
Not very/not at all important	45	45	46	49	43	45	53	43	43	47
Doesn't apply	42	43	41	39	45	43	34	46	44	41
IT COSTS TOO MUCH	%	%	%	%	%	%	%	%	%	%
Very/fairly important	6	5	7	7	5	6	14	3	11	6
Not very/not at all important	33	34	31	32	33	34	52	26	33	33
Doesn't apply	59	59	59	59	60	56	33	70	59	59
DON'T APPROVE OF THE ONE I COULD JOIN	%	%	%	%	%	%	%	%	%	%
Very/fairly important	5	6	4	5	6	3	15	1	7	4
Not very/not at all important	18	15	22	18	19	16	44	9	18	19
Doesn't apply	75	77	72	77	72	78	40	89	73	76
Weighted	808	411	397	338	381	88	226	572	335	469
Unweighted	815	406	409	336	387	92	234	574	333	477

BASE: EMPLOYEES WHO ARE NOT UNION/STAFF ASSOCIATION MEMBERS

2.5 UNION ACTIVITY (Q909c)
by type of membership and party identification

	TOTAL	TYPE OF MEMBERSHIP			PARTY IDENTIFICATION			
		Pre-entry closed shop	Post-entry closed shop	Open	Conservative	SLD/ SDP	Labour	Non-aligned
PROPORTION WHO HAVE EVER:	%	%	%	%	%	%	%	%
Attended a union or staff association meeting	74	86	73	72	67	78	81	65
Voted in a union or staff association election or meeting	75	78	75	74	71	85	80	53
Put forward a proposal or motion at a union or staff association meeting	24	31	21	24	21	29	28	13
Gone on strike	36	50	38	33	25	30	50	20
Stood in a picket line	21	34	22	19	11	15	34	10
Served as a lay representative such as a shop steward or branch committee member	17	20	17	16	10	21	23	9
BASE: EMPLOYEES WHO ARE UNION/STAFF ASSOCIATION MEMBERS *Weighted*	*624*	*69*	*138*	*405*	*202*	*78*	*236*	*47*
Unweighted	*647*	*75*	*137*	*423*	*215*	*78*	*247*	*50*

3 Women and the family

*Jacqueline Scott**

> A final way in which the nuclear family has been giving way to the post-modern family we might call 'the destruction of the nest' . . . The major unsettlers of the nest have been the women themselves. (Edward Shorter, *The Making of the Modern Family*, 1976).

> It seems possible that a new, more loosely structured, less emotionally and sexually cohesive, and far more temporary family type is already being added to the number of options available. (Lawrence Stone, *The Family, Sex and Marriage in England, 1500–1800*, 1979).

Everyone knows about the crisis of the modern family. The divorce rate is staggeringly high: on current forecasts about 20 per cent of children in Britain will experience family break-up by the age of 16. Sexual relationships seem as commonplace outside marriage as within. Writing for the National Family Trust (1989), Richard Whitfield voices his concern about the erosion of stable family life upon which personal well-being and social cohesion largely depend. Yet the belief that family life is crumbling rests implicitly not only on an absolute notion of what the 'ideal' family should be, but also on the assumption that family life has undergone such radical changes only recently.

The family is not, and never has been, an unchanging institution. As Stone (1979) reminds us, it has throughout history shown a remarkable resilience and an ability to evolve to meet the requirements of changing social and economic circumstances.

In this chapter we examine a wide range of attitudes towards family life,

* Senior Assistant Director (Research), ESRC Research Centre on Micro-social Change, University of Essex.

drawing mainly on data from the module on women and the family, which was fielded in the 1989 survey, as well as in comparable surveys carried out in the member countries of the *International Social Survey Programme* (ISSP).* The module includes questions on a range of family issues, including gender-roles, marriage, cohabitation, childrearing, single-parenting and divorce. We shall discuss the findings, and also examine trends, drawing on data from standard *British Social Attitudes* questions and from the American *General Social Survey*.

Our main purpose is to look for answers to three basic questions. First, how have beliefs about the role of women in the family changed, and in what ways have they stayed the same? Trend data for Britain are somewhat limited but, where possible, we show how attitudes have changed over time. Secondly, we examine how British attitudes towards family life compare with those held by people in other countries. We give particular attention to the USA, not just because comparable trend data are available, but also because the USA is often portrayed as a harbinger of family decline and an object lesson for other nations. We also compare current British attitudes with those of the Irish, the Hungarians and the Dutch. Further cross-national comparisons can be found in Harding, 1989.

Thirdly, we ask whether there is consensus or conflict in what people believe acceptable family behaviour to be. Some alternative family life-styles (for instance, cohabitation) may now be widely seen as acceptable, whereas others (for instance, the legal marriage of homosexual couples) may not. The dividing line is likely to be thin, and on issues that fall close to it we might expect people's attitudes to be polarised.

The American historian, Edward Shorter, has claimed that it is women rather than men who are disrupting the stable family unit. In one sense, Shorter is clearly wrong. After all, the great majority of men have always devoted far more time and energy to work than to their families. Since this is taken for granted, it is not suggested that men are unsettling the cosy family nest. When women start to take on the traditional male role by going out to work, however, sociologists talk of the disruption to family life, psychologists write about the serious consequences of maternal deprivation, and pollsters ask the public whether they think that the children of the marriage will suffer. Much less emphasis is placed on the economic pressures that drive many women into (often low-paid and repetitive) jobs; or on the many potential advantages of a paid job, such as financial independence, career-building and enjoyment of the company of colleagues or workmates.

Nevertheless Shorter is, in another sense, right; for it is women who, by entering the labour market in ever-increasing numbers, have thrown previously accepted norms of family behaviour into question. One-third of mothers with children under five years old are now in the paid labour force (OPCS, 1987), which raises the practical problem of who should look after the children. Moreover, by participating in the labour force, women gain at least a measure of economic independence which may challenge the traditional power relationships within the family.

---

* The ISSP member nations which have fielded this module to date are Austria, Britain, Hungary, the Republic of Ireland, Italy, the Netherlands, the USA and West Germany. At the time of writing, however, only unweighted data were available from Austria, Italy and West Germany, so these countries have been excluded from the analyses.

What are the effects of such changes on people's attitudes to family life? Do women tend to embrace these changes in traditional family roles more readily than men do? If so, is it women in general who are adopting these new values in respect of family life, or is the change confined to those women who are themselves in paid employment? Is it only the younger generation whose attitudes towards family behaviour have changed? We will consider different aspects of family life in turn, before attempting to discuss the relationships between them.

Changing roles within the family

In Britain the incentives for married women to work, or to return to work, have been increasing. Rising inflation has exerted economic pressure, at the same time as a reduction in the number of school-leavers has created employment opportunities for married women (Scott & Duncombe, forthcoming). Yet social pressure in recent years may be working in the opposite direction, as the rhetoric of politicians emphasises the virtues of family life, and as the media insist that motherhood is once again 'fashionable'. Whether or not British women take up the new employment opportunities may thus depend at least as much on attitudes as on economic pressures, especially on those attitudes to do with the woman's place in work and family life.

Women's work and the family

We have only a relatively limited set of trend data for monitoring changes in gender-role attitudes in Britain. In 1980, the Women and Employment Survey – WES (Martin and Roberts, 1984) asked a series of questions about the woman's role, and some of these items were replicated in the British Social Attitudes surveys of 1984, 1987 and 1989. As the table below shows, women have adopted more egalitarian attitudes on some measures but not on others.

% of women taking 'egalitarian' stance on each proposition:[†]	1980*	1984	1987	1989
Wife's job is to look after home and family (% disagreeing)	33%	50%	44%	69%
Job is all right but what women really want is home and children (% disagreeing)	34%	n/a	57%	61%
Job is best way for a woman to be independent (% agreeing)	67%	70%	65%	66%
A woman and her family will all be happier if she goes out to work (% agreeing)	29%	n/a	12%	22%

* WES data are based on women aged 16–59. The data for other years are from British Social Attitudes surveys, but – for comparative purposes – based only on women aged 18–59.

† On this and on other similar tables in this chapter, the percentage is of those who agree ("strongly" or "just") or disagree ("strongly" or "just") with each proposition including those who said "neither" or "can't choose" or who did not answer.

Women have increasingly rejected the traditional view that a woman's place is in the home with her children. And although there has been hardly any change since 1980 in the proportion believing that a job is the best way for a woman to be independent, this may be partly a 'ceiling effect', since around two-thirds of women always did endorse this proposition. Acceptance of women's working, therefore, appears to be steady and high. In contrast, however, only a small (and reducing) minority thinks that "the woman and her family will all be happier if she goes out to work". Perhaps, as Witherspoon (1988) suggests in *The 5th Report* (p.190), this reflects a greater awareness of the real role-conflicts involved in juggling family responsibilities and employment demands. We can explore this suggestion in more detail as we examine further gender-role items in the 1989 module. First, however, it is important to examine the extent to which women's gender-role attitudes are associated with age. As the next table shows, age does make a difference to some attitudes but not to others.

	Total	Aged 18–29	Aged 30–39	Aged 40–49	Aged 50–59	Aged 60–69	Aged 70+
% of women taking 'egalitarian' stance on each proposition:							
Wife's job is to look after home and family (% *disagreeing*)	58%	80%	79%	61%	41%	32%	19%
Job is all right but what women really want is home and children (% *disagreeing*)	51%	71%	70%	54%	32%	34%	10%
Job is best way for a woman to be independent (% *agreeing*)	65%	62%	72%	62%	72%	65%	56%
A woman and her family will all be happier if she goes out to work (% *agreeing*)	22%	18%	30%	20%	21%	24%	18%

On the first two propositions, older women hold far more traditional views. Interestingly, however, there is no clear age relationship with respect to the other two items; the inclusion of older women (aged over 60) in this table makes little difference to the total proportion agreeing with the last two propositions. Moreover, on both of these it is apparent that the youngest cohort (18–29 year olds) is *not* the most liberal. Rather, it is women who are aged 30–39 who are most likely to endorse the view that work brings independence and happiness. One obvious explanation for this is that, for many women around the age of 30, childbearing is over and childrearing has begun in earnest. So some measure of independence from the demands of childrearing may have become a more attractive possibility. Another reason could be that this cohort of 30–39 year old women was heavily influenced by the peak period of achievements for the women's movement (for instance, the Sex Discrimination Act was passed, and the National Women's Federation and the National Abortion Campaign were launched in 1975, when these women would have been aged 16–25). There is, of course, considerable evidence to suggest that people are at their most impressionable during this period of their lives, especially in terms of their social identities and political consciousness (see Schuman and Scott, 1989). We shall see later if a similar pattern emerges in this cohort's attitudes towards other aspects of family life.

Attitudes and gender

In the 1989 module, the four items already discussed were part of a battery of nine questions, which can be used together to form a gender-role index.* A factor analysis pointed to three different aspects of this index: role-conflict, role-segregation and role-combination. The first four items below question whether there is a conflict between a woman's job and the needs of her family and, in particular, the needs of her children. The next three (segregation) items gauge attitudes towards the traditional division of labour between men and women. The final two items tap beliefs about women combining both family responsibilities and paid employment.

% taking 'egalitarian' stance on each proposition	Men	Women
Role-conflict		
A working mother can establish just as warm and secure a relationship with her children as a mother who does not work (% agreeing)	51%	63%
All in all, family life suffers when the woman has a full-time job (% disagreeing)	37%	43%
A pre-school child is likely to suffer if his or her mother works (% disagreeing)	29%	40%
A woman and her family will all be happier if she goes out to work (% agreeing)	14%	22%
Role-segregation		
A husband's job is to earn money; a wife's job is to look after the home and family (% disagreeing)	47%	57%
A job is all right, but what most women really want is a home and children (% disagreeing)	41%	51%
Being a housewife is just as fulfilling as working for pay (% disagreeing)	33%	36%*
Role-combination		
Having a job is the best way for a woman to be an independent person (% agreeing)	59%	65%
Both the husband and wife should contribute to the household income (% agreeing)	50%	56%*

Note: all differences are statistically significant except those marked*.

The prediction that women would be more egalitarian than men in their gender-role attitudes is proved correct for almost all the items. The gender difference fails to be significant for only two items, one of which may be ambiguous anyway. That similar proportions of men and women agree that being a 'housewife' is just as fulfilling as working for pay may be because choice for women is also very much part of the feminist *credo*. Thus the homemaker's role is not to be disparaged. On all the remaining items, however, women are more egalitarian

---

* The reliability of the scale is high (Cronbach's alpha = 0.80).

than men, especially when it comes to role-clash concerns.

Further analysis shows that women who are employed (in either full-time or part-time work) are far more egalitarian in their gender-role attitudes on all nine measures than are women who are full-time homemakers (see **Table 3.1**). The positive relationship between employment and a more egalitarian gender-role stance is hardly surprising: after all, working women tend to be younger and, as we have seen, on most measures younger women are more egalitarian anyway. We cannot tell, however, whether the less 'traditionalist' women are more likely to go out to work, or whether employment undermines traditional gender-role beliefs; it is likely that both processes are occurring.

Interestingly, husbands of women in paid employment are considerably more egalitarian in their attitudes than those who are sole breadwinners (again see **Table 3.1**). In particular, men whose wives go out to work are far less likely than other men to subscribe to the view that women's employment will harm children or families. It could be argued that these men enjoy the material benefits that their working wives bring, and that their attitudes merely reflect self-interest. It is also plausible, however, that men's personal experience of these arrangements lays to rest some of their fears about the negative consequences of women's employment on family life. Or it may simply be that egalitarian men and women tend to marry each other.

Cross-national comparisons

When we compare Britain and the USA, we see a quite different pattern of attitudes. While the British are far more likely than Americans to assert that pre-school children and family life suffer if the mother is working, Americans are more traditional in their attitudes *vis-à-vis* role-segregation and role-combination, as the table below shows. In fact, Britain is the most egalitarian of all five countries in respect of role-segregation. A higher proportion of the British public than that of any of the other countries surveyed rejects the notion that most women would or should choose homemaking in preference to a job.

% of respondents taking 'egalitarian' stance on each proposition	Britain	USA	Republic of Ireland	Netherlands	Hungary
Role-conflict					
A working mother can establish just as warm and secure a relationship with her children as a mother who does not work (% *agreeing*)	58%	64%	54%	55%	52%
All in all, family life suffers when the woman has a full-time job (% *disagreeing*)	40%	48%	37%	32%	24%
A pre-school child is likely to suffer if his or her mother works (% *disagreeing*)	35%	43%	39%	24%	18%
A woman and her family will all be happier if she goes out to work (% *agreeing*)	18%	16%	21%	25%	35%

% of respondents taking 'egalitarian' stance on each proposition	Britain	USA	Republic of Ireland	Netherlands	Hungary
Role-segregation					
A husband's job is to earn money; a wife's job is to look after the home and family (% *disagreeing*)	53%	50%	45%	53%	40%
A job is all right, but what most women really want is a home and children (% *disagreeing*)	46%	37%	30%	38%	11%
Being a housewife is just as fulfilling as working for pay (% *disagreeing*)	34%	22%	21%	30%	5%
Role-combination					
Having a job is the best way for a woman to be an independent person (% *agreeing*)	62%	43%	57%	42%	54%
Both the husband and wife should contribute to the household income (% *agreeing*)	53%	48%	64%	23%	84%

The British are also the most likely to agree that a job is the best way for a woman to achieve her independence. Interestingly, on this item Americans are among the least egalitarian; but this may be an artifact of the question wording.

Hungary is almost always the outlier among the five countries, with the Hungarians being the most traditional in their attitudes. In contrast, however, an overwhelming 84 per cent of Hungarians believe that both the husband and wife should contribute to the family income. It seems likely that this stems from economic necessity, and that this factor also makes the Hungarians most likely to agree that a woman and her family will be happier if the woman works. Of course, these readings were taken some time before the recent political changes in Hungary. We shall test whether or not attitudes have shifted by the time this questionnaire module is next asked as part of the ISSP programme; but if responses reflect economic necessity, as seems very likely, we shall not see any short-term changes in the attitudes of Hungarians towards working mothers.

Working mothers and childcare

In response to another set of questions, the British are the most likely among people in these five nations to insist that a mother should stay at home when there is a child under school age. This may to some degree reflect the lack of pre-school childcare provision in Britain, compared with that available in other countries. For as the table below shows, once the child has reached school age, the overwhelming preference of the British is for women to work part time. In Britain, part-time work has increased much more than in most other industrialised countries (Dex, 1988) and taking a part-time job is clearly one way in which women can combine employment with responsibilities for children. (Part-time work, however, has costs as well as benefits, and often women suffer downward occupational mobility as a result.)

Should a woman work . . . when her children are under school age?	Britain	USA	Republic of Ireland	Nether-lands	Hungary
	%	%	%	%	%
No, stay at home	64	48	52	53	51
Yes, work part time	26	30	33	32	40
Yes, work full time	2	10	9	10	8
Don't know	6	10	5	3	1
. . . when her children have started school?	%	%	%	%	%
No, stay at home	11	11	25	13	18
Yes, work part time	68	45	49	62	49
Yes, work full time	13	31	21	19	32
Don't know	7	11	4	3	1

In striking contrast to the views of the British, we see that nearly a third of Americans think that women should work full-time when their children have started school. And indeed a high proportion of American women *do* work full-time (Morris, 1990).

If mothers are to work then some childcare provision must be arranged. Recently there has been increasing pressure on the government to put more money into state day-nurseries, and on employers to establish workplace crèches. Respondents were asked about how suitable they feel each of a number of childcare arrangements are for a child aged under three whose parents both work full time. According to our data most people would prefer informal childcare arrangements that involve other family members. The British, and also the Americans and Irish, were more likely to say that to leave the child with a relative was suitable than any of the other arrangements asked about. Of course, respondents may not be answering in terms of what would be *ideal* for them but rather what is the best *practical* solution given other considerations such as the current availability and cost of different childcare arrangements.

	Britain	USA	Republic of Ireland	Nether-lands	Hungary
% of respondents saying each form of childcare is very suitable					
A relative	39%	50%	56%	22%	3%
Private crèche or nursery	30%	31%	18%	n/a	3%
State or local authority nursery	29%	19%	8%	20%	3%
Childminder or babysitter	16%	26%	24%	22%	3%
A neighbour or friend	10%	26%	34%	8%	*

The Dutch are not very keen on any of the arrangements; and the Hungarians are even less so – despite their widely-held views that *both* parents should contribute to the household income. Responses to a new series of questions asked in the 1990 *British Social Attitudes* survey will tell us more about childcare preferences in this country. We shall report these results in a future volume.

Sexual relationships, marriage and children

Having touched on attitudes towards women's roles in the home and in the labour market, and preferred childcare arrangements, we now turn to a range of other aspects of family life – such as attitudes to marriage and children. But first we look at the issue of sexual relationships before and outside marriage.

Sexual relationships and cohabitation

Attitudes towards pre-marital and extra-marital relationships have been investigated since the series began in 1983, with a set of questions similar to the ones used in the US *General Social Survey*.* Respondents are asked to say whether each sort of relationship is "always", "mostly", "sometimes" or "rarely" wrong. In Britain, tolerance of sex before marriage is widespread, with only around a fifth of respondents saying that it is "always" or "mostly" wrong. In contrast, however, over four in five disapprove of adultery in similar terms. In *The 5th Report*, we noted that attitudes towards pre-marital sex had remained largely stable over the years, but that there had been an increase in the proportion censuring sex outside marriage (Harding, 1988; Brook, 1988). The 1989 survey data indicate that these more disapproving attitudes may have moderated somewhat (as apparently have those towards homosexual relationships) though the vast majority is disapproving. As the table below shows, on both issues, but especially with respect to pre-marital sex, Americans are considerably *less* tolerant in their views than the British.

% saying always or mostly* wrong	1983	1984	1985	1986	1987	1988	1989
Pre-marital relations:							
USA*	36%		36%	36%		36%	35%
Britain	28%	27%	23%		25%		22%
Extra-marital relations:							
USA*		87%	87%		89%	91%	90%
Britain[†]	83%	85%	82%		88%		84%

* In the USA, "almost always". Source: *GSS Cumulative Codebook* 1972–1989. Not all questions were asked every year.

† The item wording in 1983 referred to husband and wife separately. The answers were almost identical, so averaged responses are given here.

---

* A parallel question is also asked about attitudes towards homosexual relationships, and we report the British results in Chapter 5.

One possible explanation is the strong traditionalist strain that runs through American society. As Davis (1986) has noted in *The 1986 Report*, Americans tend to be more religious and thus morally more traditional, especially with respect to sexual conduct (see also Davis and Jowell, 1989).

In *The 1984 Report*, we noted that in general, men are more likely to hold permissive attitudes in respect of pre-marital and extra-marital sexual relationships. By 1989, however, these gender differences are much less marked and, in the case of extra-marital relationships, have all but disappeared. Now we can explore gender differences further, since in 1989 for the first time we asked further questions about attitudes to cohabitation. We asked respondents what advice they would give – first to a young woman, then to a young man – as to whether they should live alone, live with a steady partner without marrying, live together and then marry, or marry without living together first. As the table below shows, by a small margin respondents would advise cohabitation before marriage.* Moreover there is no evidence of a double standard of morality, at least from our survey data; the advice that they would give is the same irrespective of the young person's sex.

	Advice would give to . . .	
	young woman	young man
	%	%
Live with a steady partner for a while and then marry	43	42
Marry without living together first	37	36
Live alone without a steady partner	4	5
Live with a steady partner, without marrying	4	5
Can't choose	11	11

On this issue, as on those of pre- and extra-marital sexual relationships, the attitudes of men and women are very similar: men are no more likely than women to recommend cohabitation as a prelude to, or in place of, marriage. It is only when we look at the views of people of different ages and (to a lesser extent) of different educational backgrounds and religions that differences emerge. As **Table 3.2** shows, older people are much more likely to disapprove of cohabitation before marriage, as are the less educationally qualified and those who belong to a religious denomination.

As before, cross-national comparisons are instructive. On the issue of cohabitation, the Americans again are noticeably more traditional in their attitudes: only about a quarter support the idea of couples living together before they marry. And only about a third of the Irish would recommend this course of action. Of course, both these nations have much higher proportions of people who belong to a religion.

---

* Behavioural data on cohabitation support our findings. Estimates from the *General Household Survey* suggest that the proportion of women aged 18–49 who were cohabiting almost tripled between 1979 and 1988 (CSO, 1990).

	Advice would give to a young woman*				
			Republic of	Nether-	
	Britain	**USA**	**Ireland**	**lands**	**Hungary**
	%	**%**	**%**	**%**	**%**
Live with a steady partner for a while and then marry	43	26	32	45	40
Marry without living together first	37	46	59	24	46
Live alone without a steady partner	4	9	2	2	3
Live with a steady partner, without marrying	4	3	1	8	7
Can't choose	11	14	5	20	3

* The advice that would be given to a young man is substantially the same.

The Irish too, by a wide margin, are the most likely to advise young couples to marry without living together first, while the Dutch are the least likely to give this advice. Only very small minorities in any of the five countries reject marriage outright.

Since the module also has a series of questions on marriage, we can go on to examine why, despite the widespread acceptance of cohabitation, marriage remains such a popular institution.

Marriage

For the British (and even more conspicuously for the Dutch), the answer is clearly *not* that marriage is equated with happiness – only a third of British respondents agree that "married people are generally happier than unmarried people". Moreover a large majority of the British (in common with citizens of the five other countries) reject the proposition that "it is better to have a bad marriage than no marriage at all".

			Republic		
% agreeing with each proposition			of	Nether-	
	Britain	**USA**	**Ireland**	**lands**	**Hungary**
People who want children ought to get married	70%	72%	82%	51%	65%
Married people are generally happier than unmarried people	33%	51%	46%	16%	54%
The main purpose of marriage . . . is to have children	20%	12%	32%	17%	66%
The main advantage of marriage is . . . financial security	18%	16%	22%	16%	42%
Personal freedom is more important than the companionship of marriage	12%	15%	16%	9%	13%
It is better to have a bad marriage than no marriage at all	2%	4%	5%	2%	11%

A sizeable majority of the British (and the Americans, Dutch and Irish too) rejects the suggestion that the main purpose of marriage is to have children, although this notion does find favour among a third of the Irish and an astonishing two-thirds of Hungarians. The Hungarians are outliers too in that two-fifths see the main advantage of marriage as bringing financial security – a proposition which receives much lower levels of support elsewhere.

So what is it about marriage that has such appeal? Our data suggest two answers. First, it is clear that the companionship that marriage brings is regarded as very important: only 12 per cent of the British (and similar proportions in the other four countries) agree that "personal freedom is more important than the companionship of marriage". Data from the *British Social Attitudes* 1986 survey strongly support this finding. Asked which factors were important to a successful marriage, large majorities nominated "mutual respect and appreciation" and "understanding and tolerance" – well above the proportion nominating a happy sexual relationship (Ashford, 1987). Secondly it appears that, while most people do not regard having children as the main purpose of marriage, there is nonetheless strong agreement across the five national samples that "people who want children ought to get married".

Of course, there may be other reasons for the enduring popularity of marriage. For instance, financial security might play a bigger part than people admit, especially when linked with the desire to have children. Peer group and parental pressures may also count (the latter particularly when a baby is on the way). But we did not – nor could not, on a structured self-completion questionnaire – investigate all these sorts of motivations.

On the whole, the British and the Americans hold very similar views about marriage – but with one exception: Americans are more traditional than the British in their belief that married people are generally happier than unmarried people. Half of the American respondents believe this, compared with only a third of the British.

The USA has gone further than any country except Sweden in making marriage easy to end. That being so, we might expect unhappy marriages to be less common in the USA than elsewhere. But this suggestion cannot explain the apparent difference in attitudes. For instance, the Netherlands also has 'no-fault' divorce, and yet the Dutch are by far the most sceptical about married people's happiness. The Dutch also downplay the importance of marriage for people who want children. Yet as we have seen, in the Netherlands (just as in the other four countries) the overwhelming advice to a young person is either to marry, or to live together and then marry.

Marriage then clearly has a different meaning in different countries, and to different groups within any one country. The feminist writer Jessie Bernard (1973) goes further still and argues that, even within the same partnership there are really two marriages: the husband's and the wife's. Much research has confirmed that husbands and wives give discrepant responses when supposedly talking about the same marriage – for example when describing who does the various household chores (see, for example, Witherspoon, 1988). It seems plausible, therefore, that men and women would differ in their beliefs about marriage. Surprisingly, however, we do not find this to be the case, in Britain anyway.* True, men are

---

* The complete ISSP datatape had not been archived at the time of writing, so we cannot yet look for gender differences among people of the four other countries.

somewhat more likely than women to believe that the main purpose of marriage is to have children, and that married people are happier than unmarried people, but in other respects there are no gender differences to speak of.

% agreeing that:	Men	Women	Women Home-makers	Employed
People who want children ought to get married	72%	69%*	73%	60%
Married people are generally happier than unmarried people	36%	31%	33%	24%
The main purpose of marriage . . . is to have children	21%	19%	22%	13%
The main advantage of marriage is . . . financial security	18%	18%*	21%	12%
Personal freedom is more important than the companionship of marriage	10%	13%*	10%	13%*
It is better to have a bad marriage than no marriage at all	3%	2%*	3%	1%

All differences are statistically significant except those marked*.

That men are more likely to say marriage brings happiness may, of course, reflect a difference in experience. It has been argued, for instance, that marriage is more beneficial to the psychological well-being of men than it is to women (Gove, 1972). And it may also have material advantages for men, at least as far as household chores are concerned.

However, as the table above shows, views about marriage also differ considerably between women who are full-time homemakers and women who are in paid employment. Homemakers are more likely to agree that married people are happier, that the main advantage of marriage is financial security, that the main purpose of marriage is to have children and that people who want children should get married. But multivariate analysis would be needed to examine whether going out to work is indeed the key factor: employment is undoubtedly related to other background factors such as the woman's age, the number and age of her children, and her educational attainment (see Joshi, 1987). All we can say at present is that our data lend support to the claim that women who are in paid work (and with the resources to give themselves at least a degree of financial independence) are less likely to hold traditional marital beliefs. Women who are homemakers differ little from men in their views.

Children

As we have seen, a widespread traditional belief is that a key purpose of marriage is procreation. We asked about ideal family sizes and about the importance of children in a family. In Britain the preference for two children is very marked, with 60 per cent feeling that two children is the ideal number for a family to have. (For a discussion of attitudes towards family size in a cross-national context, see Harding in *The 6th Report*.) People differ, however, in the value they place on children. The module included a series of six questions designed to tap the importance of children in people's lives. We show below the proportions in each of the five countries taking a pro-children (or anti-childlessness) stance. The items are ordered according to the magnitude (in Britain) of the pro-children stance:

% taking pro-children stance:	Britain	USA	Republic of Ireland	Nether-lands	Hungary
It is better *not* to have children because they are such a heavy burden (% *disagreeing*)	87%	83%	93%	87%	92%
Children are more trouble than they are worth (% *disagreeing*)	86%	84%	92%	77%	68%
Watching children grow up is life's greatest joy (% *agreeing*)	81%	85%	87%	73%	95%
Having children interferes too much with the freedom of parents (% *disagreeing*)	72%	73%	83%	67%	52%
A marriage without children is not fully complete (% *agreeing*)	45%	44%	48%	34%	90%
People who have never had children lead empty lives (% *agreeing*)	23%	16%	29%	17%	82%

On the first four items, the picture is one of cross-national consensus. Majorities in all five countries willingly accept the burdens that parenthood can bring and agree that watching children grow up is life's greatest joy, though the Dutch and Hungarians are rather more ambivalent than are the British or Americans. There is rather more scepticism about the last two items which postulate that life or marriage in the absence of children is inadequate. The Hungarians again are rank outliers in their overwhelming endorsement of both these items. People in the other four countries, including Britain, may be pro-children but they do not take the view that childlessness is a curse. A factor analysis confirmed that the first four items measured positive attitudes towards having children, and the last two measured negative views about not having them.

In Britain, there are no gender differences on the first four items but, surprisingly perhaps, men are far more likely than women to regard children as an essential part of marriage. This may be because, for most men, childrearing makes fewer demands upon them than it does on women. The table below shows, first, how similar men and women are on all but this one item; and secondly, how the attitudes of women in jobs differ in some important respects from women who are homemakers.

	All	Men	Women	Women Home-makers	Employed
% taking pro-children stance:					
It is better *not* to have children because they are such a heavy burden (% *disagreeing*)	87%	88%	87%*	88%	88%*
Children are more trouble than they are worth (% *disagreeing*)	86%	86%	86%*	87%	86%*
Watching children grow up is life's greatest joy (% *agreeing*)	81%	80%	82%*	87%	77%**
Having children interferes too much with the freedom of parents (% *disagreeing*)	72%	71%	73%*	76%	70%*
A marriage without children is not fully complete (% *agreeing*)	45%	51%	41%	49%	29%
People who have never had children lead empty lives (% *agreeing*)	23%	25%	23%	27%	15%

Differences are statistically significant except those marked*.

** Not statistically significant (P<.10) because employed women adopt a neutral position on this item, rather than disagree.

As before, women who are in the paid labour force are far more likely than those who are not to reject traditional beliefs. For instance, employed women are almost twice as likely as homemakers to reject the assumption that a woman must be a mother if her marriage and life are to be complete. And, as **Table 3.3** shows, there is a strong generational effect, with older women being more likely than younger women to endorse these views. Also, as before it is women of 30–39, rather than those in the youngest age group, who most firmly reject the belief that children are essential to marriage. This cohort of women who came of age at the high point of the women's movement is again the most likely to take a rather less romantic view of the nuclear family.

Broken families

Divorce

Divorce remains a subject over which there is considerable ambivalence. This is hardly surprising since divorce laws generally attempt to achieve two somewhat conflicting aims: to allow people to end a marriage that has broken down; and to ensure that marriages are not ended lightly. This conflict is apparent in people's responses to questions on divorce. In our British sample (1989), a majority (61 per cent) agrees not only that "couples don't take marriage seriously enough when divorce is easily available", and that "in general the law makes it easy for people who want to get divorced" (75 per cent); but also that the divorce laws "should remain as they are" (53 per cent), with only three in ten wanting divorce to be harder to get than now.

In England and Wales at present, although technically divorce is only granted because of an irretrievable breakdown in the marriage, in practice the most common way of demonstrating the breakdown is for one partner to prove fault, either by adultery or 'unreasonable behaviour'. This is very different from the 'no-fault' divorce laws of most American states, where one spouse only has to say that differences are irreconcilable for the divorce to be granted.

Interestingly, attitudes towards the divorce laws in Britain and the USA differ sharply, and these differences have been relatively stable across time. Using a question similar to the one used in the US *General Social Survey*, the *British Social Attitudes* survey regularly asks if "divorce (in Britain/Scotland) should be easier to obtain than it is now, more difficult, or should things remain as they are?" As noted above, around a half of the British think that the laws should remain as they are now. Most Americans, however, say they want divorce to be made more difficult.

% saying that divorce should	1983	1984	1985	1986	1987	1988	1989
. . . be easier							
USA*	24%		23%	26%		24%	25%
Britain	11%	13%			10%		13%
. . . be more difficult							
USA*	52%		53%	52%		48%	51%
Britain	31%	30%			38%		30%
. . . remain as it is							
USA*	19%		19%	18%		22%	18%
Britain	55%	54%			50%		53%

* Source: *GSS Cumulative Codebook*, 1972–1989. The question was not asked every year.

It is clear that on this issue Americans are more polarised and less in favour of the *status quo* than the British. In both countries, the balance of opinion is two to one in favour of making divorce more difficult rather than making it easier, but in Britain a clear majority would prefer things to stay as they are. Fewer than one in five Americans support the *status quo* there.

Although the British public is content with the divorce laws *generally*, further questioning reveals that people would like the law to differentiate between couples with and without young children. Only 17 per cent feel that divorce should be easy for couples with young children, compared with 46 per cent who would support easy divorce for couples without young children. There has been considerable discussion in recent years of a 'children-first' principle to guide divorce legislation (Eekelaar, 1986; Glendon, 1987). It seems, on our evidence, that a change in this direction would be favourably received.

Our cross-national data also demonstrate the complexity of attitudes towards divorce, as people struggle to reconcile their recognition that divorce is sometimes needed, with their belief that marriage should not be ended lightly, especially when young children are involved. Responses to any one question would give a highly misleading picture. It is not a matter of being in favour of or opposed to divorce. Rather, divorce is regarded as the best of bad alternatives, when a marriage has failed.

We asked: "When a marriage is troubled and unhappy, do you think it is

generally better for the *children* if the couple stays together or gets divorced?"
Then we asked whether it was generally better for the *wife* and, after that, for
the *husband*. In all five countries, most people feel that it is better not only for
the husband and wife, but also for the children, if an unhappy marriage is ended.

% saying much better or better to end an unhappy marriage:	Britain	USA	Republic of Ireland*	Nether-lands	Hungary
For children	60%	55%	48%	65%	66%
For wife	66%	56%	55%	77%	76%
For husband	66%	57%	57%	76%	70%

* In the Republic of Ireland a middle alternative, "neither better nor worse", was offered and
around 14 per cent took it. This undoubtedly deflated positive responses.

Even with this conservative estimate of sentiment in the Irish Republic, it is
striking that in a country where 63 per cent of the voters rejected the introduction
of divorce in the 1986 referendum, a majority feels nonetheless that divorce is
a better alternative for both husband and wife than continuing in an unhappy
marriage.

One-parent families

Our final issue, the one-parent family, is closely tied to divorce although, of
course, divorce is not its sole cause. In the great majority of cases, it is the
mother who is the lone parent. Often, single mothers and their children have to
rely on state benefits as their main source of income. Not surprisingly, therefore,
there is considerable concern about how children fare in these families. A question
in the module simply asks whether people agree or disagree that "a single mother
can bring up her child as well as a married couple". The same question is
repeated for a single father. Except in the Netherlands, the balance of opinion
is that children need both their parents; and even the Dutch, on balance, do not
see the father as an adequate substitute for the two-parent family.

A single mother can bring up her child as well as a married couple:	Britain %	USA %	Republic of Ireland %	Nether-lands %	Hungary %
Strongly agree/agree	30	37	42	43	25
Disagree/strongly disagree	51	45	47	34	58
A single father can bring up his child as well as a married couple:	%	%	%	%	%
Strongly agree/agree	24	31	26	30	13
Disagree/strongly disagree	57	49	64	46	68

The two questions were put contiguously to encourage evenhandedness in response.
As can be seen, however, answers in all five countries are unabashedly sexist,
with mothers being judged the more competent to bring up a child alone. The
Dutch and the Americans are the least sexist in their attitudes and the Hungarians

the most, with the British and Irish in the middle. The 'new man' who is supposed to be more intimately involved in parenting and homemaking is not yet a reality outside the world of the image-makers – at least, according to the majority of ISSP respondents.

We might expect this bias in favour of single mothers to be more marked among female respondents. But as **Table 3.4** shows, in Britain at least, this is not the case. Both men and women are more likely to agree that the mother is the better sole parent. Nevertheless women are more likely than men to believe that either a single mother or a single father can bring up a child as well as a couple. Even so, a clear majority of women too believe that children fare better with two parents.

Conclusions

Our first goal was to determine whether attitudes towards women and the family have changed. And, although there have been changes, our data do not show any clear breaks with the recent past. People still think that there are conflicts for a woman in combining family responsibilities with full-time work, especially when children are young. Most people still believe that marriage is the preferred way of living, that the ideal number of children is two, and that children should ideally be reared by couples.

Nonetheless, traditional beliefs about family behaviour *are* being challenged. Even in the last decade, for instance, there has been a steady shift to more egalitarian attitudes in respect of the traditional division of labour within the family. The majority view in 1980 was that the husband's job is to earn the money and the wife's to look after the home. Now this is the opinion of only a small (and mainly elderly) minority. Also, attitudes towards pre-marital sexual relationships have become rather more liberal since 1983, when our trend data began. Although we have no earlier data on attitudes towards cohabitation, it seems highly probable that the present majority support for the idea of living together before marriage is a fairly new development. Moreover, people nowadays tend to support further relaxation in the divorce laws for couples without children.

There are, however, limits to British tolerance: condemnation of adultery remains as strong as in 1983; and there is widespread agreement that people who want a family should get married first. This is not to say that people do not do the things they disapprove of. As Harding (1988) notes, "adultery is still one of the most widely cited grounds for divorce in Britain". Moreover, one in four children in Britain is born out of wedlock (CSO, 1990).

Our second goal was to determine how British attitudes towards family life compare with those of other countries. Our cross-national comparison of gender-role attitudes yields mixed findings. Britain is the most egalitarian of the five nations studied (and considerably more egalitarian than the USA) on many points of principle, such as role-segregation within the home and the desirability of women combining family and work roles. However, the British are far more traditional than Americans when it comes to measures of role-conflict, being more inclined to believe that families suffer when the mother goes out to work. Consistent with this belief, the British are more likely than the Dutch, Irish, Hungarians or Americans, to urge a mother of a pre-school child to stay at home.

People in all five nations have quite similar views when it comes to marriage and children. However, the British differ markedly from Americans in their attitudes towards sexual morality and divorce. Hollywood's depiction of American morality, or rather immorality, is clearly misleading, because Americans are markedly less permissive than the British in their attitudes towards adultery, homosexuality (see Chapter 5) and pre-marital sex. Given the prodigiously high rates of divorce in America, one might think that, on this issue at least, Americans would be more tolerant. However, the British are far more likely than the Americans to say that divorce is more desirable than an unhappy marriage, and a majority of Americans (compared with only one in four of the British) believe that divorce should be made more difficult to obtain than now.

Our third goal was to discover whether there is consensus or conflict in contemporary British beliefs about the family. There is both. On some things nearly all are agreed: no marriage is better than a bad marriage; watching children grow up is a joy; women should not work full-time when there are young children; extra-marital sex is wrong. On other matters, however, there is only a thin line between acceptable and unacceptable alternative family life-styles. Co-habitation appears to have crossed the line and become acceptable: more people recommend living together before marriage than recommend marrying without living together first. But the right of homosexual couples to marry one another is still regarded by a majority as deviant.

Finally, we suggested that women may be more likely than men to challenge traditional family beliefs. This is true. Women, especially those in their thirties, are far more likely than men to endorse egalitarian attitudes in respect of family life and work outside the home, and are more likely to uphold a single parent's competence to raise children. They are also less likely than men to believe that marriage is incomplete and life empty without children, and less likely to agree that marriage is necessary for happiness.

So what should we now make of Shorter's suggestion that it is women who are unsettling the family nest? If the family nest is equated with marriage, children, a male breadwinner and a wife who stays at home, then it is certainly true that women's changing attitudes are unsettling. This is particularly true of the attitudes of women who are in paid work. On the other hand, if the family's survival depends on its adapting to changing social and economic circumstances, then the less traditional and more egalitarian views of women may well turn out to be its lifeline.

References

AIREY, C., 'Social and moral values', in Jowell, R., and Airey, C., (eds) *British Social Attitudes: the 1984 Report*, Gower, Aldershot (1984).
ASHFORD, S., 'Family matters', in Jowell, R., Witherspoon, S. and Brook, L. (eds), *British Social Attitudes: the 1987 Report*, Gower, Aldershot (1987).
BERNARD, J., *The Future of Marriage*, Bantam, New York (1973).
BROOK, L., 'The public's response to AIDS', in Jowell, R., Witherspoon, S. and Brook, L. (eds), *British Social Attitudes: the 5th Report*, Gower, Aldershot (1988).
CSO (Central Statistical Office), *Social Trends 20*, HMSO, London (1990).
DAVIS, J.A., 'British and American attitudes: similarities and contrasts', in Jowell, R., Witherspoon, S. and Brook, L., (eds), *British Social Attitudes: the 1986 Report*, Gower, Aldershot (1986).

DAVIS, J.A. and JOWELL, R., 'Measuring national differences', in Jowell, R., Witherspoon, S. and Brook, L., (eds), *British Social Attitudes: special international report (6th Report)*, Gower, Aldershot (1989).

DEX, S., *Women's Attitudes to Work*, Macmillan, London (1988).

EEKELAAR, J., 'Divorce English-style – a new way forward?', *Journal of Social Welfare*, vol.8 (1986), pp. 226–36.

GLENDON, M.A., *Abortion and Divorce in Western Law*, Harvard University Press, Cambridge (Mass.) (1987).

GOVE, W., 'The relationship between sex-roles, marital status and mental illness', *Social Forces*, vol. 51, (1972), pp. 34–44.

HARDING, S., 'Trends in permissiveness', in Jowell, R., Witherspoon, S. and Brook, L. (eds), *British Social Attitudes: the 5th Report*, Gower, Aldershot (1988).

HARDING, S., 'Interim report: the changing family', in Jowell, R., Witherspoon, S. and Brook, L. (eds), *British Social Attitudes: special international report (6th Report)*, Gower, Aldershot (1989).

JOSHI, H., 'The cost of caring', in Glendinning, C. and Millar, J. (eds), *Women and Poverty in Britain*, Wheatsheaf Books, London (1987).

MARTIN, J. and ROBERTS, C., *Women and Employment: A Lifetime Perspective*, HMSO, London (1984).

MORRIS, L., *The Working of the Household*, Polity Press, Cambridge (1990).

NATIONAL FAMILY TRUST, *Facing up to Family Income: Reversing the Economic Divestment of the Family*, National Family Trust Publications, London (1989).

OPCS (Office of Population Censuses and Surveys), *General Household Survey*, *17*, HMSO, London (1987).

SCHUMAN, H, and SCOTT, J., 'Generations and collective memories', *American Sociological Review*, vol. 54, (June 1989), pp. 359–81.

SCOTT, J. and DUNCOME, J., 'A cross-national comparison of sex-role attitudes: do families suffer when women go out to work?', in Arber, S. and Gilbert, N. (eds), *Women and Working Lives: Division and Change*, Macmillan, London (forthcoming).

SHORTER, E., *The Making of the Modern Family*, Fontana/Collins, Glasgow (1976).

STONE, L., *The Family, Sex and Marriage in England, 1500–1800*, Harper, New York (1979).

WITHERSPOON, S., 'Interim report: a woman's work', in Jowell, R., Witherspoon, S. and Brook, L. (eds), *British Social Attitudes: the 5th Report*, Gower, Aldershot (1988).

ZA (Zentralarchiv für empirische Sozialforschung), *International Social Survey Programme: Family and Changing Sex Role – 1988*, Codebook ZA – No. 1700, first edition, Cologne (1990).

Acknowledgements

The author and editors are indebted to colleagues in the member countries of the *International Social Survey Programme* for collecting the data on which much of this chapter is based; and to Irene Mueller, Rolf Uher and other staff of the *Zentralarchiv* in Cologne for making these data available through the first edition of their ISSP 1988 Codebook (ZA, 1990).

Besides SCPR, the national teams whose surveys contributed to this chapter are:

Hungary:	Társadalomkutatási Informatikai Egyesülés (TARKI), Budapest.
Republic of Ireland:	Department of Social Sciences, University College, Dublin.
Netherlands:	Sociaal en Cultureel Planbureau (SCP), Rijswijk.
USA:	National Opinion Research Center (NORC), University of Chicago, Chicago.

3.1 ATTITUDES TOWARDS WOMEN'S WORK (A201 a-i)
by sex, marital status, working status of women and working status of wife

	TOTAL	SEX		MARITAL STATUS			WORKING STATUS OF WOMEN			WORKING STATUS OF WIFE — MARRIED MEN	
		Men	Women	Married/ living as married	Widowed/ divorced/ separated	Single	Full-time	Part-time	Not working	Wife works	Wife doesn't work
A WORKING MOTHER CAN ESTABLISH JUST AS WARM AND SECURE A RELATIONSHIP WITH HER CHILDREN AS ONE WHO DOES NOT WORK	%	%	%	%	%	%	%	%	%	%	%
Strongly agree/agree	58	51	63	57	58	62	78	68	55	63	40
Neither agree nor disagree	12	13	11	10	16	15	9	10	11	12	11
Strongly disagree/disagree	28	35	23	31	24	22	12	19	31	25	47
ALL IN ALL, FAMILY LIFE SUFFERS WHEN THE WOMAN HAS A FULL-TIME JOB											
Strongly agree/agree	42	45	39	44	44	30	15	44	50	34	57
Neither agree nor disagree	17	17	16	16	15	21	20	14	16	16	15
Strongly disagree/disagree	40	37	43	39	39	48	65	37	33	49	27
A PRE-SCHOOL CHILD IS LIKELY TO SUFFER IF HIS OR HER MOTHER WORKS											
Strongly agree/agree	46	53	42	49	45	38	28	41	49	41	64
Neither agree nor disagree	17	16	17	16	15	21	13	16	19	20	12
Strongly disagree/disagree	35	29	40	35	31	39	58	42	30	37	22
A WOMAN AND HER FAMILY WILL ALL BE HAPPIER IF SHE GOES OUT TO WORK											
Strongly agree/agree	18	14	22	14	15	10	27	30	17	21	12
Neither agree nor disagree	38	37	40	42	42	50	46	38	36	42	25
Strongly disagree/disagree	39	45	34	42	30	34	21	27	44	35	59
A HUSBAND'S JOB IS TO EARN MONEY; A WIFE'S JOB IS TO LOOK AFTER THE HOME AND FAMILY											
Strongly agree/agree	28	32	26	28	44	18	5	19	39	18	46
Neither agree nor disagree	18	21	16	19	20	14	9	15	19	20	23
Strongly disagree/disagree	53	47	58	52	35	68	86	65	40	61	30

3.1 ATTITUDES TOWARDS WOMEN'S WORK (A201 a-i) continued

	TOTAL	SEX		MARITAL STATUS			WORKING STATUS OF WOMEN			MARRIED MEN WORKING STATUS OF WIFE	
		Men	Women	Married/ living as married	Widowed/ divorced/ Separated	Single	Full- time	Part- time	Not working	Wife works	Wife doesn't work
A JOB IS ALL RIGHT BUT WHAT MOST WOMEN REALLY WANT IS A HOME AND CHILDREN	%	%	%	%	%	%	%	%	%	%	%
Strongly agree/agree	31	35	28	31	47	22	12	27	39	23	45
Neither agree nor disagree	19	20	18	21	13	15	14	11	22	20	24
Strongly disagree/disagree	46	41	51	46	35	58	72	56	37	56	26
BEING A HOUSEWIFE IS JUST AS FULFILLING AS WORKING FOR PAY	%	%	%	%	%	%	%	%	%	%	%
Strongly agree/agree	41	37	45	42	48	35	28	43	54	26	47
Neither agree nor disagree	21	25	17	21	18	22	25	9	17	30	22
Strongly disagree/disagree	34	33	36	35	30	36	46	45	27	42	26
HAVING A JOB IS THE BEST WAY FOR A WOMAN TO BE AN INDEPENDENT PERSON	%	%	%	%	%	%	%	%	%	%	%
Strongly agree/agree	62	59	65	62	64	62	71	73	59	66	52
Neither agree nor disagree	16	17	15	16	12	18	14	11	17	17	19
Strongly disagree/disagree	20	21	19	21	19	16	14	13	23	16	28
BOTH THE HUSBAND AND WIFE SHOULD CONTRIBUTE TO THE HOUSEHOLD INCOME	%	%	%	%	%	%	%	%	%	%	%
Strongly agree/agree	53	50	56	51	63	55	63	62	51	55	45
Neither agree nor disagree	24	27	22	25	14	29	24	18	21	31	23
Strongly disagree/disagree	20	21	20	22	20	14	11	16	26	12	29
BASE: A RESPONDENTS											
Weighted	1274	568	705	906	162	205	187	125	368	204	217
Unweighted	1307	587	720	908	183	216	189	122	383	202	223

3.2 ADVICE TO A YOUNG WOMAN ON COHABITATION AND MARRIAGE (A204a)
by age within sex, highest educational qualification and religion

	TOTAL	AGE WITHIN SEX — MEN 18-34	35-54	55+	WOMEN 18-34	35-54	55+	HIGHEST EDUCATIONAL QUALIFICATION — Degree	Profes-sional	A Level O Level CSE	Foreign Other None	RELIGION — Roman Catholic	C of E/ Anglican	Other Christian	No Religion
	%	%	%	%	%	%	%	%	%	%	%	%	%	%	%
Live with a steady partner for a while, and then marry	43	61	48	20	60	47	22	50	49	50	34	37	42	25	54
Marry without living together first	37	17	30	64	18	33	60	23	30	30	48	43	41	56	22
Live alone without a steady partner	4	4	2	3	3	6	6	5	4	5	4	7	3	5	4
Live with a steady partner, without marrying	4	5	6	1	8	4	*	7	4	5	3	2	3	2	6
Can't choose	11	14	13	9	11	10	10	15	12	12	10	10	10	12	13
BASE: A RESPONDENTS Weighted	1274	191	189	188	237	241	225	111	162	456	540	141	475	185	447
Unweighted	1307	189	196	202	232	259	226	113	169	463	556	142	496	187	457

3.3 ATTITUDES TOWARDS CHILDREN (A208)
by age within sex and presence of children in household

		MEN						WOMEN						CHILDREN IN HOUSEHOLD		
	TOTAL	18-29	30-39	40-49	50-59	60-69	70+	18-29	30-39	40-49	50-59	60-69	70+	Aged Under 5	Aged 5-15 under 16	No children under 16
IT IS BETTER NOT TO HAVE CHILDREN BECAUSE THEY ARE SUCH A HEAVY BURDEN	%	%	%	%	%	%	%	%	%	%	%	%	%	%	%	%
Strongly agree/agree	3	2	4	1	-	2	2	4	3	2	2	3	5	2	*	3
Neither agree nor disagree	8	8	11	17	4	7	5	11	7	4	4	8	10	5	6	9
Strongly disagree/disagree	87	88	85	82	95	89	87	84	90	92	92	87	79	92	92	85
CHILDREN ARE MORE TROUBLE THAN THEY ARE WORTH	%	%	%	%	%	%	%	%	%	%	%	%	%	%	%	%
Strongly agree/agree	4	4	7	3	-	3	3	5	4	3	.	2	4	2	1	3
Neither agree nor disagree	9	11	9	9	8	13	4	10	12	5	6	10	11	4	9	11
Strongly disagree/disagree	86	83	83	88	91	83	89	85	84	89	88	86	82	94	89	83
WATCHING CHILDREN GROW UP IS LIFE'S GREATEST JOY	%	%	%	%	%	%	%	%	%	%	%	%	%	%	%	%
Strongly agree/agree	81	72	76	81	82	92	87	74	80	83	84	90	92	89	84	79
Neither agree nor disagree	13	18	19	15	14	6	7	16	15	11	10	8	3	9	11	14
Strongly disagree/disagree	4	6	4	4	2	2	3	7	4	5	5	-	1	2	4	4
HAVING CHILDREN INTERFERES TOO MUCH WITH THE FREEDOM OF THE PARENTS	%	%	%	%	%	%	%	%	%	%	%	%	%	%	%	%
Strongly agree/agree	9	13	12	6	7	6	5	16	9	6	9	9	8	11	8	9
Neither agree nor disagree	17	24	20	24	21	17	7	17	21	13	9	9	10	17	15	17
Strongly disagree/disagree	72	63	68	70	71	77	84	66	69	78	80	79	74	22	76	71
A MARRIAGE WITHOUT CHILDREN IS NOT FULLY COMPLETE	%	%	%	%	%	%	%	%	%	%	%	%	%	%	%	%
Strongly agree/agree	45	31	40	49	60	66	84	26	32	34	49	61	64	39	41	48
Neither agree nor disagree	20	27	22	20	19	17	2	28	23	23	17	16	8	26	22	18
Strongly disagree/disagree	32	40	37	29	18	14	10	44	45	40	34	22	20	33	35	32
PEOPLE WHO HAVE NEVER HAD CHILDREN LEAD EMPTY LIVES	%	%	%	%	%	%	%	%	%	%	%	%	%	%	%	%
Strongly agree/agree	23	10	12	19	31	39	59	11	18	19	27	33	38	19	18	26
Neither agree nor disagree	21	25	23	34	29	26	13	22	18	15	16	15	16	22	23	21
Strongly disagree/disagree	51	60	60	47	37	29	22	64	63	63	54	46	35	57	57	49
BASE: A RESPONDENTS																
Weighted	1274	137	102	103	81	86	61	167	150	125	81	103	78	199	211	863
Unweighted	1307	137	100	103	90	95	62	167	146	134	90	101	79	194	214	899

Column header note: AGE WITHIN SEX

3.4 SINGLE PARENTHOOD (A205 g and h)
by sex, age, marital status within sex and presence of children in household

| | TOTAL | SEX | | AGE | | | MARITAL STATUS WITHIN SEX | | | | | | CHILDREN IN HOUSEHOLD | | |
| | | | | | | | MEN | | | WOMEN | | | | | |
		Men	Women	18-34	35-54	55+	Married/ living as married	Widowed/ divorced/ separated	Single	Married/ living as married	Widowed/ divorced/ separated	Single	Aged Under 5	Aged 5-15	No children under 16
	%	%	%	%	%	%	%	%	%	%	%	%	%	%	%
A SINGLE MOTHER CAN BRING UP HER CHILD AS WELL AS A MARRIED COUPLE															
Agree/strongly agree	30	25	35	41	31	19	23	27	34	30	43	49	42	33	27
Neither agree nor disagree	17	16	18	19	17	15	16	18	15	18	18	16	13	19	17
Disagree strongly/ disagree	51	58	45	39	50	64	60	50	49	50	36	33	44	46	53
A SINGLE FATHER CAN BRING UP HIS CHILD AS WELL AS A MARRIED COUPLE	%	%	%	%	%	%	%	%	%	%	%	%	%	%	%
Agree strongly/agree	24	19	28	35	26	11	18	22	25	25	28	42	35	28	20
Neither agree nor disagree	18	15	20	22	17	14	14	16	17	19	23	17	18	21	17
Disagree strongly/ disagree	57	65	51	42	55	73	67	58	56	54	47	39	46	51	61
BASE: A RESPONDENTS															
Weighted	1274	568	705	427	430	414	421	49	98	485	113	107	199	211	863
Unweighted	1307	587	720	421	455	428	425	57	105	483	126	111	194	214	899

4 Living under threat

*Ken Young**

In the first part of this chapter, we examine current attitudes towards a wide range of environmental issues, from atmospheric pollution and the future of the countryside, to nuclear power. We then go on to discuss the linked issues of the risks of nuclear war and its aftermath, and the direction of Britain's defence policy. We explore fluctuations in opinion over the past few years and try to discern trends in attitudes – within the population as a whole and among subgroups within it. All the topics covered have received wide coverage in the media and have been close to the top of the political agenda. Our data reveal how responsive the public at large has been to the various debates – for instance on the threat to the global environment and on Britain's defence stance in a rapidly changing Europe.

We can chart responses to some questions – for instance, on environmental threats and nuclear defence – back to 1983. Other questions, notably on concern for the countryside, were introduced between 1985 and 1987. Those on the likelihood of a nuclear war with the USSR and its possible consequences were first asked in 1985 and repeated in 1989. So we have time-trends on all of them.

As we shall show, it is too soon to tell whether or not the public's fear of nuclear catastrophe, especially pronounced in the early 1980s, will be matched and possibly replaced in the early 1990s by a similar apprehension about calamitous change in the physical environment. But there is evidence from these findings and others that public concern about nuclear issues – defence policies as well as nuclear energy – is linked, to some extent at least, with concern about certain forms of atmospheric pollution and other threats to the world's natural environment.

---

* Professor of Politics, Queen Mary and Westfield College, University of London.

Concern about the environment

In the second half of the 1980s, there has been unprecedented media discussion both of broad environmental issues – most notably the effects on the earth's atmosphere of fossil-fuel power generation and of industrial pollution – and of the farmers' role as a provider of food and as the custodian of the countryside.

Concern about the impact of pollution on the global environment was dramatically revived, as evidence of ozone depletion accumulated and with the discovery in 1985 of a seasonal 'hole' in the ozone layer over Antarctica. Four issues in particular now engage widespread attention: damage to the ozone layer itself; the build-up of 'greenhouse gases' (mainly carbon dioxide) leading to global warming; the pace of the destruction of the tropical rainforests; and trans-boundary acid rain pollution.

The frequency with which concerted international action to combat these threats is discussed and (less often) agreed has sustained media attention and public awareness. The discovery of the Antarctic hole prompted a meeting of 31 countries in Montreal in September 1987, under the auspices of the United Nations Environment Programme. The American delegation, concerned in particular about predictions of the rise in the incidence of skin cancer, sought an almost total ban on chlorofluorocarbon (CFC) production; but after representations by other countries, the US substantially modified this proposal.

In the following two years, however, the sense of urgency grew. In 1989 the EC agreed to eliminate CFC production and use by the end of the century; and this decision was echoed by the Montreal signatories when, with more than 40 other nations, they met in Helsinki in May that year. The US manufacturer Du Pont subsequently announced its decision to discontinue CFC production and switch to the less environmentally damaging hydrochlorofluorocarbons (HCFCs). Public awareness in Britain of the need for urgent action was doubtless heightened by the 'Save the Ozone Layer' conference in March 1989, convened by the Prime Minister. Meanwhile the environmental lobby has been highly critical of what it regards as the piecemeal and voluntaristic nature of the British approach.

In contrast with measures to preserve the ozone layer, international action on global warming has been more cautious. Climatic disturbances may have become more frequent since the early 1970s (Gribbin, 1978). But the relative influence of natural (solar and seismic) changes and those which are man-made (notably changes in the earth's atmospheric sunshield) is still contested. Internationally, no agreements have yet been reached to combat the build-up of atmospheric and greenhouse gases. This inaction has been in part due to controversy over the nature of the 'greenhouse effect' itself. First identified as long ago as 1903, and attributed even then to emissions from Europe's rapidly increasing industrial plant, its very existence has lately been disputed by some scientists (notably Sherwood Idso) who argue that the build-up of industrial pollution may equally well have a cooling effect (Kemp, 1990). Professed scepticism on the part of the US government has sustained a cautious approach, although a recent shift in the American position is likely to speed the pace of international action.

The policy implications of global warming for Britain are now recognised to be considerable (Boyle and Ardill, 1989). In September 1988, in a speech to the Royal Society of Arts, the Prime Minister declared a need for both domestic legislation and international action to protect the environment. In 1989, the UK permanent representative at the UN – himself a pioneer writer on climatic change

(Tickell, 1978) – called for international guidelines for 'good climate behaviour'. However, Britain may be less likely than other European countries to see a surge of support for 'green politics'. Britain's non-proportional voting system – distinct among the concerned industrial nations of Europe – may well limit the impact of the Green Party, at least in contrast to the successes scored by Green candidates in West Germany, the Netherlands and elsewhere. This may well serve to temper political demands in Britain for stringent action on environmental protection (Ward, Samways and Benton, 1990, pp. 222–4). The main political parties appear to be adopting the environmental cause in response to increasing public concern about environmental problems. However it remains to be seen how environmental imperatives will be integrated with their existing policies and translated into effective action.

The depletion of the tropical forests is a matter of contention between the developed and less developed nations, with the World Bank exercising increasing leverage upon the latter. The burning of the forests adds to atmospheric carbon dioxide levels, while the depletion of forests itself restricts the potential for carbon dioxide absorption. Rainforest depletion has been the subject of considerable media attention through the 1980s, alerting public opinion to high annual rates of loss (estimated at 0.6 per cent annually between 1981 and 1985) and the clearance policies of such countries as Brazil (with the largest area of forest and a high rate of clearance) and Indonesia.

Finally the increasing problem of acid rain, arising for the most part from sulphur dioxide emissions from power stations and nitrogen oxide from motor vehicles, has led to sharp divisions between Britain and the mainland European countries. Britain was not party to the Sofia protocol of 1988, and has not joined the movement to reduce sulphur dioxide levels to 30 per cent of 1980 levels by 1993. The environment ministers of the EC nevertheless agreed in June 1988 to seek a 60 per cent reduction by the year 2003. For Britain, the problem is inseparable from the larger issues of energy policy: it is estimated that about half of Britain's sulphur dioxide contribution arises from coal-fired power stations. International pressures continued during 1990, with the report from the Intergovernmental Panel on Climate Change and the preparation of a new White Paper on the environment. The government's position, however, has been firm on the need to avoid both the adoption of stringent pollution reduction goals (which are likely to be ignored in practice) and the adoption of measures which will raise industrial costs or consumer prices (*Economist*, May 1990). Early expectations, following publication of the Pearce Report (Pearce, 1989), of a radically new approach to valuing environmental protection, appear to have been confounded.

Environmental hazards

Throughout this series we have asked a set of questions about the environmental impact of various forms of pollution; and at each round we have found that concern about atmospheric pollution and effluent has been high and, on the whole, rising. The table below shows the proportions naming each as "very serious" over the life of the survey series.

	1983	1986	1989
% regarding each hazard as very serious:			
Industrial waste in rivers or sea	62%	65%	75%
Cutting down tropical rainforests	n/a	n/a	68%
Certain aerosol chemicals in the atmosphere	n/a	n/a	67%
Waste from nuclear electricity stations	63%	72%	67%
Industrial fumes in the air	41%	46%	60%
Acid rain	n/a	54%	57%
Lead from petrol	48%	42%	45%
Noise and dirt from traffic	23%	25%	31%
Noise from aircraft	8%	9%	9%

Add to these figures the proportions of people who regarded each threat as "quite" serious, and we find that more than four-fifths of the population are concerned about eight of the nine threats – the exception being aircraft noise.[1]

Indeed, concern about global environmental pollution has risen over the course of the series to such an extent that further increases in the proportions regarding them as serious are difficult to envisage. Moreover, in response to questions introduced for the first time in 1989, more than two-thirds of respondents already believe that the environmental effects of ozone-depleting gases and the destruction of tropical rainforests are "very" serious.

These remarkably high levels of concern may well reflect the growing sense of urgency conveyed in recent media coverage of these issues. As Kemp (1990) observes:

> The spectre of thousands of cases of skin cancer linked to a seemingly innocuous product like hairspray or deodorant was sufficiently startling that it excited the media and, through them, the general public (p.130).

Environmental issues are perhaps distinctive in this respect, having the capability to link familiar, everyday phenomena to global events.

Protecting the countryside

Another series of questions, addressing the extent to which people's *behaviour* reflects their concern about various 'green' issues, is being asked for the first time in 1990. Responses to that series will provide a more direct measure of 'green consumerism' and will be reported next year.

For the moment, however, we can assess strength of feeling on only a limited range of environmental issues to do with the countryside, and the measures people endorse to protect it. Concern about the countryside can to some degree serve as a proxy measure for more general environmental attitudes, although locality and circumstances will clearly influence attitudes to some extent. Some of our questions asked respondents to choose between pairs of alternatives: countryside protection *versus* lower food prices; and countryside protection *versus* employment opportunities. We also asked respondents whether looking after the countryside was "too important to be left to the farmers" or whether "farmers should be left to decide what's done on farms". Responses to all three questions show sharp increases in levels of concern about the future of the British countryside:

	1985	1986	1987	1989
% agreeing that:				
Industry should be prevented from causing damage to the country-side, even if this sometimes leads to higher prices	78%	82%	83%	88%
The countryside should be protected from development even if this sometimes leads to fewer jobs	n/a	n/a	60%	72%
Looking after the countryside is too important to be left to the farmers	34%	34%	38%	46%

In earlier reports we have noted that, on matters of countryside protection, and indeed on a range of other environmental issues, the views of men and women and of people in different age groups differ quite markedly. Education and political partisanship sometimes also appear to shape attitudes. So we looked at the latest figures for evidence of subgroup differences:

	Industry should be prevented from causing damage	Countryside should be protected	Looking after countryside too important to be left to farmers
Total:	88%	72%	46%
Men:			
18–34	90%	74%	55%
35–54	92%	78%	63%
55+	85%	72%	48%
Women:			
18–34	87%	68%	33%
35–54	91%	70%	42%
55+	83%	71%	36%

The general picture is one of consensus rather than of division. Only on the issue of 'trusting the farmer' were opinions somewhat divided with women – especially younger women – markedly more content than men to leave farm development in farmers' hands.

Respondents with higher educational qualifications tended to be less trusting of the farmer, and rather less inclined to favour jobs and lower prices at the expense of the countryside. Labour identifiers are rather more likely than Conservatives to favour jobs and lower prices. This suggests that the Labour Party may have some difficulty in persuading its supporters to pay the price of environmental protection. These and other differences are shown in **Table 4.1**.

The most marked increase in concern is among graduates, who increasingly favour protecting the countryside at the expense of job opportunities; younger respondents (aged 18–34) tend to share this concern. But graduates' responses to the other two related questions were much the same as in 1985, with the result that the educational divisions that were so noticeable then were, by 1989, considerably less marked.

Our findings on changing attitudes towards countryside protection are echoed in responses to a series of statements about the role of the farmer. We asked respondents to say how much they agreed or disagreed with each of these statements:

Government should withhold some subsidies from farmers and use them to protect the countryside, even if this leads to higher prices.

Modern methods of farming have caused damage to the countryside.

All things considered, farmers do a good job in looking after the countryside.

Here we find consistent and quite marked shifts since 1985 towards support for government action, and a slight decline in the longstanding belief in the farmer as custodian of countryside interests.

	1985	1987	1989
% agreeing that:			
Government should withhold subsidies from farmers	48%	51%	61%
Modern farming damages the countryside	64%	67%	72%
Farmers look after the countryside well	76%	74%	72%

Subgroup differences appear but none is dramatic. Men, especially those in the middle age-range, tend to be less supportive of the farmer on this measure, as are graduates and non-Conservatives. Since 1985, concern about damage to the countryside has grown especially rapidly among older men (aged 55+), the less well educated and Labour identifiers, the effect of which has been to make the divisions of opinion that do exist noticeably less pronounced than they were.

Concern about nuclear power

Since the early years of the survey series, we have asked a number of questions about nuclear power generation, covering both energy policy options and, more specifically, the perceived safety of nuclear reactors. On both issues, public attitudes have proved to be volatile.

Energy policy options

Each year we have asked:

Which of these three possible solutions to Britain's electricity needs would you favour most?

We should make do with the power stations we have already; OR
We should build more coal-fuelled power stations; OR
We should build more nuclear power stations.

As the following table shows, increased reliance on nuclear power generation has never been popular – and never less so than in 1986, around the time of the Chernobyl disaster. But the most startling change is that between 1987 and 1989: an increase from 25 to 44 per cent in the proportion in favour of making do with the power stations we already have.

	Energy policy options 1983–1989					
	1983	1984	1985	1986	1987	1989
	%	%	%	%	%	%
We should:						
Make do with power stations we have	32	38	34	34	25	44
Build more coal-fuelled power stations	47	44	41	52	48	37
Build more nuclear power stations	19	15	23	11	22	16

It is unlikely to be a coincidence that in recent years unprecedented media attention has been focused on the environmental threats posed by carbon fuel emissions. The debate has centred on the relative significance of carbon dioxide gases in contributing to the greenhouse effect, and on the contribution to it made by coal-fired power stations. The Prime Minister has argued in favour of nuclear power as the least polluting form of electricity generation, while on the other hand the coalfields lobbyists claim that coal-fired production "is the greenest option available" (O'Keefe *et al*, 1989). But it appears that coal-fired stations are now regarded by fewer people as a 'safe' alternative to nuclear reactors. Publicity about global warming and acid rain is, it seems, beginning to influence attitudes, and the relative risks of alternative sources of power are coming to be seen as less clear cut (Fremlin, 1987).

As **Table 4.2** shows, the rise in support for making do with the power stations we already have is more or less uniform across most subgroups. People in different age groups with differing levels of education and with different party identification have all, it seems, changed their attitudes in unison. True, younger people (particularly younger women) aged under 35 are still conspicuous in their opposition to building more power stations, but the fairly large age differences evident in 1987 have, two years later, become less marked.

That nuclear power is still, however, a politically-charged issue is clear from the following table:

Energy policy options 1987–89

	Conservative		SLD/SDP		Labour	
	1987	1989	1987	1989	1987	1989
	%	%	%	%	%	%
We should:						
Make do with power stations we have	24	43	26	47	22	42
Build more coal-fuelled power stations	31	31	57	32	66	48
Build more nuclear power stations	39	24	15	17	7	6

Opposition to nuclear power stations could scarcely be higher among Labour identifiers; supporters of the 'centre' parties are only barely more enthusiastic. But it is the fall in support for nuclear reactors among Conservatives that is perhaps the most intriguing: the policy options they support are the reverse of those they advocated two years earlier. And Labour identifiers, still the strongest advocates of coal-fired stations, were in 1989 much more muted in their support.

The costs of nuclear power generation received considerable media coverage in the wake of the Sizewell B enquiry. The government's fluctuating plans for electricity privatisation also served to place the issue firmly on the political agenda. Of course, the cancellation of the post-Sizewell PWR programme and the withdrawal of existing nuclear power plants from privatisation plans followed our 1989 fieldwork round; but nonetheless it is likely that respondents were more aware than in earlier years of the problems that the nuclear power industry was having in living up to its claims. With *British Social Attitudes* surveys showing little enthusiasm for privatisation (only 14 per cent in 1989 favouring complete freedom of the industry from government control), it seems likely that the issue will continue to be one which divides voters on party political lines – though perhaps to a decreasing extent and in changing forms.

Risks posed by nuclear reactors

A further series of questions has been included regularly, to monitor public concern about the *risks* posed by nuclear power generation. The following table summarises the overall responses over the period of the survey series:

	Perceptions of risks posed by nuclear power					
	1983	1984	1985	1986	1987	1989
Waste from nuclear electricity stations has a very or quite serious effect on the environment	83%	87%	82%	90%	83%	89%
Nuclear power stations create very or quite serious risks for the future	63%	67%	61%	78%	64%	73%
A serious accident at a British nuclear power station is very or quite likely in next ten years	45%	53%	n/a	59%	52%	58%

As we can see 1986 – the year of Chernobyl – was the high point of anxiety on all these measures. The only other discernible feature is that the level of concern in 1989 is higher than 1983. Since 1987, of course, there has been renewed controversy over the health hazards of living near, or working at, nuclear installations. Anxiety about the present and future safety of nuclear reactors is remarkably widespread, in sharp contrast to the overwhelmingly reassuring line taken on the safety of British and Western European power generation by both government and scientific experts in the wake of the Chernobyl disaster (OECD, 1987; Fremlin, 1987; Warley and Lewins, 1989).

We expected to find changes among subgroups since 1987 similar to those evident on the issue of future energy policy, and by and large we did. Perceptions of the risks of nuclear power stations have risen most sharply among the over 55s (and especially the over 65s). Women still tend to be more anxious than men, but gender and age differences are now much less apparent than they were in 1987. And, in parallel with the changes along party political lines already noted, Conservative identifiers in 1989 were markedly more worried than before about the possible dangers of nuclear reactors:

Perceptions of risks posed by nuclear power stations

	Conservative		SLD/SDP		Labour	
	1987	1989	1987	1989	1987	1989
	%	%	%	%	%	%
% saying create:						
Very serious risks for the future	21	26	40	39	55	56
Quite serious risks for the future	23	34	34	39	26	30

Since government support for nuclear power generation has also cooled nowadays – with plans to build three new reactors following the construction of Sizewell B now shelved – nuclear power will probably find it increasingly difficult to find advocates. On the other hand, coal-fuelled power is unlikely to be the beneficiary of this change, as might have been the case two or three years ago.

More generally, as suggested in *The 1987 Report*, public concern about the risks of nuclear power generation, and the disposal of its associated waste products, remains largely impervious to official reassurances; anxiety

> remains strong and deep-rooted and involves a very powerful fear of radioactivity, cancer and genetic disorders, and also of the industry associated with it (Openshaw, 1986, p.11).

As the long-term implications of decommissioning and waste disposal become more apparent, we may expect this underlying suspicion to surface in fierce conflicts over the siting of nuclear power stations and waste disposal facilities (Openshaw, Carver and Fernie, 1989).

Before moving on to people's attitudes towards defence in general – and towards nuclear defence in particular – it is worth noting that there is a strong correspondence between attitudes to civil and to military nuclear issues. Those people who oppose British nuclear armaments tend to be much more pessimistic as regards the risks posed by civil nuclear power: for instance 74 per cent of them expect a serious nuclear accident at a British power station, compared with only 51 per cent of the rest of the population. Similarly, 76 per cent of them believe that nuclear power stations pose "very" or "quite" serious risks for the future, compared with 64 per cent of others. In *The 1985 Report* we speculated about the significance of 'uncontrollability' in perceptions of the nuclear threat. In confirmation, we find that in 1989 one-half of those who feel that US nuclear weapons on British soil make Britain a less safe place to live also believe that nuclear power stations pose very serious risks for the future (compared with just over a quarter of those who are more sanguine about the US nuclear presence). In other words, 'anti-nuclear' associations run right through the dataset, cross-cutting other green concerns. Further analysis of this phenomenon would reap rich returns.

War scares and a changing world

In the early 1980s, shortly before the *British Social Attitudes* series began, popular concern about the prospect of war rose steeply to that of earlier cold war levels. Against the background of a sharpening political debate about NATO's defence capability, and a renewed and bitter superpower confrontation following the occupation of Afghanistan by Soviet troops, war scenarios became popular reading. General Sir John Hackett's *The Third World War* (1978) sold three million copies in ten languages over the next few years; and the television dramas *Threads* and *The Day After*, depicting the aftermath of a nuclear holocaust, were watched by millions.

The defence debate in the late 1970s began with mounting concern about the numerical weakness of NATO forces in relation to those of the Warsaw Pact. On both sides of the Atlantic, partisan debate about defence matters played a large part in the campaigning and subsequent election of Margaret Thatcher in 1979 and of Ronald Reagan the following year. Increased public awareness of, and concern about, the Western nations' military capability undoubtedly helped secure political support for the modernisation of NATO's nuclear arsenal (Sabin, 1986). But in Britain the victory of the nuclear defence lobby also led to a revival of pacifism and anti-militarism on the left during the first half of the decade: there was a sustained campaign of direct action (most notably against the deployment of cruise missiles at US bases) and an increase in anti-American sentiment more generally.

This polarisation of opinion probably helped to feed a general rise in levels of war anxiety, reflecting both a sense of the increased probability of war and a belief that it would take the form of a cataclysmic nuclear convulsion (as claimed by the anti-nuclear movement). The political effects of the new 'doomsday scenario' were also considerable. Membership of the Campaign for Nuclear Disarmament increased seven-fold between 1980 and 1983, while the Labour Party formally adopted a unilateralist position. The sense of living in a dangerous age was coupled with a new suspicion that great power rivalry and impetuousness, rather than Soviet aggression alone, threatened to tip the world into an unsought nuclear conflict; to many the threat to peace was no longer seen as a Soviet monopoly, but more of an inevitable consequence of the 'superpower system' itself.

In the event the predicted 'decade of danger' proved to be something less. By 1985, with the accession of Mikhail Gorbachev to the Soviet leadership and with the retreat from bellicosity in President Reagan's second term, *détente* was gradually renewed and the apparent risk of a major conflict between Russia and the West steadily receded (Cox, 1985). The agreement on intermediate nuclear force limitations in Europe represents a shift back from the tensions which had accompanied the deployment of SS20s and cruise missiles in the early 1980s. Agreement on short-range nuclear forces followed quickly but by the spring of 1989, when our fieldwork was undertaken, radical disagreements as to the interpretation of the agreement threatened to divide the NATO governments, with the US and Britain holding a firm line against the so-called 'zero-option' of no land-based missiles. The Prime Minister's earlier image as the 'Iron Lady' was revived through the firmness of her resistance to West German pressure for a denuclearised Germany.

How have British public attitudes responded to these events? As if to underline the speed of the change, it is sobering to note that the collapse of the Communist regimes in central and eastern Europe, the virtual dismantling of the Warsaw Pact, and the rapid moves towards German unification all came too late to be reflected in our 1989 survey. We look forward with keen interest to assessing the extent of the effects of these developments in future rounds of the series (and we may plausibly expect popular opinion to change slowly and to lag behind changes in the international situation). For the moment, we can examine only the impact upon popular expectations of the relaxation of international tension during the second half of the 1980s and ask to what extent trends that are already visible might reasonably be expected to carry through – perhaps accelerated by the recent political changes in Europe – to 1990 and beyond.

Expectations of war

In each survey year (except 1985) we have presented respondents with a list of predictions, and asked them to say how likely they thought each was to come about "within the next ten years". As the table below shows, in the earlier years of the series gloom about the likelihood of war was widespread, with around a quarter of respondents thinking that a world war "involving Britain and Europe" was likely within the space of a decade:

Likelihood of a world war in next ten years

	1983	1984	1986	1987	1989
	%	%	%	%	%
Very likely	6	3	5	2	1
Quite likely	18	18	18	9	7
Not very likely	52	50	52	56	55
Not at all likely	24	25	24	29	34

But the change in mood since 1986 is striking. By 1989, only eight per cent of respondents thought the prospect of a world war involving Britain to be likely.

These remarkable changes are paralleled in responses to a question about the specific and threatening prospect of "a *nuclear* war between Russia and the West before the end of the century"; in 1985 only 16 per cent of respondents deemed this "not at all likely", but by 1989 that proportion had risen steeply to 38 per cent. Once again only a handful now regard the prospect of a nuclear war as likely, compared with nearly a quarter of the population only four years earlier.

Likelihood of a nuclear war between Russia and the West

	1985	1989
	%	%
Very likely	5	2
Quite likely	18	5
Not very likely	47	45
Not at all likely	16	38
Can't choose	13	9

But the great powers are not the only nations capable of detonating a nuclear bomb. Less powerful nations – for instance Israel, Iraq and Pakistan – are believed to have nuclear weapons too, or at least the technology to develop and deliver them. So it is of interest to see whether a lessening of anxiety about superpower conflict is accompanied by similar optimism about the nuclear capabilities and intentions of lesser powers.

**Likelihood that "a nuclear bomb will be dropped
somewhere in the world"**

	1984	1986	1987	1989
	%	%	%	%
Very likely	9	8	6	4
Quite likely	26	27	22	20
Not very likely	38	39	39	45
Not at all likely	24	25	29	28

The figures suggest that some respondents at least are aware that the likelihood of a nuclear calamity is not solely to do with relations between the superpowers. True, the later 1980s is seen as a time when a nuclear engagement "somewhere in the world" is seen as less and less likely; only around a quarter of respondents now appear to fear such a disaster. But, this figure is much higher than the proportions who believe a *world war* is likely within the next decade (eight per cent) and those who believe that the USA and USSR will become involved in a nuclear engagement (seven per cent).

A superficial conclusion to be drawn from these marked shifts is that recent political changes within the Soviet Union, and the thawing of relations between the great powers, has led to parallel shifts in prevailing patterns of beliefs and expectations about the prospects for peace. However, the evidence from trend data going back before 1983 suggests that something more than this is at work. Comparisons between recent *British Social Attitudes* results and Gallup poll data stretching back to 1951 suggest that public fears of a world war, despite fluctuations associated with events such as the Korean War, remained low for a period of nearly 30 years, and rose again to 'Korean War levels' only in the early 1980s (Sabin, 1986, p.154). So while recent international developments have, beyond doubt, led to a marked decrease in expectations of war, it would be an exaggeration to say that our findings so far suggest a sea-change in public attitudes. World events are moving so fast nowadays – particularly in eastern Europe – that public attitudes are bound to be somewhat volatile on these issues for a while.

Nonetheless, the size of the changes since 1986 prompted us to look for subgroup differences. Are all sectors of the population moving in unison, or are some noticeably more optimistic now than others? Our own earlier analyses (Young, 1986, p.74) suggested that younger people tended to be more pessimistic than older people, and that women were either more pessimistic or more uncertain (according to their generation) than men. Moreover, these differences appeared to be systematically related to other age and gender differences on a range of potentially life-threatening issues.

Here we confine ourselves to analysing the responses given in 1985 and 1989 to the question on nuclear war with the USSR, first looking at age and gender differences. We see that women, especially young women, are still more gloomy than men, though a large majority now believes that war is unlikely.

**Nuclear war between Russia and the West
before end of the century**

% saying not very or not at all likely	1985	1989	% increase
Total	63%	83%	+20%
Men:			
18–34	62%	90%	+28%
35–54	77%	90%	+13%
55+	72%	94%	+22%
Women:			
18–34	52%	71%	+19%
35–54	67%	81%	+14%
55+	49%	73%	+24%

While much more optimistic in 1989 than in 1985, as many as 16 per cent of young women still consider such a war to be "very" or "quite" likely, a view held by only six per cent of men in the same age group. No other discernible demographic group shares this pessimism. This type of comparison is often bedevilled by differential responses between men and women of different generations – older women, for instance, being less willing on the whole to make any prediction at all. Young women remain the most pessimistic of all age groups about nuclear war.

Although expectations of nuclear war are now confined to very low levels (generally well below 10 per cent), marked differences do remain, especially between those with educational qualifications and those without. The least highly educated respondents remain the least optimistic.

**Nuclear war between Russia and the West
before end of the century**

% saying not very or not at all likely	1985	1989	% increase
Total	63%	83%	+20%
Highest educational qualification:			
Degree	74%	97%	+23%
Professional	74%	87%	+13%
'A' level	66%	90%	+24%
'O' level/CSE	63%	84%	+21%
None	57%	77%	+20%

Whereas in 1985 almost a quarter of graduates thought that a nuclear war with Russia within 15 years was likely, now not a single graduate gave this response. More highly educated respondents probably follow world affairs more closely, thus translating changes in events more quickly into hopes for the future. Their greater optimism may well have 'trickled' to other groups by the time of the next round.

In 1985 we found striking partisan differences, with Labour identifiers far more pessimistic than either Conservative or 'centre' party identifiers (Young, 1986). These differences persist, but in 1989 they were far less marked (see **Table 4.3**). As we have discovered, political partisanship still tends to shape attitudes towards nuclear issues generally but, so it appears, less so on nuclear *defence* than it used to.

The effect of a continuing decline in anxiety about nuclear war could be far-reaching. For instance, Sabin (1986) argues that it is undesirable (even if it were possible) fully to defuse war anxieties, since a minimum level of informed concern is necessary to promote a sensible and realistic defence debate. Expenditure on defence has, however, consistently been a low priority among the British public (in 1989, only one per cent nominated it as a first priority for extra government spending). In a climate of increasing optimism, public pressure for a sizeable 'peace dividend' – perhaps to improve the core welfare services – could become increasingly difficult for governments of any persuasion to resist.

Consequences for Britain of nuclear war

We have seen that people are much more optimistic about the prospects for peace; but is this matched by a change in their evaluations of the consequences, should nuclear war break out? After all, a perception that the risk of war is lower need not lead to a more sanguine view of its aftermath.

Interpreting public images of war is, of course, complicated by the vagueness of the concept of superpower conflict. People's expectations of what might happen may (quite understandably) vary; some might envisage a limited and conventional encounter involving few civilians while, at the other extreme, some might imagine a full-scale and mutually devastating nuclear exchange. In *The 1986 Report* we examined for the first time responses to a series of questions about the nature and consequences of such a war, and we repeated these questions in 1989. First, we asked:

> *If there was a nuclear war between Russia and the West, which of these statements best describes what you think would happen to Britain?*
>
> > *Battlefield nuclear weapons would be used, but there would be few civilian deaths; OR*
> > *Some British cities would be destroyed, but much of the country would pull through; OR*
> > *Much or all of Britain would be destroyed.*

As the table below shows, we find that the greater optimism expressed by respondents about the likelihood of nuclear war is reflected – though to a more limited extent – in their expectation of the nature and consequences of such a war.

	1985	1989
	%	%
In the event of nuclear war:		
There would be few civilian deaths	2	3
Much of the country would pull through	12	17
Britain would be destroyed	72	62
Can't choose	13	16

Overall, around the same (minuscule) proportion of respondents in both years envisaged a tactical nuclear war with few civilian deaths. But the proportion of those believing that much or all of Britain would be destroyed has decreased by some 10 percentage points.

A less pessimistic attitude towards the consequences of nuclear war is apparent among all subgroups within the 1989 sample; but the fall in the proportion predicting a nuclear holocaust is tempered by a smaller rise (among younger respondents particularly) in the proportion unable to choose between any of the alternatives offered. It is predictable, perhaps, in a world where international tension is noticeably more relaxed than it was four years earlier, that fewer people feel able to think about the consequences of a nuclear cataclysm. There appears then to have been a generalised reduction in levels of anxiety, with the apocalyptic visions of the early 1980s television productions being replaced for some by rather greater confidence in the future and for others by simple uncertainty.

However, anxiety about the probability of war, and anxiety as to its consequences, appear to be distinct phenomena. We find, for instance, that the relationship between education level and optimism about war is inverted in respect of the likely consequences of nuclear war: graduates are far *more* inclined than non-graduates to believe that a nuclear war would bring complete destruction. Not surprisingly, perhaps, the better educated are also better able to distinguish between probability and consequences.

Likely consequences of nuclear war

	1985	1989
% saying much or all of Britain would be destroyed		
Total	72%	62%
Highest educational qualification:		
Degree	85%	80%
Professional	73%	67%
'A' level	75%	64%
'O' level/CSE	76%	61%
None	67%	58%

Environmental impact of nuclear war

A related question about the effects of a nuclear war on the physical environment helps cast light on these complex patterns of expectation and belief. In 1989, as in 1985, we presented respondents with a 'doomsday' scenario of "a nuclear war [which] would result in a world-wide 'nuclear winter' with hardly any sunlight and little chance of survival", and asked them whether they thought that it was "highly exaggerated" or "slightly exaggerated", or "more or less true". Here again we find evidence of a rather greater confidence in the future than was apparent four years earlier. Nonetheless, in both years, around two-thirds of respondents (67 per cent in 1985 and 63 per cent in 1989) believed that the dire nuclear winter scenario was "more or less true".

As we have seen, the lessening of international tension has gone hand in hand with a decline in anxiety about war; this may reflect a realistic assessment of diminishing risks, or it may be of independent origin. Similarly, the slight falling off in anxiety about the prospect of a nuclear winter may be an indicator of a general reduction in fear of nuclear conflict, or it may just reflect the fact that the issue is now dormant. Indeed, the prospect of a nuclear winter has also been regarded with increasing *scientific* scepticism in recent years, since the publication of the first major study of the impact of nuclear weapons on the global climate (Turco *et al*, 1983). The scientific consensus has now generally downgraded the postulated effect to, at most, a 'nuclear autumn' (Kemp, 1990, p.178), with each later and more sophisticated study predicting a lesser, and shorter, period of temperature and light reduction. Recently John Maddox (1988), editor of *Nature*, asked rhetorically, "What happened to nuclear winter?"

It will be interesting to see if this particularly arcane and speculative topic of scientific debate continues to affect public attitudes in future years; the possibility certainly exists that the very notion of a nuclear winter has had the effect of sensitising people to the prospect of man-made global disasters, influencing attitudes to some of the topics discussed earlier in this chapter.

As in 1985, attitudes differ according to level of education, with the most highly educated respondents being the most pessimistic, and *vice versa*. We also find quite strong associations with age and gender, with women much more despondent than their male peers about the prospects of human survival following a nuclear holocaust. Again older people (of both sexes) are the most sanguine, and young women are again the least likely to consider the nuclear winter scenario exaggerated (see **Table 4.4**). The age differences are, however, much less marked than they were four years earlier.

Civil defence and nuclear war

We might perhaps expect a lessening anxiety about the likelihood of nuclear conflict and its possible consequences to be reflected in attitudes towards civil defence measures. We reintroduced a question asked in 1985:

> *At the moment, the British government publishes advice on how people should prepare for survival in the event of a nuclear war. Which of the following statements comes closest to your view on what the government should do?*
>
> *It is pointless for the government to do anything, because so few people would survive; OR*
> *The government should continue to provide only advice on how people can protect themselves; OR*
> *The government should also provide nuclear shelters to increase people's chances of survival.*

As the following table shows, there has been very little change from 1985. There are still more people who favour the provision of shelters than those who do not, but it is far from an overwhelming level of support.[2]

Civil defence measures

	1985	1989
	%	%
Government should:		
Do nothing	31	29
Provide advice	16	19
Build shelters	44	40
Can't choose	8	10

Taking these findings as a whole, it seems that the receding prospect of nuclear war makes people more confident about the likelihood of human survival in the event of such a war. This greater sense of security on defence matters might well lead to a shift in policy preference; but in which direction? Will it bring greater confidence in Britain's current defence policies or, conversely, will it foster the view that strong defence is irrelevant? The debates over the direction of defence policy in the run-up to the next general election – and, in particular, those over the need for a British nuclear deterrent – are likely to reflect these two points of view. In particular there is likely to be increasing support for attempts to reap the 'peace dividend' as a means of increasing Britain's economic strength and regenerating a neglected infrastructure. So we next examine perceptions of the great military power blocs, and of Britain's relations with the USA, NATO and the European Community.

Unfreezing the cold war

Superpower threats

If public attitudes towards, and expectations of, the possibility of nuclear war are becoming more sanguine, we might anticipate changes in respondents' perceptions of the great powers themselves. Since 1984 we have been monitoring responses to a question about the extent to which America and the USSR constitute threats to world peace. As the table below shows, there has been a marked decline in the proportions regarding the USSR as a threat, and (until 1987) a slow but steady rise in concern about the dangers of the military stance of the USA. In 1989, with the launch of political and economic reforms in Hungary and Poland, the first tangible signs of a transformation of Soviet relations with eastern Europe began to appear. The result is a substantial rise in the proportion who consider *neither* superpower a threat to world peace.

Threats to world peace

	1984	1985	1986	1987	1989
	%	%	%	%	%
America is a greater threat to world peace	11	13	16	18	14
Russia is a greater threat to world peace	26	24	18	17	16
Russia and America are equally great threats	54	55	54	54	47
Neither is a threat	5	6	9	8	20

Do these shifts imply a fundamental reassessment of international conflict? Or might this revised view of the superpowers be no more than a corollary of the fading of anxiety about the possibility of war? If it is the former, we would expect to find consequential changes in attitudes towards the Atlantic alliance, and perhaps some shift in views about the extent to which closer links should be sought with Britain's continental European neighbours. We would surely also expect to see some change in attitudes towards British membership of NATO. If, on the other hand, the better explanation is a receding fear of war, then public attitudes towards Britain's present international alignments might well retain the stability shown in past rounds of this series. As we shall see, the evidence appears to support the latter view.

The Atlantic alliance

Although public fears about the military threat posed by the two superpowers have receded quite markedly since 1983, whether this change has resulted in a popular reappraisal of Britain's position in relation to Western Europe and the United States is unclear.

The Atlantic alliance

	1983 %	1984 %	1985 %	1986 %	1987 %	1989 %
% saying that Britain's interests are better served by:						
Closer links with Western Europe	n/a	53	48	55	57	50
Closer links with America	n/a	21	18	18	18	17
Both equally	n/a	16	20	17	14	20
% saying that Britain should:						
Continue to be a member of NATO	79	79	74	76	79	79
Withdraw	13	11	15	13	11	11

Around one-half of respondents favour closer links with Western Europe, much the same proportion as in 1984. Meanwhile, however, the agenda for European integration has changed substantially. The single market, proposals for monetary union and discussion of political union raise the prospect of deeper and further-reaching European integration than was envisaged in 1984. Public support for continued membership of the EC is strong, having risen from a low point of 48 per cent in 1984 to 68 per cent in 1989.

In contrast, enthusiasm for closer links with the US is, if anything, more muted than it was in the early 1980s. More surprisingly, perhaps, the changes in central and eastern Europe – which of course accelerated only after fieldwork on the 1989 survey had ended – have not (yet) been reflected in changed views of NATO: support has remained at a high and fairly stable level throughout the life of the survey series.

As in earlier years, support for NATO and for closer links with Western Europe tends to be especially marked among those with educational qualifications and among those in Social Classes I–III, while younger people (18–24 year olds) are conspicuously less enamoured of NATO. These and other subgroup differences may be inspected in **Table 4.5**. But, as we see later when examining subgroup differences, the link between attitudes towards Britain's defence policies and towards its international alignments appears to be weak.

Nuclear weapons and defence policy

Missile bases in Britain

The receding public anxiety about nuclear war prompts us to turn to responses to our questions on the siting of British and American nuclear missiles at bases in this country. We speculated in earlier *Reports* that the deployment of cruise missiles in Britain might have stimulated some of the increase in distrust of nuclear weapons in general, and of US weapons in particular, among young respondents (and especially among young women). The unexpectedly rapid implementation of the US–Soviet Intermediate Range Nuclear Forces Treaty saw the early withdrawal of cruise missiles from Britain, the weapons at Molesworth being flown out in September 1988.

As earlier *Reports* have shown, a majority has always regarded *British* nuclear missiles as contributing to the nation's security, while only a minority has been in favour of *US* nuclear weapons on British soil. Overall, more than half of our respondents consider that British weapons enhance security, while only just over a third take this view of the presence of US missiles. But the year-on-year figures are instructive, as can be seen from the table below. Between 1983 and 1986 there was a marked and fairly steady decline in confidence both in the effectiveness of Britain's nuclear capability and in the value of the American 'nuclear umbrella'.* But these trends reversed sharply in 1987, and it is too soon to tell whether or not the slight fall off in support for British-based nuclear weapons registered in 1989 marks the beginning of another trend similar to that evident in the early to mid-1980s.

	Nuclear missiles on British soil					
	1983	1984	1985	1986	1987	1989
	%	%	%	%	%	%
American nuclear missiles:						
Make Britain a safer place	38	36	36	29	39	36
Make Britain less safe	48	51	53	60	50	52
	%	%	%	%	%	%
British nuclear missiles:						
Make Britain a safer place	60	56	54	52	58	55
Make Britain less safe	29	33	34	37	31	34

The marked change in 1987 needs an explanation. Our 1987 fieldwork was carried out in the weeks leading up to the last general election, when the Labour Party's defence policy was one of the main campaign issues. We cannot be sure,

---

* It is clear that the sharp increase in concern about the US military presence in Britain which followed the bombing of Libya in April 1986 (see Young, 1987) was a fluctuation of no lasting consequence.

but it is likely that the then-current anxiety about the nuclear defence stance of a future Labour government contributed to this renewed support for nuclear weapons on British soil.

The Labour Party's 1983 election manifesto had been notable for its commitment to establish a non-nuclear defence policy for Britain and to "remove all existing nuclear bases and weapons". The 1987 manifesto offered a rather different emphasis, promising to decommission Polaris, cancel Trident and strengthen conventional defences. Only if the superpowers' arms talks failed would a Labour government have insisted on the withdrawal of US nuclear weapons. Despite these qualifications, the next party conference reaffirmed its commitment to a non-nuclear defence policy and to unilateral disarmament. The 1989 policy review therefore represented a major shift back towards a bipartisan defence policy, merely forswearing the first use of nuclear weapons and insisting that Britain's nuclear capability should be negotiable. Now the Labour Party is a multilateralist party again.

Although shifts in attitudes since 1983 have been modest and far from consistent, it is useful to look at the results for that year and for 1989 to see among which subgroups scepticism about the protection afforded to Britain by nuclear missile bases is most marked. Gender differences on the issue of arms deployment are now familiar: generally women express more anxiety about nuclear weapons than do men. We find that it is among women, especially younger women, that distrust is most widespread *and* has risen most sharply. And women of all ages are more distrustful than are their male peers (and growing increasingly so) of the contribution of the American nuclear umbrella to national security (see **Table 4.6** for full details).

A comparison of the attitudes of men and women in 1983 and 1989 shows a widening 'gender gap' (Norris, 1986) on the issue of arms deployment among the youngest age group in the sample (18-24 year olds). And as is evident from the table below, young women are still much more concerned about British nuclear weapons than are young men.

Nuclear missiles on British soil
Gender differences, 1989

	British missiles make Britain less safe %	US missiles make Britain less safe %
% difference* between views of men and women aged:		
18–24	+10	+17
25–34	+10	+15
35–44	+ 7	+16
45–54	+ 4	+14
55–64	+ 2	+12
65+	− 4	+16

* A plus sign represents the excess of men over women agreeing with each proposition.

Moreover, while the gender gap diminishes with age on attitudes to British missiles (and, owing to a high incidence of "don't knows" among older women, becomes negative among the oldest group of respondents), it remains consistently high throughout the age range as far as *US* missiles are concerned. Of course, partisan differences on the issue of nuclear weapons are of primary importance in view of the sharply-differing policies of the two main political parties, even with the Labour Party's shift away from unilateralism. As the table below shows, since 1986 there has been a general shift among identifiers with all three political party groupings towards thinking that both countries' weapons jeopardise safety, but the change is not large – certainly less pronounced than the one we reported between 1983 and 1986. While Conservative identifiers have not been immune to this trend, it is Labour supporters whose attitudes between 1983 and 1989 have proved to be the most volatile – thus accentuating the pre-existing partisan differences on this issue.

	1983	1986	1989
% saying that British nuclear missiles on British soil make Britain less safe			
Total	29%	37%	34%
Party identification			
Conservative	16%	20%	18%
SLD/SDP	30%	42%	39%
Labour	39%	50%	47%
% saying that US nuclear missiles on British soil make Britain less safe			
Total	48%	60%	52%
Party identification			
Conservative	34%	39%	36%
SLD/SDP	56%	66%	60%
Labour	59%	75%	67%

Nuclear disarmament

A question of continuing political relevance concerns support for unilateral nuclear disarmament. In every year of the series we have asked respondents whether Britain should "rid itself of nuclear weapons while persuading others to do the same" or "keep its nuclear weapons until it can persuade others to reduce theirs". Responses have been unequivocal throughout the time-series, with a continuing decisive (but somewhat narrowing) majority in favour of Britain's retention of a nuclear deterrent.

Unilateralism *versus* multilateralism

	1983	1984	1985	1986	1987	1989
	%	%	%	%	%	%
Britain should:						
Rid itself of nuclear weapons	19	23	27	28	25	26
Keep its nuclear weapons	77	73	68	69	72	72
Difference	58	50	41	41	47	46

As in previous years, younger respondents are still somewhat more likely to favour the unilateral alternative. Just under one-third of respondents aged 34 or under think Britain should renounce its nuclear weapons, while only one in five of those aged 55 or over support this view. These figures are much the same as in 1987.

The political implications of these patterns of opinion have never been clear cut since many voters support parties at the polling booth despite, rather than because of, their policy positions – on defence, or on any other matter. Between 1983 and 1986, there was a steady rise in the proportion of Labour identifiers adopting a unilateralist position. Subsequently, however, there has been a slight shift back towards multilateralism among Labour identifiers, probably reflecting the Party's movement away from unambiguous unilateralism.

Support for unilateral disarmament

	1983	1986	1989
Total	19%	28%	26%
Party identification			
Conservative	8%	13%	11%
SLD/SDP	22%	27%	31%
Labour	29%	42%	38%

Nonetheless, nuclear defence remains an issue upon which Labour party identifiers remain deeply divided (see Heath and Evans, 1988).

Defence policy and party preferences

General support for Conservative defence policies has risen steadily since 1985 when we first asked: "Which political party's views on defence would you say comes closest to your own views?"

	1985	1986	1987	1989
	%	%	%	%
% saying each party's views on defence are closest to own				
Conservative	33	35	42	44
SLD/SDP	11	11	10	6
Labour	24	24	20	23
Other/none	5	3	3	5
Don't know	27	27	21	22

The Conservative advantage runs throughout the sample, Labour enjoying greater support than the Conservatives for their defence policy only among those in Social Class V. Even among Labour identifiers, one in five prefers Conservative Party defence policy to that of their 'own' party. Conservative identifiers are, on the other hand, much more united on this issue. Willingness to state a preference is related to educational level, and Conservative policy enjoys about twice the level of support accorded to Labour in all groups of respondents who hold an educational qualification (see **Table 4.7**).

Although Conservative policy is strongly preferred to that of the Labour Party in all age groups, there are important gender differences: the Conservative advantage is smaller among younger women (aged under 45) than among any other group. Overall, men are substantially more inclined to support the Conservative

Party on defence than are women; but as the following table shows, the gender gap on this measure varies from one age group to another.

Conservative advantage over Labour on defence policy

	Men	Women
Total	24%	18%
Age:		
18–24	14%	3%
25–34	21%	10%
35–44	28%	14%
45–54	33%	31%
55–64	20%	25%
65+	28%	24%

A more searching analysis is required to determine whether this advantage reflects robust support for Conservative defence policies or merely generalised distrust of – or vagueness about – Labour's (changing) position. In either case the Conservatives appear to have a continuing electoral advantage on defence, and one which may well persist even following Labour's policy review. Doubtless, much will depend in future upon the perceived relevance of defence policies of whatever colour in a world of changing tensions and shifting alignments.

Conclusions

It seems distinctly possible that, as the war scare of the early 1980s recedes, increased concern about the physical environment may take its place. In the short term, this concern will express itself in opposition to those forms of localised pollution that affect people in their everyday lives. Clearly therefore, the Environmental Protection Bill is timely, and wider measures to protect the environment are likely to enjoy very high levels of popular support. Although high levels of concern are registered in response to new questions on global environmental issues, we cannot tell how far this will translate itself into *active* concern. In particular, we do not yet know what price people are willing to pay for long-term measures, the benefits of which only the next generations may live to see. We have included questions in the latest round of the series to tap this dimension and will report on the findings next year.

Notes

1. Preliminary factor analyses conducted by the Joint Centre for Survey Methods have indicated only a weak association between concern about traffic and aircraft pollution on the one hand, and atmospheric pollution and effluent on the other. This suggests that worries about the former are *localised*, to do with noise and dirt in the respondent's immediate neighbourhood.
2. However, further analysis casts doubt on whether this question is in fact measuring solely attitudes to civil defence. Factor analysis indicates that it is, to some extent, measuring the same underlying attitudes as those tapped in two earlier questions designed to gauge attitudes towards countryside protection. Although, superficially, these questions appear to have little in common with our question about civil defence, it is interesting that all have alternatives which imply government intervention (or lack of it) and that all could lead to despoliation of the countryside, including the building of shelters.

References

BOYLE, S. and ARDILL, J., *The Greenhouse Effect*, Hodder and Stoughton, London (1989).

COX, M., 'The rise and fall of the "Soviet Threat" ' *Political Studies*, vol. 33, no. 3 (1985), pp. 484-98.

ECONOMIST, 'Cutting back on greenery' (19 May 1990) pp. 23–4.

FREMLIN, J.H., *Power Production: What are the Risks?* OUP, London (1987).

GRIBBIN, J., *The Climatic Threat*, Fontana, London (1978).

HACKETT, Sir J., *The Third World War, August 1985: A Future History*, Sidgwick and Jackson, London (1978).

HEATH, A. and EVANS, G., 'Working class Conservatives and middle class socialists', in Jowell, R., Witherspoon, S. and Brook, L., *British Social Attitudes: the 5th Report*, Gower, Aldershot (1988).

KEMP, D.D., *Global Environmental Issues*, Routledge and Kegan Paul, London (1990).

MADDOX, J., 'What happened to nuclear winter?', *Nature*, no. 333 (1988), p.203.

NORRIS, P., 'Conservative attitudes in recent British elections: an emerging gender gap?', *Political Studies*, vol. 34, no. 1 (1986), pp.120–28.

OECD (Organisation for Economic Cooperation and Development), *Chernobyl and the Safety of Nuclear Reactors in OECD Countries* (Report by the Nuclear Energy Agency Group of Experts), OECD, Paris (1987).

O'KEEFE, P.J., CHADWICK, M.J., HILL, R. and ROBINSON, D., *How Green is my Power Station?*, Coalfield Communities Campaign (1989).

OPENSHAW, S., *Nuclear Power: Siting and Safety*, Routledge and Kegan Paul, London (1986).

OPENSHAW, S., CARVER, S. and FERNIE, J., *Britain's Nuclear Waste: Siting and Safety*, Bellhaven, London (1989).

PEARCE, D., *Blueprint for a Green Economy*, Earthscan Publications, London (1989).

SABIN, P.A.G., *The Third World War Scare in Britain*, Macmillan, Basingstoke (1986).

TICKELL, C., *Climatic Change and World Affairs*, Pergamon, Oxford (1977).

TURCO, R.P., TOON, O.B., ACKERMAN, J.P., POLLACK, J.B. and SAGAN, S., 'Nuclear winter: Global consequences of multiple nuclear explosions', *Science*, no. 222 (1983), pp. 1283-92.

WARD, H., SAMWAYS, D., and BENTON, T., 'Environmental politics and policy' in Dunleavy, D., Gamble, A. and Peale, G. (eds), *Developments in British Politics 3*, Macmillan, Basingstoke (1990).

WARLEY, N. and LEWINS, J., *The Chernobyl Accident and its Implications for the UK* (Watt Committee Report No. 19), London, Elsevier (1989).

YOUNG, K., 'A green and pleasant land', in Jowell, R., Witherspoon, S. and Brook L., (eds), *British Social Attitudes: the 1986 Report*, Gower, Aldershot (1986).

YOUNG, K., 'Nuclear reactions', in Jowell, R., Witherspoon, S. and Brook L., (eds), *British Social Attitudes: the 1987 Report*, Gower, Aldershot (1987).

Acknowledgement

The Countryside Commission provided funding for the survey series between 1985 and 1987, and (together with the ESRC) is doing so again between 1990 and 1992 to allow us to continue monitoring attitudes to countryside issues. We are grateful to the Commission and to the ESRC for their support.

4.1 PROTECTING THE COUNTRYSIDE (B236a,b; B238)
by sex, highest educational qualification, party identification and social class

WHICH OF THESE TWO STATEMENTS COMES CLOSEST TO YOUR OWN VIEWS?	TOTAL	SEX		HIGHEST EDUCATIONAL QUALIFICATION				PARTY IDENTIFICATION				SOCIAL CLASS			
		Men	Women	De-gree	Profes-sional	A level O level CSE	Foreign Other None	Cons	SLD/ SDP	Lab	Non-aligned	I/II	III non manual	III manual	IV/V
	%	%	%	%	%	%	%	%	%	%	%	%	%	%	%
Industry should be prevented from causing damage to the countryside, even if this sometimes leads to higher prices	88	89	87	96	93	91	81	91	94	83	80	94	93	87	77
OR															
Industry should keep prices down even if this sometimes causes damage to the countryside	10	9	10	3	5	7	15	6	4	14	17	5	6	8	19
The countryside should be protected from development even if this sometimes leads to fewer jobs	72	75	70	78	76	74	68	75	82	65	69	75	74	73	63
OR															
New jobs should be created, even if this sometimes causes damage to the countryside	23	22	24	19	21	23	26	21	14	29	26	21	22	22	30
Looking after the countryside is too important to be left to farmers - government authorities should have more control	46	56	38	64	54	48	38	47	49	49	38	59	42	44	36
OR															
Farmers know how important it is to look after the countryside - there are enough controls	37	31	42	17	32	35	44	35	27	37	41	27	39	40	45
BASE: B RESPONDENTS															
Weighted	1255	586	669	79	211	475	490	522	156	387	87	333	305	287	266
Unweighted	1297	598	699	79	219	491	507	551	161	394	90	344	318	295	273

4.2 POSSIBLE SOLUTIONS TO BRITAIN'S ELECTRICITY NEEDS, 1987 AND 1989 (1989:B235a) by age within sex, highest educational qualification and party identification

	TOTAL	AGE WITHIN SEX MEN 18-34	MEN 35-54	MEN 55+	WOMEN 18-34	WOMEN 35-54	WOMEN 55+	HIGHEST EDUCATIONAL QUALIFICATION Degree	Profes-sional	A level/O level/CSE	Foreign/Other/None	PARTY IDENTIFICATION Cons.	Alliance/SLD/SDP	Labour	Non-aligned
1987	%	%	%	%	%	%	%	%	%	%	%	%	%	%	%
We should make do with the power stations we have already	25	27	22	10	42	27	19	38	16	28	23	24	26	22	31
We should build more coal-fuelled power stations	48	43	41	51	45	56	52	37	39	47	55	51	57	66	48
We should build more nuclear power stations	22	24	33	34	11	14	20	22	41	22	16	39	15	7	18
BASE: B RESPONDENTS *Weighted*	*1181*	*185*	*198*	*174*	*201*	*222*	*200*	*100*	*160*	*437*	*482*	*465*	*225*	*352*	*68*
Unweighted	*1212*	*181*	*203*	*185*	*201*	*236*	*205*	*96*	*164*	*446*	*504*	*480*	*225*	*362*	*72*
1989	%	%	%	%	%	%	%	%	%	%	%	%	%	%	%
We should make do with the power stations we have already	44	43	41	34	60	44	43	48	43	48	40	43	47	42	51
We should build more coal-fuelled power stations	37	34	30	42	30	40	43	26	32	34	43	30	32	48	33
We should build more nuclear power stations	16	18	27	21	7	12	11	20	24	16	12	24	17	6	15
BASE: B RESPONDENTS *Weighted*	*1255*	*194*	*208*	*183*	*194*	*277*	*195*	*79*	*211*	*475*	*490*	*522*	*156*	*387*	*87*
Unweighted	*1297*	*192*	*216*	*188*	*200*	*285*	*210*	*79*	*219*	*491*	*507*	*551*	*161*	*394*	*90*

4.3 LIKELIHOOD OF NUCLEAR WAR, 1985 AND 1989 (1989:B240a)
by age within sex, highest educational qualification, party identification and social class

THE LIKELIHOOD OF A NUCLEAR WAR BETWEEN RUSSIA AND THE WEST BEFORE THE END OF THE CENTURY:	TOTAL	MEN 18-34	MEN 35-54	MEN 55+	WOMEN 18-34	WOMEN 35-54	WOMEN 55+	Degree	Professional	A level/O level/CSE	Foreign Other None	Cons	Alliance/SLD/SDP	Lab	Non-aligned	I/II	III non-manual	III manual	IV/V
1985	%	%	%	%	%	%	%	%	%	%	%	%	%	%	%	%	%	%	%
Very likely	5	4	5	8	5	3	7	3	4	5	6	4	5	6	8	3	5	4	8
Quite likely	18	26	13	10	26	16	13	20	15	20	16	10	19	24	19	14	18	21	17
Not very likely	47	43	56	54	41	52	37	54	54	49	42	53	51	44	31	54	49	49	37
Not at all likely	16	19	21	18	11	15	12	20	20	14	15	22	16	10	17	20	11	17	17
Can't choose N/A	14	8	5	10	17	14	31	3	6	11	20	12	9	16	25	9	17	9	21
BASE: ALL RESPONDENTS																			
Weighted	1502	239	242	218	292	269	240	102	172	541	687	472	275	549	108	333	352	319	362
Unweighted	1530	236	248	214	299	288	245	100	180	555	695	495	279	550	110	339	369	314	373
1989	%	%	%	%	%	%	%	%	%	%	%	%	%	%	%	%	%	%	%
Very likely	2	1	1	1	4	3	-	-	1	1	2	1	1	3	8	1	*	1	4
Quite likely	5	5	4	*	12	4	6	-	4	6	7	1	3	6	10	3	7	4	7
Not very likely	45	43	42	45	46	49	42	31	43	48	45	45	45	47	31	42	47	48	45
Not at all likely	38	47	48	49	26	31	32	66	44	38	32	42	44	33	29	50	34	37	28
Can't choose N/A	10	4	4	5	13	12	20	3	8	8	14	7	8	11	23	4	12	9	17
BASE: B RESPONDENTS																			
Weighted	1255	194	208	183	194	277	195	79	211	475	490	522	156	387	87	333	305	287	266
Unweighted	1297	192	216	188	200	285	210	79	219	491	507	551	161	394	90	344	318	295	273

4.4 OUTCOME OF NUCLEAR WAR, 1985 AND 1989 (1989:B240b)
by age within sex, highest educational qualification, party identification and social class

IF THERE WAS A NUCLEAR WAR BETWEEN RUSSIA AND THE WEST, WHAT DO YOU THINK WOULD HAPPEN TO BRITAIN?	TOTAL	AGE WITHIN SEX						HIGHEST EDUCATIONAL QUALIFICATION				PARTY IDENTIFICATION				SOCIAL CLASS			
		MEN			WOMEN			De-gree	Profes-sional	A level O level CSE	Foreign Other None	Cons	Alliance/ SID SDP	Lab	Non-aligned	I/II	III non-manual	III manual	IV/V
		18-34	35-54	55+	18-34	35-54	55+												
1985	%	%	%	%	%	%	%	%	%	%	%	%	%	%	%	%	%	%	%
Battlefield nuclear weapons would be used, but there would be few civilian deaths	2	2	3	1	*	1	3	1	2	1	2	3	2	2	-	2	1	1	4
Some British cities would be destroyed, but much of the country would pull through	12	12	15	18	6	10	13	9	16	11	12	17	10	7	9	14	12	13	8
Much or all of Britain would be destroyed	72	82	75	69	77	75	53	85	73	76	67	65	80	76	69	76	70	75	70
Can't choose	13	4	5	10	16	14	27	4	8	11	17	14	8	14	19	7	16	9	16
BASE: ALL RESPONDENTS																			
Weighted	1502	239	242	218	292	269	240	102	172	541	687	472	275	549	108	333	352	319	362
Unweighted	1530	236	248	214	299	288	245	100	180	555	695	495	279	550	110	339	369	314	373
1989	%	%	%	%	%	%	%	%	%	%	%	%	%	%	%	%	%	%	%
Battlefield nuclear weapons would be used, but there would be few civilian deaths	3	5	2	4	4	3	2	5	3	4	2	5	2	2	2	2	3	4	2
Some British cities would be destroyed, but much of the country would pull through	17	18	20	25	13	12	19	5	17	19	18	20	17	16	16	16	17	17	19
Much or all of Britain would be destroyed	62	67	68	56	62	68	48	80	67	62	58	57	70	65	60	68	64	59	56
Can't choose	16	10	10	13	20	16	29	10	13	14	21	17	12	16	19	14	14	17	22
BASE: B RESPONDENTS																			
Weighted	1255	194	208	183	194	277	195	75	211	475	490	522	156	387	87	333	305	287	266
Unweighted	1297	192	216	188	200	285	210	75	219	491	507	551	161	394	90	344	318	295	273

4.5 EUROPE AND THE ATLANTIC ALLIANCE (Q5, Q4a,b)
by age within sex, highest educational qualification, party identification and social class

	TOTAL	AGE WITHIN SEX — MEN 18-34	MEN 35-54	MEN 55+	WOMEN 18-34	WOMEN 35-54	WOMEN 55+	HIGHEST EDUCATIONAL QUALIFICATION — Degree	Profes-sional	A level O level CSE	Foreign Other None	PARTY IDENTIFICATION — Cons	SLD/SDP	Lab	Non-aligned	SOCIAL CLASS — I/II	III non-manual	III manual	IV/V
BRITAIN'S INTERESTS ARE BETTER SERVED BY:	%	%	%	%	%	%	%	%	%	%	%	%	%	%	%	%	%	%	%
Closer links with Western Europe	50	56	60	53	43	47	45	75	56	53	42	47	67	53	36	61	49	49	42
Closer links with America	17	18	14	19	21	18	16	4	15	17	21	20	12	18	17	11	19	19	22
Both Equally	20	20	22	21	19	20	17	17	22	20	19	24	13	15	24	21	19	22	15
Neither	3	2	2	3	2	2	5	2	2	2	4	2	3	3	6	3	2	3	4
Don't know	10	4	3	4	15	13	17	2	5	7	14	7	5	11	18	5	10	7	17
BRITAIN SHOULD:	%	%	%	%	%	%	%	%	%	%	%	%	%	%	%	%	%	%	%
Continue to be a member of the EC	68	74	74	69	76	63	55	92	77	74	55	73	71	65	54	79	70	63	57
Withdraw from the EC	26	19	23	28	16	31	37	5	17	20	37	22	27	29	31	17	24	32	34
Don't know	6	7	3	3	8	6	8	3	5	5	7	4	3	6	14	3	6	5	8
	%	%	%	%	%	%	%	%	%	%	%	%	%	%	%	%	%	%	%
Continue to be a member of NATO	79	81	89	90	71	75	69	86	87	82	72	88	86	71	64	86	78	83	67
Withdraw from NATO	11	13	7	6	14	12	12	8	7	9	14	4	7	16	17	8	9	10	15
Don't know	10	6	3	4	14	12	19	5	5	8	14	7	7	12	17	5	12	7	16
BASE:																			
ALL RESPONDENTS Weighted	2930	452	466	437	479	585	506	212	407	1055	1250	1157	330	982	208	734	695	637	689
Unweighted	3029	449	486	459	484	612	529	216	424	1085	1295	1198	335	1017	215	764	725	659	702

4.6 NUCLEAR MISSILES ON BRITISH SOIL, 1983 AND 1989 (1989:Q6a,b) by age within sex, highest educational qualification, party identification and social class

1983

	TOTAL	MEN 18-34	MEN 35-54	MEN 55+	WOMEN 18-34	WOMEN 35-54	WOMEN 55+	Cons	Alliance	Lab	Non-aligned	I/II	III Non-manual	III manual	IV/V
	%	%	%	%	%	%	%	%	%	%	%	%	%	%	%
THE SITING OF AMERICAN NUCLEAR MISSILES IN BRITAIN MAKES BRITAIN:															
A safer place to live	38	41	46	47	28	33	38	52	29	31	31	42	37	41	37
A less safe place to live	48	46	43	44	61	52	40	34	56	59	51	42	51	49	51
Don't know	12	8	8	7	10	14	20	11	12	9	15	12	10	8	11
HAVING ITS OWN INDEPENDENT NUCLEAR MISSILES MAKES BRITAIN:															
A safer place to live	50	54	65	67	54	59	63	73	60	53	45	60	62	61	60
A less safe place to live	29	36	26	27	34	29	22	16	30	39	37	27	29	30	29
Don't know	9	7	7	4	10	11	14	8	9	7	17	10	7	8	9
BASE: ALL RESPONDENTS Weighted	1719	258	285	250	274	309	337	664	252	565	137	334	268	365	300
Unweighted	1751	256	294	257	269	329	350	676	258	584	139	343	281	362	316

1989

	TOTAL	MEN 18-34	MEN 35-54	MEN 55+	WOMEN 18-34	WOMEN 35-54	WOMEN 55+	Degree	Professional	A level O level CSE	Foreign Other None	Cons	SLD/SDP	Lab	Non-aligned	I/II	III non-manual	III manual	IV/V
	%	%	%	%	%	%	%	%	%	%	%	%	%	%	%	%	%	%	%
THE SITING OF AMERICAN NUCLEAR MISSILES IN BRITAIN MAKES BRITAIN:																			
A safer place to live	36	40	42	49	28	29	29	27	37	38	34	53	25	22	33	38	35	37	33
A less safe place to live	52	46	45	39	62	60	53	59	48	51	52	35	60	66	51	49	53	52	53
Don't know	11	11	10*	10	9	10	16	9	10	10	13	10	12	11	15	10	11	10	13
HAVING ITS OWN INDEPENDENT NUCLEAR MISSILES MAKES BRITAIN:																			
A safer place to live	55	55	59	61	45	52	57	43	58	57	54	72	49	41	46	55	55	57	52
A less safe place to live	34	33	31	29	43	37	28	42	31	33	34	18	39	47	39	35	32	32	36
Don't know	10	10	8	7	11	10	15	10	8	9	12	8	10	10	13	7	12	10	12
BASE: ALL RESPONDENTS Weighted	2530	452	466	437	479	585	506	212	407	1055	1250	1157	330	982	208	734	695	637	689
Unweighted	3029	449	486	459	484	612	529	216	424	1085	1295	1198	335	1017	215	764	725	659	702

4.7 DEFENCE AND PARTY POLITICS (Q8)
by age within sex, highest educational qualification, party identification and social class

WHICH POLITICAL PARTY'S VIEWS ON DEFENCE WOULD YOU SAY COMES CLOSEST TO YOUR OWN VIEWS?

	TOTAL	AGE WITHIN SEX						HIGHEST EDUCATIONAL QUALIFICATION				PARTY IDENTIFICATION				SOCIAL CLASS			
		MEN			WOMEN			Degree	Profes- sional	A level O level CSE	Foreign Other None	Cons	SLD/ SDP	Lab	Non- aligned	I/II	III non- manual	III manual	IV/V
		18-34	35-54	55+	18-34	35-54	55+												
	%	%	%	%	%	%	%	%	%	%	%	%	%	%	%	%	%	%	%
Conservative	44	43	52	52	32	42	44	47	53	46	39	80	24	4	18	52	50	42	32
Labour	23	25	22	27	24	21	20	25	19	20	26	4	13	53	9	18	19	27	29
SLD/Liberal	3	3	6	5	2	3	3	6	6	4	2	1	22	2	1	6	3	3	1
SDP	2	2	3	2	2	2	2	8	3	2	1	1	12	1	1	4	2	2	1
Other party	1	2	1	1	1	1	1	4	1	1	1	*	*	1	1	2	1	1	*
None	4	7	3	4	4	4	3	3	4	5	4	2	4	3	21	4	4	4	5
Don't know	22	18	11	9	35	27	26	7	14	23	26	12	25	21	48	13	22	21	31
BASE: ALL RESPONDENTS Weighted	2930	452	466	437	479	585	506	212	407	1055	1250	1157	330	982	208	734	695	637	689
Unweighted	3029	449	486	459	484	612	529	216	424	1085	1295	1198	335	1017	215	764	725	659	702

5 AIDS and the moral climate

*Kaye Wellings and Jane Wadsworth**

In the two years between fieldwork for the first *British Social Attitudes* questionnaire module on AIDS, and the second in 1989, the context has changed considerably. Our 1987 survey took place soon after an intensive publicly-funded campaign, unprecedented in the field of health education and designed to bring AIDS to the forefront of the public's consciousness. At that time, expert scientific predictions were that the incidence of AIDS would continue to grow exponentially and would before long become endemic in the heterosexual population. The interest of the media in 1987 was apparently insatiable, and the tenor of much of the reporting, especially in the tabloid press, was highly censorious.

This atmosphere would have been difficult to sustain, even if there had been a consensus in the scientific community on the likely future spread of the disease. As it turned out, there was not. Occasional articles began to appear in the medical press (for example, Evans, 1987) which threw into question the possibility of widespread heterosexual transmission of HIV; these began to fuel debate in the mass media over whether current levels of alarm were justified, at least as far as the general population was concerned. The tone of subsequent health education campaigns became less alarmist and more muted; meanwhile press coverage, in response perhaps to these new doubts about the nature of the disease, became characterised more and more by straight reportage rather than by moralistic comment. To some extent then, the hysteria of the mid-1980s was gradually replaced by a more customary concern for a disease which, though serious, seemed unlikely to spread according to the most dire predictions.

To some extent this calmer mood is reflected, perhaps even to the point of near-complacency, in responses to the 1989 survey. An important question, however, is whether changes in public attitudes to AIDS are linked to changes

* Kaye Wellings is a Wellcome Research fellow, and Jane Wadsworth is Senior Lecturer in Medical Statistics, in the Academic Department of Public Health, St Mary's Hospital Medical School, University of London.

in the moral climate generally, or whether the two issues are unrelated. So we begin by examining attitudes towards sexual relationships (also touched on in a different context in Chapter 3) and, in particular, levels of tolerance towards homosexuals.

The moral climate

Attitudes towards sexual relationships

Sexual relationships outside marriage have long attracted censure (Gorer, 1970) – although the extent of public disapproval predictably varies according to the nature of the relationship. The *British Social Attitudes* surveys have regularly included questions on attitudes towards pre-marital, extra-marital and homosexual relationships. The degree of public disapproval for each is by no means the same, as **Figure 5.1** shows.

Figure 5.1 Attitudes towards sexual relationships

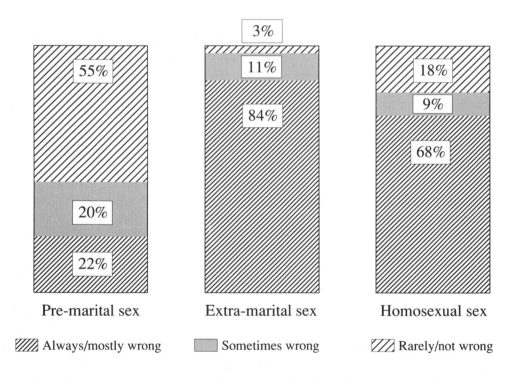

People reserve their greatest condemnation for extra-marital sex (which more than four out of five see as "always" or "almost always" wrong). They are slightly less disapproving about sexual relations between those of the same sex (which two-thirds think are wrong). By contrast, there is a good deal of tolerance of pre-marital sex (which only just over one in five believe to be wrong).

Permissiveness is strongly related to age. The youngest age group is the least disapproving of all three types of sexual relationship, but the age difference is most marked in respect of pre-marital sex (see **Table 5.1**). There are fairly clear gender differences too, men being less disapproving of sex before and outside marriage, and women more tolerant of homosexual sex. Yet despite different levels of tolerance, changes in attitudes towards each tend to move fairly consistently in the same direction.

When results from these questions were last reported the trend seemed to be towards greater censoriousness (Harding, 1988), and the question was raised as to whether we might be witnessing a longer-term return to more puritanical values, or whether the trend over the past few decades towards more liberal attitudes was facing only a temporary reversal – related perhaps to fear about the spread of AIDS.

Our evidence tends to lend more weight to the latter view: public alarm about AIDS appears to have led to a short-term hardening of moral attitudes surrounding sex. As anxiety about AIDS abates, opinions on sexual matters are once again becoming more relaxed.

As **Table 5.1** shows, the proportion disapproving of extra-marital sex remained fairly stable between 1983 and 1985 (except among younger people of both sexes); and the already small minority believing pre-marital sex to be wrong was declining. Yet over the same period disapproval of homosexual relations was, in contrast, growing – particularly among women (Brook, 1988, p.73). Since the first case of AIDS in Britain was reported in December 1981 and this series of questions has been asked only from 1983 onwards, we have no exact point of comparison for the 'pre-AIDS era'. However, data from earlier surveys suggest that this rise in disapproval of homosexual relations did indeed mark the reversal of an earlier trend. For instance, in answer to a Gallup poll question "Do you think that homosexual relations between consenting adults should or should not be legal?", the proportion of respondents favouring legality remained stable (at around 62 per cent) between 1979 and 1981*. In this respect at least then, public attitudes at the start of the 1980s seemed to be rather more permissive towards homosexuality than they were by the middle of the decade.

Between 1985 and 1987 there was certainly a hardening of attitudes against homosexuality. But there was also a sizeable increase in this period, especially among men, in disapproval of extra-marital sex, related perhaps to the growing realisation that heterosexuals were also at risk from HIV. Amongst men, and older women, we also saw for the first time an increase in the proportion who believed sex before marriage to be wrong (again see **Table 5.1**).

However, in the most recent two-year period for which we have data (1987 to 1989), all the trends seem to have changed direction again. Levels of disapproval of homosexuality are already settling back to their mid-1980s levels, although not (as yet) to those prevailing in the early part of the decade. Similarly, the proportion of people believing extra-marital sex to be wrong, while still high, has also decreased slightly during this period, particularly among men aged under 55. Even attitudes to pre-marital sex, which have in contrast been fairly stable, are rather more permissive than they were in the early 1980s: only a quarter of women believe pre-marital sex to be wrong, compared with a third in 1983, and only one in 20 women between the ages of 18 and 34 believe this. Now, only among the over 65s (both men and women), is majority opinion against sex before marriage.

---

* Unpublished figures, Bob Wybrow, Gallup, personal communication.

	Pre-marital relations		Extra-marital relations		Homosexual relations	
	1987	1989	1987	1989	1987	1989
% saying always or mostly wrong						
Total	25%	22%	88%	84%	74%	68%
Men: total	22%	20%	88%	83%	77%	72%
18–34	5%	6%	86%	78%	65%	60%
35–54	17%	15%	90%	82%	74%	70%
55+	47%	39%	91%	89%	95%	88%
Women: total	27%	25%	88%	84%	72%	65%
18–34	7%	5%	85%	82%	56%	49%
35–54	23%	17%	84%	80%	73%	60%
55+	54%	50%	96%	91%	89%	85%

So it does seem as if moral disapproval of sexual relationships outside heterosexual marriages may have peaked in 1987 and is now in decline. Of course it is too early to talk about a firm trend, but the evidence from *British Social Attitudes* tends to support the view that the flurry of concern over a possible future AIDS epidemic, and the attendant wave of moral censure and homophobia, might prove to have been transient. We can only speculate as to the reasons for the recent change in attitudes. Certainly AIDS has slipped from its prominent position in the public's consciousness, and the previously high levels of public anxiety have abated.

We may also be seeing, in the return of more tolerant attitudes towards sexual relationships, the effects of a growing realisation that it is not so much the type of sexual relationship which presents the risk of infection, as 'unsafe' sexual practices. An optimistic view is that a more temperate treatment of AIDS in the media may have made it easier for people to distinguish between the moral and the practical issues. When the disease was strongly equated with homosexuality and promiscuity, heterosexual monogamy (or chastity) seemed the only obvious method of preventing its spread.

There is further support for the belief that the public may now be less inclined to see AIDS in moral terms. Respondents were, in 1989 as in 1987, asked to express their agreement or disagreement with two statements designed to test the extent to which people see AIDS as a moral issue. A comparison of the results for the two survey years shows a slight decline in the public's perception of AIDS as a moral matter rather than a medical or humanitarian concern.

AIDS is a way of punishing the world for its decline in moral standards

	1987		1989	
	%		%	
Agree strongly	10	} 29	7	} 26
Agree	19		19	
Neither agree nor disagree	25		22	
Disagree	24	} 46	29	} 49
Disagree strongly	22		20	

Official warnings about AIDS should say that some sexual practices are morally wrong

	1987		1989	
	%		%	
Agree strongly	31	} 66	23	} 62
Agree	35		39	
Neither agree nor disagree	13		15	
Disagree	14	} 19	18	} 22
Disagree strongly	5		4	

Further analysis has shown that, predictably perhaps, these two moralistic views tend to be held by the same sorts of people (see Brook, 1988). Many of these people probably see moral exhortations not only as appropriate in principle, but also as a practical way of gaining greater compliance with the underlying health education messages. The evidence, however, is that such messages would *not* be too well received by the main target audience of young people in their late teens and early twenties. Little over a third of those in the youngest age group (18–24) support a moralistic tone in AIDS publicity, with the proportion rising steadily with age. Among people aged over 64, almost nine out of ten would approve of a campaign with a moral content. So although opinion may have softened somewhat, the issue of AIDS still has a strong moral dimension.

Discrimination against homosexuals

A number of questions in the series provide an opportunity to see if and how moral disapproval manifests itself in practice. For example, respondents are asked, in addition to whether they think homosexual relations are right or wrong, how acceptable it is for a "homosexual person" to be a teacher in a school or in higher education, or to hold "a responsible position in public life". As the table below shows, the trend towards greater tolerance (noted in *The 5th Report*) has continued. The public is more or less evenly divided on whether homosexuals should be allowed to teach in schools, but sizeable majorities regard it as acceptable for homosexual people to hold posts in higher education and in public life.

Is it acceptable for a homosexual person . . .	1983	1985	1987	1989
. . . to be a teacher in a school?	%	%	%	%
Yes	41	36	43	45
No	53	54	50	47
Depends/other answer	6	10	7	8
. . . to be a teacher in a college or university?	%	%	%	%
Yes	48	44	51	55
No	48	48	44	39
Depends/other answer	4	8	5	5
. . . to hold a responsible position in public life?	%	%	%	%
Yes	53	50	54	58
No	42	41	39	37
Depends/other answer	5	9	7	4

Curiously, perhaps, the relationship between tolerance of homosexual sex on the one hand and of homosexuals in public office on the other, is not straightforward. True, between 1983 and 1985, when public opinion was becoming more disapproving of sexual relations between people of the same sex, attitudes also appeared to harden slightly against allowing gays and lesbians access to positions of responsibility. But as disapproval of homosexual sex rose further between 1985 and 1987, it was not accompanied by a growth in support for discrimination against homosexuals themselves. Now the trends on both measures are moving in the same, more liberal, direction.

Groups at risk

It may well be by now that the British public knows more about AIDS than about any other disease. Certainly this seemed to be so in 1987 when, shortly after the first public education campaign, very high proportions of *British Social Attitudes* respondents were aware of the sorts of people most at risk of contracting HIV. Thus well before these questions were repeated in 1989, the level of public knowledge about HIV and AIDS was already so high that there was little scope for further increases.

In the two years since the first questionnaire module on AIDS, the public has been exposed to two further waves of public education about the disease, each presenting more information and reinforcing messages about the main routes by which the virus may be transmitted. In both these campaigns the emphasis has moved away from 'high-risk groups' towards the dangers to the general population, with warnings about avoiding risky practice. The messages have thus been more mixed than they were during the first campaign which took place just before the 1987 fieldwork round. Then the mood was almost universally one of pessimism that AIDS would reach epidemic proportions within the general population. By 1989, things had changed.

First, as we have noted, there was far less consensus among experts as to whether the worst initial fears would be realised. The scientific and medical community was also more inclined than before to stress that the heterosexual majority was also at risk. They had help from television programmes such as *Suzie's Story* which underscored the dangers to people outside recognised high-risks groups.

The line adopted by the national press in this period was far less consistent. Whilst the 'quality' press generally supported the main health education messages,* some of the tabloids continued hotly to dispute the idea that anyone outside the categories of high risk groups was in danger, often issuing hefty broadsides against the Government campaign ('Spreading the false message of AIDS – who are these publicly funded advertising moguls trying to kid?', *Daily Express*, 18 February 1988). The *Daily Mail* carried a four-page feature headlined 'A disease that's hard for us to catch' in which the campaign directed at heterosexuals was described as a 'lie, a waste of funds and energy and a cruel diversion' (*Daily Mail*, 19 October 1989).

In the face of such conflicting and confusing messages, we might have expected to see some erosion of the previously high levels of belief (95 per cent in 1987)

---

* For example, '"Second wave" of AIDS spreads beyond high risk groups', *Guardian*, 9 February 1988; 'The need for action to prevent a heterosexual spread', *Independent* 17 February 1988.

that heterosexuals with large numbers of partners were "greatly" or "quite a lot" at risk. However, those involved in health education can take comfort from the fact that their message does not seem to have been undermined. Very large majorities are still convinced both that heterosexuals with many different partners and that gay men *are* at risk from AIDS. Moreover, a staggering 99 per cent of people realise that injecting drug users are vulnerable.

% saying each group is greatly or quite a lot at risk from AIDS	1987	1989
People who inject themselves with drugs using shared needles	99%	99%
Male homosexuals – that is, gays	98%	96%
People who have sex with many different partners of the opposite sex	95%	96%
Female homosexuals – that is, lesbians	60%	65%
Married people who occasionally have sex with someone other than their regular partner	64%	60%
People who have a blood transfusion	36%	37%
Doctors and nurses who treat people who have AIDS	23%	42%
Married couples who have sex only with each other	1%	1%

The distinctions people are making seem to reflect a consistent awareness that people can protect themselves from infection, that safer sex practices can reduce (although not eliminate) the risks of hetero- or homosexual transmission of AIDS. By the same token, a shared needle is inherently risky. It appears that (as **Table 5.2** illustrates) the health education messages are getting across, especially to the educationally well-qualified.

Gay men are (still) thought of as being at greater risk than highly active heterosexuals, but beliefs about the vulnerability of both groups to AIDS seem to be converging among all population subgroups. This shift may be partly the result of the publicity given to the fact that AIDS is not exclusively a gay disease, but may also owe something to reports of the adoption of safer sex practices on the part of gay men. In any event, it shows that people are increasingly thinking in terms of risky practices instead of risky people.

Despite evidence to the contrary, lesbian women are seen by around two-thirds of respondents (a rather higher proportion than in 1987) as being vulnerable – a consequence perhaps of equating unorthodox sexualities with disease. Three-quarters of the over 55s were of this opinion and, surprisingly perhaps, men and women held very much the same views. In contrast, respondents were almost unanimous, as they had been in 1987, in the knowledge that couples who stick together and have sexual relations exclusively with each other are not at risk. Nonetheless, respondents were a little *more* inclined than two years earlier to believe that the odd fling would not be a serious health hazard.

People's misunderstandings of routes of transmission of HIV are perhaps as important as correct identification of routes, though for different reasons. Misinformation about contagion and infection contributes substantially to the degree of prejudice and discrimination against those with HIV. The *British Social Attitudes* surveys do not ask questions about the most common transmission myths – for instance, through sharing eating and drinking utensils, touching and kissing – though other surveys show such beliefs to be fairly firmly fixed in the minds of a small section of the public (DHSS, 1987).

However, our series does include a question about the likelihood of catching AIDS through a blood transfusion; and it must be worrying for the medical profession that fears about the risk from this source persist in the minds of more than a third of respondents, both in 1987 and 1989. After all, it is some five years since the introduction of screening procedures has all but eliminated donor blood as a source of infection. Educational level is a fairly reliable predictor on this issue (as on many to do with attitudes to AIDS): only 18 per cent of graduates believe that the virus can still be contracted through contaminated blood, compared with nearly half of those with no formal educational qualifications (see **Table 5.2**).

The Blood Transfusion Service has so far resisted publicity aimed at countering any residual worries about infection, in the belief that association with HIV in the public mind might be counterproductive. But the time may be right for a reappraisal.

By far the most striking change in the public's assessment is in the risks that health care professionals are thought to face. The proportion of people who believe "doctors and nurses who treat people with AIDS" to be "greatly" or "quite a lot" at risk virtually doubled between 1987 and 1989 (from 23 per cent to 42 per cent). Among some sections of the population (older women, for instance) this view is even more widespread. But this marked shift may be at least partly the result of the widespread press coverage, in early 1988, of the death from AIDS of a doctor with no exposure to the disease other than his medical treatment of AIDS patients in Africa.

Perceptions of the spread of AIDS

In 1989, as in 1987, respondents were asked two questions designed to probe perceptions of the future pattern of the AIDS epidemic in this country. The first related to the scale of the epidemic, the second to the possibility of discovering a vaccine. The two statements, with the responses for both years, are given below:

Within the next five years	1987	1989
. . . AIDS will cause more deaths in Britain than any other single disease	%	%
Highly exaggerated	11	14
Slightly exaggerated	27	31
More or less true	60	53
. . . doctors will discover a vaccine against AIDS	%	%
Agree strongly	4	3
Agree	30	31
Neither agree nor disagree	45	45
Disagree	16	18
Disagree strongly	3	2

Although around one half of respondents still believe that AIDS will become Britain's biggest killer disease, there has (not surprisingly) been a fall since 1987 in the proportion taking this pessimistic view. For this prediction to be realistic, AIDS would by 1994 have to be responsible for over 160,000 deaths annually (the number of British heart disease fatalities per year) – an unlikely prospect given that by the end of July 1990 (only) just over 3,500 AIDS cases had been reported in Britain. Expert estimates of the future scale of the epidemic were in fact revised downwards well before our last fieldwork round (Department of Health and the Welsh Office, 1988). The public's apparent over-estimation of the extent of the future spread of AIDS is no doubt a legacy from two or three years earlier when the publicity campaigns and media attention were at their height.

Hopes for a vaccine remained virtually unchanged during this period. Scarcely more than half of respondents in both years were prepared to make a prediction; of those who did, many more were optimistic than pessimistic. We shall monitor both these measurements with interest over the coming years since they will serve as guides to the prevailing mood of the population. After all, despondency about the future course of AIDS and about the possibility of a vaccine may help to keep alive a responsible attitude to safer sex.

Attitudes towards AIDS patients

Lack of sympathy for such a devastating disease has been perhaps one of the most disturbing revelations of all the studies of attitudes to AIDS. On the other hand, findings from the 1987 *British Social Attitudes* survey indicated that a majority (although by no means a large one) felt that "people who have AIDS get much less sympathy from society than they ought to get". It was speculated then, on the basis of other survey evidence too, that this majority would increase. But this is scarcely borne out by the most recent findings: about the same proportion of the population still held this view in 1989 (62 per cent compared with 60 per cent in 1987). As we can see from the following table, there are some very marked age differences on this issue, and some gender differences too.

	AIDS sufferers get much less sympathy than they ought
% agreeing	
Total	62%
Men:	
18–34	65%
35–54	68%
55+	51%
Women	
18–34	60%
35–54	74%
55+	45%

It is people in their middle years (aged 35–54) who are most likely to agree that society is too unsympathetic towards people with AIDS; other than among this age group, women in general are less inclined to take this view. But we are slightly wary of this item as a measure of people's *own* feelings, since it refers in essence to more general attitudes. It may well be that women, who are on the whole more tolerant than men on this issue (as we have seen, they are more tolerant of homosexuality), are less aware of society's lack of sympathy for sufferers from AIDS. So they may be less willing to endorse the implied criticism of public attitudes in the statement. We shall attempt to design a complementary measure for the next round of questions.

The belief that AIDS is largely self-inflicted is nonetheless still prevalent. Much the same proportion of respondents in 1989 as in 1987 (55 per cent and 57 per cent respectively) feel that "most people with AIDS have only themselves to blame". As we can see from the table below, women are once again more tolerant, being less inclined than men to censure AIDS sufferers. But the most notable differences are those between people of different ages; on this item the young (18–34 year olds, and especially the under 25s) are the least censorious, and the oldest age group by far the most – a return to the usual pattern on these sorts of issues:

	AIDS sufferers have only themselves to blame
% agreeing:	
Total	55%
Men	
18–34	41%
35–54	57%
55+	79%
Women	
18–34	40%
35–54	49%
55+	67%

So people are able to separate their views on the cause of infection from their views on its outcome for the sufferer. Compassion for the plight of people with AIDS seems to coexist for many people with a lack of sympathy for the lifestyle through which the disease is thought to have been acquired.

Two further sets of questions were included to probe how far sympathy for AIDS patients goes. One set asks about the legal rights of people with AIDS in situations where they might face discrimination; another set explores attitudes towards increased resources for care for those suffering from the disease and research to find a cure.

In *The 5th Report*, Britain was compared favourably with certain other countries in terms of its record on safeguarding the civil rights of people with AIDS, and in general the comparison is still valid two years later. As in the 1987 survey, three areas of possible discrimination were chosen, with respondents being asked whether . . .

> . . . *employers should or should not have the legal right to dismiss people who have AIDS*
> . . . *doctors and nurses should or should not have the legal right to refuse to treat people who have AIDS*
> . . . *schools should or should not have the legal right to expel children who have AIDS.*

At present, none of these legal rights exists in Britain, although the AIDS charity, the Terrence Higgins Trust, deals with about one hundred cases a year of alleged discrimination against employees (The *Independent*, 17 October 1989). Moreover, none of the more draconian measures adopted in some other countries – such as quarantining AIDS sufferers or involuntarily testing the blood of people entering the country – have been instituted in Britain.

On our evidence, however, a sizeable minority of the British public would like to see changes, and levels of support have hardly altered since 1987. Those who express libertarian sentiments on all these issues still outnumber those who take a harder line by roughly two to one; nonetheless between a quarter and a third of the adult population feel that there should be a legal right to discriminate against AIDS sufferers in the workplace, in health care and at school.

	Should there be a legal right to					
	... dismiss employees?		... refuse treatment?		... expel children?	
	1987	1989	1987	1989	1987	1989
	%	%	%	%	%	%
Definitely	13	13	11	11	8	9
Probably	25	23	20	21	16	18
Probably not	29	30	26	28	30	29
Definitely not	28	28	41	37	40	39
Don't know/not stated	5	6	2	3	6	6

In general people take a more benign view in respect of children being able to stay in school than they do about adult sufferers being able to stay in work – no doubt a reflection of public perceptions of innocence and guilt as to the way in which the virus is contracted. But a surprisingly large number of people feel that doctors and nurses should have a right to withhold treatment. We might plausibly see a link here with the perceived exposure to risk of HIV infection of health care professionals, but there may be other explanations too. Certainly, concern in some parts of the medical profession about this issue is growing, but on our evidence a persistent two-thirds of the public would *not* be sympathetic to any move which involved the right to withhold treatment.

On these questions, there are few marked subgroup variations other than by education. Women once again are slightly more supportive than men of the rights of employees and of schoolchildren, but rather less so of patients. But the differences are small. As in 1987, it is graduates who are the most libertarian in their views:

	Degree		No degree	
	1987	1989	1987	1989
Employers should have legal right to dismiss:	%	%	%	%
Definitely	6	3	14	14
Probably	13	14	26	23
Doctors and nurses should have legal right to refuse to treat:	%	%	%	%
Definitely	3	6	11	11
Probably	16	19	21	21
Schools should have legal right to expel:	%	%	%	%
Definitely	1	3	9	9
Probably	11	12	17	18

Moreover, the gap between graduates and non-graduates has, if anything, widened on the issue of employees' rights. There are important implications here for health education. Public sympathy and practical concern for AIDS sufferers affect more than simply the level of care and kindness accorded to those who are ill. In a discriminatory and unsympathetic climate possible sufferers from the disease are less likely to show themselves and the problem is more likely to be driven underground. Fostering greater sympathy can therefore be justified not only on humanitarian grounds, but also on pragmatic ones, since open disclosure of HIV status is a prerequisite for preventive practices. In some countries, notably Switzerland and France, AIDS public education programmes include messages aimed at increasing levels of tolerance and sympathy. There may be a lesson for British health educators in their efforts.

One possible reason for the apparent lack of compassion may be that most people have never as yet come across anyone with HIV or AIDS, and so are unable to put a human face to the disease. For the first time in 1989, respondents were asked if they had met someone with HIV; only one in twenty claim to have done so. The question wording is careful to specify "met" rather than "know", to try to reduce the possibility that people would include well-known figures with the syndrome, whom respondents merely "know of". The actual question is: "As far as you know, have you ever met anyone who was confirmed as having the virus that causes AIDS?" As the numbers of those with AIDS and HIV increases, so too will the proportion of people who have met someone with the virus, and it will be interesting to see whether attitudes to AIDS sufferers change with their increasing visibility.

Younger respondents are, unsurprisingly, more likely to have met someone with the AIDS virus. So too, it seems, are those in Social Classes I and II and those with degrees or professional qualifications – perhaps because friends and acquaintances of people in these groups are less likely, or less able, to hide their condition.

Resources for those with HIV and AIDS

We included two questions designed to find out the sorts of practical measures people endorsed to cope with the mounting problem of AIDS: on the interview questionnaire, we asked about resources for the care of those dying from AIDS, and on the self-completion supplement about research to discover a cure for the disease. As the figures below show, a clear majority in both years favours the more generous option of more rather than less spending on both. Support for care of the dying has hardly changed (although rather more people are undecided than two years before). However, in relation to more generous funding for research into a cure, public attitudes have shifted quite markedly: the less philanthropic now outnumber the more charitable, though they did not in 1987.

	More NHS resources on care for the dying		More money for research into a cure	
	1987	1989	1987	1989
	%	%	%	%
Agree strongly	8	6	32	20
Agree (a little*)	34	34	26	23
Neither agree nor disagree	29	34	n/a	n/a
Disagree (a little*)	23	21	20	24
Disagree strongly	5	4	18	26

* Interview questionnaire

This shift towards a less generous spirit on this one matter is somewhat surprising, since we have found little or no reduction in sympathy on our other measures, and no change in people's expectations that a vaccine will be found. We can only hazard a guess as to why this might be so. It may be that publicity given to the high costs of developing treatments like AZT has prompted people to question whether the expenditure was indeed worth it. Perhaps the failure so far of scientists to come up with a cure may have influenced public opinion. Another explanation could be that the imminent reorganisation of the health service (see Chapter 1) may have alerted people to the scarcity of resources for health care generally.

Testing and screening for HIV

For the first time in 1989, the issue of testing for HIV was introduced into the questionnaire. Following earlier controversy over the relative merits of testing and non-testing, there was a gradual groundswell of opinion during 1988 as professional bodies such as the British Medical Association and the Health Education Authority declared themselves in favour of some system of anonymised screening of blood to provide better estimates of the size of the population infected with the virus. (Notable exceptions to this emerging consensus were the Royal College of Nursing and the Royal College of General Practitioners: both were unconvinced that all the issues had been satisfactorily resolved.)

Discussion culminated in the introduction (late in 1989) of a system of anonymised testing of blood taken from unnamed patients (who are having blood tests anyway), about whom nothing is recorded other than their age and sex, and the geographical area in which they live. So there are no opportunities for tracing donors and disclosing the results of the test. First data from this study are expected to be available in 1990 making the latest *British Social Attitudes* results especially pertinent.

Although few would doubt the importance of better estimates of the prevalence of HIV in the population, a number of ethical, scientific and practical dilemmas face those charged with implementing such a scheme. Any system of voluntary screening cannot hope to be representative of the population as a whole. It may be that those *most* at risk are the least willing to take part, or *vice versa*, leading to misleading estimates of the prevalence of HIV infection.

We asked two questions, the first relating to the principle of testing, the second to the way in which it should ideally be conducted:

As one way of getting to know how AIDS is spreading, it has been suggested that hospitals should be allowed to test any patient's blood (that has been taken for other reasons) to see whether it contains the virus that causes AIDS.

Do you agree or disagree with this suggestion?

		Agree strongly	Agree	Neither	Disagree/ disagree strongly
All	%	46	41	6	6
Men:					
18–34	%	46	37	6	8
35–54	%	49	41	6	3
55+	%	64	29	4	3
Women:					
18–34	%	37	46	7	10
35–54	%	39	47	4	10
55+	%	44	44	8	2

The results show overwhelming support for a system of testing for HIV. Nearly nine out of ten believe that hospitals should have the right to test blood, and only one in twenty disgrees. Strong agreement increases with age; even so it is interesting that few young people (who are most likely to be infected with the virus) reject the principle of testing. Women, perhaps on civil libertarian grounds or perhaps because they feel the risks to women are slighter, are rather less enthusiastic than men in their support for systematic testing.

Yet despite this strong endorsement for the principle of testing, there is less support for the chosen means of implementation. We asked:

Thinking of patients whose blood has been tested for the AIDS virus **without their knowledge** – should they . . .

Not be told the test has been carried out
*Be told about the test **but not** be told the result*
*Be told about the test, **and** have the choice of knowing or not knowing the result*
*Be told about the test, **and** be told the result.*

More than half the sample is in favour of a system in which it is obligatory for the individual to be told of both test and outcome. More than a third back the slightly milder option of the individual's being told of the test but of having the choice of whether or not to be told the result. Only one in twenty would choose the system which has been put into practice, where individuals have no knowledge that they are being tested.

Again, there are differences by age and gender, as the table below shows:

		Not be told about test	Told about test, but not result	Have choice of knowing result	Be told the result
All	%	5	1	38	54
Men:					
18–34	%	7	1	40	51
35–54	%	6	–	33	60
55+	%	6	3	28	63
Women:					
18–34	%	6	1	50	43
35–54	%	4	*	41	55
55+	%	4	2	33	58

Men of all age groups are more likely than women to say that the person should be told the result; and young people are keener than older people that the person should be given a choice. Indeed for young (18–34 year old) women, this is the preferred option.

Setting aside the practical effect of knowing if one has the HIV virus from the point of view of sexual practice, there used to be little medical reason for knowing a positive test result because there were few possibilities for remedial action. However, increasing success has been achieved in producing drugs which can delay progression to AIDS and, if such success were to continue, then the ethical balance could well shift in favour of telling the patient. In any event, the apparent divergence between the views of the public and the principles of established practice will clearly need to be addressed when results of the current screening study are made public.

Conclusions

In *The 5th Report*, Harding (1988) predicted that the trend towards more liberal attitudes to sexual morality over the past few decades was unlikely to suffer more than a temporary setback. This most recent round of data seems to prove him right so far. True, a slight swing of the pendulum back to greater tolerance of diversity in sexual relationships may or may not herald the start of a new trend, but it certainly brings a halt to the rise in censoriousness which we saw in the last *Report*, and which seemed to be linked to fears of AIDS.

There may have been those who saw the onset of AIDS as a reason to return to absolute moral values governing sexual relationships, but a sizeable minority of the population (including the young and those with a better education) seem rather to favour a brand of moral pragmatism. Certain acts are judged right or wrong according to the harm they cause, rather than the fact that they offend against a rigid and predetermined moral code. And people may be coming to realise that it is unsafe sexual practices themselves which carry a risk of AIDS, and not the kind of sexual relationship in which these practices take place.

All of this is good news for the management of the AIDS epidemic and for sufferers from it. Efforts directed at prevention and cure can easily be undermined in a moral climate characterised by stigma and prejudice. However, there is a long way to go before the level of public concern and compassion for sufferers and potential sufferers can be said to match the severity of the disease itself.

For instance, substantial minorities of the public favour discrimination against AIDS sufferers at work, at school and even in hospital. And in increasing numbers, people seem reluctant to put more resources into the search for a cure.

Moreover, there are signs – though faint as yet – that the British public is becoming more complacent about the disease. More people (especially among the young) discount the risks of occasional infidelities by couples outside their relationship; fewer now believe that AIDS will develop into an epidemic.

Some might say that the British public is at last getting the problem into proportion; others might say that this is just a first step backwards towards old habits and attitudes. Attitudes will no doubt be affected as more and more people come across AIDS sufferers themselves.

In any event, our latest findings indicate that health educators and policy makers still have a vital role in informing opinion on this issue.

Notes

1. The National Union of Journalists had, in 1985, with some success issued guidelines intended to persuade members not to report AIDS and related issues in a manner which stigmatised gay men; yet reporting with an anti-homosexual slant was, even in 1989, still all too frequent in some parts of the press.
2. It should be noted here that a quarter of the sample believe the term 'homosexuality' to refer only to sexual relations between two men, so excluding lesbians from the definition. But when we excluded this group of respondents from the analysis, the proportions supporting and opposing discrimination against homosexuals remained substantially the same as before.

References

BROOK, L., 'The public's response to AIDS', in Jowell, R., Witherspoon, S. and Brook, L. (eds), *British Social Attitudes: the 5th Report*, Gower, Aldershot (1988).

DEPARTMENT OF HEALTH AND SOCIAL SECURITY, *AIDS: Monitoring Response to the Public Education Campaign, February 1986–February1987*, Report on four surveys during the first year of advertising, HMSO, London (1987).

DEPARTMENT OF HEALTH & THE WELSH OFFICE, *Short-Term Predictions of HIV Infections and AIDS in England and Wales*, Report of a Working Group (Chairman Sir D. Cox), HMSO, London (1988).

EVANS, B.A., 'Heterosexual transmission of HIV infection', *Lancet* vol.ii (1987) p.41.

GORER, G., *Sex and Marriage in England Today*, Cresset Press, London (1970).

HARDING, S., 'Trends in permissiveness', in Jowell, R., Witherspoon, S. and Brook, L. (eds), *British Social Attitudes: the 5th Report*, Gower, Aldershot (1988).

Acknowledgement

SCPR is grateful to the Health Education Authority for providing the funding that enabled us to repeat the 1987 questionnaire module in 1989. However, responsibility for the content and wording of the module, and for the interpretation of the findings, rests with SCPR and the authors.

5.1 ATTITUDES TOWARDS EXTRA-MARITAL, HOMOSEXUAL AND PRE-MARITAL RELATIONSHIPS, 1983 TO 1989 (1989:A86)
by age within sex

ALWAYS OR MOSTLY WRONG	EXTRA-MARITAL SEX				SEX BETWEEN PEOPLE OF THE SAME SEX				PRE-MARITAL SEX			
	1983*	1985	1987	1989	1983	1985	1987	1989	1983	1985	1987	1989
TOTAL	83%	82%	88%	84%	62%	69%	74%	68%	28%	23%	25%	22%
MEN All	82%	80%	89%	83%	67%	71%	77%	72%	22%	18%	22%	20%
18-34	76%	77%	86%	78%	57%	59%	65%	60%	5%	4%	6%	6%
35-54	79%	76%	90%	82%	63%	68%	74%	70%	18%	15%	17%	14%
55+	90%	87%	91%	89%	82%	88%	93%	87%	44%	40%	47%	39%
WOMEN All	85%	84%	88%	84%	57%	67%	72%	65%	33%	27%	27%	24%
18-34	80%	85%	85%	81%	45%	59%	56%	49%	7%	9%	7%	6%
35-54	83%	81%	84%	81%	51%	61%	72%	60%	25%	24%	22%	17%
55+	92%	86%	96%	90%	73%	82%	89%	85%	60%	50%	53%	50%

* The question wording in 1983 referred to husband and wife separately. The answers were almost identical, so averaged responses are given here.

5.2 GROUPS PERCEIVED TO BE AT RISK FROM AIDS (A103) by sex, age within sex and highest educational qualification

HOW MUCH AT RISK IS EACH OF THESE GROUPS FROM AIDS?	TOTAL	SEX		AGE WITHIN SEX						HIGHEST EDUCATIONAL QUALIFICATION			
				MEN			WOMEN						
		Men	Women	18-34	35-54	55+	18-34	35-54	55+	Degree	Profess -ional	A'level/ O'level/ CSE	Foreign/ Other/ None
Female homosexuals – that is, lesbians	%	%	%	%	%	%	%	%	%	%	%	%	%
Greatly/quite a lot	65	64	65	56	62	76	56	64	76	42	55	62	74
Not very much/not at all	28	30	26	42	33	14	39	28	13	51	39	33	17
Married couples who occasionally have sex with someone other than their regular partner	%	%	%	%	%	%	%	%	%	%	%	%	%
Greatly/quite a lot	60	55	64	49	53	65	56	63	73	45	60	57	66
Not very much/not at all	37	43	33	50	47	30	44	35	20	55	40	42	29
Doctors and nurses who treat people who have AIDS	%	%	%	%	%	%	%	%	%	%	%	%	%
Greatly/quite a lot	42	37	45	33	34	44	38	48	50	22	37	38	49
Not very much/not at all	54	60	50	64	65	50	59	50	42	77	61	59	44
People who have a blood transfusion	%	%	%	%	%	%	%	%	%	%	%	%	%
Greatly/quite a lot	37	33	41	30	27	42	34	41	46	18	26	31	48
Not very much/not at all	60	65	56	69	73	53	65	58	45	82	73	67	47
BASE: A RESPONDENT'S													
Weighted	1469	660	809	223	223	214	263	273	270	125	174	518	646
Unweighted	1513	682	831	220	231	231	260	291	277	128	183	527	668

6 Self-employment and the enterprise culture

*David G. Blanchflower and Andrew J. Oswald**

The 1980s saw a remarkable growth in the numbers of the self-employed in Great Britain. In March 1980, the Department of Employment recorded the number of self-employed people as 1.9 million – nearly 8 per cent of the employed labour force. Nine years later, in March 1989, the figure stood at 3.1 million – 12 per cent of all those in work.

Some observers have interpreted this as evidence of a revival of an entrepreneurial spirit in Britain. In 1988, the then Minister for Employment was keen to stress that "according to international comparisons of self-employment in non-agricultural activities, the UK had a growth between 1979 and 1987 of 45 per cent, compared with an average of 10 per cent in all other EC countries" (*Employment Gazette*, November 1988, p.585). Has the last decade, through changed attitudes and incentives, ushered in an inherently more entrepreneurial society? Has a new 'enterprise culture' sprung up in Britain?

Economists do not usually ask where jobs come from. Typically, economic theory makes the assumption that a given number of firms and workers exist; it then considers how they interact, and explores whether some form of government intervention is required to produce a social optimum. It is not therefore surprising that while standard economics textbooks contain chapters on the worker, the firm and the trade union, they rarely include a single page on the entrepreneur. Kirzner (1973, p.ix) points to the "virtual exclusion of the entrepreneurial role from economic theory"; Johnson (1986, p.xi) notes that economists "have not been attracted into this area"; Evans and Leighton (1989, p.532) conclude that economists "have a lot to learn about entrepreneurship".

It is now more explicitly recognised than it used to be that large employers

* David Blanchflower and Andrew Oswald are Professors in the Department of Economics, Dartmouth College, New Hampshire, USA; Research Associates at the National Bureau of Economic Research, USA; and members of the Centre for Economic Performance, London School of Economics.

begin as small employers. Several government policies over the last decade have thus been designed to encourage people to start up in business. Meanwhile, public and academic interest in the role of entrepreneurship has grown apace. Efficient intervention, however, requires that it is the most suitable individuals who are induced – by financial incentives or other means – to become self-employed. This demands that we understand what 'makes' an entrepreneur and, if possible, how to predict who will be successful at running his or her own business.

The last few years have seen an increase in research on self-employment and entrepreneurship. Rees and Shah (1986) use the *General Household Survey* and show that the probability of being self-employed is greatest in middle age, is more likely among those working in construction and manufacturing, and more likely among those living outside London and the North. Evans and Jovanovic (1989), using the *US National Longitudinal Survey*, find that the probability of a person being self-employed rises with the level of family assets and the number of past jobs, and falls as a function of the past wage level. They provide some evidence too that a spell of past unemployment encourages self-employment. Blanchflower and Oswald (1990) using data from a British birth cohort (the *National Child Development Study*) find that the probability of self-employment is higher if an individual has received an inheritance.

In this chapter, we use data from the *British Social Attitudes* surveys between 1983 and 1989 to examine the characteristics and attitudes of the self-employed. Our aims are to see what kinds of individuals run their own businesses, whether people move from unemployment into self-employment, and whether the self-employed are more enterprising than employees. We then try to assess the reasons for the growth in self-employment activity in Britain during the 1980s. Is there indeed a new, dynamic enterprise culture, with increasing numbers of employees feeling empowered to start their own businesses, or can the rise in the numbers of self-employed be explained simply by changes in the composition of the workforce (say, changes in age or the types of industrial sector in which people work)? We examine the data to look for other unexplained factors underlying the growth in self-employment – factors which might plausibly have resulted in a change in the cultural climate which is more favourable to enterprise.

Characteristics and attitudes of the self-employed

The *British Social Attitudes* series allows us to look at the proportion of people who say they are self-employed in each year between 1983 and 1987, and in 1989.* (There are, however, no data for 1988, since the survey was not carried out in that year). In the table below, we compare the survey data with the Employment Department's official statistics: both show the self-employed as a percentage of all individuals aged 18 or over in paid work.

---

* In the main questionnaire respondents who say they are in paid work for at least 10 hours a week are asked: "In your (main) job are you an employee or self-employed?"

% of employed workforce in self-employment

	Survey estimates*	Official statistics†
1983	11.5%	9.9%
1984	10.2%	10.5%
1985	12.1%	10.8%
1986	10.6%	11.0%
1987	12.3%	11.4%
1989	13.3%	12.2%

† Computed from seasonally-adjusted figures for Britain; 'employed workforce' does not include those on government training programmes or schemes.

Both sets show an increase over the period in the proportion of self-employed, the largest increase coming in the two years from 1987 to 1989.

To put these figures in historical perspective, according to official statistics the proportion of the workforce that was self-employed held virtually steady between 1973 and 1979, at around 7.9 per cent. Hence there was an increase of about two percentage points between 1979 and 1983 in the numbers of self-employed, and an increase of just over this amount in the six years from 1983 to 1989.

Who are the self-employed?

As there are relatively few self-employed people in any single *British Social Attitudes* survey, we have combined data from the six surveys carried out between 1983 and 1989. This gives us a larger sample of self-employed to compare with employees, and so more confidence in the data.

According to these figures, the self-employed are much more likely than employees to be men (see also Curran and Burrows, 1989). The proportion of men among all employees in the sample is 55 per cent, while among the self-employed, it is 78 per cent. The self-employed are also predominantly older rather than younger. As a percentage of all those in work, the age distribution of the self-employed in *British Social Attitudes* samples is as follows:

	Self-employed
Total workforce	12%
Age:	
18–24	7%
25–40	12%
41–54	13%
55 or over	16%

Note: the data are from 1983–1987 and 1989.

This difference is unsurprising since younger people tend not to have access either to the capital or to the social networks which make self-employment more of a possibility.

---

* The survey estimates are well within sampling error of the official statistics.

In terms of qualifications and length of schooling, however, the differences between the self-employed and employees are slight.

Years of schooling:	In self-employment	Employees
	%	%
10	44	40
11	26	29
12	9	10
13	6	8
14 and above	15	14

Highest educational qualification:	In self-employment	Employees
	%	%
None	33	31
CSE	9	9
'O' levels	20	23
'A' levels	13	11
Professional	16	16
Degree	9	10

Note: the data are from 1983–1987 and 1989.

As we have noted, a common theme in the growing literature on self-employment is that people may be encouraged into self-employment by an experience of unemployment (see for example, Evans and Leighton, 1989). In each of the surveys the self-employed and employees were asked whether, in the last five years, they had been unemployed and seeking work for any period. In the combined sample, 18 per cent of the self-employed answered 'yes', compared with 21 per cent of employees. So there is little evidence that the self-employed are disproportionately more likely to have suffered from unemployment, or that unemployment provides a spur towards enterprise. We return to this issue later.

As might be expected, the self-employed are not evenly distributed across industries. Over the 1983–89 period the distribution was as follows:

Proportion of self-employed and of employees in *selected* industries

	In self-employment	Employees
	%	%
Construction	25	5
Retail distribution	14	9
Business services	9	4
Agriculture	7	1
Other transport	6	2
Hotels and catering	5	3
Personal services	4	1
Recreational	4	2
Medical	3	7
Repair of goods	4	1

Note: the data are from 1983–1987 and 1989.

More than a third of self-employment in Britain is thus accounted for by those in construction and in the retail sector. Business services and agriculture are other industries with large numbers of the self-employed.

We asked both the self-employed and employees how many hours a week they normally worked: the data suggest that those who work for themselves put in long hours. The self-employed in our combined sample report working 48.6

hours a week on average; employees report working around 11 hours a week less on average (37.7 hours).*

One expected but nonetheless striking difference between the employed and the self-employed is the relative absence among the latter of trade union members. Nearly two-thirds of employees (63 per cent) are, or have been, union members compared with only 41 per cent of the self-employed. Since trade union membership is not only an 'objective' characteristic, but also a reflection of people's attitudes, we turn now to other attitudes which divide the self-employed and employees.

Attitudes of the self-employed

It is now a standard finding that the self-employed are strong supporters of the Conservative Party (see, for example, Heath, Jowell and Curtice, 1985; Curtice, 1986). In confirmation, our combined sample shows the following figures:

	In self-employment	Employees
Party identification:	%	%
Conservative	56	36
Labour	18	33
Centre/Alliance	11	14

Note: the data are from 1983–1987 and 1989.

Since the self-employed are disproportionately drawn from the working class, which is normally predisposed to vote Labour, this difference is even larger than it first appears. Further, as Witherspoon (1989) has noted, the self-employed are less likely to be left-wing in their political attitudes generally. For instance, they do not favour redistribution of income; they are more likely to believe that welfare benefits encourage dependency, and so on. The table below underlines these differences.

Attitudes of the self-employed

% agreeing with each of the following statements:	In self-employment	Employees
Government should redistribute income from the better off to those who are less well off	36%	48%
Big business benefits owners at the expense of workers	42%	54%
Ordinary working people do not get their fair share of the nation's wealth	50%	65%
There is one law for the poor and one for the rich	56%	67%
Most people on the dole are fiddling in one way or another	37%	31%
If welfare benefits weren't so generous people would learn to stand on their own two feet	37%	29%

Note: the data are from 1987 and 1989.

In each case, the self-employed are less likely, often markedly so, to agree with the left-wing alternative.

---

* The standard deviations on these two estimates are, however, high (18.5 and 12.1 respectively).

We also looked for evidence as to whether the self-employed differ from employees in the way they view work *per se*. The survey asked both groups to choose, from a long list of job characteristics, the one that would be most important to them *personally* if they were looking for a new job. We show below a number of those characteristics in their order of importance to the self-employed.

Most important characteristics in any new job

	In self-employment	Employees
	%	%
Interesting work	37	29
Good pay	14	14
Convenient working hours	14	15
Job security	12	18
Get on with work your own way	9	4
Work that helps others	4	4
Possibility of promotion	3	6
Friendly people	3	4

Note: the data are from 1989.

The self-employed are more likely than employees to say that interesting work is their first priority, and somewhat more likely to stress the ability to get on with work in their own way. They are less likely than employees to mention job security and promotion prospects. Here then is a little evidence of a more entrepreneurial, risk-taking personality.

Advantages of being self-employed

We asked all the self-employed (in 1985) about the advantages for them of being self-employed. Admittedly, the sample base is small (111 cases), but the indications are clear enough. Broadly speaking, the advantages may be divided into two categories. First, individuals may enjoy the independence of being their own boss. Second, they may earn more by running their own business than by working for somebody else. Money does not appear to be by any means the overriding reason. The table below contains the proportions of self-employed people giving each response.

Advantages of being self-employed, 1985*

	%
Flexible hours	43
No supervision	41
Money	30
Freedom	17
Work for self	8
Fits with domestic responsibilities	7
Flexibility for customers	3
Security	3
No advantages	11
Other	9
Don't know/not answered	3

* Respondents could give more than one reason; hence the percentages add up to more than 100.

This picture may help to explain the political beliefs of the self-employed. Hardy individualists, they prefer the flexibility and potential financial rewards of self-reliance, even if it brings greater risks. Of course, we do not know if these beliefs *cause* people to become self-employed or if they develop them as a *result* of self-employment. Our data measure possible associations, not causes.

Why then do more people *not* become self-employed? In most years, the survey asked those in employment at the time of interview how seriously they had considered self-employment. Excluding those workers who had in fact been self-employed at some point during the preceding five years (four per cent), 16 per cent of employees over the time period reported that they had "very seriously" or "quite seriously" considered becoming self-employed; 71 per cent said they had *not* considered it at all seriously. Why then had those people who *had* considered self-employment not taken it up? In the 1983, 1984 and 1986 surveys, they were asked precisely that question.

Of a total of 485 would-be entrepreneurs, around one half said that they were constrained by a shortage of capital; a further 16 per cent were in the end unwilling to take the risk.

Reasons for not becoming self-employed

% saying:	%
Lack of capital	52
Risk involved	16
Economic climate	1
Other reason	31

Note: the data are from 1983, 1984 and 1986.

As the table shows, these were the only two dominant reasons, the largest constraint by far being a practical one rather than any simple personality factor.

Evidence of an 'enterprise culture'

We use two methods to examine the hypothesis that an enterprise culture flourished in Britain since 1983. First, we look directly at answers to a survey question discussed briefly above, to discover how seriously employees have considered setting up on their own during the last five years, and whether there has been any clear rise in the number of people seriously considering this course of action. In other words, was there over time a growing tendency among employees even to *think* about becoming self-employed?

The second method uses econometric techniques to examine whether, over the period 1983–89, there has actually been an upward trend in self-employment which is not accounted for by objective changes either in the labour force or in Britain's economic performance. If this is indeed the case, it is therefore likely to have been brought about by some abstract change in 'culture'. The statistical analysis also produces information about the possible determinants – or, more accurately, the correlates – of self-employment.

The table below shows the year-on-year trends in response to the question about how seriously employees had considered self-employment.

% of employees who have considered self-employment

		. . . very seriously	. . . quite seriously	. . . not very seriously	. . . not at all seriously
1983	%	5	12	13	70
1984	%	7	10	13	71
1986	%	6	10	14	70
1987	%	5	10	14	71
1989	%	6	10	12	73
All years	%	6	10	13	71

Base: employees who had not themselves been self-employed within the preceding five years.

There is no evidence at all here of any increase in the *desire* among employees for self-employment. Thus, between 15 and 17 per cent of employees in each year said they had seriously considered self-employment. What is remarkable about these figures is the stability in every column of the table.

The remainder of the evidence in this section relies on a number of statistical experiments.* The aim is to see whether, after controlling for a range of personal and economic circumstances identified earlier in this chapter, the data provide evidence for an otherwise unexplained upward trend in self-employment. If we find that the growth in self-employment is not accounted for *either* by changes in the economic characteristics of those in the labour market, *or* by changes in the economy as a whole, we may conclude that some other factor – a growing entrepreneurial culture, perhaps – is at work. The statistical analysis we have used (known as probit analysis) attempts to determine the probability of an individual being self-employed. (Details of the method are given at the end of the chapter. We describe only the broad conclusions here.)[1]

In order to look at trends, we need to discount macroeconomic and labour market influences, and particularly the business cycle, which might create a more favourable environment for those taking the risk of becoming self-employed. Thus we controlled for regional differences in unemployment – one macroeconomic indicator – to see whether local economic circumstances were associated with the propensity to be self-employed. If they were, then it was possibly economic factors rather than any change in 'culture' which led to the growth in self-employment.

Our analysis suggests that the *rise* in self-employment at the *end* of the 1980s seems to be attributable to the *fall* in unemployment during that period. This might be because people are more likely to enter self-employment when they feel they are likely to find a job should their business fail. Alternatively, it might be because falling unemployment is simply an indicator that the economy is buoyant, as it was in the latter part of the 1980s, and likely to provide a favourable market for products and services.

We also examined whether changes in the *types* of people in the labour market, rather than any cultural shift, account for any of the growth in self-employment. We looked in particular at gender, ethnic origin and age – three pre-determined

* The results we report are based on the pooled sample in employment from 1983–1987 inclusive and in 1989. This gives a sample of 8109, 12.1 per cent of whom were self-employed in their main occupation.

demographic characteristics which, of course, could not change in response to any change in 'culture'. In line with our previous findings, we found that males are much more likely than females to be self-employed. We also found that the probability of running one's own business goes up with age and then down again *beyond* retirement age: this is because some people choose self-employment in preference to retirement. Ethnic origin made little difference, though Asians were more likely to be self-employed than other ethnic groups. Once again, however, these factors had not significantly altered *over time*, so they could not explain the *growth* in self-employment. It seems to be the buoyancy of the economy during the middle and late 1980s that best accounts for the growth in self-employment in that period.

We then tested for possible changes over time in other personal characteristics, such as union membership, the kind of work people did (manual or non-manual) and people's experience of unemployment. These variables are unlikely to be exogenous to self-employment status – that is, they are likely to be causally related to self-employment. As might be expected, however, our findings remain the same. People who have been union members, and non-manual workers, are less likely than average to be self-employed, but no more or less so over the period in question.

Finally, we amalgamated regions with similar coefficients on unemployment, in order to look for trends, but the time trend was still small and not statistically significant. We found that those living in areas of high unemployment were less likely to be self-employed. But economic recovery, rather than any cultural shift, proved to be more important in accounting for growth in self-employment in the 1980s. There may of course have been an earlier cultural shift between 1979 and 1983, since in that period self-employment and unemployment rose together. Unfortunately our data do not go back that far, so we cannot rule out the possibility that there was a growth of an entrepreneurial mood in Britain in the years of the first Thatcher term in government.

Taken as a whole, however, these results support the idea that since 1983 Britain has experienced a renaissance of an entrepreneurial spirit. The upward movement in the self-employment figures is accounted for by our statistical analysis as a response to macroeconomic forces. Self-employment as a proportion of employees was counter-cyclical in the middle and late 1980s. When unemployment in a region is low, its self-employment rate is high.

We cannot explain from these data why this occurs, but it is likely that people are inhibited from starting their own businesses in depressed economic conditions, and more willing to take risks when there are plenty of jobs to fall back upon if their enterprise fails. But the result itself is important because it helps to explain why in the *later* 1980s there was such a big growth in self-employment: according to government statistics, unemployment halved over the second part of the decade. Once this effect is allowed for, there is no compelling evidence of a post-1983 upward trend in self-employment in Britain.

Conclusion

One in eight British workers run their own businesses. They are disproportionately male, older, and working in the construction and retailing sectors. They work long hours, typically vote Conservative, believe that state welfare benefits encourage dependency, and are less concerned than employees about job security.

People say they are self-employed mainly because it provides flexible hours and lets them be their own boss, but also because of its financial rewards. Employees say they are put off from being self-employed by the difficulty of raising start-up capital, and to a lesser extent, by the risks involved.

According to the survey data, between 1983 and 1989 there was no increase in the proportion of employees who were tempted to consider self-employment. Moreover, after allowing for the effects of the decline in unemployment during the latter part of the decade, our econometric analysis can detect no rising trend in self-employment. We cannot say from these data whether an enterprise culture was stimulated between 1979 and 1983, but we find no evidence of an underlying upward trend in self-employment from 1983 to 1989.

Notes

1. This note describes a number of statistical experiments, the aim of which is to see whether, after controlling for personal and economic characteristics, the data provide evidence for an underlying upward trend in self-employment. All of these results are based on the pooled sample of adults in employment from 1983–89 inclusive. This gives a sample base of 8109, 12.1 per cent of whom were self-employed in their main occupation.

   In **Table 7.1**, different probit equations are estimated. Each of these is a statistical attempt to determine the probability of an individual being self-employed. The explanatory variables are defined in Note 2. A preliminary look at the data is provided by *Specifications 1 and 2*. *Specification 1* enters only a time trend and a constant, and reveals a rising trend in self-employment in *British Social Attitudes*, as in Department of Employment data. The inclusion, in *Specification 2*, of a full set of regional dummy variables leaves the time trend virtually unaltered. Thus far, this is consistent with the idea of a 'Thatcher-effect' on self-employment which filtered through over the period.

   However, to control for macroeconomic and labour market influences, and particularly the business cycle, *Specifications 3 and 4* include regional unemployment as an extra explanatory variable. While *Specification 3* – omitting regional dummy variables – continues to find a strong time trend, this breaks down in *Specification 4*. It includes as regressors a time trend, a regional unemployment variable, and a set of regional dummy variables. In this specification the significance of the time trend collapses: it enters with an asymptotic t-statistic of 0.05 and a coefficient 30 times smaller than in the earlier specifications. Regional unemployment itself now appears negatively with a t-statistic of 2.1 (Johnson *et al*, 1988, reports a positive effect using a short annual time series). Thus the rise in self-employment seems, from this specification, to be attributable to the fall in unemployment.

   Specification 5 allows for some personal characteristics, ones that we have already seen are significantly associated with self-employment. It includes:
   1. Male: a male/female dummy
   2. White: a white/black dummy
   3. Asian: a dummy for those of Asian/other non-white origin
   4. Age, and age squared.

   These are assumed to be predetermined or exogenous variables. In line with *British Social Attitudes* findings, males emerge on this model as being much more likely than females to be self-employed. The probability of being self-employed emerges as an increasing concave function of age, which reaches a maximum point beyond normal working age. The Asian and White variables correlate positively with self-employment, although the coefficient on the latter is not strongly significant. The time trend coefficient is still well below conventional levels of significance. Although regional unemployment weakens to a t-statistic of 1.7, its coefficient is little changed.

   Specification 6 adds the following extra variables.
   5. Ever union: a dummy for having been a trade union member
   6. Non-manual: a dummy for non-manual occupations
   7. Ever unemployed: a dummy for having been jobless in the last five years.

   These variables are unlikely to be exogenous to self-employment status, rather are likely to be causally related to it. People who have been union members, and non-manual workers, are less likely than average to be self-employed, though our basic results are unaltered; the effect of unemployment is, however, considerably weaker in this specification.

Specification 7 is an attempt to provide a condensed form, by amalgamating the insignificant regional dummy variables (Scotland, Yorkshire, West Midlands, North and London). The result is a time trend which is still small and statistically not significant, but a much better determined unemployment effect – an unemployment coefficient approximately double that of *Specification 6*, and significant at conventional levels.

To check whether the inclusion of a linear trend is crucial, *Specifications 8 and 9* rework *Specifications 1 and 6*, with time dummies instead of a trend. *Specification 8* reveals the importance of 1989 in generating the upward trend in self-employment. *Specification 9* suggests that there is little or no evidence for an unexplained upward trend in self-employment in this period. *Specification 10* also has time dummies instead of a time trend. It amalgamates regional dummies and, as before, the regional unemployment rate then appears statistically important.

When taken as a whole, these results show that the strong upward movement in the raw data on self-employment is explained statistically as a response to macroeconomic forces. Self-employment as a proportion of employees is apparently counter-cyclical: when unemployment in a region is low, its self-employment rate is high. This explains the growth in self-employment in the late 1980s, as unemployment fell.

2. Definition of variables

		Mean	SD
SE	a (1,0) dummy variable set to 1 if self-employed and 0 if an employee	.121	.326
Time trend	Variable set to 1 in 1983, 2 in 1984 etc.	4.298	1.997
Year 84	a (1,0) dummy variable set to 1 if year is 1984	.106	.308
Year 85	a (1,0) dummy variable set to 1 if year is 1985	.118	.323
Year 86	a (1,0) dummy variable set to 1 if year is 1986	.213	.409
Year 87	a (1,0) dummy variable set to 1 if year is 1987	.191	.393
Year 89	a (1,0) dummy variable set to 1 if year is 1989	.259	.438
Ever Union	a (1,0) dummy variable set to 1 if ever union	.603	.489
Nonmanual	a (1,0) dummy variable set to 1 if nonmanual	.544	.498
Ever unemployed	a (1,0) dummy variable set to 1 if ever unemployed	.203	.402
SCOT	a (1,0) dummy variable set to 1 if lives in Scotland	.087	.282
IRELAND	a (1,0) dummy variable set to 1 if lives in N. Ireland (1989)	.052	.222
YORKS	a (1,0) dummy variable set to 1 if lives in Yorkshire/Humberside	.085	.279
WMID	a (1,0) dummy variable set to 1 if lives in West Midlands	.093	.290
NORTH	a (1,0) dummy variable set to 1 if lives in North of England	.053	.224
EMID	a (1,0) dummy variable set to 1 if lives in East Midlands	.064	.245
EANG	a (1,0) dummy variable set to 1 if lives in East Anglia	.045	.207
SW	a (1,0) dummy variable set to 1 if lives in South West	.094	.292
LONDON	a (1,0) dummy variable set to 1 if lives in London	.107	.310

		Mean	**SD**
WALES	a (1,0) dummy variable set to 1 if lives in Wales	.044	.206
MALE	a (1,0) dummy variable set to 1 if male	.576	.494
WHITE	a (1,0) dummy variable set to 1 if white	.912	.283
ASIAN	a (1,0) dummy variable set to 1 if Asian or other non-white race	.020	.140
MARRIEDS	a (1,0) dummy variable set to 1 if married	.747	.435
UNEMP	Regional unemployment rate (Source: *Regional Trends*)	10.398	3.481
RAGE	Age	38.934	12.618

References

BLANCHFLOWER, D. and OSWALD A.J., *What Makes a Young Entrepreneur?*, Working Paper No. 3252, National Bureau of Economic Research, (1990).

CURRAN, R. and BURROWS, R., 'National profiles of the self-employed', *Employment Gazette*, July 1989, pp. 376–386.

CURTICE, J., 'Political partisanship', in Jowell, R., Witherspoon, S., and Brook, L. (eds.), *British Social Attitudes: the 1986 Report*, Gower, Aldershot (1986).

EVANS, D. and JOVANOVIC, B., 'An estimated model of entrepreneurial choice under liquidity constraints', *Journal of Political Economy*, 97, 4 (1989) pp. 808–827.

EVANS, D. and LEIGHTON, L., 'Some empirical aspects of entrepreneurship', *American Economic Review*, 79 (1989) pp. 519–535.

HEATH, A., JOWELL, R. and CURTICE, J., *How Britain Votes*, Pergamon, Oxford (1985).

JOHNSON, P., *New Firms: An Economic Perspective*, Allen and Unwin, London (1986).

JOHNSON, S., LINDLEY, R. and BOURLAKIS, C., *Modelling Aggregate Self-employment: a Preliminary Analysis*, Institute for Employment Research, University of Warwick, December 1988.

KIRZNER, I.M., *Competition and Entrepreneurship*, University of Chicago Press, Chicago (1973).

REES, H. and SHAH, A., 'An empirical analysis of self-employment in the UK', *Journal of Applied Econometrics*, 1 (1986), pp. 95–108.

WITHERSPOON, S., 'The self-employed and the enterprise culture', mimeo, SCPR, London (1988).

Acknowledgement

The authors have relied on a number of sources including government statistics and the BSA dataset. The interpretations are of course those of the authors alone.

6.1 PROBIT EQUATIONS ON SELF-EMPLOYMENT

Specification 1

Variable	Coefficient	Asymptotic S.E.	Asymptotic T Stat
TIME TREND	0.0255	0.0088	2.8696
CONSTANT	-1.2789	0.0429	-29.8125

Likelihood Ratio Test   11.0298

Specification 2

Variable	Coefficient	Asymptotic S.E.	Asymptotic T Stat
TIME TREND	0.0220	0.0094	2.3274
SCOTLAND	-0.0286	0.0710	-0.4029
IRELAND	0.1656	0.0876	1.8903
YORKS	-0.0462	0.0716	-0.6464
WMID	-0.0695	0.0698	-0.9953
NORTH	-0.2023	0.0926	-2.1828
EMID	0.1138	0.0738	1.5407
EANG	-0.1062	0.1038	-1.0231
SW	0.1040	0.0692	1.5028
LONDON	-0.0065	0.06507	-0.1002
WALES	0.2713	0.0842	3.2207
CONSTANT	-1.2806	0.0520	-24.6211

Likelihood Ratio Test   41.1377

Specification 3

Variable	Coefficient	Asymptotic S.E.	Asymptotic T Stat
TIME TREND	0.0216	0.0099	2.1695
UNEMPLOYMENT RATE	-0.0061	0.0057	-1.0716
CONSTANT	-1.2020	0.0892	-13.4629

Likelihood Ratio Test   11.8706

6.1 PROBIT EQUATIONS ON SELF-EMPLOYMENT (continued)

Specification 4

Variable	Coefficient	Asymptotic S.E.	Asymptotic T Stat
TIME TREND	0.0025	0.0133	0.1868
SCOTLAND	0.0406	0.0788	0.5159
IRELAND	0.3117	0.1125	2.7696
YORKS	-0.0040	0.0749	-0.0543
WMID	-0.0292	0.0733	-0.3985
NORTH	-0.1170	0.1024	-1.1419
EMID	0.1201	0.0739	1.6246
EANG	-0.1387	0.1046	-1.3256
SW	0.0939	0.0696	1.3489
LONDON	-0.0264	0.0657	-0.4021
WALES	0.3348	0.0901	3.7135
UNEMPLOYMENT RATE	-0.0182	0.0088	-2.0591
CONSTANT	-1.0339	0.1303	-7.9324

Likelihood Ratio Test   45.4609

Specification 5

Variable	Coefficient	Asymptotic S.E.	Asymptotic T Stat
TIME TREND	0.0092	0.0137	0.6746
SCOTLAND	0.0393	0.0811	0.4855
IRELAND	0.5356	0.2097	2.5538
YORKS	0.0023	0.0775	0.0297
WMID	-0.0172	0.0747	-0.2311
NORTH	-0.0874	0.1031	-0.8479
EMID	0.1122	0.0760	1.4750
EANG	-0.1515	0.1096	-1.3816
SW	0.0838	0.0721	1.1624
LONDON	-0.0046	0.0680	-0.0677
WALES	0.3338	0.0944	3.5338
MALE	0.5420	0.0406	13.3379
WHITE	0.2517	0.1773	1.4193
ASIAN	0.4926	0.2142	2.2993
UNEMPLOYMENT RATE	-0.0160	0.0091	-1.7484
AGE	0.0327	0.0086	3.7733
AGE SQUARED	-0.0002	0.0000	-2.6581
CONSTANT	-2.5428	0.2881	-8.8236

Likelihood Ratio Test 304.2959

6.1 PROBIT EQUATIONS ON SELF-EMPLOYMENT (continued)

Specification 6

Variable	Coefficient	Asymptotic S.E.	Asymptotic T Stat
TIME TREND	0.0081	0.0142	0.5715
SCOTLAND	0.0429	0.0820	0.5228
IRELAND	0.4881	0.2171	2.2480
YORKS	0.0224	0.0795	0.2817
WMID	-0.0057	0.0769	-0.0746
NORTH	-0.0788	0.1060	-0.7440
EMID	0.1327	0.0786	1.6881
EANG	-0.1885	0.1093	-1.7243
SW	0.0918	0.0743	1.2352
LONDON	0.0047	0.0685	0.0688
WALES	0.3809	0.1005	3.7885
MALE	0.6065	0.0421	14.4002
WHITE	0.2382	0.1842	1.2928
ASIAN	0.3748	0.2214	1.6923
UNEMPLOYMENT RATE	-0.0090	0.0093	-0.9629
AGE	0.0591	0.0090	6.5320
AGE SQUARED	-0.0005	0.0001	-5.2696
EVER UNION	-0.6388	0.0396	-16.1062
NONMANUAL	-0.1274	0.0393	-3.2396
EVER UNEMPLOYED	0.0676	0.0499	1.3554
CONSTANT	-2.8197	0.3011	-9.3643

Likelihood Ratio Test 568.2178

Specification 7

Variable	Coefficient	Asymptotic S.E.	Asymptotic T Stat
TIME TREND	0.0078	0.0122	0.6435
IRELAND	0.5476	0.1996	2.7430
EMID	0.1150	0.0715	1.6079
EANG	-0.1508	0.1075	-1.4023
SW	0.0856	0.0683	1.2528
WALES	0.3403	0.0859	3.9606
MALE	0.5422	0.0404	13.4035
WHITE	0.2516	0.1743	1.4434
ASIAN	0.4962	0.2121	2.3396
UNEMPLOYMENT RATE	-0.0171	0.0072	-2.3797
AGE	0.0328	0.0086	3.8042
AGE SQUARED	-0.0002	0.0000	-2.6798
CONSTANT	-2.5319	0.2692	-9.4052

Likelihood Ratio Test 302.8755

6.1 PROBIT EQUATIONS ON SELF-EMPLOYMENT (continued)

Specification 8

Variable	Coefficient	Asymptotic S.E.	Asymptotic T Stat
YEAR84	-0.0768	0.0788	-0.9740
YEAR85	-0.0121	0.0754	-0.1614
YEAR86	-0.0469	0.0672	-0.6974
YEAR87	0.0345	0.0674	0.5120
YEAR89	0.1118	0.0638	1.7520
CONSTANT	-1.1908	0.0538	-22.1209

Likelihood Ratio Test 14.8726

Specification 9

Variable	Coefficient	Asymptotic S.E.	Asymptotic T Stat
YEAR84	-0.0822	0.0822	-0.9999
YEAR85	0.0237	0.0777	0.3049
YEAR86	-0.0348	0.0696	-0.5004
YEAR87	0.0339	0.0705	0.4820
YEAR89	0.0226	0.1003	0.2254
SCOTLAND	0.0398	0.0879	0.4525
IRELAND	0.5363	0.2342	2.2902
YORKS	0.0022	0.0808	0.0280
WMID	-0.0171	0.0784	-0.2182
NORTH	-0.0901	0.1129	-0.7978
EMID	0.1119	0.0763	1.4656
EANG	-0.1531	0.1110	-1.3799
SW	0.0837	0.0722	1.1601
LONDON	-0.0047	0.0682	-0.0701
WALES	0.3339	0.0998	3.3438
MALE	0.5426	0.0407	13.3099
WHITE	0.2518	0.1769	1.4232
ASIAN	0.4913	0.2138	2.2971
UNEMPLOYMENT RATE	-0.01566	0.0125	-1.252
AGE	0.0327	0.0087	3.7438
AGE SQUARED	-0.0002	0.0001	-2.6379
CONSTANT	-2.5067	0.2906	-8.6239

Likelihood Ratio Test 307.1436

6.1 PROBIT EQUATIONS ON SELF-EMPLOYMENT (continued)

Specification 10

Variable	Coefficient	Asymptotic S.E.	Asymptotic T Stat
YEAR84	-0.0823	0.0821	-1.0026
YEAR85	0.0214	0.0775	0.2765
YEAR86	-0.0337	0.0696	-0.4853
YEAR87	0.0320	0.0697	0.4591
YEAR89	0.0101	0.0831	0.1221
IRELAND	0.5571	0.2105	2.6454
EMID	0.1145	0.0717	1.5951
EANG	-0.1545	0.1090	-1.4177
SW	0.0844	0.0687	1.2290
WALES	0.3419	0.0866	3.9456
MALE	0.5432	0.0406	13.3664
WHITE	0.2527	0.1744	1.4485
ASIAN	0.4959	0.2120	2.3385
UNEMPLOYMENT RATE	-0.0174	0.0085	-2.0406
AGE	0.0328	0.0087	3.7712
AGE SQUARED	-0.0002	0.0001	-2.6569
CONSTANT	-2.4928	0.2684	-9.2861

Likelihood Ratio Test 305.6436

7 Recipes for health

Aubrey Sheiham, Michael Marmot,
Bridget Taylor and Andrew Brown*

When the second *British Social Attitudes* questionnaire module on health and diet was fielded in spring 1989, food was making headline news. There had been a salmonella scare and 'listeria hysteria'. They soon died down, but other dietary issues continued to preoccupy the media and, it seems, aroused levels of public interest and concern inconceivable only a few years earlier. Food irradiation and additives, while perhaps not the subject of everyday conversation, are now certainly debated by an increasingly informed and worried minority. More recent fears about Bovine Spongiform Encephalopathy (BSE) – too recent to be reflected in the 1989 fieldwork round – have fuelled heated debate about the relationship between government and farmers. Calls for a new Ministry of Food, mandated to safeguard the health of the consumer rather than the interests of the producer, have become more and more sustained. Public scepticism about sources of information on food and diet is widespread (McCluney, 1988). Public confidence seems to be low, whether in farming, food manufacturing or food retailing.

Such wide public interest in the recent headline-making stories must be set against a lively background debate on healthy eating. Throughout the 1980s, nutrition education designed to encourage the British public to alter its eating habits has played an important part both in forming policy decisions and in changing the food production and retailing industries in many directions. More recently, anxiety about food safety, and a rapidly growing 'green' consumer consciousness, have forced both government and industry to become more responsive to public pressure. There is ample evidence too that increasing numbers

* Aubrey Sheiham is Professor of Community Dental Health and Dental Practice, University College London; Michael Marmot is Professor of Community Medicine, University College London; Bridget Taylor is a Researcher at SCPR on the *British Social Attitudes* survey series; Andrew Brown is a research student at Nuffield College, Oxford.

of people have understood and acted on the nutrition messages of the 1980s. There is now widespread public appreciation of the links between food and health.

Tracking trends in dietary habits

The 1986 survey in this series contained for the first time a module of questions about diet and health. It included questions both on attitudes and on eating behaviour. Respondents to the main questionnaire were asked a series of questions about several types of food (such as meat, eggs, fruit and vegetables) so that we could find out whether and how their consumption of each had changed in the recent past. Those who had changed were asked why. We also probed for details about particular changes in eating habits in both healthy and unhealthy directions. In the self-completion questionnaire we explored attitudes to and beliefs about a number of issues to do with diet and health, and the relationship between them.

Our preliminary findings in *The 1987 Report* presented an encouraging picture of attitudes to food and its preparation (Sheiham *et al*, 1987). People of all social classes reported recent changes in the directions recommended by nutritionists and health educators. For instance, many reported eating less meat, eggs and sugar, more fruit and vegetables, grilling rather than frying their food, drinking more semi-skimmed or skimmed milk, and eating more wholemeal bread in preference to white bread. The majority of respondents were not put off by putative barriers to 'healthy eating'. They had mainly decided to change their eating patterns for reasons of good health or to control their weight. Women led men in positive attitudes to healthy eating.

In 1989 we repeated most of the questions, but made some minor changes and additions. For instance, among the foods we asked about we added "biscuits, pastries and cakes"; we also asked about chips and roast potatoes instead of potatoes generally; and we added a question about consumption of sweets and chocolates. We omitted an open-ended question about reasons for changing eating habits. But on most measures we can look with confidence for evidence of time-trends.

We examine below the extent to which increased awareness and concern about food and diet seem to be matched by changes in behaviour.

Complacency and concern

The findings from this survey and others reveal that many people are still uncertain about the nutritional quality and importance of the foods they eat. It seems that single-issue nutrition messages (for instance, that sugar gives one energy), designed to sell particular products, have led to misunderstanding and confusion. The advertising industry and the mass media have therefore played an important role both in informing and in misleading consumers. Expenditure on food advertising is huge, most of it aimed at encouraging people to eat foods which are *not* recommended as part of a healthy diet. So far, improvements in food labelling have been limited and selective and do not seem to have helped greatly in increasing public understanding of the nutritional qualities of food. So some consumers who are keen to change to a healthier diet may well make the wrong choices. Others with good intentions may be inhibited by lack of money or lack of choice of healthy foods.

Responses to the 1989 survey provide evidence of discrepancies between attitudes and behaviour. Around a quarter of respondents (28 per cent) say that they are "very" or "fairly" worried about the sorts of foods they eat. Yet only one in ten of those who are worried say they would probably change their diets. The rest feel either that they have done enough already or that they would simply not get round to it.

Worry about food and propensity to change

	All	Very or fairly worried about what they eat
% saying:	%	%
I have never felt any need to change	26	9
I have already changed as much as I'm going to	41	44
I ought to change more but probably won't	28	37
I will probably be changing soon	4	10

Changes in attitudes

Now that we have results from two rounds of the survey, we can begin to look at *changes* in attitudes towards diet and health. We are also able to examine the extent to which eating patterns have altered over a three-year period during which publicity to do with food and health has been so prominent. We are also in a position to explore further the relationship between attitudes and behaviour with respect to diet. We attempt to measure how far increased awareness of the healthy and unhealthy properties of different foods are being translated into healthier eating habits.

We begin by looking at perceptions of the importance of diet to health, the images which different types of food have, and attitudes towards what constitutes a proper meal. Then we look at the extent to which these attitudes and images have remained the same or changed between 1986 and 1989. In each case, we examine various subgroups to discover where changes in attitudes have been greatest.

In 1989, over one quarter of respondents believed that, provided one takes enough exercise, it does not matter what one eats. Just over one half of respondents disagreed – a slightly higher level of disagreement than in 1986.

We have already noted that in 1989 more than a quarter of respondents were worried about the sorts of food they ate. However, the extent of concern varies between different groups in the population, particularly according to age: just 20 per cent of those aged 55 or over say that they are "very" or "fairly" worried about the food they eat, compared with 34 per cent of 18–34 year olds. In both these age groups the differences between men and women are small. In the middle age group (35–54 year olds) however, women (35 per cent) are more

likely to be worried about the sorts of food they eat than men (28 per cent).
These findings tie in with those of other studies, which have found that women
tend to be more preoccupied with their weight than men, and to feel more guilty
about what they eat (Hodgkinson, 1989).

There is no linear relationship between attitudes and social class, but education
has some bearing on levels of concern: 31 per cent of those with educational
qualifications say that they are worried about the food they eat, compared with
25 per cent of those without qualifications. These findings are reflected in slight
regional variations too. **Table 7.1** gives full details.

Images of food

We also find evidence that considerable confusion still exists about the health
properties of foods. In both 1986 and 1989, we asked respondents whether they
thought various foods were "good for people", "bad for people" or "neither"
(the question was asked only of people who had changed their eating patterns).*
The table below gives the results.

	Good for people*		Neither		Bad for people*	
	1986	1989	1986	1989	1986	1989
Fresh fruit and vegetables	95%	94%	3%	3%	*	*
Fish	91%	89%	8%	8%	*	1%
Eggs	73%	67%	23%	28%	4%	3%
Bread	70%	69%	26%	26%	3%	2%
Beef, pork or lamb	66%	57%	30%	35%	3%	6%
Processed meat	23%	22%	61%	58%	15%	17%
Potatoes	64%	n/a	30%	n/a	5%	n/a
Chips or roast potatoes	n/a	21%	n/a	38%	n/a	39%
Biscuits, pastries & cakes	n/a	19%	n/a	37%	n/a	42%

*"Good for *one*", "bad for *one*" in 1986.

Fish, and fruit and vegetables are thought to be good for people by about nine
in ten of those asked the question in both years, a result which must provide
some comfort to nutritionists. Moreover, only about one in five respondents
believe that processed meat "such as sausages, ham and tinned meat", or chips
and roast potatoes, or biscuits, pastries and cakes (not asked about in 1986) are
good for people. This too must be reassuring for health professionals. Less
reassuring, perhaps, is the fact that red meat and eggs are thought to be good
for people by about two-thirds of those asked this question in each year. These,
of course, are all traditional, standard items in the British diet, but nutritionists
have increasingly been advising people to cut down on their consumption of
meat and to increase the amount of potatoes and (wholemeal) bread in their diet.

Our results suggest that images of different foods changed little between 1986
and 1989, with two exceptions. The proportion saying that eggs are good for people
fell from 72 per cent in 1986 to 65 per cent in 1989. This decline may in part be

---

* The fact that we did not ask *all* respondents this question (and we may remedy this in future
rounds of the survey) means that the proportion of our respondents answering this question differs
between 1986 and 1989 for each type of food.

attributable to warnings from nutritionists about excessive consumption of eggs, but they continue to recommend eggs in moderation. There has, in fact, been a steady decline in egg consumption in Britain during the 1980s (National Food Survey, 1988), but our results were probably also influenced by the scare over salmonella. In October 1988 Environmental Health Departments had warned the public not to eat raw eggs and in November there had been a call for a consumer boycott of eggs. In early December, the then junior Health Minister asserted on television that most egg production in the UK was contaminated with salmonella – a remark she later retracted; as a result egg sales plummeted. News coverage continued to be extensive in the months before and during fieldwork for the 1989 survey.

The image of eggs took the hardest knocking among those in the youngest age group. The proportion of 18–24 year olds saying that eggs are good for people fell from 83 per cent in 1986 to 57 per cent in 1989. In contrast, among older respondents (particularly those aged 60 or over) eggs by and large maintained their healthy image.

The other shift since 1986 was in the reduced proportion of respondents saying that beef, pork and lamb were good for people – from 65 per cent in 1986 to 57 per cent in 1989. This suggests that the messages from diet and health specialists about the high saturated fat content of these meats, and their associated detrimental effects on health, may well be making some headway. (News coverage of BSE came too late to affect our results.)

Since 1986, there has been a slight decline also (from 62 per cent to 58 per cent) in the proportion of the population who believe that "a proper meal should include meat and vegetables" – which suggests that messages from nutritionists that meat (especially meat with a high fat content) is in some respects unhealthy, and that protein can be derived from alternative foods, may gradually be making some inroads into traditional ideas. Nonetheless, on our evidence they still have a considerable way to go. As the table below shows, women in the middle age group (35–54) appear to be least resistant to changing their views: among this group agreement with the view that a proper meal should include meat and vegetables fell from 58 per cent in 1986 to 47 per cent in 1989. Among older women the traditional view is stronger (two-thirds of them supported it), and shows no sign of declining, while among men aged 55 or over the proportion agreeing with this view in fact rose between 1986 and 1989, though this movement may not be statistically significant.

	A proper meal should include meat and vegetables	
% agreeing (strongly or just)	1986	1989
Total:	62%	58%
Men:		
18–34	63%	56%
35–54	58%	56%
55┐	66%	70%
Women:		
18–34	57%	56%
35–54	58%	47%
55+	67%	66%

When we isolated men aged 65 or more, the most traditional group, we found that three-quarters reported a proper meal as incomplete without meat and vegetables (see **Table 7.2**). Social class is positively associated with more 'informed' attitudes as is education, and the gap between those with qualifications and those without is becoming larger. Detailed breakdowns by all these are given in **Table 7.2**.

The message from the experts

Confusion about what constitutes a healthy diet is still widespread, and the messages getting through are evidently conflicting. In 1986 nearly three-quarters of our sample believed that experts contradict each other about what makes for a healthy diet, and this proportion has remained fairly stable over the three years to 1989. The enormous publicity given to food safety and healthy living in recent years has apparently failed to dispel confusion about the best advice to follow. Subgroup differences on this question are largely predictable. The likelihood of believing that experts contradict each other tends to increase with age and to decline with education. Less predictably, perhaps, the proportion critical of expert opinion actually rose in Scotland (from 62 per cent to 71 per cent) despite (or perhaps because of) a series of major health promotion campaigns in Scotland in the interim.

Changes in eating patterns

Attitudes towards food and diet did not, of course, change dramatically between 1986 and 1989; indeed, it would have been surprising if they had done so in such a short period. However, there does appear to have been *some* change in attitudes, mainly towards a healthier diet. But we need to examine how far this shift is reflected in positive changes in behaviour, leading to healthier eating habits.

In both rounds of the survey, we asked two sets of questions about changes in diet. First, for certain types of food we asked respondents about changes in their consumption. In the table below we have categorised changes as 'healthy' or 'unhealthy' according to current orthodoxy. (People's recent changes in diet and earlier ones are combined since the great majority of respondents report having changed within the last two or three years.)

	'Healthy change'		No change		'Unhealthy change'	
	1986	1989	1986	1989	1986	1989
Processed meat, like sausages, ham or tinned meat*	37%	35%	56%	59%	7%	5%
Fresh fruit and vegetables†	26%	27%	66%	66%	7%	6%
Beef, pork or lamb*	27%	28%	66%	64%	7%	7%
Eggs*	24%	32%	67%	59%	10%	7%
Fish†	20%	15%	62%	69%	18%	14%
Chips or roast potatoes*	n/a	33%	n/a	62%	n/a	5%
Biscuits, pastries and cakes*	n/a	34%	n/a	59%	n/a	6%

* = less now; † = more now. Percentages are based on all respondents, not (as in the table on p.108 of *The 1987 Report*) on those saying they have ever eaten that food.

In 1989 (as in 1986), while most respondents reportedly made no changes in the quantities of each of these foods consumed, such changes as there were have been in a healthy direction. Proportions making healthy changes were similar in both years in the case of most foods, suggesting that healthier eating behaviour is being sustained or is increasing. An exception is consumption of fish. The proportion claiming to eat more fish fell by five percentage points between 1986 and 1989; as many as 14 per cent actually report eating less nowadays. Nutritionists have certainly been pushing the claims of fish, but apparently unsuccessfully. It could well be that the availability and price of fresh fish are inhibiting factors.

The figures for reported change in egg consumption also deserve comment. The proportion saying they were eating fewer eggs rose by six percentage points over the three years. However, as suggested above, this change in a healthy direction may be less a sign that nutritionists' advice to eat fewer eggs is being heeded than a result of the 'egg scare'. If so, levels of consumption may have risen again since our survey was in the field.

We also asked in both rounds about the habit of taking sugar in hot drinks. Our data suggest that this is becoming less widespread, providing further evidence of a continuing change towards healthier eating. The proportion of respondents taking sugar in hot drinks fell from 54 per cent in 1986 to 49 per cent in 1989. Moreover, of those taking sugar this way in 1989, a third said they were using less compared with two or three years earlier.

An important exception to healthier eating is consumption of confectionery (not asked about in 1986). In 1989, 85 per cent of our respondents said that they sometimes ate sweets or chocolates. Although many of these (43 per cent) said they were consuming less confectionery than two or three years earlier, the market still appears to be expanding. Over the five years to 1988, the average annual growth in the retail confectionery market was eight per cent and sales were at an all-time high. Nutritionists, health experts and dentists clearly have an uphill task ahead in persuading people to cut down on, or give up, eating confectionery.

In a further set of questions, in both 1986 and 1989 respondents were asked whether or not they had made a number of changes to their diet in the recent past. In 1989 we added an item about potatoes – chips and roast potatoes *versus* boiled and baked potatoes. Also in 1989, we fielded two versions of all these questions (one on each version of the questionnaire): one asked about changes in a 'healthy' direction, the other about 'unhealthy' changes.

In asking about changes in behaviour, it is necessary to tie questions to some specified (and fairly short) time period; in these questions we chose to ask about changes over the last two or three years. This, of course, presents a problem since some people would have changed their behaviour longer ago. Others may have been 'healthy eaters' since childhood or youth: radical changes in eating patterns have been afoot and spreading for many years now. Thus respondents who were in the vanguard of healthy eating fail to appear among our count of those who have made healthy changes in their diet. It is important to bear this in mind in interpreting these particular results, as it may explain what might otherwise appear to be anomalies.

The table below shows proportions of respondents in both years who said that they had recently made healthy changes in their diet:

Compared with two or three years ago would you say you are now . . .

	% answering "yes"	
	1986	**1989**
eating more grilled food instead of fried food?	56%	61%
eating more wholemeal bread instead of white bread?	56%	55%
using more low-fat spreads or soft margarine instead of butter?	54%	60%
eating more fish and poultry instead of red meat?	44%	45%
drinking or using more semi-skimmed or skimmed milk instead of full-cream milk?	33%	43%
eating more boiled or baked potatoes instead of chips or roast potatoes?	n/a	56%

The proportions making each healthy change are substantial in both years. Majorities said that they are eating more grilled food instead of fried food, more low-fat spreads instead of butter, more wholemeal instead of white bread, and (in 1989) more boiled or baked potatoes instead of chips or roast potatoes. Further, for some items the proportions making healthy changes are significantly higher than three years before. This supports our other evidence that progress towards healthier diets is continuing and becoming more widespread.

The largest rise is in the proportion using more reduced-fat milk now instead of full-cream milk. Change to use of reduced-fat milk was not as widespread in 1986 as other reported changes, but the proportion of respondents claiming to have switched rose by 10 percentage points over the three years. Nonetheless, despite strong encouragement to people to buy semi-skimmed or skimmed milk, by 1988 reduced-fat milk represented only one quarter of milk consumption in Britain. The proportions eating more grilled food instead of fried food, and using more low-fat spreads instead of butter, also rose between 1986 and 1989, but less steeply.

So we have evidence of healthy changes, particularly towards reducing intake of dairy and saturated fats, which suggests that medical advice on this issue is proving influential. Indeed, data from the National Food Survey shows a recent marked change in the types of fat used. In 1987, butter accounted for just over half of spreading fats used; only a year later, it accounted for just under a third (Van den Berghs, 1989). In contrast wholemeal bread does not appear to have won additional converts in recent years. Other evidence suggests that the trend towards eating wholemeal bread between the late 1970s and mid-1980s appears to have halted; in 1987 white bread (including wrapped and sliced) still accounted for over half of bread sales in the UK (FAB, 1988).

In order to investigate unhealthy changes in diet, in 1989 these same questions were asked in reverse on the second version of our questionnaire. As many as 18 per cent of respondents say that they are now eating more white bread instead of wholemeal, and 16 per cent report consuming more red meat instead of fish and poultry, and more full-cream milk instead of reduced-fat milk. Smaller proportions say they are using more butter instead of low-fat spreads (13 per cent), more chips and roast potatoes (again 13 per cent) and more fried food instead of grilled food (eight per cent). These figures show that, although the news for nutritionists is generally good, a small minority of people are changing their diet in unhealthy directions.

An overwhelming majority of respondents claim recently to have made at least one of the five healthy changes asked about both in 1986 and 1989: 86 per cent and 88 per cent respectively. Moreover, many respondents say that they made *several* healthy changes in the last two or three years. The average number of healthy changes made was 2.4 in 1986 and 2.7 in 1989. Bearing in mind that some people who made healthy changes longer than three years ago are lost from our figures, these figures are encouraging indeed.

| | % of respondents changing | |
	1986	1989
Number of healthy changes made within the previous two or three years*	%	%
None	14	12
One	18	14
Two	20	19
Three	18	22
Four	18	19
Five	11	14
Average 'change score'	*2.4*	*2.7*

* Omitting new item "... more boiled or baked potatoes instead of chips or roast potatoes", (added in 1989).

Whose eating habits are changing?

To look for variations in the extent of recent healthy changes in diet between different groups in the population, we calculated the average number of changes that they made, this time using all six items asked about in 1989, including the item on potatoes. The average change score rose to 3.2. Once again, the range in the number of changes registered by various subgroups is not wide; the smallest is 2.8 and the largest is 3.5. Overall, women have made on average rather more healthy changes recently than men. This greater propensity of women to change holds across all age groups, as the table below shows:

	1989 Average 'change score'*
Total	3.2
Men: total	3.0
18–34	3.0
35–54	3.3
55+	2.8
Women: total	3.4
18–34	3.3
35–54	3.5
55+	3.2

* Calculated on all six changes to healthy eating.

Middle-aged respondents tend to have made the most changes, followed by those aged 18–34, with respondents aged 55 or over making fewest.

Behaviour also differs by social class and level of educational qualification.

Respondents in manual occupations have made on average 3.1 recent healthy changes compared with 3.4 amongst classes I and II, and those with CSEs or without qualifications average 3.0 changes compared with 3.5 among those with a degree or professional qualification. Respondents living in the Midlands and Wales average 3.4 recent changes compared with just 3.1 amongst those in southern England, although this might once again be a result of southerners having changed too long ago to register.

Importantly, however, the rise between 1986 and 1989 in the number of healthy changes made tends to be greatest among those groups who registered the smallest number of changes in 1986, such as younger men and older respondents, those in manual social classes and the least highly qualified. Conversely, the number of changes is smallest among those groups who registered the most changes in 1986, notably women in the middle age range, those in social class I and the most highly qualified. This pattern is, as we have noted, partly a function of our question wording, which asks only about *recent* changes in diet. Nonetheless, it suggests that the 'healthy diet' messages are slowly reaching those whose eating patterns have traditionally been the least healthy.

We have looked more closely at changes in eating patterns by carrying out some multivariate analyses. First, we performed a cluster analysis on the responses in the main questionnaire to the six questions about recent healthy changes in diet. On this basis, we divided our sample into two groups: the first group comprised the *'new healthy eaters'* who made predominantly 'healthy changes' to their diets in recent years; and the second group comprised those who either made no recent healthy changes or only a few. Half the sample fell into the 'healthy group' and half into the other group. Cross-tabulation of group membership by a number of other variables provides us with profiles of those belonging to each group (shown in **Table 7.3**).

These results broadly confirm those of our initial cross-tabulations. Those in the healthy group are slightly more likely to be women than men, middle-aged rather than young or elderly and living in Scotland, the Midlands or Wales. While the proportion in the healthy group varies little between social classes, 52 per cent of those with higher educational qualifications ('O'levels or above) fall into this group compared with 46 per cent of those with CSEs or without qualifications. We also found that 46 per cent of those living alone are in the healthy group, compared with 50 per cent of those living in families or other groups; there is no difference between respondents in households with children and those without.

Then, using logistic regression, we analysed further the responses of people who have made healthy changes to attempt to discover the relative importance of different influences on dietary changes. The results show the effect of each characteristic, net of the effects of the other factors. We found that the level of educational qualifications has an influence over healthy changes in diet which just reaches statistical significance.* The influences of other factors, such as sex and age, are not statistically significant. Interestingly, respondents with a professional qualification or degree are no more likely than those with 'O'levels or 'A'levels to have made healthy changes recently: this seems to indicate that the influence of education levels off beyond a certain standard. Once again, however, it may also be that some of those with the highest qualifications made healthy changes in diet more than two or three years ago, and so escaped our time-limited definition of healthy eating.

---

* Its coefficient was 0.08 and its Z-score (coefficient divided by standard error) 2.0.

An exception to the lack of significant gender differences in healthy eating behaviour is the habit of taking sugar in hot drinks. In 1986, 65 per cent of men took sugar in hot drinks, compared with only 44 per cent of women, and by 1989 these proportions had fallen to 61 per cent and 39 per cent respectively. The difference between men and women on this item is much larger than variations between, for example, respondents with different levels of education, or those from different regions or from different social classes. When we added this variable (taking sugar or not) into our analyses, gender emerged as a significantly stronger influence on behaviour than education. Thus, the tendency for men to take sugar in hot drinks is the only behavioural characteristic (of those we asked about) on which women are significantly more likely than men to make healthy dietary changes.

Not only were fewer women than men in both years taking sugar in hot drinks, but women are somewhat more likely than men to report changing their behaviour. In 1986, 30 per cent of women said they were using less sugar in hot drinks than two or three years earlier, compared with 25 per cent of men (though by 1989 this gap had narrowed).

Certainly the overall market for sugar in Britain has declined sharply (a fall of 27 per cent between 1984 and 1988). At the same time, there has been a strong growth in sales of artificial sweeteners (Mintel, 1989). Clearly, consumers have cut back on their direct intake of sugar. Equally clearly, though, they have not perceived the extent to which they are replacing direct intake of sugar with indirect intake. Despite declining retail sugar sales, the total industrial tonnage of sugar has remained static since 1983; so the industry has been successful in switching sales to food manufacturing markets.

Reasons for dietary change

In 1986, though not in 1989, we asked respondents who said they had given up or cut down on sugar in hot drinks why they had done so. We invited them to choose from a number of listed reasons including "none of these"; respondents could cite as many reasons as they chose. The major differences in choice between men and women are, first, that women are somewhat more likely than men to give weight control as a reason (a third of women said this compared with just over a quarter of men). Secondly, a third of men nominated "wanting to keep healthy" as a reason, compared with only one in five women.

Despite this difference, about the same proportion of women as men still eat sweets and chocolates (86 per cent of women and 83 per cent of men in 1989 reported eating sweets or chocolates nowadays). Even so, women are once again somewhat more likely than men to say that their intake of confectionery is less than two or three years earlier: 45 per cent of women say this compared with 40 per cent of men.

Respondents who had changed their consumption of any of the other types of food asked about were likewise asked, in 1986 and 1989, for each one, why they had changed. In 1986, the main reasons given for making healthy changes in eating patterns were to keep healthy and to help control weight; few respondents said that they were "told to change for medical reasons". In 1989, health and weight control were again commonly cited reasons – for example, for reducing consumption of chips and roast potatoes, and of cakes and biscuits, and for eating more fresh fruit and vegetables. Concern to keep healthy is also a common reason given for eating less beef, pork and lamb, and more fish (suggesting that the messages from nutritionists about the benefits of eating fish are getting through to some at least). The proportion giving health as a reason for eating fewer eggs rose steeply from 18 per cent in 1986 to 31 per cent in 1989; and for eating less processed meat from 26 per cent in 1986 to 33 per cent in 1989. But as before, these changes may be due, in part at least, to the salmonella outbreak and other food scares in 1988 and early 1989.

Weight control is a common reason given for eating less bread, while almost no one gives this as a reason for eating more bread. So outdated ideas that starchy foods are fattening are, it seems, still prevalent.

In order to look more rigorously at reasons for changes in diet, we first compressed the seven listed reasons into three categories: health reasons (help in weight control, concern to keep healthy and 'doctor's orders'); financial reasons (poor, or good, value for money); and reasons of personal taste ("I just like it more", and "I just don't like it as much").* Then we cross-tabulated membership of the two groups identified earlier through cluster analysis ('healthy eaters' and others) by the three types of reasons. As the table below shows, while majorities in both groups cite health reasons for changing, a much higher proportion of 'healthy eaters' do so; only about a quarter give taste as a reason. In contrast, of those who have not made healthy changes recently two in five give taste as a reason.

| | | Changed dietary habits recently for | | |
		. . . health reasons	. . . financial reasons	. . . reasons of personal taste
Healthy eaters	%	71	5	24
Others	%	53	9	39

Relatively few in either group report changing their eating habits for financial reasons.

When we look at the profiles of those giving different sorts of reasons for changing their eating habits, we find no gender differences. However, health reasons are cited relatively more frequently among respondents in the middle age group, and among those in social classes I and II.

| | | Changed dietary habits recently for | | |
		. . . health reasons	. . . financial reasons	. . . reasons of personal taste
Age:				
18–34	%	54	5	41
35–54	%	71	6	23
55+	%	64	8	28
Social class:				
I/II	%	69	6	24
III Non-manual	%	64	5	31
III Manual	%	65	7	28
IV/V	%	57	8	36

Health reasons are also more often mentioned by graduates and those with professional qualifications. Reasons of taste are relatively more important for

---

* Respondents could give more than one reason. The figures in the two tables above are based on the number of individual reasons given, not on the number of repondents.

respondents in social classes IV and V and for the youngest age group (aged under 35). Size of household also appears to be a factor. Respondents living alone are much less likely than others to give health reasons and more likely to cite personal taste. But, of course, it is predominantly elderly people who live on their own, so it may be age that is at play here.

Finally, a multivariate (logit) analysis was performed on the types of reasons given for changes in eating patterns. The model used compares those who give health reasons with those giving reasons of personal taste (since these two account for the great majority of the variance in responses). The results show that social class and level of educational qualifications are the only characteristics to have a significant influence on the kind of reason given for making dietary changes.* The influence of social class is straightforward. The tendency to give health reasons for changes in diet increases in a linear way from social classes IV/V to social class I; conversely the tendency to give personal taste as a reason decreases from classes IV/V to class I. The effect of education, however, seems more complicated.[1]

Obstacles to change

Earlier we reported evidence of a discrepancy between *attitudes* towards diet and health, and eating *behaviour*. Moreover, many respondents feel that the advice from food experts on what makes a healthy diet is contradictory. Nonetheless, our findings suggest that, with notable exceptions, most people's images of particular food types are broadly in line with the views of nutritionists. However, there may be other constraints which inhibit people from making healthy changes to their diet.

Barriers to healthy eating

In 1986 and 1989 we asked respondents about a number of overt barriers to buying, serving and eating healthy food. It does not appear that these barriers have diminished much during the three-year period.

	% of respondents perceiving barriers:	
	1986	**1989**
Food that is good for you is usually more expensive (% *agreeing*)	49%	49%
Healthy food doesn't usually taste as nice as other food (% *agreeing*)	–	26%
Food that is good for you generally tastes nicer than other food (% *disagreeing*)	37%	–
Food that is good for you generally takes too long to prepare (% *agreeing*)	19%	16%
It is hard to find food that is good for you in supermarkets (% *agreeing*)	–	17%
Food that is good for you is easy to find in supermarkets (% *disagreeing*)	19%	–
Mothers would eat healthier food if the rest of their families would let them (% *agreeing*)	–	26%

* With coefficients of 0.34 and 0.28 and Z-scores of 4.1 and 2.2 respectively.

In both years around half the sample say that healthy food is usually more expensive. This is the most widely perceived barrier of those asked about. Yet it is somewhat ironic, since vegetables, fruit, bread and pulses tend to be cheaper than less healthy foods like meat and dairy products. On the other hand, the image is probably attributable to the inflated prices charged by some retailers of 'specialist' healthy foods.

Although finding healthy food in supermarkets does not apparently present a problem to a majority of respondents, it is surprising that there was no change between 1986 and 1989. On the face of it, supermarkets now handle a good deal more 'healthy' food than they used to. Nevertheless, one in six respondents in 1989 still believed this to be an obstacle. The time required to prepare healthy food was a barrier to even fewer respondents and their numbers show signs of diminishing. In 1989, a quarter of respondents believed that mothers would eat healthy food if their families would let them; so for a substantial minority family pressure is also a barrier.[2]

Predictably, some subgroups within the population are more inclined than others to see barriers (see **Table 7.4**). In particular, the manual social classes are the more likely to be sensitive to *all* the possible barriers to healthy eating. Likewise, awareness of barriers is particularly widespread among older people (those aged 55 and over) and those who are the least well educated.

But since these groups overlap, we can get a better overall picture of the relative importance of these barriers to different sorts of people by carrying out multivariate analysis. We divided respondents into two categories according to the extent to which they perceived barriers to healthy eating. A logistic regression was performed to measure the influence of various characteristics on perception of barriers. The results show that the strongest characteristic with influence is age, older respondents tending to be daunted by barriers to healthy eating while younger people apparently find them easier to overcome (although this just failed to reach statistical significance).*

Fatalism and health

Unless people believe that they can influence their own good health they are unlikely to stick to 'healthy' habits. So, in 1986 and 1989, we presented respondents with two statements designed to measure the strength of 'fatalistic' views of health,

> *Good health is just a matter of good luck*
>
> *If heart disease is in your family, there is little you can do to reduce your chance of getting it*

and asked them to say how much they agreed or disagreed with each. It is reassuring that agreement with either statement is confined to a small – and diminishing – minority: 17 per cent in 1986 and 14 per cent in 1989 agreed with the first statement, while 15 per cent and 12 per cent respectively agreed with the second. Around three-quarters disagreed with each.

As **Table 7.5** shows, fatalistic attitudes tend to be held more by certain groups in the population than by others. Once again, respondents in older age groups,

---

* With a coefficient of 0.08 and Z-score of 1.9.

those in manual social classes, (especially classes IV and V) and those with lower educational qualifications or none at all are more likely to be fatalistic about health.

Again with multivariate analysis, we can get a clearer overall picture of the characteristics which dispose people towards fatalistic attitudes towards health. We divided the sample into 'fatalists', that is those agreeing with either of the two statements, and others, and performed a logistic regression to measure the influence of personal characteristics on fatalistic attitudes. Four of the characteristics we investigated had a significant effect in determining fatalistic attitudes. Whereas neither gender nor region are significant factors, once again education did matter, and indeed had the strongest influence:* respondents without 'O'levels or higher qualifications are much more likely than those with qualifications to have fatalistic attitudes towards health. The factor with the next strongest influence is household type: respondents living alone are more likely than those living in a family or other group to have fatalistic views.** The other significant factors are age and social class – in the expected directions.

An interesting question however, is whether respondents with fatalistic attitudes about health and heart disease differ in their perceptions of barriers to healthy eating. It appears that they do – a great deal.

% agreeing (strongly or just):	'Fatalists'	'Non-fatalists'
Healthy food doesn't usually taste as nice as other food	41%	23%
Food that is good for you is usually more expensive	66%	45%
Food that is good for you generally takes too long to prepare	32%	12%
It is hard to find food that is good for you in supermarkets	30%	13%
Mothers would eat healthier food if the rest of their families would let them	37%	23%

On all items, fatalists are *much* more likely than non-fatalists to perceive barriers to healthy eating – almost to the point of inventing constraints which suit their general disposition. The reassuring fact is that fatalists are a minority. Most people now believe that good health is not only in our stars but in ourselves – and that it is influenced by sensible eating.

Notes

1. The relationship between level of educational qualifications and the tendency to give health reasons, as opposed to personal taste, for dietary changes is not linear: 72 per cent of respondents with a degree or professional qualification cited health reasons, compared with 64 per cent of those with 'A' or 'O' levels, and 68 per cent of those without qualifications. A possible explanation for this pattern is that two separate mechanisms are at work. It may be that the more highly qualified respondents are better informed than others about health and diet, leading them to change their diet for reasons of health. The least well qualified respondents, meanwhile, who tend generally also to be less well off and to have poorer health, may be more likely than others to change their diet on medical advice.

---

* With a coefficient of 0.37 and a Z-score of 4.8.
** With a coefficient of 0.25 and a Z-score of 2.1.

2. In 1986, when this statement referred to "many people", 42 per cent of respondents agreed with it, compared with only 26 per cent agreeing when we asked about "mothers", in 1989. This is a somewhat unexpected result.

References

FAB, *The Bread and Flour Report*: 3, Flour Advisory Bureau, London (1988).
HODGKINSON, N., 'Britain's Hunger for Good Health', *Sunday Times*, (1 October 1989).
McCLUNEY, J., *Answering Back: Public Views on Food and Health Information*, Food Policy Research Unit, University of Bradford, (1988).
MINTEL, 'Sugar and Artificial Sweeteners', *Market Intelligence*, London (1988).
NATIONAL FOOD SURVEY, 'Household Food Consumption and Expenditure', *Annual Report of the National Food Survey Committee*, MAFF, HMSO, London (1988).
SHEIHAM, A., MARMOT, M., RAWSON, D. and RUCK, N., 'Food values: health and diet' in *British Social Attitudes, The 1987 Report*, Jowell, R., Witherspoon, S. and Brook, L. (eds), Gower, Aldershot (1987).
VAN DEN BERGHS, *In Touch with People's Tastes – Yellow Fats Market Review and Merchandising Guide*, Van den Berghs, (1988).

Acknowledgement

We are grateful to the Health Education Authority for its financial support for the questionnaire module on attitudes to food, diet and health. SCPR must however accept the final responsibility for question wording and, with the authors, for the interpretation of the findings.

7.1 LEVELS OF CONCERN ABOUT DIET (A.228)
by age within sex, social class, highest educational qualification and region

7.1 A.228

HOW WORRIED ARE YOU ABOUT THE SORTS OF FOOD YOU EAT?	TOTAL	AGE WITHIN SEX						SOCIAL CLASS				HIGHEST EDUCATIONAL QUALIFICATION			REGION			
		MEN			WOMEN			I/II	III non-manual	III manual	IV/V	Degree/ Profes-sional	A level/ O level/ CSE	Foreign/ Other/ None	Scotland	Northern England	Midlands & Wales	Southern England
		18-34	35-54	55+	18-34	35-54	55+											
	%	%	%	%	%	%	%	%	%	%	%	%	%	%	%	%	%	%
Very worried	4	5	5	4	4	4	5	4	4	3	6	2	4	6	4	3	4	5
Fairly worried	24	29	23	16	30	31	15	27	22	22	21	29	26	20	25	23	21	27
Not particularly worried	50	47	53	48	56	49	48	53	54	50	47	55	53	46	51	52	52	49
Not at all worried	21	20	19	32	9	16	31	16	20	22	25	13	17	28	20	22	22	19
BASE: A RESPONDENTS																		
Weighted	1274	191	189	188	237	240	226	321	302	264	308	273	456	544	115	345	296	517
Unweighted	1304	189	196	202	232	259	226	332	315	272	311	282	463	556	121	363	298	525

7.2 ATTITUDES TOWARDS THE CONTENT OF A PROPER MEAL (A.227k) by age within sex, social class and highest educational qualification

	TOTAL	AGE WITHIN SEX								SOCIAL CLASS				HIGHEST EDUCATIONAL QUALIFICATION		
		MEN				WOMEN				I/II	III non-manual	III manual	IV/V	Degree/ Profes-sional	A level/ O level/ CSE	Foreign/ Other/ None
		18-34	35-54	55-64	65+	18-34	35-54	55-64	65+							
A PROPER MEAL SHOULD INCLUDE MEAT AND VEGETABLES	%	%	%	%	%	%	%	%	%	%	%	%	%	%	%	%
Agree strongly/ just agree	58	56	56	61	76	56	47	56	73	46	55	64	69	40	55	71
Neither agree nor disagree	14	20	19	14	6	14	14	11	7	15	15	15	11	17	17	11
Just disagree/ disagree strongly	27	23	24	24	18	29	39	31	19	38	30	21	20	43	28	18
BASE: A RESPONDENTS																
Weighted	*1274*	*191*	*189*	*80*	*108*	*237*	*240*	*89*	*137*	*321*	*302*	*264*	*308*	*273*	*456*	*544*
Unweighted	*1304*	*189*	*196*	*90*	*112*	*232*	*259*	*90*	*136*	*332*	*315*	*272*	*311*	*282*	*463*	*556*

7.3 CHANGES IN EATING BEHAVIOUR (CLUSTER MEMBERSHIP) (A.91a–f)
by sex, age, region, social class, highest educational qualification and household type

CHANGES IN EATING BEHAVIOUR (CLUSTER MEMBERSHIP)

	TOTAL	SEX		AGE			REGION			
		Men	Women	18-34	35-54	55+	Scotland	Northern England	Midlands & Wales	Southern England
	%	%	%	%	%	%	%	%	%	%
'New healthy eaters'	49	47	51	49	51	47	52	49	53	46
Others	51	53	49	51	49	53	48	51	47	54
BASE: A RESPONDENTS Weighted	1424	640	787	469	485	470	130	374	331	593
Unweighted	1469	662	807	462	510	494	141	396	330	602

	I/II	III non-manual	III manual	IV/V	Degree/ Profess-ional	A level/ O level/ CSE	Foreign/ Other/ None	Single person household	Family/ group
	%	%	%	%	%	%	%	%	%
'New healthy eaters'	48	51	49	48	51	52	46	45	50
Others	52	49	51	52	49	48	54	56	50
BASE: A RESPONDENTS Weighted	346	333	294	362	293	502	626	166	1261
Unweighted	360	347	303	366	304	511	647	202	1267

7.4 PERCEPTION OF BARRIERS TO HEALTHY EATING (A.227a–e) by sex, age, social class and highest educational qualification

	TOTAL	SEX		AGE			SOCIAL CLASS				HIGHEST EDUCATIONAL QUALIFICATION		
		Men	Women	18-34	35-54	55+	I/II	III non-manual	III manual	IV/V	Degree/ Profess-ional	A level/ O level/ CSE	Foreign Other/ None
	%	%	%	%	%	%	%	%	%	%	%	%	%
HEALTHY FOOD DOESN'T USUALLY TASTE AS NICE AS OTHER FOOD													
Agree strongly/just	26	27	26	25	23	31	19	22	31	34	16	25	33
Neither agree nor disagree	28	30	25	27	23	32	25	26	33	27	23	25	32
Disagree strongly/just	45	43	47	48	52	34	56	51	37	37	62	49	34
FOOD THAT IS GOOD FOR YOU IS USUALLY MORE EXPENSIVE													
Agree strongly/just	49	47	50	47	46	53	39	42	54	58	36	44	59
Neither agree nor disagree	14	15	14	14	12	17	17	14	17	11	18	12	14
Disagree strongly/just	36	37	35	39	41	28	44	43	29	30	46	42	26
FOOD THAT IS GOOD FOR YOU GENERALLY TAKES TOO LONG TO PREPARE													
Agree strongly/just	16	15	17	15	13	19	14	13	21	17	11	12	21
Neither agree nor disagree	26	29	24	26	23	29	21	23	30	31	23	26	28
Disagree strongly/just	58	56	59	59	62	52	65	63	49	51	66	61	51
IT IS HARD TO FIND FOOD THAT IS GOOD FOR YOU IN SUPERMARKETS													
Agree strongly/just	17	15	18	13	14	22	15	13	19	19	9	14	22
Neither agree nor disagree	18	23	14	18	16	20	16	13	24	18	17	15	21
Disagree strongly/just	65	61	68	68	70	56	68	73	56	61	74	70	56
MOTHERS WOULD EAT HEALTHIER FOOD IF THE REST OF THEIR FAMILIES WOULD LET THEM													
Agree strongly/just	26	25	27	22	27	29	29	24	25	27	24	25	28
Neither agree nor disagree	31	37	26	31	27	34	30	26	33	34	32	31	30
Disagree strongly/just	42	37	47	46	45	35	41	48	42	37	44	42	41
BASE: A RESPONDENTS Weighted	1274	568	705	427	430	414	321	302	264	308	273	456	544
Unweighted	1307	587	720	421	455	428	332	315	272	311	282	463	556

7.5 FATALISTIC ATTITUDES TOWARDS HEALTH (A.227j,g)
by sex, age, social class and highest educational qualification

	TOTAL	SEX		AGE			SOCIAL CLASS				HIGHEST EDUCATIONAL QUALIFICATION		
		Men	Women	18-34	35-54	55+	I/II	III non-manual	III manual	IV/V	Degree/ Profess-ional	A level/ O level/ CSE	Foreign Other/ None
	%	%	%	%	%	%	%	%	%	%	%	%	%
GOOD HEALTH IS JUST A MATTER OF GOOD LUCK													
Agree strongly/just	14	15	14	8	11	23	13	8	16	20	8	8	23
Neither agree nor disagree	13	12	15	14	12	14	9	16	15	16	9	15	14
Disagree strongly/just	71	72	71	78	77	60	78	76	69	63	83	77	61
IF HEART DISEASE IS IN YOUR FAMILY, THERE IS LITTLE YOU CAN DO TO REDUCE YOUR CHANCES OF GETTING IT													
Agree strongly/just	12	10	13	7	10	18	6	7	15	19	4	7	19
Neither agree nor disagree	12	14	11	11	7	21	8	8	17	15	5	10	17
Disagree strongly/just	75	76	75	81	82	63	86	84	68	64	90	83	62
BASE: A RESPONDENTS *Weighted*	1274	568	705	427	430	414	321	302	264	308	273	456	544
Unweighted	1307	587	720	421	455	428	332	315	272	311	282	463	556

8 Individualism

John Rentoul*

British Social Attitudes reports have consistently produced data which cast doubt on the conventional wisdom that, under Margaret Thatcher, there has been a transformation in the political values of the British people. It appears that successive Conservative governments have won and retained power for over a decade despite espousing many values at odds with the 'social democratic' character of much of the electorate.

The explanation of this apparent paradox is partly a matter of economic expectations. The Conservatives' success was partly the political dividend from a period of sustained economic growth. Equally, the Labour Party's spectacular rise in the opinion polls between spring 1989 and spring 1990 coincided with a policy review founded explicitly on the claim that 'Labour values are our values', but the main *cause* of the surge was probably the faltering of the economy at the end of the 1980s. Economic optimism has been shown (Curtice, 1986) to be a powerful predictor of party identification among people with similar values. And economic pessimism was probably more important in the Conservative opinion poll decline and Labour's rise than any sudden realisation by the electorate that its values were in tune with the Labour Party's.

So does this mean that British political fortunes rise and fall independently of the electorate's deeply-held values? That would be a curious conclusion at which to arrive after 11 years of a government so committed to entrenching and furthering a distinctive set of values among the British people. But now, with six years of survey data covering what might be described as the high-water-mark of 'Thatcherite individualism', it ought to be possible to reach an interim judgement on whether or not, or to what extent, the values so closely associated with the Prime Minister herself have been adopted by the public.

---

*   John Rentoul is a reporter for BBC Television's *On the Record*.

Individualist values

First we need to define her values, and the alternative. Here, we call her values 'individualist', the opposite of 'collectivist'. The classic text of 'Thatcherite individualism' is its author's interview with *Woman's Own* on 31 October 1987:

> Too many people have been given to understand that if they have a problem it's the government's job to cope with it . . . . They're casting their problem on society. And, you know, there's no such thing as society. There are individual men and women, and there are families. And no government can do anything except through people, and people must look to themselves first. It's our duty to look after ourselves and then, also, to look after our neighbour.

As a political doctrine, individualism is an extension of Adam Smith's insight into the working of a market economy: that "self-love and social" can be the same. 'Thatcherite individualism' is the belief that it is generally better for people to look after themselves (and their families) than for them to combine as a society to provide for themselves collectively.

The political programme of individualism is that taxes should be reduced, and people should provide for themselves; for the few who cannot look after themselves, charity should provide. The state should supply a safety net only as a last resort, in the regrettable cases where the charitable impulse is not as strong as it ought to be.

This kind of individualism is not the same as Conservatism. There is a long tradition of Conservative collectivism which views society as an organic whole, held together by the ties of hierarchy and social responsibility; but it was not in the name of this tradition that Mrs Thatcher claimed her place in history.[1]

Nor does the division between individualist and collectivist values exactly fit ordinary people's views of political issues, which are often more pragmatic than ideological – for instance, supporting the party they think will manage the economy better in the short to medium term. On the other hand, previous *British Social Attitudes* surveys have identified two dimensions of value differences which underlie political partisanship in Britain. In *The 1986 Report*, John Curtice describes the primary one as centred on "the value of collective action to achieve equality" (p.50) – in other words whether or not people are in favour of more redistribution of income and wealth. This value is clearly related to the class divide in British politics.[2] The second dimension reflects the difference between moral liberalism and traditionalism, or between libertarian and authoritarian values and attitudes. This dimension reflects differences in education and was shown to divide Conservative identifiers from those of the 'centre' parties within the middle classes.

Mrs Thatcher's individualism provides a rhetorical link between these two value dimensions, enabling her to fight on two ideological fronts at once – against *both* egalitarian collectivism *and* moral liberalism. But the sentiment which provides the backbone of individualism is a moral disapproval of the 'nanny' welfare state and the dependency it supposedly engenders.[3]

Two questions in this series (both asked on and off since 1983) almost explicitly address this sort of moral repudiation of social democratic values – expressing the view that the welfare state is debilitating rather than uplifting. We show below the proportion of the population in alternate years who support these individualist propositions.

	1983	1985	1987	1989
% agreeing/strongly agreeing:				
The welfare state makes people nowadays less willing to look after themselves	53%	44%	52%	39%
The welfare state encourages people to stop helping each other	37%	36%	40%	32%

There is a third statement in the battery, introduced first in 1987 and supported by an even smaller proportion of the population (30 per cent in 1989), which says: "If welfare benefits weren't so generous, people would learn to stand on their own two feet". We suspect, however, that its greater level of rejection may be due in part to disagreement with the conditional clause which implies that welfare benefits are generous in the first place.

In any event, the data show two things. First, they reveal that the public in 1989 divides fairly evenly in its reaction to the two propositions, with around a quarter of respondents choosing the neutral "neither agree nor disagree" option. Overall, more people reject than support the notion that the welfare state is undermining the nation's moral fibre, but not many more. Secondly, they reveal that support for an individualist philosophy has been falling rather than increasing, though in the election year of 1987 the trend was interrupted somewhat. In 1983, there was a clear majority for the individualist standpoint on these measures. By 1989 it had disappeared.

Privatisation of interests

If the 'Thatcher revolution' has not (yet) influenced the core value of individualism, that does not necessarily negate its political success. Policy changes since 1979 have been in an individualist direction, the aim being to produce a permanent increase in people's self-provision. So even if the public still supports collective provision in principle, there is another aspect to the individualist appeal, and that is self-interest. The rhetoric says it is acceptable to be self-interested because that is what makes society work. If people provide for themselves they are likely over time to become less enamoured of collective provision, or at any rate less willing to pay for it through taxation.

In other words, the strategy of the Conservative governments since 1979 has been to transform British society and its values and not just to beat the Labour Party. In short, the strategy is to eliminate socialism and its look-alikes. Even though the Labour Party itself has clearly not been eliminated, there is a view among commentators that the 'centre of gravity' of British politics has nonetheless now shifted decisively to the right, with the Labour Party's acceptance of market economics and trade union reform.

Through the 'privatisation of interests' – for example wider ownership and opting out of state control – people acquire an economic motive for individualism. The Conservative governments throughout the 1980s have thus encouraged people to take out private health insurance, to own their homes and to buy shares. In time, if not immediately, the argument runs, people's political values will surely be shaped by their material interest in private rather than public provision.

There are four key policy areas where this 'privatisation of interests' could foster support for individualism.

Health care

Public opinion on the subject of health care in Britain is predominantly collectivist, as previous *British Social Attitudes* reports have testified (see also Chapter 1). Support for the principles of the National Health Service is overwhelming, although in most cases non-ideological – most people would have private health insurance *as well* (not instead) if they could afford it (Rentoul, 1989, p.69). However, a majority also sees private medicine as potentially undermining the NHS, and prefers to see the private and public sectors kept apart (presumably so that NHS doctors are not distracted from NHS work by private practice). The prevailing view of private health care is thus one of tolerant suspicion, mixed perhaps with a bit of envy.

The present government hopes that the spread of private health insurance will encourage support for increased private provision of health care. Indeed, those people who are covered by private insurance do hold more individualist views on the subject. Of those with private insurance, 55 per cent believe that "private medical treatment in private hospitals is a good thing for the NHS", while only 36 per cent of those who are not insured agree. There is a similar difference, although at much lower levels of support, on the more sensitive question of private treatment *within* NHS hospitals: 38 per cent of those with private insurance say it is good for the NHS, as against 21 per cent of those who are not insured.

These figures do not necessarily tell us anything about the relationship between private health insurance and political attitudes. Such attitudes are likely to be class-related, and middle-class people are more likely to be able to afford insurance than working-class people. The full breakdown of the answers to these questions, given in **Table 8.1**, confirms that middle-class people (in the 'salariat') are much more likely to have private insurance than are working-class people, and also that middle-class respondents are more likely to believe that private treatment is "a good thing for the NHS" than working-class ones.

However, when attitudes *within* classes are analysed (to control for the prior effects of class interest), those with private insurance are still consistently more individualist in their views. For instance, within the salariat, 58 per cent of those who are covered by private health insurance support private hospitals as opposed to 43 per cent of those without it.

These figures show that membership of private health insurance schemes is associated with the belief that private medicine is socially beneficial. This is perhaps not particularly surprising, since this belief equates self-interest with public interest, which is a comfortable view to hold. It is still some distance from support for privatising health care as a political principle. That would require health care *generally* to be provided privately (as in the USA), a proposition tested in this question:

> *It has been suggested that the National Health Service should be available only to those with lower incomes. This would mean that contributions and taxes could be lower and most people would take out medical insurance or pay for health care. Do you support or oppose this idea?*

In 1989, only 22 per cent said they supported the idea of a 'two-tier' NHS, and 74 per cent opposed it. But again, if we look at the responses of those with and without private health insurance, there does appear to be an 'interest effect': the idea of mainly private health care with a 'safety-net' NHS is supported by

28 per cent of those with insurance, compared to 20 per cent of those without it. The full breakdown (in **Table 8.1**) confirms that there is a difference between the insured and the uninsured even when class is taken into account. But the 'interest effect' of private health insurance is smaller on this question than it was on more specific ones. And, even among those with a vested interest in private provision, there is still only minority support for a private system *per se*. People with private health insurance are certainly in favour of its existence, but not as an alternative to NHS provision for all – or, for that matter, for themselves when they need it.

But the key question remains: does the 'privatisation of interests' lead to a change in attitudes over time? No amount of data can prove that one causes the other, since it could be that those who hold individualist views are more likely to take out insurance anyway, or *vice versa*. At least some evidence for the causal mechanism, however, would be some concurrence between the spread of private medical insurance and an increase in individualist attitudes to health care. For instance, a *prima facie* case could be constructed by looking at trends in responses to the two-tier NHS question back to 1983, since which time there has been a rise from 11 per cent to 15 per cent in the proportion of respondents covered by private health insurance. One might anticipate that this growth in take-up would be accompanied by a growth in support for the principle of private medicine. Yet, as the table below shows, support for the privatisation of health care actually reached a six-year low in 1989, and opposition reached a six-year high.

	1983	1984	1986	1987	1989
	%	%	%	%	%
% supporting and opposing 'two-tier'					
health provision:					
Support	29	23	27	26	22
Oppose	64	70	67	68	74

There is, of course, some fluctuation from year to year, but there is certainly no evidence of a shift towards the individualist position; on the contrary, the trend appears to be in the opposite direction. This is confirmed in answers to two questions which touch more directly on the interests of those with private health insurance, and which might be expected to show an even greater 'interest effect' over the five-year period. Here the movement is less marked; but, once again, it is certainly not in an individualist direction.

	1984	1989
% agreeing that private medical	%	%
treatment . . .		
. . . should be abolished	9	12
. . . should be allowed (only) in private		
hospitals	48	50
. . . should be allowed in private and		
NHS hospitals	39	35
% agreeing that GPs . . .	%	%
. . . should be free to take on private		
patients	59	54
. . . should not be free to do so	36	41

Chapter 1 charts the steady rise in general dissatisfaction with the NHS between 1983 and 1989. As dissatisfaction with public provision increases, we might expect to have seen support for private provision growing too. It is even more surprising then that this does not appear to have happened. So the spread of private health insurance should not be confused with the spread of Thatcherite individualism. More people may be having private operations now, because they can afford insurance and it is in their interest to jump the queue. But the majority of people still believes it is in both their own and the public's interest to have more resources spent on the NHS to prevent it from being undermined by either competition or attrition.

Education

Attitudes towards private education are similar to those towards private health care. Broadly, public opinion accepts private schools, but is not keen to see the private sector expand. We have no figures for 1989 because this module of questions was not fielded in that year. However, attitudes in 1987 differed little from those held in 1983 (though there were fluctuations in between), as the table below shows.

	1983	1987
There should be . . .	%	%
. . . more private schools	11	11
. . . about the same number as now	67	65
. . . fewer or no private schools	19	21
If there were fewer private schools . . .	%	%
. . . state schools would suffer	18	16
. . . state schools would benefit	18	20
. . . it would make no difference	59	60

Those who oppose private education outnumber those who support it, but the majority thinks that the balance between private and state provision is about right. Similarly, those who see the private sector as a threat to the quality of state education slightly outnumber those who take the opposite view, but the majority thinks that the amount of private education makes no difference.

Not surprisingly, people with children at private schools are more likely to say there should be more private schools, and less likely to say they should be abolished or their number restricted. Thus, in 1987, 20 per cent of parents with children at state schools said there should be "fewer" or "no private schools at all", as against only seven per cent of parents of private-school children. Conversely, only nine per cent of state-school parents wanted "more private schools", as against 22 per cent of private-school parents.* Further details are shown in **Table 8.2**.

However, these questions measure only a direct interest in private education. Another question tests the principle rather better. Effectively it asks respondents to choose between strict egalitarianism on the one hand and the admission of inequality on the other – in the provision of education, as well as in health care and pensions. We first asked:

---

* Because of the small numbers of parents with children at private schools it is not possible to control for the effects of class.

Do you think that health care should be the same for everyone, or should people who can afford it be able to pay for better health care?

The question was then repeated in respect of "the quality of education" and "pensions".

	1986	1989
Health care should be:	%	%
Same for everyone	46	50
Better for those able to pay	53	49
The quality of education should be:	%	%
Same for everyone	47	52
Better for those able to pay	52	46
Pensions should be:	%	%
Same for everyone	36	33
Better for those able to pay	61	63

These questions are not strictly a test of individualism *versus* collectivism. Those replying "same for everyone" are clearly collectivists on these issues. But those who say people should be "able to pay" for better quality are not all individualists. As we have seen, strong support for collective provision can co-exist with a toleration of, and even a desire for, private provision. So those who say that people *should* be able to pay for better provision include liberal collectivists as well as true individualists.

The balance of opinion on the question of equality in education is remarkably similar to that on health care – evenly divided, and in both cases showing a small swing towards egalitarianism between 1986 and 1989 (although too much should' not be made of just two readings). The balance of opinion on pensions is against egalitarianism, though perhaps the size of the 'leveller' minority here is surprisingly large, given the difficulty in practice of *preventing* people from providing themselves with their own pensions.

In **Table 8.3**, the 1989 answers on education and health are analysed by those with children at private schools and those with children at state schools, and those with and without health insurance. Once again the subsample of private-school parents is too small to be reliably representative, although an 'interest effect' appears to operate here, as it does on the question on health care. It is possible that collectivist attitudes to education are harder to undermine than those to health care, since private schools may be seen to confer a permanent social advantage, while private health care is seen as more of a perk. However, the evidence here is inconclusive.

Council housing sales

The most apparently successful of Conservative policies designed to change people's values and votes by a strategy of 'privatisation of interests' is the sale of council houses. This strategy is recognised by supporters and opponents alike. The Marxist argument on home ownership is put most simply by Cynthia Cockburn (1977, p.45): "Successive governments have used owner-occupation purposively as an inducement to workers to identify with bourgeois values."

The sale of a million and a half homes since 1979 has had a noticeable effect on the pattern of tenure in Britain, and an impact on a significant slice of the electorate. Of our 1989 sample, eight per cent owned a home they had bought as council tenants, and a further four per cent were tenants who said they were "likely to buy at some time in the future".

However, since 1983 at least, attitudes to the 'right to buy' policy have been stable. Only a small minority (one in ten) would abandon the policy altogether, although a further third would impose some restrictions on sales. More than half think council tenants should generally be allowed to buy their homes. This distribution of attitudes has been more or less unchanged between 1983 and 1989, and Gallup poll evidence suggests that attitudes have been stable over a period of more than 20 years. In 1979, 74 per cent thought "selling more council houses to tenants" was a good idea (Gallup Political Index, May 1979); in 1967, exactly the same percentage approved of "local authorities willing to sell council houses to the occupiers" (Gallup, 1976).

Council tenants . . .	1983 %	1985 %	1989 %
. . . should not be allowed to buy	11	9	11
. . . should be allowed to buy only in areas with no housing shortage	31	29	33
. . . should generally be allowed to buy	57	60	56

Despite this stability, there is a very strong association between a personal interest in, and support for, council house sales. On this issue, those people who have bought their council homes or who might do so, are nearly unanimous in their individualism:

		1989 Pro-sales	Anti-sales*
Buyers and likely buyers	%	89	11
Other renters	%	53	47
Other owners	%	50	48

*Including those who want to restrict sales in areas of housing shortage

It is interesting that those who have no direct interest in council house sales have similar views – evenly divided between 'individualists' and 'collectivists' – regardless of whether they own or rent. The detailed breakdown (in **Table 8.4**) shows further that attitudes to council house sales do not vary according to class.

What we do *not* know is whether having an interest in council house sales affects general political values. As Heath, Jowell and Curtice (1985, pp.46–8) point out, people who were already inclined to the Conservatives may well be those most inclined to buy their homes. Nonetheless, their work does establish that housing tenure is associated with political values independently of (though less strongly than) class. In particular, they note that attitudes to the redistribution of income and wealth are highly associated with housing tenure. Even so, they establish through panel data (Heath *et al*, forthcoming) that the short-term political consequences of buying a council house are rather small. The effect does not seem to be to *increase* their propensity either to vote Conservative or to adopt individualist values on issues *other than* housing.

Kemeny (1981) argues that differing levels of owner-occupation explain differing levels of support for state welfare provision. Using Australia, Sweden and Britain as examples, he points out that Australia has a high level of owner-occupation and low support for welfare, while Sweden has a low rate of owner-occupation and high support for welfare. But Britain does not properly fit the scheme: it has a high rate of owner-occupation and middling attitudes to welfare.

Saunders (1990) is unable to find a relationship between tenure and attitudes to welfare spending in general. But he does raise the interesting question of the effect of housing inheritance on political attitudes. A long-term panel survey would be needed to establish whether or not there is such a link, but it would be fascinating to monitor the impact over time, if any, of inheritance on the long-run attitudes of the home-owning majority of the population. Over the limited time-span of the *British Social Attitudes* series, we find no evidence of a causal link between ownership and individualism.

State ownership and share ownership

According to Gallup (1976), further nationalisation has been unpopular since 1948, although it took the Labour Party 40 years to acknowledge it. The *British Social Attitudes* surveys took to the field just in time to witness the beginnings of its partial rehabilitation. From being very unpopular in 1983, it is now only mildly unpopular, as further privatisation is too. A majority favours leaving things as they are.

State ownership of industry

% saying:	1983 %	1984 %	1985 %	1986 %	1987 %	1989 %
There should be less	49	36	31	30	30	24
There should be more	11	10	13	16	16	18
There should be about the same amount as now	33	50	51	49	48	53
Don't know	7	4	5	5	5	5

Clearly, the responses to this question have been affected by the extent of the privatisation programme: people believe there is simply less and less for the government to sell anyway. However, was the government right in believing that the sale of shares in privatised companies to the wider public would help to create new values, converting people to what the present Conservative Party chairman approvingly calls "acquisitive individualism"?

There is some *prima facie* evidence for an 'interest effect' on share owners. In 1989, twice as many share owners (29 per cent) thought there should be less state ownership of industry as thought there should be more (14 per cent), while non-share owners were more or less equally divided. The full breakdown in **Table 8.5** confirms that share owners are more individualist regardless of class. But, once again, as Heath *et al* (forthcoming) point out, the people who went ahead and bought shares were probably more individualist in the first place. They find little evidence from their panel data to show that share purchase has transformed the political values of the purchasers.

There is another route through which the 'interest effect' could operate. Those who work (or whose partner works) in nationalised industries may have different attitudes to privatisation from those of other employees. The breakdown, given in full in **Table 8.5**, confirms that they are more likely to oppose privatisation, perhaps seeing their job security enhanced by state ownership. In 1989, the views of those who worked for a nationalised industry, or were married to or living with a worker in a nationalised industry, were almost the reverse of the population as a whole. Among them, less state ownership was supported by 18 per cent, more state ownership by 25 per cent. But even so the great majority of this group supports the *status quo*.

As in other areas, however, the 'interest effect' does not seem to have changed attitudes, at least in the short term. Nor does it appear to have an influence over voting behaviour. Curtice (1987) reports that in the 1987 general election, voters who had acquired shares since 1983 voted no differently from those who had not, and this finding is confirmed in the panel data from 1983–1987, reported in Heath *et al*, (forthcoming).

Conclusion

Successive Conservative governments since 1979 have tried to change public values in respect of issues such as private health care, private schools, the sale of council homes and share ownership, in order to recruit new supporters to the ideology of individualism. We have to report that so far the strategy does not appear to have succeeded.

True, those who have an interest in private health or education or whatever are more likely to support it in principle. But that is hardly surprising. The point is that the major growth in private provision and private ownership over the past 10 years does not seem to have led to increased support for individualism. Instead, it seems, the very people who *already* hold views favourable to private provision and ownership are the ones who tend to 'go private'. So the net effect on values is almost nil.

On the basis of work by Heath, Jowell and Curtice (1985), we might expect the social changes that derive from home ownership and the decline in trade union membership to harm the Labour Party and help the Conservatives in the long run. But that is a different causative chain. What we have examined here, in these preliminary analyses, is the effect of the 'enterprise culture' on the national psyche, the extent to which the present government seems to have won the hearts and minds of the electorate to its individualist values. And our conclusion is that it has not done so – at least not yet.

Moreover, as environmental problems and 'green' issues grow in prominence (see Chapter 4) it may be that the popularity of individualism as a credo will decline. After all, pollution and congestion are classic examples of what Hirsch (1977) called the "tyranny of small decisions". Increasingly, people may be driven to accept that a key role of government is to limit individual actions that adversely affect us collectively. The fact that younger people are especially inclined to these sorts of views makes it even less likely that the ideology of individualism will gain ground over time. On the contrary, collectivist values appear still to be deeply rooted.

Notes

1. Equally individualism need not necessarily be a Conservative value. If it is morally liberal, it produces libertarianism, shading into anarchism. It is the combination of moral traditionalism and individualism that is associated with free-market conservatism (see Note 3 below).
2. Earlier *British Social Attitudes* surveys confirm that class interest, and not moral values (such as attitudes to welfare dependency), is the most important factor dividing the parties in British politics. Of the 18 statements which most sharply divided Labour from Conservative supporters in 1985 and 1986, 14 were to do with class interest – the other four were to do with American nuclear weapons on British soil and socialist planning *versus* private enterprise (*The 1986 Report*, p.48; *The 1987 Report*, p.174).
3. Heath *et al*, (1987, p.28) show how attitudes to social security are more closely related to authoritarian attitudes than to views about redistribution. This demonstrates how moral individualism can provide the basis for an economic philosophy of the free market.

References

COCKBURN, C., *The Local State*, Pluto Press, London (1977).

CURTICE, J., 'Political partisanship', in Jowell, R., Witherspoon, S. and Brook, L., *British Social Attitudes: the 1986 Report*, Gower, Aldershot, (1986).

CURTICE, J., 'Must Labour lose?', *New Society* (19 June 1987).

GALLUP, G.H. (ed.), *The Gallup International Public Opinion Polls: Great Britain 1937-1975*, Random House, New York (1976).

HEATH, A., JOWELL, R. and CURTICE, J., *How Britain Votes,* Pergamon Press, Oxford (1985).

HEATH, A., JOWELL, R., CURTICE, J. and WITHERSPOON, S., *British Election Study Follow-up Interviews*, SCPR, London (1987).

HEATH, A., JOWELL, R., CURTICE, J., EVANS, G., FIELD, J. and WITHERSPOON, S., *Understanding Political Change: the British Voter 1964–1987*, Pergamon Press, Oxford (forthcoming).

HIRSCH, F., *The Social Limits to Growth*, Routledge & Kegan Paul, London (1977).

KEMENY, J., *The Myth of Home Ownership*, Routledge & Kegan Paul, London (1981).

RENTOUL, J., *Me and Mine: The Triumph of the New Individualism?*, Unwin Hyman, London (1989).

SAUNDERS, P., *A Nation of Home Owners*, Unwin Hyman, London (1990).

8.1 PRIVATE MEDICAL TREATMENT AND THE NHS (Q75a,b Q78) by compressed Goldthorpe class schema within respondent's private medical insurance

	TOTAL	NOT INSURED				RESPONDENT HAS PRIVATE MEDICAL INSURANCE			
		All	Salariat	Intermediate	Working	All	Salariat	Intermediate	Working
	%	%	%	%	%	%	%	%	%
THE EXISTENCE OF PRIVATE MEDICAL TREATMENT IN NATIONAL HEALTH SERVICE HOSPITALS IS:									
A good thing for the NHS ('INDIVIDUALISTS')	24	21	27	25	15	38	41	40	28
A bad thing for the NHS ('COLLECTIVISTS')	47	49	47	47	51	37	36	35	44
Makes no difference to the NHS	24	25	23	23	27	22	19	23	24
THE EXISTENCE OF PRIVATE MEDICAL TREATMENT IN PRIVATE HOSPITALS IS:	%	%	%	%	%	%	%	%	%
A good thing for the NHS ('INDIVIDUALISTS')	38	36	43	40	29	55	59	59	34
A bad thing for the NHS ('COLLECTIVISTS')	21	22	27	19	23	16	15	14	28
Makes no difference to the NHS	36	38	31	37	41	27	24	28	33
THE NATIONAL HEALTH SERVICE SHOULD BE AVAILABLE ONLY TO THOSE WITH LOWER INCOMES:	%	%	%	%	%	%	%	%	%
Support ('INDIVIDUALISTS')	22	20	15	21	23	28	24	36	16
Oppose ('COLLECTIVISTS')	74	75	82	74	71	69	74	61	84
Don't know	4	5	3	4	6	3	3	3	-
BASE: ALL RESPONDENTS									
Weighted	*2930*	*2490*	*490*	*887*	*964*	*439*	*199*	*174*	*50*
Unweighted	*3029*	*2563*	*509*	*910*	*988*	*463*	*207*	*184*	*57*

8.2 PRIVATE EDUCATION, 1987 (Q73a)
by compressed Goldthorpe class schema within children's education

1987	TOTAL	CHILD AT STATE SCHOOL					CHILD AT PRIVATE SCHOOL			
		All	Salariat	Intermediate	Working		All	Salariat	Intermediate	Working
	%	%	%	%	%		%	%	%	%
THERE SHOULD BE:										
More private schools	11	9	11	11	7		22	(28)	(19)	(22)
About the same number as now	65	67	65	69	67		70	(63)	(74)	(69)
Fewer private schools	11	11	11	7	13		2	(2)	(2)	(-)
No private schools at all	11	9	11	8	10		5	(5)	(5)	(9)
Other	1	1	1	1	1		2	(2)	(-)	(-)
Don't know	2	3	1	3	3		-	(-)	(-)	(-)
BASE: ALL RESPONDENTS Weighted	2766	958	204	348	378		112	(48)	(43)	(11)
Unweighted	2847	966	197	361	379		120	52	(46)	(13)

8.3 PRIVATE MEDICAL TREATMENT AND PRIVATE EDUCATION (B95a,b) by compressed Goldthorpe class schema within respondent's private medical insurance or children's education

SHOULD HEALTH CARE BE THE SAME FOR EVERYONE, OR SHOULD PEOPLE WHO CAN AFFORD IT BE ABLE TO PAY FOR BETTER HEALTH CARE?

	TOTAL	NOT INSURED				PRIVATE INSURANCE			
		All	Salariat	Intermediate	Working	All	Salariat	Intermediate	Working
	%	%	%	%	%	%	%	%	%
Same for everyone ('COLLECTIVISTS')	50	52	55	48	53	39	38	31	(51)
Better for those able to pay ('INDIVIDUALISTS')	49	46	44	51	45	61	62	69	(49)
Don't know	1	2	1	1	2	-	-	-	(-)
BASE: B RESPONDENTS Weighted	1461	1213	255	429	474	248	100	97	(27)
Unweighted	1516	1269	262	446	486	246	106	103	(30)

SHOULD THE QUALITY OF EDUCATION BE THE SAME FOR ALL CHILDREN, OR SHOULD PARENTS WHO CAN AFFORD IT BE ABLE TO PAY FOR BETTER EDUCATION?

	TOTAL	CHILD AT STATE SCHOOL				CHILD AT PRIVATE SCHOOL			
		All	Salariat	Intermediate	Working	All	Salariat	Intermediate	Working
	%	%	%	%	%	%	%	%	%
Same for everyone ('COLLECTIVISTS')	52	57	54	52	64	43	(51)	(39)	(18)
Better for those able to pay ('INDIVIDUALISTS')	46	42	44	48	34	57	(49)	(56)	(82)
Don't know	1	2	2	1	2	2	(-)	(5)	(-)
BASE: B RESPONDENTS Weighted	1461	489	112	190	175	53	(25)	(20)	(8)
Unweighted	1516	495	108	195	180	56	(28)	(19)	(9)

8.4 COUNCIL HOUSE SALES (B224b)
by compressed Goldthorpe class schema within housing tenure

Council tenants...	TOTAL	OTHER HOMEOWNERS*				LOCAL AUTHORITY BUYERS/ LIKELY BUYERS+				OTHER RENTERS**			
		All	Salariat	Intermediate	Working	All	Salariat	Intermediate	Working	All	Salariat	Intermediate	Working
	%	%	%	%	%	%	%	%	%	%	%	%	%
should not be allowed to buy their houses or flats	10	12	13	11	9	*	(-)	(*)	-	15	(13)	(11)	15
should be allowed to buy but only in areas with no housing shortage	33	37	38	38	36	11	(6)	(12)	11	32	(36)	(26)	35
ALL 'COLLECTIVISTS'	43	48	50	49	45	11	(6)	(12)	11	47	(50)	(38)	50
should generally be allowed to buy their houses or flats ('INDIVIDUALISTS')	56	50	49	51	53	89	(94)	(88)	89	53	(51)	(63)	50
BASE: B RESPONDENTS Weighted	1255	791	264	338	156	161	(17)	(49)	93	213	(20)	(45)	135
Unweighted	1297	826	274	356	163	162	(17)	(49)	94	220	(19)	(48)	138

*   OTHER HOMEOWNERS = Respondent's household currently owns accommodation and did not buy from the local authority as a tenant

+   LOCAL AUTHORITY BUYERS/LIKELY BUYERS = Current accommodation was bought from the local authority as a tenant, OR respondent rents from local authority and is very or quite likely to buy current accommodation at some time in the future

** OTHER RENTERS = Respondent's household currently rents accommodation (not from the local authority), OR rents from the local authority but is not likely to buy the accommodation

8.5 STATE OWNERSHIP OF INDUSTRY (Q16)
by compressed Goldthorpe class schema within share ownership, and employment in nationalised industry

ON THE WHOLE, WOULD YOU LIKE TO SEE MORE OR LESS STATE OWNERSHIP OF INDUSTRY, OR ABOUT THE SAME AMOUNT AS NOW?	TOTAL	NON-SHARE OWNER				SHARE OWNER			
		All	Salariat	Intermediate	Working	All	Salariat	Intermediate	Working
	%	%	%	%	%	%	%	%	%
More ('COLLECTIVISTS')	18	19	22	17	19	14	13	11	19
Less ('INDIVIDUALISTS')	24	22	26	23	20	29	33	30	19
About the same amount	53	52	50	54	53	55	52	55	60
Don't know/not answered	6	7	2	6	8	3	1	4	3
Base: All respondents									
Weighted	2930	2147	389	746	878	761	291	309	133
Unweighted	3029	2195	401	761	897	810	306	327	145

	TOTAL	NOT EMPLOYED IN NATIONALISED INDUSTRY				RESPONDENT/PARTNER WORKS IN NATIONALISED INDUSTRY			
		All	Salariat	Intermediate	Working	All	Salariat	Intermediate	Working
	%	%	%	%	%	%	%	%	%
More ('COLLECTIVISTS')	18	17	18	15	17	25	(20)	20	30
Less ('INDIVIDUALISTS')	24	24	29	26	20	18	(36)	17	14
About the same amount	53	54	52	54	54	53	(42)	60	49
Don't know/not answered	6	5	1	6	8	4	(2)	3	6
Base: All respondents									
Weighted	2930	2409	623	858	882	296	(45)	115	128
Unweighted	3029	2486	643	881	915	298	(48)	116	126

9 The Northern Irish dimension

John Curtice and Tony Gallagher*

Northern Ireland is an integral part of the United Kingdom. Yet most supposedly 'nationwide' surveys are limited to England, Scotland and Wales. This is true not only of major academic studies such as the *British General Election Study* series, but also of some government time-series such as the *General Household Survey* (for which there is a complementary but separate survey in Northern Ireland). The European Commission, for its surveys such as the *Eurobarometer* series, treats the United Kingdom (uniquely among the member states of the EC) as two separate entities – Britain and Northern Ireland.

The first five surveys in the *British Social Attitudes* series did not extend to Northern Ireland either. However, this omission was rectified in 1989 when, with funding from the Central Community Relations Unit and the Nuffield Foundation, we were able to conduct a separate social attitudes survey in Northern Ireland (and shall do so again in two further rounds of the series). Many of the questions included on the *Northern Ireland Social Attitudes* questionnaire were also asked in one or both versions of the questionnaire fielded in Britain. So we have an unusual opportunity to compare the attitudes of people living in Northern Ireland with those in Britain, across a wide range of social, economic and political issues.

On some matters there is much to support the claim that Northern Ireland is different from Britain – and that the difference matters. Different political parties dominate elections from those in Britain. The United Kingdom (matched in Europe only by Belgium) is thus a single state with two separate party systems. Moreover, the rhetoric of political debate in Northern Ireland is dominated by disagreements about its constitutional position – whether or not the province should indeed remain part of the United Kingdom, and if so what its relationship with Westminster should be. Indeed this controversy has, since 1969, occasioned

* John Curtice is Senior Lecturer in Politics, University of Strathclyde; Tony Gallagher is a Research Officer in the Centre for the Study of Conflict, University of Ulster.

some of the most serious and sustained intercommunal violence in the developed world. Although constitutional questions and issues of national identity are not entirely absent from politics in the rest of the United Kingdom, they have not so far posed any substantial threat to the ability of the state to maintain civil order. In any event, such issues have nearly always been subsidiary to the debates over socio-economic concerns which are articulated by the Conservative and Labour parties. A comparison of social attitudes in Northern Ireland and Britain is thus of considerable academic and practical interest.

We approach our task under six main headings. First, we compare and contrast the social composition of the populations of Northern Ireland and Britain. How different are they in terms of their religious affinities and practices, the economic position of their members and so on. Secondly, we focus on one area of apparent obvious difference between the two parts of the UK – the political parties and the substance of political controversy. Thirdly, we look at the distribution of class and national identities. Fourthly, we examine social attitudes more generally, and compare the two populations' attitudes to a range of economic, social and moral issues. Fifthly, we return to the more distinctive issues of Northern Irish society, and consider attitudes on both sides of the Irish Sea to a number of constitutional questions, including trust in government and beliefs about the evenhandedness of institutions in the province. And finally we consider the current state of relations between Protestants and Catholics.

Social background

Religion

The political and social divide in Northern Ireland is commonly described as being between Protestant and Catholic communities. Religion has remained at the forefront of political and social life to a far greater extent than in most of the rest of Western Europe, and certainly more than in Britain. For instance, in 1989, only 12 per cent of people in Northern Ireland said that they did not have a religion, compared with 34 per cent in Britain. Further, 54 per cent of people in Northern Ireland claimed to attend church at least once a week, compared with just 13 per cent in Britain. Indeed, church attendance in Northern Ireland is higher than anywhere else in Western Europe (including Italy and Spain) except for the Republic of Ireland (Harding and Phillips, 1986).

While Northern Ireland, unlike the Republic, is predominantly Protestant, the size of the Catholic minority there is much greater than it is in Britain.[1] Within the Protestant denominations Presbyterians form the largest group, reflecting the fact that many Protestants are descended from immigrants from Scotland where Presbyterianism is the established denomination.*

---

* The Anglican Church in Northern Ireland is the Church of Ireland.

	Northern Ireland %	Great Britain %
% giving religious affiliation as:		
Catholic	36	11
Protestant (total)	(49)	(49)
Presbyterian	23	5
Anglican	18	37
Other Protestant	8	7
Other Christian (unspecified)	2	4
Non-Christian	*	2
None	12	34

In Northern Ireland, as is generally the case (including in Britain), Catholics are much more frequent church attenders than are Protestants. But the importance of religion in Northern Irish life is underscored by the fact that religious attendance by Catholics in the province is far higher than that of their counterparts on the other side of the Irish Sea.

	Northern Ireland	Great Britain
% of each denomination attending church at least once a week:		
Catholic	86%	42%
Protestant (total)	(44%)	(15%)
Anglican	35%	7%
Other Protestant	49%	32%

But church attendance is not the only measure of the importance of religion in Northern Irish life. In a number of areas of social life, contact between Protestants and Catholics is very limited, a situation which is often thought to exacerbate the division between them (see also Whyte, 1986). Most striking is the lack of intermarriage between members of the two religions.* Only six per cent of married people in Northern Ireland say that their spouse is not of the same religion, compared with 20 per cent in Britain. Similarly only five per cent say that their mother's religion is different from their father's, compared with 15 per cent in Britain.

Moreover, nearly all schools in Northern Ireland reflect either a Protestant or a Catholic ethos. The last major piece of research into the extent of educational segregation in the province (Darby et al, 1977) found that 71 per cent of schools were either wholly Protestant or wholly Catholic, that only five per cent of Protestant schools had more than 1 in 20 Catholic pupils, and that only two per cent of Catholic schools had more than 1 in 20 Protestant pupils. We asked respondents whether they had ever attended "a mixed or integrated school, with fairly large numbers of both Catholics and Protestants". Just 24 per cent claim to have attended such a school, many of whom are probably referring to schools where there was in fact no more than a small minority-group presence. A similar proportion of those with school-age children say that their child or children attends (or has attended) a mixed school.

In other areas of social life the separation of the two religions is not quite

---

* We use the term 'religion' in both the questionnaire and this chapter to denote the distinction between Protestantism and Catholicism in Northern Ireland.

so stark. For instance, only a minority of employees report that all or most of their colleagues or workmates belong to the same religion as themselves, and four out of five respondents report that they have at least one friend of a different religion. But neighbourhood segregation in the province remains, with a majority of respondents saying that all or most of the people in their neighbourhood belong to the same religion as themselves.

All this being so, the description of Northern Ireland as being divided into Protestant and Catholic 'communities' is clearly apt. The degree of social interaction between the two communities is very limited.

		Northern Ireland		
		Religious affiliation		
	All	Catholic	Protestant	None
% saying all or most are same religion as themselves	%	%	%	%
Relatives:				
All	42	42	47	22
Most	41	41	40	46
Neighbours:	%	%	%	%
All	31	35	30	22
Most	31	27	35	25
Friends:	%	%	%	%
All	18	18	19	10
Most	47	45	51	37
Workmates:	%	%	%	%
All	16	23	13	11
Most	25	21	29	24

Yet although religion is clearly a predominant (and divisive) feature of Northern Irish life, there are some signs that its hold may have weakened a little. Up to now, Ireland – North and South – has been exceptional in Western Europe for having apparently held out against the gradual decline in religious attendance and in adherence to church teachings experienced elsewhere. However, comparison of the results of this latest survey with two earlier academic surveys – one in 1968 (Rose, 1971) and one in 1978 (Moxon-Browne, 1983) – reveals that there has been some weakening in the importance of religion in the province.

The first indication is in the proportion of people who profess no religion. Only 4 out of the 1,291 persons interviewed in the 1968 survey said that they did not have a religion. By 1978, three per cent of respondents claimed to have no religious affiliation, while in our survey, 12 per cent say they have no religion.

The second piece of evidence is the reported level of church attendance, although the story is not entirely straightforward. Among the population as a whole the reported level of regular church attendance has remained steady since 1978 (though lower than in 1968). But the slow decline among Catholics between 1968 and 1978 continued. And while regular attendance among Protestants has increased since 1978, there has also been a continued increase in the proportion of Protestants who never go to church (from five per cent in 1968 to 15 per cent in 1989).

Northern Ireland

| | All+ | Religious affiliation | |
		Catholic	Protestant
Church attendance:			
1968*	%	%	%
Once a week or more	66	95	46
Never	4	1	5
1978**	%	%	%
Once a week or more	53	90	39
Never	10	3	10
1989	%	%	%
Once a week or more	54	86	44
Never	16	3	15

* Source: Rose (1971); ** Source: Moxon-Browne (1983).
+ Total column includes those who have no religion.

Finally, we should also note that, as is usual elsewhere in Western Europe, younger people are less likely to be religious than older people. Nineteen per cent of those aged under 35 never attend church, compared with 14 per cent of those aged over 54; moreover, 47 per cent of young people attend once a week or more compared with 61 per cent of those aged 35–54 and 55 per cent of the over 55s.

It would appear that some younger people are deciding not to follow their parents' religion, or any other religion. It is, of course, possible that these younger people will become more religious with age. But we could well have evidence here that parents are now somewhat less able to transmit their religious beliefs to their children. If so, we can anticipate a further decline in the overall level of church attendance as the more religious older generation is replaced by a less religious new one.[2]

Each of these pieces of evidence has to be treated with caution. There are, in particular, some methodological differences between the two earlier studies and ours which vitiate exact comparability.[3] Nonetheless, together our findings lend considerable weight to the argument that some secularisation of Northern Irish society has taken place. They certainly point to the existence of a sizeable non-religious minority in Northern Ireland.

There are also indications that the influence of religion on the social life of the province may have declined a little. Although still uncommon, intermarriage seems to have become a little more frequent in Northern Ireland over the last 20 years. In the 1968 survey (Rose, 1971) just three per cent of respondents said that their spouse was not of the same religion compared with six per cent now. Further, while 42 per cent of our respondents report that all their relatives belong to the same religion as themselves, the comparable proportions were 65 per cent in the 1978 survey (Moxon-Browne, 1983) and 70 per cent in the 1968 survey.

It also appears that the extent of neighbourhood segregation has diminished in recent years and returned to the level it was before the outbreak of the 'Troubles'. The proportion saying that all or most of their neighbours belong to the same religion is around 10 percentage points lower than in the 1978 survey and similar to that in the 1968 survey. Integration of workplaces also seems to have increased somewhat.[4] None of the changes is large, and Northern Ireland is clearly still a society deeply divided by religion. But in general the results of our survey point to some narrowing in recent years of the divide between the two communities.

Social class

Just as religion is considered to be the most important feature of social and political life in Northern Ireland, so social class is often reckoned to be the most important source of social division in Britain – although the extent to which this is true and, indeed, what is meant by social class have been the subject of considerable dispute (see, for example, Franklin, 1985; Marshall *et al*, 1988, and Heath, 1981). Our data show differences between Northern Ireland and Britain in their respective class profiles, but they are not nearly so marked as in the case of religion. Northern Ireland does though have a larger working class and a smaller salariat than Britain.[5]

	Northern Ireland	Great Britain
Social class:	%	%
Salariat	17	23
Routine non-manual	16	23
Petty bourgeoisie	14	8
Foremen and technicians	5	6
Working class	39	35

In addition, 18 per cent of people in Northern Ireland are self-employed in their current or last job compared with 13 per cent in Britain, reflecting to some extent the greater importance of agriculture in the Northern Irish economy. Six per cent of the Northern Irish labour force are farmers – who form part of the 'petty bourgeoisie', and a further one and a half per cent are agricultural workers; these two groups combined form only one per cent of the British workforce.

Despite the somewhat larger working class than Britain, the penetration of trade unions (traditionally the organised expression of working class interests) is rather weaker. Eighteen per cent of respondents in Northern Ireland state that they are trade union members compared with 23 per cent in Britain. Again, this difference is not very large but since white collar workers in Northern Ireland are, according to our data, *more* likely to be trade union members than are manual workers, the extent of working class trade unionism in the province is even lower than the overall figures imply.

Income and social benefits

It is not surprising to discover that, on a number of indicators, Northern Ireland is poorer than Britain. Throughout the post-war period unemployment has been persistently higher in Northern Ireland than in the rest of the UK.* On our

* In April 1989 when our two surveys were in the field, government figures put the rate of unemployment in Northern Ireland at 15.6 per cent compared with 6.4 per cent in Britain.

figures, average household income in Northern Ireland is substantially lower than the average for Britain:

	Northern Ireland	Great Britain
Household income before		
deductions:	%	%
Less than £5,000 pa	26	18
£5,000–£7,999 pa	19	13
£8,000–£11,999 pa	14	14
£12,000–£17,999 pa	14	17
£18,000 pa or more	16	25

One consequence of the weaker economic structure of Northern Ireland is that the state is a more important source of income compared with Britain. For example, in 1989, seven per cent of Northern Irish respondents were in receipt of Family Credit, compared with under three per cent in Britain; 19 per cent received Income Support compared with 11 per cent in Britain. This pattern continues right through to retirement: just over half (57 per cent) of retired people in Britain reported that they were in receipt of a pension from their former employers, compared with just over a third (35 per cent) in Northern Ireland.

Moreover, the importance of the state in the economy of Northern Ireland is not confined to transfer payments: it is also a more dominant source of employment and a larger provider of services than it is in Britain. For instance, central and local government employ a higher proportion of the workforce in the province than in Britain, and council housing accounts for a higher proportion of tenures. Similarly, while 15 per cent of people in Britain reported (in 1989) that they had private health insurance, only six per cent did so in Northern Ireland.

The importance of the state in the Northern Irish economy indicates that the constitutional position of the province is not just of symbolic significance. Its residents have, of course, access to UK welfare provision which is at a higher level than afforded by the Republic, and overall the province benefits from a substantial net inflow of government expenditure. Not surprisingly, unionist politicians have cited these factors in favour of a continued link with Britain.

Linking religion, class and income

All these differences between the social *characteristics* of Britain and Northern Ireland clearly raise a number of important questions about how social *attitudes* might differ between the two countries. Does, for instance, the importance of religion in Northern Irish life influence attitudes to other issues? And does Northern Ireland's more working class character, together with the greater involvement of the state in the province, lead to greater support for government intervention in welfare and in the economy?

Before addressing these issues, however, we should briefly consider how far religion and other social characteristics are interrelated – that is, whether the religious divide is distinct from, or coincidental with, the class divide? It has widely been argued that Protestants have used their economic and political power in Northern Ireland to advance themselves *vis-à-vis* Catholics. How far then are divisions of class, sector and income associated with religion?

First, Catholics are disproportionately located in working-class occupations and are under-represented in the salariat. The association though is modest (see also Eversley, 1989). Forty-seven per cent of the Catholics in our survey were in the working class, compared with 33 per cent of Protestants. And there is indeed also a difference in the class composition of Anglicans (38 per cent working class) and other Protestants (31 per cent). Secondly, one in six economically active Catholics in our survey in 1989 were registered as unemployed compared with only one in ten Protestants. But this is a smaller gap between the two communities than found in earlier surveys and would appear to confirm other evidence that the gap may have narrowed somewhat in the recent past, though it should be treated with some caution.[6] It is also not nearly so wide as the gap between the salariat (four per cent unemployed) and the working class (25 per cent). Thirdly, as the table below indicates, Protestants have somewhat higher average household incomes than Catholics. But even so nearly one half of Protestants reported household incomes of less than £8,000 a year and there were almost as many households with an income of less than £5,000 a year among Protestants as among Catholics. In fact the group with the highest average household income in Northern Ireland is the one professing no religious affiliation.

Northern Ireland

| | | Religious affiliation | | |
	All	**Catholic**	**Protestant**	**None**
Social class:	%	%	%	%
Salariat	17	13	18	30
Working class	39	45	33	44
Gross household income:*	%	%	%	%
Less than £8,000 pa	50	59	47	42
£18,000 pa or more	18	15	21	20

But the gap between Catholic and Protestant living standards is rather wider than these overall figures imply. First, on our data, Protestant households contain on average only 2.7 persons compared with 3.6 persons in the case of Catholics – so Protestant incomes do not in general have to stretch quite as far as Catholic ones do. Secondly, the gap looks artificially narrow because Protestants are much more likely to be past retirement age. If we look only at respondents aged under 65, around two in five Protestant households have incomes below £8,000 a year compared with over half of Catholic ones. Similarly, around a quarter of Protestant households had incomes over £18,000 a year compared with around one in six Catholic ones.

It is nonetheless the case that although not dramatic the associations between religion and class, and between religion and income, are clearly stronger in Northern Ireland than in Britain. In Britain Protestants and Catholics are almost equally likely to be members of the salariat or members of the working class. The income gap between Catholics and Protestants is also narrower in Britain than in Northern Ireland. So our data certainly suggest that one's religion has an important influence on one's life chances in the province.

* Those respondents who did not report their income – who were significantly more numerous among Catholics than among Protestants – were excluded from the base on which these percentages were calculated.

Party politics

As we have noted, one of the most striking differences between Britain and Northern Ireland is their party systems. The Labour Party refuses to allow people resident in the province to become members, while the Conservative Party fought the unionists in a parliamentary election for the first time only in 1990. The Liberal Party did fight Northern Irish elections in the 1960s, but more recently the Liberal Democrats have concentrated on fostering relations with the Northern Ireland Alliance Party instead of contesting elections in the province.

Support for 'mainland' parties

Even so, 'mainland' parties are not without support in Northern Ireland. This emerges from responses to our questions on political partisanship which are identical to those asked in Britain. Respondents are asked for their party identification and, since the question does not specify any particular parties, respondents to the *Northern Ireland Social Attitudes* survey are free to name British parties. As many as 27 per cent did. Their choices were as follows:

Political partisanship

	Northern Ireland
% nominating each 'mainland' party:	**%**
Conservative Party	19
Labour Party	7
SLD/SDP	2
Green Party	*

Indeed the Conservative Party received more support than any other single party, surpassing both the Official Unionists (17 per cent) and the SDLP (15 per cent). The Conservative Party has for some time been regarded by many unionist politicians with deep suspicion, following the decisions of successive Conservative governments to implement direct rule, then the Sunningdale Agreement and, more recently, the Anglo–Irish Agreement. Given all this it commands a surprising level of support. Thus the decision by the Conservative Party to contest elections in Northern Ireland may prove more of a threat to the established Northern Irish parties than its initial failure in the 1990 Upper Bann by-election suggested. And the general level of support for mainland parties is an indication that the hold of the Northern Irish parties upon their voters is perhaps not so firm as the intensity of the political conflict in Northern Ireland might lead us to anticipate.

We also wanted to discover the balance of support for the exclusively Northern Irish parties within the province. So those respondents who named a British party in response to our party identification questions were then asked a follow-up question:

> If there were a general election in which only Northern Ireland parties were standing, which one do you think you would be most likely to support?

Responses reveal that Conservative partisans are overwhelmingly unionist, a choice reflecting the party's historic links with unionism before the implementation of direct rule in 1972. Almost half (48 per cent) opted for the Official Unionists (OUP) and 19 per cent for the Democratic Unionists (DUP). Fifteen per cent opted for the non-sectarian Alliance Party, but none chose the main nationalist party, the Social Democratic and Labour Party (SDLP), let alone Sinn Fein. The 59 Labour partisans in the sample were in contrast rather more mixed in their Northern Irish party preferences. Only about a quarter opted for the SDLP (a fellow member of the Socialist International) while the rest spread their support between the other parties (except Sinn Fein) in a manner not dissimilar to that of the now defunct Northern Ireland Labour Party (Rose, 1971).

Support for Northern Irish parties

We summarise below the overall pattern of partisanship for the Northern Irish parties alone:

Political partisanship

	Northern Ireland
%nominating each Northern Ireland party*	**%**
Unionist (total)	(39)
Official Unionist (OUP)	27
Democratic Unionist (DUP)	11
Other Unionist	1
Non-aligned (total)	(10)
(Northern Ireland) Alliance	10
Other	*
Nationalist/Catholic (total)	(23)
SDLP	17
Sinn Fein	3
Workers' Party	3
None	20

* Nine per cent were either unwilling or unable to answer.†

The *Northern Ireland Social Attitudes* survey is not designed to chart or predict voting intentions. Our aim instead is to measure partisanship (or party identification). And a striking finding to emerge from our data is that 20 per cent of people in Northern Ireland say that they do not have a party identification – that is, no longstanding and relatively stable attachment to any one political party or grouping; among Catholics this figure reaches as high as 28 per cent. It contrasts with just seven per cent in Britain – further evidence of the weak hold of the Northern Irish parties upon the electorate. Even among those who *do* identify with a party the reported strength of their identification is rather weaker than in Britain:

	Northern Ireland	Great Britain
Strength of party identification:	**%**	**%**
Very strong	10	12
Fairly strong	30	37
Not very strong	55	47

† The low proportion of Sinn Fein identifiers in our sample means that this survey cannot be used to analyse the attitudes of this section of opinion in the province. Some Sinn Fein identifiers may have been particularly reluctant to declare their allegiance.

Party identification was weak among all Northern Irish parties. It was especially weak however among Alliance identifiers of whom only eight per cent are very strong identifiers. In fact, as with other surveys, the level of Alliance support we recorded is higher than its performance in recent elections; some of the Alliance's potential support would appear to be too frail to withstand the heat of an election battle. In contrast the DUP has a lower proportion of identifiers than voters, suggesting that the personal appeal and charisma of its founder and leader, the Reverend Ian Paisley, have been more important to the Party's electoral success than the enduring appeal of the party *per se*.

It should however be borne in mind that the existing Northern Irish party system is barely 20 years old. Three of the most important parties, the DUP, the SDLP and the Alliance Party were founded only in the years immediately following the outbreak of the troubles in 1968. At the same time, the formerly close relationship between the OUP and the Conservative Party was broken in 1972. Since party identification theory emphasises the importance of a long-term socialisation process in the development and maintenance of party identification, the low level of partisanship in Northern Ireland may reflect no more than the infancy of the parties themselves. However, although the parties may have changed, the issues that dominate Northern Irish politics have not.

Ideological identity

Indeed, rather than form an attachment to a particular political party, people in Northern Ireland appear more inclined to identify with an ideology – either unionist or nationalist. We asked:

> *Generally speaking, do you think of yourself as a unionist, a nationalist or neither?*

Fifty-four per cent of respondents say that they are either unionist or nationalist, compared with just 35 per cent of respondents who declare themselves to be partisans of a particular political party.* This level of ideological identity is similar to the proportion of partisans (51 per cent) in Britain. This tendency to adhere to a general ideological symbol rather than a specific institutional means for its expression has been found in other Western European countries with longstanding political cleavages but unstable party systems (see, for example, Lancaster, forthcoming).

Protestants are, however, more likely to form an ideological identity than are Catholics. Seventy-one per cent of Protestants declare themselves to be unionist, as against the 40 per cent of Catholics who say that they are nationalist. Overall, declared unionists in the population (39 per cent) far outnumber declared nationalists (15 per cent).

The social basis of party politics

Religion is the primary social basis of party politics in Northern Ireland, while social class serves the same role in Britain. So much is commonplace. But it is

---

* 'Partisans' are those identifiers who name a party in response to the first of the sequence of questions used to elicit party identification.

important to underline just how much wider the religious divide is in Northern Ireland than the social class divide is in Britain.[7]

	Northern Ireland Religious affiliation		
	Protestant	Catholic	None
Party identification:	%	%	%
Official Unionist	50	1	13
Democratic Unionist	19	1	10
Alliance	10	7	17
SDLP	–	44	8
Sinn Fein	–	7	1
Workers' Party	2	5	5
None	10	28	33

In Northern Ireland, not a single Protestant respondent reports an SDLP identification (let alone one with Sinn Fein), and only a handful of Catholics support one of the unionist parties. A Protestant or Catholic who does not support one of the sectarian parties associated with his or her community will either support a cross-sectarian party, principally the Alliance, or no party at all. In contrast, in Britain, a quarter of those in the working class identify with the traditional party of the 'middle classes' (that is the Conservative Party), and one fifth of the salariat express support for Labour. Cross-class voting in Britain is common. Cross-sectarian voting in Northern Ireland is virtually non-existent.

	Great Britain Social class		
	Salariat	Intermediate	Working
Party identification:	%	%	%
Conservative	48	49	23
SLD/SDP	15	10	10
Labour	24	26	46
None	5	6	10

These differences help to account for the very different nature of party competition in the two parts of the United Kingdom. In Northern Ireland the major parties can hope to gain support only by capturing votes from other parties *within* their community, or by getting more of their supporters to turn out. By contrast, the two 'class' parties in Britain compete effectively for each other's 'natural' supporters.

Social class is not, however, entirely absent from the pattern of Northern Irish partisanship. For instance, while the level of OUP support is largely similar across all classes, support for the DUP is much stronger in the working class than in the salariat or lower non-manual occupations (thereby appealing to just those elements in Protestant society which were least well represented in the upper echelons of the traditional Unionist Party; see also Moxon-Browne, 1983). In contrast, while nearly a quarter of Protestant members of the salariat support the Alliance, only a handful (five per cent) of the Protestant working class does. Support is also skewed among Catholics, making the Alliance by far the most middle-class party in Northern Ireland. Evidently the Alliance's non-sectarian message flourishes most easily among those who are relatively economically secure and perhaps have also been subject to the liberalizing influence of higher or further education.

Just as class plays a role in Northern Irish politics, so religion is not entirely absent from British politics – though here the divide is not simply between Protestant and Catholic. Historically, of course, the Liberal Party has been associated with the nonconformist churches, and the Conservative Party with the Church of England. The Irish issue, among others, traditionally gave cause for Catholics not to vote for the anti-Home Rule Conservatives. Indeed in 1989 we find that Labour Party identification remains highest among Catholics (47 per cent compared with 34 per cent in the sample as a whole); SLD and SDP support is highest among nonconformists while the Conservatives attract dispro-portionate support among Anglicans. These differences cannot simply be accounted for by the differences in the class composition of the different religious groups, though they are much stronger within the salariat than within the working class (see Heath *et al*, forthcoming). But as with class in Northern Ireland, the religious divide in Britain is clearly only a sub-theme.

The substance of party politics

Not only do the Northern Irish parties have a different social base from those in Britain, but the issues which most divide the parties are also different. Not surprisingly, Catholics and Protestants (and therefore different party groupings) in Northern Ireland are most divided by issues to do with the constitutional status of the province. In Britain, the issues that divide the classes (and therefore the parties) are those that tap attitudes towards economic equality and the role of the state in the economy (see Curtice, 1986; Curtice, 1987). Further, the gap between party identifiers on the most divisive issues in Northern Ireland is much wider than the equivalent gap in Britain, underlining the difficulty of acquiring *cross-party* support for any major policy initiative in the province. Importantly, however, not just the constitutional question, but economic issues also divide party identifiers in Northern Ireland.

We illustrate these points by looking at the distribution of answers to four questions, two relating to the constitutional position of Northern Ireland and two which form part of a scale of items on attitudes towards economic equality. Respondents were asked:

> *Do you think the long-term policy for Northern Ireland should be for it to remain part of the United Kingdom or to reunify with the rest of Ireland?*

And later on in the questionnaire, they were asked:

> *If there was self-rule, how much do you think you would generally trust a Stormont government in Belfast to act in the best interests of Northern Ireland?*

(We also asked about other possible constitutional arrangements and report on responses later in this chapter.)

The extent of the party division on these items in Northern Ireland is clearly very substantial:

	Northern Ireland Party identification				
	Alliance	OUP	DUP	SDLP	None
% of respondents:					
Favouring reunification	14%	3%	1%	67%	25%
Prepared to trust Stormont just about always/most of the time	36%	76%	68%	25%	23%

Only a handful of unionists support reunification, while in contrast a sizeable minority of SDLP supporters do not support reunification. So far as attitudes towards Stormont are concerned, no party grouping is completely united, but overall the sharpness of the division between the two main political camps is very clear.

In Britain, in contrast, the constitutional position of Northern Ireland does not divide people clearly along party lines, although there is somewhat greater support for reunification among Labour and SLD/SDP identifiers than among Conservatives:

	Great Britain Party identification			
	Conservative	SLD/SDP	Labour	None
% of respondents:				
Favouring reunification	48%	58%	61%	56%
Prepared to trust Stormont just about always/most of the time	38%	35%	35%	23%

On the whole, these issues do not divide the British electorate to anything like the same degree as do issues of economic equality (see Curtice, 1987, p.174). But even the differences between the party supporters on economic issues in Britain never approach the size of those between the SDLP and the unionist parties in Northern Ireland on constitutional issues. For in Britain a sizeable minority of Conservatives take a 'left-wing' position on our economic equality items, and a sizeable minority of Labour identifiers 'a 'right-wing' position.

Issues to do with economic equality also divide party identifiers in Northern Ireland. Indeed, they partly cut across the sectarian divide.

	Northern Ireland Party identification				
	Alliance	OUP	DUP	SDLP	None
% agreeing that:					
Government should redistribute income from the better off to those who are less well off	46%	39%	70%	70%	58%
Ordinary working people do not get their fair share of the nation's wealth	55%	58%	80%	80%	69%

The issue of economic equality serves to drive one of the biggest wedges between DUP supporters (who, as we have seen, are particularly likely to be working class) and supporters of the OUP. Indeed supporters of the SDLP are no more left-wing on this issue than those of the DUP. So the political parties in Northern Ireland represent not just one ideological divide (on religion) but two. In so far as the rhetoric of Northern Irish parties is influenced by the attitudes of their supporters, the relative absence of economic issues from the Northern Irish political debate reflects not so much the absence of an economic divide between the parties as the intensity of the constitutional divide.

Social identities

We now turn to the relative importance of class and national identity in Northern Ireland and Britain.

Class and community identity

According to our data, the relationship between 'objective' class and 'subjective' class is as strong in Northern Ireland as in Britain. Overall, social class appears to have the same resonance in Northern Ireland as in Britain. Moreover, despite the emphasis in much of the public debate in the province on religious differences rather than on economic issues, much the same proportions in Northern Ireland as in Britain regard social class as an important influence on people's life-chances. Respondents were asked:

To what extent do you think a person's social class affects his or her opportunities today?

	Northern Ireland	Great Britain
	%	%
A great deal	30	27
Quite a lot	34	42
Not very much/not at all	33	29

People in Northern Ireland appear then to have a class identity as well as a religious identity. Indeed, as the following table shows, there is more social solidarity in Northern Ireland generally than there is in Britain. The figures are from a set of questions which asked respondents to say which social groups they personally felt close to.

	Northern Ireland	Great Britain	Difference
% saying they feel very or fairly close to:			
People who have the same social class background	65%	59%	6%
People who have the same religious background	64%	36%	28%
People of the same race	64%	56%	8%
People born in the same area	58%	49%	9%
People who live in the same area now	58%	46%	12%
People who have the same political beliefs	50%	34%	16%

People in Northern Ireland are more likely on every measure to feel close to people of the same background as themselves than are their counterparts in

Britain. In part, this simply reflects the fact that some of the criteria (certainly area and political beliefs) overlap with religion. And the term "race" may well for some respondents in Northern Ireland encompass the distinction between Protestants of Scots and English extraction and the indigenous Catholic population. But the pattern of responses also strongly suggests that social identities engender a greater degree of community and social solidarity in Northern Ireland than in Britain, (see also Budge and O'Leary, 1973). Whereas, in Britain, only race apparently matches class as a source of social identity, in Northern Ireland religion, class and race are apparently of equal importance.[8]

National identity

How far is the religious and constitutional divide in Northern Ireland underpinned by different national identities? We asked:

> *Which of these best describes the way you usually think of yourself: British, Irish, Ulster or Northern Irish?*

The pattern of responses clearly underlines the extent to which national identities bolster (or are bolstered by) the religious divide. Two-thirds of Protestants say they are British, while nearly three in five of Catholics say they are Irish.

	Northern Ireland			
		Religious affiliation		
	All	**Protestant**	**Catholic**	**None**
% thinking of themselves as:	%	%	%	%
British	44	66	10	55
Irish	25	4	60	12
Ulster	7	10	2	9
Northern Irish	20	16	25	22
Sometimes British/sometimes Irish	3	3	4	2

Indeed, our survey confirms the finding from earlier research that, since the outbreak of the Troubles, Protestants have been much more likely to adopt a British identity than they once were (Moxon-Browne, 1983, p.6). On the other hand, neither community is *united* around either national identity: around a quarter of Protestants say they are either "Ulster" or "Northern Irish" suggesting that perhaps for them Northern Ireland is something of a separate society (see also Moxon-Browne, 1983).[9] Similarly, around a quarter of Catholics also say "Northern Irish" (although hardly any said "Ulster"), suggesting that perhaps for them there may be some degree of psychological distance from the Republic.

Economic, social and moral attitudes

We turn now from political and social identities to other social attitudes, concentrating on two particular topics – economic equality and the role of the state, and moral issues (including questions of sexual *mores*).

Economic equality and the role of the state

Both the British and the Northern Irish questionnaires asked a wide range of questions about attitudes towards the role of the government in the economy and towards the role of the welfare state. From these we can develop a good picture of the similarities and differences between Northern Irish and British attitudes.

For instance, we asked about a number of possible measures that might improve the UK's economy and found that those living in Northern Ireland are rather more willing to endorse measures which require active intervention by the government than are those living in Britain.

	Northern Ireland	Great Britain
% supporting:		
Government to set up construction projects to create more jobs	90%	87%
Government action to cut interest rates	87%	84%
Government control of hire purchase and credit	82%	79%
Government schemes to encourage job-sharing	76%	67%
Control of prices by law	67%	56%
Increase in government subsidies to private industry	66%	53%
Control of wages by law	36%	28%

People in Northern Ireland are also more likely to endorse calls for greater welfare spending by the government, though these differences are for the most part rather smaller. However, this greater Northern Irish commitment to government intervention is a pragmatic one. It is not, it seems, an indicator of a greater commitment to a more socialist or egalitarian society. For instance, a smaller proportion of Northern Irish respondents than British respondents support more state ownership of industry, and fewer support more state spending on social benefits.

We can look more closely at underlying attitudes towards greater economic equality using the egalitarianism scale (Heath *et al*, 1986) which we have described before in this series (for example Curtice, 1987; Harding, 1988).[10] The pattern of responses to the scale items indicates that the two societies are identical in their ideological positions on the issue of economic equality. So the greater involvement of the public sector on the ground in Northern Ireland does not appear to be associated with any strong ideological commitment to the pursuit of economic equality there.

But if Northern Ireland as a whole appears similar on this count to Britain, what of particular subgroups? We have shown earlier that, in Britain, attitudes towards economic equality are closely associated with social class. Is this also true in Northern Ireland, and to what extent does religion come into play? We attempt to answer these questions by conducting an analysis of variance of the scale scores in the two surveys. This technique enables us to identify the extent to which differences in scores are associated with the particular religion or social class group to which the respondent belongs.[11]

The first important conclusion to emerge from this analysis is that social class is at least as strongly associated with attitudes towards economic equality in

Northern Ireland as it is in Britain. Indeed, as the table below shows, the difference between the mean scale score for members of the salariat and members of the working class is actually somewhat greater in Northern Ireland. This is because the salariat in Northern Ireland is politically slightly to the right of the salariat in Britain. The proportion of the total variance in scale score accounted for by class (controlling for the impact of religion) was also a little higher in Northern Ireland than in Britain.

	Mean economic equality scale score	
	Northern Ireland	Great Britain
Social class:		
Salariat	14.7	13.9
Intermediate	12.9	12.8
Working class	11.3	11.3

Note. The scale ranges between 5 and 25 (see Note 10 at the end of this chapter.) For the derivation of social class and religion see Note 11.

Secondly, although religion is more strongly correlated with attitudes towards economic equality in Northern Ireland than in Britain, it is not as influential as social class. Catholics in Northern Ireland are clearly to the left of Protestants and to the right of those without any religion.* But the differences are narrower than those between the salariat and the working class in the province.

These results are striking. After all, religion is the main source of division in Northern Ireland and the most dominant subject of political rhetoric there. In contrast, in Britain, it is class that is the principal social divide, and attitudes towards economic equality are central to the political debate between the Conservatives and Labour. Yet our results show that people identify with a class as much in Northern Ireland as they do in Britain, and that attitudes towards economic equality are as strongly related to class on both sides of the Irish Sea. It appears then that the *potential* for class-based politics in Northern Ireland is as strong as it is in Britain, and that it is only the strength of the religious divide in the province which prevents a version of Britain's class-based party system from dominating politics there too.

Social and sexual morality

While Britain and Northern Ireland are similar in their attitudes towards economic equality, they remain very different in their moral attitudes. Indeed, it is attitudes towards sexual morality in particular which most sharply and consistently distinguish the two parts of the UK. Northern Ireland is a far more conservative society.

For example, respondents were asked whether and to what extent pre-marital, extra-marital and homosexual relationships are acceptable. Although, even in Northern Ireland, pre-marital sex is now consistently frowned upon by only a minority (around one in three), there is still considerably greater disapproval in the province on this and on the other items than in Britain.

---

* The mean scale score for Catholics was 11.5, for Protestants 13.7, and for those without any religion 11.0.

	Northern Ireland	Great Britain
% saying each is always wrong		
Pre-marital sexual relationships	30%	12%
Extra-marital sexual relationships	77%	55%
Homosexual relationships	76%	56%

Homosexual relations remained illegal in Northern Ireland until 1987, so it is perhaps not surprising that disapproval is much greater there than in Britain. Indeed, there is also a greater reluctance in the province to allow homosexuals to teach in schools (55 per cent oppose it in Northern Ireland, compared with 47 per cent in Britain), or in higher education (49 per cent and 39 per cent oppose it, respectively).

On other moral issues too, the Northern Irish adopt a much more conservative stance than people in Britain do. For instance, there is much greater opposition to abortion, particularly where an abortion might be for social reasons. Indeed, such abortions are not legally permitted in the province.

	Northern Ireland	Great Britain
% saying law should not allow		
an abortion if:		
The couple cannot afford any more children	70%	38%
The woman is not married and does not want to marry the man	68%	38%
The woman decides on her own that she does not wish to have the child	67%	46%
The couple agree they do not wish to have the child	65%	35%
There is a strong chance of a defect in the baby	35%	10%
The woman became pregnant as a result of rape	24%	6%
The woman's health is seriously endangered by the pregnancy	19%	5%

There is also greater opposition in the province to forms of medical intervention which could help childless couples to conceive. For example, 55 per cent of Northern Irish respondents would *not* permit artificial insemination using an anonymous donor, compared with 43 per cent in Britain. And 22 per cent would not allow the implantation of a test-tube embryo compared with 10 per cent in Britain.

More people in Northern Ireland than in Britain also want the law to stop the publication of pornographic magazines and books: 55 per cent say such material should be banned altogether compared with 39 per cent in Britain. And 29 per cent strongly agree that "censorship of films and magazines is necessary to uphold moral standards", compared with only 19 per cent in Britain.

But, importantly, just as these *differences* between people in Northern Ireland and Britain are striking, so are the *similarities* between Protestants and Catholics in the province. Except on the question of abortion, Protestants and Catholics are not far apart. The large division of opinion is between Christians on the one side and those with no religion on the other.

	Northern Ireland Religious affiliation		
% saying:	Catholic	Protestant	None
Pre-marital sex always wrong	32%	34%	10%
Homosexual relations always wrong	75%	82%	53%
Homosexuals should not teach in a college or university	46%	54%	36%
Abortion should not be allowed if couple cannot afford any more children	84%	60%	58%
Abortion should not be allowed if there is a strong chance of a defect in the baby	62%	19%	17%
Pornography should be banned altogether	60%	54%	29%

Conservatism in respect of sexual mores certainly makes Northern Ireland culturally distinct from Britain. But that distinctiveness is founded on the greater importance of religion in the province, not on denominational differences.

Indeed, religious observance is also associated with conservatism on these matters in Britain (see also Harding, 1988; Heath, 1986; Airey and Brook, 1986; Airey, 1984). For instance, those in Britain who attend a religious service regularly are more likely to have conservative views than those who do not attend at all. But the level of conservatism in Northern Ireland, compared with Britain, cannot be accounted for simply by the larger number of practising Christians in the province. Both frequent and infrequent churchgoers in Northern Ireland are more conservative than their counterparts in Britain.

	Attends religious service		
	. . . at least once a week	. . . at least twice a year	. . . less than twice a year
Pre-marital sex always wrong:			
Northern Ireland	40%	21%	15%
Great Britain	30%	9%	9%
Homosexual relations always wrong:			
Northern Ireland	81%	82%	59%
Great Britain	70%	54%	54%
Homosexuals should not teach in a college or university:			
Northern Ireland	50%	54%	42%
Great Britain	46%	36%	39%
Abortion should not be allowed if couple cannot afford more children:			
Northern Ireland	82%	61%	54%
Great Britain	65%	38%	32%
Abortion should not be allowed if there is a strong chance of a defect in the baby:			
Northern Ireland	50%	17%	17%
Great Britain	25%	9%	6%
Pornography should be banned altogether:			
Northern Ireland	69%	45%	33%
Great Britain	65%	41%	34%

Social attitudes are, of course, derived not only from an individual's personal characteristics but also from his or her social context (see for example, Curtice, 1988). It would appear that the high level of religious observance in Northern Ireland creates a social context in which attitudes (such as towards sexual matters) tend to be influenced by religious teachings, even among those who are not themselves religious. Few people in Northern Ireland can avoid hearing (and being influenced by) the message of the churches on moral issues.

We might expect Northern Ireland to differ sharply from Britain on other moral issues too, such as euthanasia – and indeed it does. But it is perhaps surprising that people in Northern Ireland are more liberal on the question of capital punishment than are people in Britain. While only around one in five British people oppose the death penalty, around two in five do so in Northern Ireland. This is true even when respondents are asked specifically about a murder of a police officer and about terrorist crimes, both of which are, because of the Troubles, much more prevalent in the province than in Britain.

	Northern Ireland	Great Britain
% against the death penalty for:		
Murder in the course of a terrorist act	39%	19%
Murder of a police officer	39%	23%
Other murders	44%	26%

Further, while 59 per cent of people in Northern Ireland agree that "for some crimes, the death penalty is the most appropriate sentence", 74 per cent do so in Britain.

The reason for this apparent conundrum is that the death penalty is strongly opposed by Catholics in Northern Ireland: while 71 per cent of Catholics are against the death penalty for terrorist murders, only 19 per cent of Protestants oppose it – the same proportion as among all respondents in Britain. The division on this issue between the two religious communities – and thus the political parties – is as sharp as on any issue we have examined. In comparison, majorities among the supporters of all the main parties and religious denominations in Britain are in favour of the death penalty. It appears that the minority community in Northern Ireland has deep reservations about capital punishment, possibly because they feel Catholics might be more under threat from it. Clearly then, we cannot conclude our examination without looking further at attitudes towards the province's constitutional position and at relations between the communities.

Constitutional questions

We have seen the extent to which attitudes towards the constitutional question divide the Protestant and Catholic communities. On this issue there is a fundamental disagreement between British and Northern Irish public opinion too.

Reunification

As the table below shows, whereas in Britain reunification of Ireland is widely supported (though its popularity has fallen slightly since 1983), in Northern Ireland as a whole it is much less popular. Over two-thirds of the population (and over 90 per cent of Protestants) believe that Northern Ireland should remain part of the United Kingdom, and only around a quarter favour unification with the Republic.

	In favour of	
	. . . reunification	. . . withdrawal of British troops
Great Britain: total	55%	59%
Religious affiliation:		
Protestant	51%	58%
Catholic	65%	63%
None	58%	61%
Northern Ireland: total	24%	33%
Religious affiliation:		
Protestant	3%	18%
Catholic	56%	55%
None	13%	30%

Moreover, it is striking that support for the reunification of Ireland is as strong in Britain as a whole as among Catholics alone in Northern Ireland, only a bare majority of whom support reunification.

In Britain, reunification of Ireland is, as one might expect, most likely to be opposed by Conservative identifiers, but even among this group only 37 per cent are in favour of maintaining the Union with Britain, and almost half favour reunification. Similarly, while there is greater support for reunification with the Republic among British Catholics than among Protestants, a majority of Protestants in Britain nonetheless supports reunification.

Further, nearly 60 per cent of the British public, including 52 per cent of Conservative identifiers, favour the withdrawal of troops from Northern Ireland. Among the Northern Irish public, only a third hold this view, and that proportion rises to only 55 per cent even among Catholics.

It appears then, on our evidence that the United Kingdom of Great Britain and Northern Ireland rests on somewhat shaky foundations. British governments clearly lack widespread public support for Britain's continued association with, and involvement in, the province. As yet however, Northern Ireland has not become a major electoral issue in Britain, not least because all of the political parties have maintained a commitment to the Union, at least for the foreseeable future. But if that party consensus were to break down – or if public concern about Northern Ireland were to be heightened – then the strains on the Union could become even greater.

Whatever their views about the desirability of a united Ireland, however, the British public believes that it is unlikely to happen for the foreseeable future. Just 18 per cent think it is likely to come about in the next 20 years. On this prediction, people on the two sides of the Irish Sea are in agreement. In Northern Ireland only 23 per cent think that it is likely to happen, and on this Catholics are in complete agreement with Protestants.

Trust in government

We investigated the constitutional issue further by asking respondents (in both Northern Ireland and Britain) how much trust they have in the present arrangements.

We asked:

> *Under direct rule from Britain, as now, how much do you generally trust* **British governments** *of* **any** *party to act in the best interests of Northern Ireland?*

We then asked two parallel questions about possible future arrangements:

> *If there was self-rule, how much do you think you would generally trust a* **Stormont government** . . .

> *And if there were a united Ireland, how much do you think you would generally trust an* **Irish government** . . .

As the table below shows, it is clear that none of the possible constitutional arrangements we depicted for Northern Ireland currently has the confidence of more than one of the potential parties to an agreement (see also Rose, McAllister and Mair, 1978).

		Trust each government to act in best interests of Northern Ireland				
		Just about always	Most of the time	Some of the time	Rarely	Never
British governments of any party:						
Northern Ireland	%	4	21	39	20	11
Great Britain	%	6	34	36	9	13
A Stormont government:						
Northern Ireland	%	11	35	26	12	9
Great Britain	%	5	30	29	11	4
An all-Irish government:						
Northern Ireland	%	3	16	29	20	22
Great Britain	%	6	30	30	10	5

Only a quarter of people in Northern Ireland say that they trust British governments to act in the interests of Northern Ireland "just about always" or "most of the time". Catholics are particularly lacking in confidence, with 15 per cent saying they trust British governments, but even among Protestants this figure rises to only 33 per cent. In Britain itself, only two in five respondents say they trust British governments to look after Northern Ireland's interests. Conservative identifiers (54 per cent) voice much more confidence than Labour identifiers (27 per cent) do, but this is probably only because they trust the present government more, not because of any particular confidence in direct rule.

We saw earlier that, although a clear majority of unionists would trust a Stormont government to act in the best interests of Northern Ireland in the event of self-rule, most SDLP supporters and those of no political persuasion would not. The British public shares the concern of the Catholic community. Indeed, it would trust such a Stormont government no more than it would trust an all-Irish government. Only about a third say they would trust either "just about always" or "most of the time".

But perhaps most surprisingly, not even the Catholic community in Northern Ireland has much trust an all-Irish government. Indeed, trust in such a government is no higher than in Britain. Even among supporters of the SDLP or among the small number of declared Sinn Fein identifiers in our sample no more than half say that they would trust an all-Irish government.

A potentially strong influence upon the future of Northern Ireland is the European Community: both the Republic of Ireland and the UK are, of course, members. If the planned moves towards monetary, economic and political union in the Community eventually bear fruit, then some policies affecting Northern Ireland, Britain and the Republic will be decided increasingly by institutions of the Community. It is interesting to note, therefore, that support for the UK's continued membership of the Community is greater in Northern Ireland than in Britain. Just 17 per cent of respondents in Northern Ireland want the UK to withdraw, compared with 26 per cent in Britain. Support for withdrawal from the EC is slightly higher among Protestants in Northern Ireland than among Catholics, but for both communities it is well below the 47 per cent who favoured withdrawal in 1978 (Moxon-Browne, 1983).[12]

Evenhandedness of institutions

The attitudes of the Northern Irish towards the present constitutional arrangements in the province were explored further in a set of questions which asked people to consider how fairly they thought various institutions treated Protestants and Catholics. The National Health Service, government unemployment schemes, and the courts (when dealing with non-terrorist offences) are seen by large majorities of both communities to be operating evenhandedly. But the security forces (the Ulster Defence Regiment (UDR), the Royal Ulster Constabulary (RUC) and the army) all lack the confidence of a large section of the Catholic community. Indeed, there is doubt among some Protestants too about the way in which the Ulster Defence Regiment (a locally recruited regiment of the British Army which only undertakes security duties in the province) operates. *Both* communities are sceptical about the evenhandedness of central government in Stormont and local councils in their treatment of job applicants.

| | Northern Ireland Religious affiliation | | |
	Catholic	Protestant	None
% saying Catholics and Protestants are treated equally:			
National Health Service in treating patients	94%	86%	90%
Government unemployment schemes in treating applicants for a place	81%	70%	74%
Courts in treating those accused of *non-terrorist* offences	76%	84%	91%
NI Housing Executive in treating applicants for a home	71%	64%	73%
Courts in treating those accused of *terrorist* offences	54%	79%	88%
Local district councils in treating job applicants	45%	55%	39%
Army in treating public	43%	74%	55%
Central government in Stormont in treating job applicants	42%	56%	55%
RUC in treating public	38%	71%	46%
UDR in treating public	22%	62%	35%

On most of these items Protestants say that Catholics are at an advantage while Catholics say that Protestants are. Thus, for example one in five Protestants think that the Housing Executive treats Catholics better than Protestants, while one in six Catholics say that it treats Protestants better than Catholics.

But in the case of Protestant attitudes towards the security forces this is not true. Even 21 per cent of Protestants say that the UDR treats Protestants better than Catholics, while 13 per cent say the RUC does so and 12 per cent the army. Only a handful of respondents say that any of these institutions treat Catholics better. There is thus a degree of cross-sectarian agreement that the security forces treat Protestants more favourably than Catholics. Attempts to change the image of the local security forces over the last 20 years do not appear to have met with much success.

We should note three other points about these figures. First, the Northern Ireland Housing Executive took over responsibility for providing municipal housing, following the outbreak of the troubles and in response to concern that local authorities were practising discrimination in the allocation of housing. The Housing Executive has evidently gained a better reputation for fairness, especially among the Catholic community.

Secondly, although around a third of Catholics believe that Protestants are treated more favourably by the courts when accused of terrorist offences, a majority of Catholics do trust the courts to operate equitably. The courts are clearly more widely trusted by the Catholics than the security forces are, despite the controversy over the abandonment of trial by jury for terrorist offences.

Thirdly, we should note that DUP identifiers are more likely to think that the two communities are treated unequally than are supporters of the OUP. This is true both of those institutions where Protestants say that Catholics are advantaged and those where they say that *Protestants* are advantaged. The DUP's supporters are often thought to have the more hardline approach of the two loyalist camps and we cannot assume that they regard the Protestant bias of the security forces with disapproval. But it is also possible that as a relatively new party its supporters are more critical of government institutions generally.

Political protest

The constitutional debate and the continuing conflict in Northern Ireland have placed considerable strains upon democratic government in the province. Not only has the Stormont parliament been prorogued, but local government too has lost much of its power. Northern Ireland is for the most part administered by politicians who come from outside the province, and in whose election the province has played no part. In both Northern Ireland and Britain, the media have been barred from broadcasting interviews with members of Sinn Fein (outside election times). And the right to hold protest marches and demonstrations has sometimes been curtailed for fear of civil disorder.

How does all this affect democratic values in Northern Ireland? On the small amount of evidence we have, it does appear that the political culture of Northern Ireland is somewhat less supportive of democratic values than is that of Britain. For instance, respondents on both sides of the Irish Sea were asked whether people should be allowed to engage in various forms of political protest commonly permitted (within limits) in democratic societies; and we find that people in

Northern Ireland are a good deal less willing to permit any of these forms of protest.

% agreeing that people should be allowed to:	Northern Ireland	Great Britain
Organise public meetings to protest against the government	55%	65%
Publish leaflets to protest against the government	55%	63%
Organise protest marches and demonstrations	49%	56%

Catholics in Northern Ireland are somewhat more libertarian than Protestants, but still less so than the British population as a whole.

We also asked respondents whether "the law should always be obeyed, even if a particular law is wrong". Overall, only six per cent more people in Northern Ireland than in Britain feel that the claims of the law are less important than those of individual conscience. But among the Catholic community in Northern Ireland, nearly half feel that way. In general, democracy and social order rely heavily upon consent and adherence to the law. So this apparent lack of support for the law among a substantial proportion of the minority community in Northern Ireland is significant indeed.

Community relations

We look finally at attitudes towards relations between the two religious communities, towards some of the institutions that appear to maintain the religious divide, and more generally at the extent of religious prejudice in the province.

People in Britain are clearly pessimistic about the state of relations between the Protestant and Catholic communities in Northern Ireland. Only 14 per cent think that relations are better now than five years ago; almost twice as many think they are worse. And on balance, they believe that relations will be worse rather than better in five years time.

In Northern Ireland, in contrast, optimists outnumber pessimists: 26 per cent believe relations will get better compared with 16 per cent who believe they will get worse. Moreover, they are rather more inclined than people in Britain to believe that relations have improved in the last five years. Nonetheless, the mood in the province now is dramatically more pessimistic than it was at the onset of the troubles in 1968; then, three-fifths thought things were improving (Rose, 1971). The events of the last 20 years have clearly taken their toll.

Perceptions of religious prejudice

There is a widespread belief in Northern Ireland that there is religious prejudice against *both* Catholics and Protestants. For example in both religious communities two-thirds believe there is *at least* a little prejudice against members of the *other* community. But people in Britain are even more likely to believe there is prejudice against Protestants and Catholics in the province.

	Northern Ireland			Great Britain
	Religious Affiliation			
	All	Catholic	Protestant	None	All
Prejudice against Catholics in Northern Ireland	%	%	%	%	%
There is a lot	33	38	27	39	58
There is a little	40	46	36	42	22
There is hardly any	21	11	30	15	6
Prejudice against Protestants in Northern Ireland	%	%	%	%	%
There is a lot	23	15	27	31	52
There is a little	44	47	42	43	25
There is hardly any	27	31	24	20	9

Within Northern Ireland, however, there is one important difference in people's perceptions of the degree of prejudice against each of the two communities. Prejudice against Catholics is perceived to be less compared with five years ago. But in the case of Protestants, it is perceived to be greater. Protestants themselves are particularly likely to take that view. This increasing sense of vulnerability among the Protestant community might perhaps be in response to the Anglo-Irish Agreement and to what they see as a weakening of commitment to the Union by the British government.

As we noted, one area in which prejudice and discrimination is thought to exist is the labour market. Certainly, there appears to be widespread belief in both religious communities in Northern Ireland that job discrimination persists. We asked:

> On the whole, do you think that Protestants and Catholics in Northern Ireland who apply for the same jobs have the same chance of getting a job, or are their chances of getting a job different?

Around half of all respondents say that job applicants have the same chance, nearly one third say that Protestants are more likely to get a job, and only one in ten believe Catholics to have an advantage. Perception of discrimination is particularly strong among Catholics, with no less than 59 per cent of them believing that Protestants have a relative advantage. Indeed, in response to a further set of questions, around half of Protestants too accept that Protestants have at least a little advantage in the job market. When Protestants and Catholics were asked why the other group had an advantage, hardly anyone believed that this was because they were better qualified. Over three-quarters say it is because of employers' prejudices in favour of one group or another.

In contrast, the existence of separate educational systems for Protestants and Catholics does not appear to arouse much concern. Respondents were asked whether Protestants and Catholics have an equal chance of going to a good primary school, a good secondary intermediate school,* a good grammar school, and of going to university. In each case more than four in five respondents say their chances are much the same.

---

* Secondary intermediate schools are the equivalent of secondary modern schools in Britain. In Northern Ireland most children take a selective examination at the age of 11 in order to determine whether they go to a grammar or a secondary intermediate school.

Segregation and integration

Despite their different views about the current state of relations between Protestants and Catholics in the province, people in Northern Ireland and Britain are in agreement that more mixing between Protestants and Catholics in the province would be better for community relations. Overwhelming majorities (90 per cent in Northern Ireland and 88 per cent in Britain) believe that better relations between the two communities would come about through more mixing. But closer examination reveals clear limits to the extent to which the two religious communities in the province would actually accept either further mixing, or measures to reduce religious discrimination.

Some forms of mixing between the two communities are more commonplace than others. As we noted, while most schools tend to be single-religion, workplaces tend not to be. This appears to reflect current preferences. Respondents were asked whether or not they would prefer to live in a mixed neighbourhood, have a job at a mixed workplace or send their children to a mixed school. This is how they answered:

	Northern Ireland			
		Religious affiliation		
	All	**Catholics**	**Protestants**	**None**
% preferring:				
Mixed religion neighbourhood	71%	75%	67%	78%
Mixed religion workplace	84%	86%	82%	89%
Mixed religion school	55%	54%	52%	79%

Mixed workplaces generate the least opposition while opposition to mixed schools is greatest. On all three items opposition among Catholics is lower than among Protestants. Mixed schooling, sometimes seen as an important mechanism for improving relations between the two communities, is strongly supported by Alliance identifiers, but is opposed by nearly two in three DUP identifiers.

But the pattern of responses to these general questions do not tell the whole story. As we shall see, the existence of opposition to more mixing of the two communities becomes clearer when respondents are asked about specific measures for encouraging intermixing. Further, although only a minority of people in Northern Ireland *express* opposition to intermixing, the proportion is still much higher than in Britain.

For example, while just over a third (37 per cent) of Northern Ireland respondents express a preference for single denominational schools, only 15 per cent do so in Britain. And while only 18 per cent of people in the province are prepared to admit being prejudiced towards people of other religions, only eight per cent of people in Britain admit this.

And when we turn to specific measures, then even on the matter of workplace discrimination, there is clear evidence of opposition to a central element of the recently introduced Fair Employment Act. We asked two differently worded questions about the monitoring of the religious composition of workforces, and the contrast in the pattern of responses is highly revealing.

First, we asked:

> *Do you generally support or oppose a* **fair employment law** *in Northern Ireland, that is a law which* **requires** *employers to keep records on the religion of their employees and make sure there is no discrimination?*

Support was only lukewarm. Only a half of respondents say that they are in favour while 40 per cent are opposed. In contrast, two-thirds of respondents in Britain are in favour of a law against *racial* discrimination.

But we approached the issue another way, asking:

> *Some people say that all employers should keep records on the religion of their employees to make sure there is no discrimination. Other people say this is not necessary. What about you – do you think that employers* **should** *or* **should not** *keep records about their employees' religion?*

Asked in this way, the opposition to the measure is much clearer: only a quarter now say they are in favour, while more than two-thirds are opposed. The key difference between the questions seems to be that the first one introduces the notion of 'fairness'. Stripped of that general value judgement, opposition to this measure seems to become more legitimate.

The extent of opposition in the province to 'mixed marriages' is particularly striking. Respondents were asked both whether "most people" and they "personally" would mind if "one of their close relatives were to marry someone of a different religion". They were also asked a parallel question about "a suitably qualified person of a different religion [being] appointed as their boss". Whereas only a handful (seven per cent) say they personally would mind having a boss of a different religion, 30 per cent say they would mind if one of their close relatives were to marry someone of a different religion (see also Moxon-Browne, 1981). In answer to the question whether they thought *other people* would mind if a close relative were to marry someone of a different religion, as many as two-thirds say they would. As previous surveys have shown, opposition to intermarriage is particularly marked among Protestants: over two in five say they would personally mind, compared with only 16 per cent of Catholics. Among those with no religion, this figure fell to 11 per cent.

There are then considerable practical barriers to achieving greater mixing between the two communities, and the reduction of discrimination and prejudice. But Northern Ireland is by no means unique in this respect. Some of the factors that divide the Protestant and Catholic communities in Northern Ireland are also present in racially-mixed societies (Lijphart, 1975) such as Britain. In the British survey, a number of questions were asked that were directly analogous to questions included in the Northern Ireland survey about religious prejudice, but which were designed to tap *racial* prejudice. The responses reveal that racial prejudice is in fact more prevalent in Britain than is religious prejudice in Northern Ireland. For example, as many as 38 per cent of white people in Britain admit to being prejudiced against people of other races, compared with the 18 per cent who admit to religious prejudice in Northern Ireland. One in five white people in Britain say that they would object to having an Asian or a black person as their boss, compared with only seven per cent in Northern Ireland who would object to someone of a different religion. And, most strikingly, a half of white people in Britain say they would object to a close relative marrying an Asian or black person; in contrast, just under a third of people in Northern Ireland are opposed to religious intermarriage.

Conclusions

There are then two clear differences between social attitudes in Britain and Northern Ireland.

First, *Northern Ireland is a religious society while Britain is a secular one.* The main implication of this is that religion rather than class is the primary source of social and political division in Northern Ireland. Indeed, in many respects Protestants and Catholics there form two separate political and social communities. Intermarriage is rare, and so is voting for a party associated with the other religion. Differences between Protestants and Catholics in Britain are minor in contrast. More important, even social class differences in Britain fail to divide people there to the extent that religion does in Northern Ireland.

But social attitudes in Northern Ireland are also distinguished from those in Britain because of certain values held *in common* by Protestants and Catholics. They share conservative moral values which sharply distinguish their attitudes from British ones. It is no accident then that social legislation has been second only to constitutional issues as a source of tension between the British government and Northern Irish MPs since the implementation of direct rule.

Even so, there are indications that religious adherence is in decline and that religion is becoming slightly less important as a source of social division in Northern Ireland than it used to be. But this has not yet manifested itself in a reduction of intensity in the political conflict in the province. Indeed, while there is support for more integration in principle, specific proposals that might reduce discrimination are still met with considerable suspicion and opposition.

Secondly, *while most people in Northern Ireland wish to remain in the United Kingdom, most people in Britain wish that in the long term it would leave.* All shades of British opinion believe that the best future for Northern Ireland would be for it to be part of a united Ireland. There is also strong support in Britain for the removal of British troops from the province. Meanwhile, in Northern Ireland, not only are Protestants virtually unanimous in support of the Union with Britain, but even among Catholics support is higher than it is in Britain. The gap between British and Northern Irish public opinion on the constitutional future of the province is as serious as that between the two communities within the province.

Alongside these serious differences we have, however, also found surprising similarities between the two societies. Most notably, *Northern Ireland and Britain are very similar in their attitudes towards class-based, economic issues.* Not only is the overall distribution of attitudes towards such issues much the same, but the strength of their association with social class is also similar. True, there is rather greater support in Northern Ireland for selective governmental intervention in the economy – in keeping with its actual role in the province – but the degree of general ideological support for action to promote economic equality is very similar on both sides of the Irish Sea. Despite the relative absence in the province of parties or political institutions which promote socialist principles, the Northern Irish working class is in general as left-wing (or as right-wing) as its British equivalent. And it is also just as likely to have a subjective working-class identity. In the end, what distinguishes Northern Ireland from Britain is not the absence of a class divide, but the overwhelming importance of the religious one.

Notes

1. The combined *Continuous Household Surveys (CHS)* for 1985 to 1987 found that 37 per cent of those aged 16 and over in the households it sampled were Catholic and 60 per cent were Protestant. The procedures used by the *CHS* to measure religion are not however directly analogous to those used in the *Northern Ireland Social Attitudes* survey and in the *CHS* only two per cent of respondents are classified as having no religion. In the *Social Attitudes* survey, however, those respondents who did not profess any religion were also asked in which religion they were brought up. If respondents are assigned to a religion on the basis of either their own or their family's religion, 38 per cent of our sample are Catholic, 57 per cent Protestant and 2 per cent unspecified Christian. The remaining differences between the two surveys are well within the bounds of sampling error. It would appear therefore that on this crucial characteristic the sample of the *Social Attitudes* survey is reasonably representative of the Northern Irish population.

2. We should also note that Catholics are more numerous among young people than older people. As many as 45 per cent of those aged under 35 are Catholic compared with just 26 per cent of those aged over 55. Indeed Catholics outnumber Protestants among those aged under 35. Just 37 per cent of those aged under 35 are Protestants compared with two-thirds of those aged over 55. These differences in the main reflect the higher fertility of the Catholic population which, without any other factor intervening, would in the long term alter the denominational balance in the province. In practice, this higher Catholic fertility has historically been counterbalanced by a higher level of emigration among Catholics than Protestants. But emigration from the province has been lower in the 1980s and this appears to be reflected in our figures. The imbalance in the age distribution of the two communities is more marked in our survey than in either the 1968 or the 1978 surveys. For example, in the 1978 survey 56 per cent of the under 35s were Protestant and just 40 per cent Catholic.

3. There are two important differences in the question wording of our survey compared with the earlier surveys. The first concerns the way in which religious denomination was ascertained. In the 1968 survey, respondents were asked, "What is your religion?", and in the 1978 survey, "Could you tell us which Church you belong to?" Both these formulations contain the presumption that the respondents do indeed have a religion. This may have inclined some people who might not otherwise have done so to report a religious denomination. In the *Social Attitudes* survey we asked, "Do you regard yourself as belonging to any particular religion?"

   The second difference is in the way in which frequency of church attendance was ascertained. In the *Social Attitudes* survey respondents were asked how often they attended services, "apart from such special occasions as weddings, funerals and baptisms". This qualification was not included in either of the two earlier surveys. This may have meant that some respondents to the earlier surveys who would otherwise have said that they never attended church said that they attended very infrequently.

4. In the earlier surveys all respondents were asked about the extent of workplace integration, irrespective of whether they themselves were working. Those not in work were asked to answer in terms of the degree of integration at their partner's workplace. In the *Social Attitudes* survey only employees currently in employment and working at least ten hours a week were asked this question. In order to compare our results with the earlier surveys we re-analysed the datasets and looked at the replies of only those who were in work.

   It is also possible that the degree of mixing in schools has increased. In the 1968 survey only 14 per cent of respondents said that they had attended a mixed school compared with 24 per cent in our 1989 survey, although the wording of the question in the 1968 survey was different. Given that the research of Darby *et al* is now 13 years old, there would appear to be a case for further research into the current situation.

5. Our findings are confirmed by the results of the *Continuous Household Survey* in Northern Ireland and the *General Household Survey* in Britain. In the 1985-7 samples of the *CHS* combined, 9 per cent of all persons aged 16 or over were in professional or managerial occupations (socio-economic groups 1,2,3,4 and 13) compared with 16 per cent in the 1987 *GHS*. Meanwhile 53 per cent were in one of the manual socio-economic groups compared with 47 per cent in the 1987 *GHS*.

6. The *Continuous Household Survey* reports similar findings on the class composition of the two communities. In the 1985–7 combined samples of the *CHS*, 57 per cent of Catholics were in one of the manual socio-economic groups compared with 48 per cent of Protestants.

A slight narrowing of the gap in Protestant and Catholic unemployment rates was revealed by the 1988 *CHS*. In the 1985–7 combined sample, 27 per cent of economically active Catholics were unemployed compared with 11 per cent of Protestants. In the 1988 sample, however, Catholic unemployment fell to 24 per cent while Protestant unemployment remained at 11 per cent. However, we are inclined to be cautious in our interpretation of these findings until corroborated by further evidence as the narrowing of the gap could be a consequence of sampling error.

7. In all of the tables in this chapter up to this point, respondents have been assigned to a social class on the basis of their own current or last occupation. The procedure adopted in the subsequent tables in the chapter in which social class is being used as an analytic concept is slightly different. Respondents are assigned to a class on the basis of their own occupation unless they are economically inactive (but not retired) and are married to someone who is economically active, in which case respondents are assigned to a class on the basis of their spouse's occupation.

8. This result suggests that one criticism made of the work of Marshall *et al* may be misplaced. This was that their findings about the importance of class as a social identity in Britain are distorted by the fact that in their questionnaire they concentrated their attention almost wholly on the subject of class, thereby artificially raising its importance in respondents' minds (Emmison and Weston, 1990; Marshall and Rose, 1990). The *British Social Attitudes* results come from a questionnaire in which little attention is paid to this subject.

9. However, the gap in the proportion of OUP and DUP supporters saying that they are British is only 5 per cent in our survey compared with 11 per cent in Moxon-Browne.

10. The five items comprising the economic equality scale are:

    The government should redistribute income from the better off to those who are less well off.
    Big business benefits owners at the expense of workers.
    Ordinary working people do not get their fair share of the nation's wealth.
    There is one law for the rich and one for the poor.
    Management will always try to get the better of employees if it gets the chance.

    Respondents are invited to say whether they agree or disagree with each of these items, using a five-point scale ranging from "strongly agree" to "strongly disagree". Previous research (Heath *et al*, 1986) has shown that these items form a Likert scale which in Britain has a satisfactory level of reliability (Cronbach's alpha for these items in the 1989 *British Social Attitudes* survey is 0.89). We can therefore safely sum the responses given by each respondent to each item to get an overall measure of his or her attitudes towards economic equality. Thus a respondent who said that he or she "strongly agreed" with each item would score 1 on each item and have a total score of 5. In contrast a respondent who said that he or she "strongly disagreed" with each item would score 5 on each item and have a total score of 25. Thus the lower the respondent's score the more in favour he or she is of economic equality.

    The scale appears to perform just as satisfactorily in Northern Ireland (Crombach's alpha = 0.89). This success in replicating the scale in Northern Ireland suggests that the validity of the scale is not dependent upon the particularities of British political culture and that it may be a useful tool in cross-national research.

11. For this purpose religion and social class were each collapsed into three categories. Religion was coded as Protestant, Catholic, or none/other. Social class was coded as salariat, intermediate (including junior non-manual, petty bourgeois and foremen) and working. In the resulting analysis, the main effect of social class accounted for 4.7 per cent of the variance in Northern Ireland and 4.0 per cent in Britain. Religion accounted for 3.6 per cent of the variance in Northern Ireland and 1.5 per cent in Britain.

12. Intriguingly, however, other aspects of existing British foreign and defence policy receive less support in Northern Ireland than in Britain. There is both greater opposition to nuclear weapons and to the United Kingdom's continued membership of NATO in the province than in Britain. This opposition is greatest among Catholics who may be influenced by the more neutralist stance of the Republic. But even so, the level of opposition among unionists is noticeably greater than among Conservative identifiers in Britain.

References

AIREY, C., 'Social and moral values', in Jowell, R. and Airey, C. (eds), *British Social Attitudes: the 1984 Report*, Gower, Aldershot (1984).

AIREY, C. and BROOK, L., 'Interim report: social and moral issues', in Jowell, R., Witherspoon, S. and Brook, L. (eds), *British Social Attitudes: the 1986 Report*, Gower, Aldershot (1986).

BUDGE, I. and O'LEARY, C., *Belfast: Approach to Crisis*, Macmillan, London (1973).

CURTICE, J., 'Political partisanship', in Jowell, R., Witherspoon, S. and Brook, L., (eds) *British Social Attitudes: the 1986 Report*, Gower, Aldershot (1986).

CURTICE J., 'Interim report: party politics', in Jowell, R., Witherspoon, S. and Brook, L. (eds), *British Social Attitudes: the 1987 Report*, Gower, Aldershot (1987).

CURTICE, J., 'One nation?', in Jowell, R., Witherspoon, S. and Brook, L. (eds), *British Social Attitudes: the 5th Report*, Gower, Aldershot (1988).

DARBY, J., MURRAY, D., BATTS, D., DUNN, S., FARREN, S. and HARRIS, J., *Education and Community in Northern Ireland: Schools Apart?*, New University of Ulster, Coleraine (1977).

EMMISON, M. and WESTON, M., 'Social class and social identity: a comment in Marshall *et al*', *Sociology*, vol.24, no.2 (1990), pp.241–53.

EVERSLEY, D., *Religion and Employment in Northern Ireland*, Sage, London (1989).

FRANKLIN, N., *The Decline of Class Voting in Britain*, Clarendon, Oxford (1985).

HARDING, S., 'Trends in permissiveness', in Jowell, R., Witherspoon, S. and Brook, L. (eds), *British Social Attitudes: the 5th Report*, Gower, Aldershot (1988).

HARDING, S., PHILLIPS, D. with FOGARTY, M., *Contrasting Values in Western Europe*, Macmillan, London (1986).

HEATH, A., *Social Mobility*, Fontana, London (1981).

HEATH, A., 'Do people have consistent attitudes?', in Jowell, R., Witherspoon, S. and Brook, L. (eds), *British Social Attitudes: the 1986 Report*, Gower, Aldershot (1986).

HEATH, A., JOWELL, R., CURTICE, J. and WITHERSPOON, S., *End of Award Report to the ESRC: Methodological Aspects of Attitude Research*, SCPR, London (1986).

HEATH, A., JOWELL, R., CURTICE, J., EVANS, G., FIELD, J. and WITHER-SPOON, S., *Understanding Political Change: Voting Behaviour in Britain 1964–1987*, Pergamon, Oxford (forthcoming).

LANCASTER, T., 'Spain', in Franklin, M., Mackie, T. and Valen, H. (eds), *Electoral Change: Responses to Evolving Social and Attitudinal Structures in Western Countries*, Cambridge University Press, Cambridge (forthcoming).

LIJPHART, A., 'Review article: the Northern Ireland problem; cases, theories, solutions', *British Journal of Political Science*, vol. 5, no. 1 (1975), pp.83–106.

MARSHALL, G., NEWBY, H., ROSE, D., and VOGLER, C., *Social Class in Modern Britain*, Hutchinson, London (1988).

MARSHALL, G. and ROSE, D., 'Out-classed by our critics', *Sociology*, vol. 24, no. 2 (1990), pp. 255–67.

MOXON-BROWNE, E., *Nation, Class and Creed in Northern Ireland*, Gower, Aldershot (1983).

ROSE, R., *Governing Without Consensus*, Faber, London (1971).

ROSE, R., McALLISTER, I. and MAIR, P., 'Is there a concurring majority about Northern Ireland?', *Studies in Public Policy*, no. 22, University of Strathclyde Centre for the Study of Public Policy, Glasgow (1978).

WHYTE, J., 'How is the boundary maintained between the two communities in Northern Ireland?', *Ethnic and Racial Studies*, vol. 9, no. 2 (1986), pp. 219–34.

Acknowledgements

The extension of the annual *British Social Attitudes* survey to Northern Ireland was made possible by funding to SCPR and to the Policy Research Institute (PRI), Belfast, from the Central Community Relations Unit and the Nuffield Foundation. We thank them both. Fieldwork for the Northern Ireland survey was carried out by the Policy and Planning Research Unit (PPRU) at Stormont, whose efficiency and patience in the face of an almost impossible timetable were remarkable.

Our thanks are also due to the PPRU interviewers who administered the questionnaire with such professionalism.

Valuable computing assistance was provided to the authors by Ann Mair of the Social Statistics Laboratory, University of Strathclyde.

Finally we acknowledge with gratitude the help extended by our colleagues at the PRI and at the PPRU in developing the questionnaires. Final responsibility for their content is, however, that of the *British Social Attitudes* team; and responsibility for the findings reported in this chapter and their interpretation is that of SCPR and the authors.

Appendix I
Technical details of the surveys

British Social Attitudes

In 1989, as in 1987 and 1986, the generosity of the Sainsbury Family Charitable Trusts enabled us to interview around 3,000 respondents, a substantial increase from the 1,700 to 1,800 interviewed in the first three years of the *British Social Attitudes* survey series. So we were again able to cover more topics in the questionnaire. Core questions were asked of all respondents, and the remaining questions were asked of a half sample of around 1,500 respondents each – version A of one half, version B of the other. The structure of the questionnaire is shown in Appendix III.

Sample design

The survey was designed to yield a representative sample of adults aged 18 or over living in private households in Britain.

For practical reasons, the sample was confined to those living in private households whose addresses were listed in the electoral registers. People living in institutions (though not in private households at such institutions) were excluded, as were households whose addresses were not on the electoral registers. Fieldwork was timed to start in mid-March, so the sample was drawn from the 1988 registers, which were just reaching the end of their period of currency.

The sampling method involved a multi-stage design, with four separate stages of selection.

Selection of parliamentary constituencies

One hundred and fifty-two parliamentary constituencies were selected from all those in England, Scotland and Wales. In Scotland, the constituencies north of the Caledonian Canal were omitted for reasons of cost.

Before selection, the constituencies were stratified according to information held in SCPR's constituency datafile. This datafile is a compilation of information gathered from OPCS *Monitors*, and includes a variety of social indicators such as population density, percentage of Labour vote at the 1987 general election, percentage of those holding professional qualifications, percentage of male un-employment and so on. The stratification factors used in the 1989 survey were:

- Registrar General's Standard Region
- Population density (persons per hectare) with variable banding used according to region, in order to make the strata roughly equal in size[1]
- Ranking by percentage of homes that were owner-occupied.

Constituencies were then selected systematically with probability of selection proportionate to size of electorate.

After the selection of constituencies, alternate constituencies were allocated to the A or B half of the sample, so that each questionnaire version was used in 76 areas.

Selection of polling districts

Within most of the selected constituencies a single polling district was chosen. Any polling district with fewer than 500 electors was combined with one or more other polling districts before the selection stage, so that in some constituencies a combination of polling districts was selected. Polling districts were chosen with probability proportionate to size of electorate.

Selection of addresses

Thirty addresses were selected in each of the 152 polling districts. The sample issued to interviewers was therefore 152 x 30 = 4560 addresses.

The addresses in each polling district were selected by starting from a random point on the list of electors and, treating the list as circular, choosing each address at a fixed interval. The fixed interval was calculated for each polling district separately to generate the correct number of addresses.

By this means, addresses were chosen with probability proportionate to their number of listed electors. At each sampled address the names of all electors given on the register were listed, and the name of the individual on which the sampling interval had landed was marked with an asterisk. (This person is known as the 'starred elector'.)

Selection of individuals

The electoral register is an unsatisfactory sampling frame of *individuals*, although it is regarded as reasonably complete as a frame of *addresses*. So a further selection stage was required to convert the listing of addresses into a sample of individuals.

Interviewers were instructed to call at the address of each starred elector and to list all those eligible for inclusion in the sample – that is, all persons currently aged 18 or over and resident at the selected household.

In households where the list of people eligible to take part in the survey was the same as the electoral register listing, the interviewer was instructed to interview the starred elector. Where there was a difference between the household members named in the register and those eligible to take part in the survey (because there had been movement into or out of the address after the compilation of the electoral register, or because some people were not registered) the interviewer selected one respondent by a random selection procedure (using a 'Kish grid'). Where there were two or more households at the selected address, interviewers were required to identify the household of the starred elector, or the household occupying the part of the address where he or she used to live, and to select a household using a Kish grid; then they followed the same procedure to select a person for interview.

Before analysis, the data were weighted to take account of any differences between the number of people listed on the register (which determined the initial selection probability) and the number found at the address. Such differences were found in about 27 per cent of addresses, in each of which data were weighted by the number of persons aged 18 or over currently living at the address divided by the number of electors listed on the register for that address. The vast majority of such weights was between 0.25 and 2.0. In only 19 cases were weights below 0.20 assigned, and in only 16 cases were weights greater than 2.0. At 73 per cent of addresses the number of persons listed on the register and the number found at the address matched, so that the effective weight was one. The unweighted base (the number of persons interviewed) was 3,029 and the weighted base was 2,930.

Fieldwork

Interviewing was carried out mainly during March, April and May 1989, with only six per cent of interviews taking place later.

As an experiment to test the effect on response rates, a letter was sent to a random half of the selected households shortly before fieldwork began. This briefly described the purpose of the survey and the coverage of the questionnaire, and asked for cooperation when the interviewer called. In the event, the effect of the advance letter on overall response was negligible.*

Fieldwork was conducted by 164 interviewers drawn from SCPR's regular panel, all of whom attended a one-day briefing conference to familiarise them with the selection procedures and questionnaires. The average interview length, for both versions of the questionnaire, was 63 minutes.

---

* The results of this experiment are to be published as a working paper by the Joint Centre for Survey Methods based at SCPR.

The final response achieved is shown below:

	No.	%
Addresses issued	4560	
Vacant, derelict, other out of scope	189	
In scope	4371	100
Interview achieved	3029	69.3
Interview not achieved	1342	30.7
Refused	1064[2]	24.3
Not contacted	148[3]	3.4
Other non-response	130	3.0

Response rates achieved with the A and B versions of the questionnaire were identical – 69 per cent. They ranged between 77 per cent in the North of England and 65 per cent in Greater London and 63 per cent in North West England.

As in earlier rounds of the series, respondents were asked to fill in a self-completion questionnaire which was, whenever possible, collected by the interviewer. Otherwise the respondent was asked to post it to SCPR. If necessary, up to two postal reminders were sent to obtain the self-completion supplement.

Four hundred and one respondents (14 per cent of those interviewed) did not return their self-completion questionnaire. Version A of the self-completion questionnaire was returned by 87 per cent of respondents, and version B by 86 per cent. Non-respondents to the self-completion questionnaire included a higher proportion of unskilled manual workers, residents of Greater London and respondents with no educational qualifications. Labour identifiers were less likely than Conservative or 'centre party' identifiers to return a self-completion questionnaire, while 25–44 year olds were more likely than other groups to do so. However, since the overall proportion returning a self-completion questionnaire was high we decided against additional weighting to correct for non-response.

Analysis variables

A number of standard analyses have been used in the tables that appear both in the text and at the end of the chapters of this report. The analysis groups requiring further definition are set out below.

Region

The Registrar General's 10 Standard Regions have been used, except that we have distinguished between Greater London and the remainder of the South East. Sometimes these have been grouped into what we have termed 'compressed region': 'Northern' includes the North, North West and Yorkshire and Humberside. East Anglia is included in the 'South', as is the South West.

Social class

Respondents are classified according to their own social class, not that of a putative 'head of household'. The main social class variable used in the analyses in this report is the Registrar General's, although Socio-Economic Group (SEG) has also been coded, and so can be used by secondary analysts with access to the datatape.

Each respondent's social class is based on his or her current or last occupation. So all respondents in paid work at the time of the interview, or waiting to take up a paid job already offered, or retired, or seeking work, or looking after the home, have their occupation (present, future or last as appropriate) classified into Occupational Unit Groups, according to the *OPCS Classification of Occupations 1980*. This method has been adopted on each survey, except for that of 1983 when we separately classified those looking after the home. The combination of occupational classification with employment status generates six social classes:

I	Professional	
II	Intermediate	'Non-manual'
III (Non-manual)	Skilled occupations	
III (Manual)	Skilled occupations	
IV	Semi-skilled occupations	'Manual'
V	Unskilled occupations	

In this report we have usually collapsed them into four groups: I & II, III Non-manual, III Manual, IV & V.

The remaining respondents are grouped as 'never worked/not classifiable', but are not shown in the tables. For some analyses, it may be more appropriate to classify respondents according to their *current* social class, which takes into account only their present employment status. In this case, in addition to the six social classes listed above, the remaining respondents not currently in paid work fall into one of the following categories: 'not classified', 'retired', 'looking after the home', 'unemployed' or 'others not in paid occupations'.

In some chapters, John Goldthorpe's schema is used. This system classifies occupations by their 'general comparability', considering such factors as sources and levels of income, economic security, promotion prospects, and level of job autonomy and authority. We have developed a programme which derives the Goldthorpe classification from the five-digit Occupational Unit Groups combined with employment status. The full Goldthorpe schema has 11 categories but the version used in this report (the 'compressed schema') combines these into five classes:

- Salariat (professional and managerial)
- Routine non-manual workers (office and sales)
- Petty bourgeoisie (the self-employed, including farmers, with and without employees)
- Manual foremen and supervisors
- Working class (skilled, semi-skilled and unskilled manual workers, personal service and agricultural workers).

There is a residual category of those who have never had a job or who have given insufficient information, but this is not shown in any of the analyses in this report.

Industry

All respondents whose occupation could be coded were allocated a Standard Industrial Classification (SIC, 1980). Two-digit class codes were applied. Respondents were also classified as working in public-sector services, public-sector manufacturing and transport, private-sector manufacturing, or private-sector non-manufacturing, by cross-analysing SIC categories with responses to a question about the type of employer for whom they worked. As with social class, SIC may be generated on the basis of the respondent's current occupation only, or on his or her most recently-classifiable occupation.

Party identification

Respondents can be classified as identifying with a particular political party, or party grouping, on one of three counts: if they consider themselves supporters of the party (Q.2a,d), or as closer to it than to others (Q.2b,d), or as more likely to support it in the event of a general election (Q.2c). The three groups are generally described respectively as *partisans*, *sympathisers* and *residual identifiers*. The three groups combined are referred to in both text and tables as 'identifiers'.

SLD/SDP identifiers (in spring 1989) included those nominating the Social and Liberal Democrat Party, the Liberal Party, the Social Democrat Party or the Alliance. Respondents saying "Alliance" were asked whether this meant Social and Liberal Democrat or SDP (Owen).

Other analysis variables

These are taken directly from the questionnaire, and to that extent are self-explanatory. The principal ones used in the in-text and end-of-chapter tables are:

Sex (Q.901a)	Economic status (Q.22)
Age (Q.901b)	Highest educational qualification obtained (Q.905)
Household income (Q.918a)	Marital status (A83a/B102)
Religion (Q.82a)	Union membership (Q.43a)
Religious attendance (Q.82b)	Open/closed shop union member (Q.40)

Sampling errors

No sample precisely reflects the characteristics of the population it represents because of both sampling and non-sampling errors. If a sample were designed as a random sample (if every adult had an equal and independent chance of inclusion in the sample) then we could calculate the sampling error of any percentage, p, using the formula:

$$s.e.\,(p) = \sqrt{\frac{p(100-p)}{n}}$$

where n is the number of respondents on which the percentage is based. Once the sampling error had been calculated, it would be a straightforward exercise to calculate a confidence interval for the true population percentage. For example, a 95 per cent confidence interval would be given by the formula:

$$p \pm 1.96 \times s.e.(p)$$

Clearly, for a simple random sample, the sampling error depends only on the values of p and n. However, simple random sampling is almost never used in practice because of its inefficiency in terms of time and cost.

As noted above, the *British Social Attitudes* sample, like that drawn for most large-scale surveys, was clustered according to a stratified multi-stage design into 152 polling districts (or combinations of polling districts). With a complex design like this, the sampling error of a percentage giving a particular response is not simply a function of the number of respondents in the sample and the size of the percentage; it also depends on how that percentage response is spread within and between polling districts.

So, in the case of a complex sample design, we need to calculate the complex standard error, taking into account how percentage response is spread between different areas. The underlying principle is that, since the areas themselves are now samples, the clustering of responses in areas is in itself a source of response variation.

Estimates of complex sampling errors for the 1989 survey were made using a different procedure from that followed for previous years. First, we chose a range of questions and then looked at the proportions answering in a certain way (for example "expect inflation to go up"), separately for each of the 152 different sampling points. These sampling points were then treated as if they were a sample of areas, and we calculated the variance of the proportions between areas. This gives an unbiased estimate of the complex sampling error for the sample as a whole. That this estimate takes into account neither the fact that different areas had different response rates, nor the improvements in precision due to stratification, means that the estimates will tend to overstate the size of the complex error, though the size of this overstatement is likely to be small.

However, the new procedure used does not allow us to calculate the *components* of sampling variation – that is, how much of it would have occurred as a result of random sampling variation even if there had been no clustering, and how much is due to clustering. This means that we cannot calculate design factors which give us a yardstick for comparing our sample with the efficiency obtained using simple random sampling. Nonetheless, we can see which variables have larger or smaller confidence intervals, which helps us interpret responses.

The table below gives examples of the complex standard errors and confidence intervals calculated.* In the case of most attitudinal questions asked of the whole sample, we can see that the confidence interval is usually around plus or minus two per cent of the survey proportion; so we can be 95 per cent certain that the true population proportion is within two per cent (in either direction) of the proportion we report. However, for certain variables (those most associated with the area a person lives in) we find that the confidence interval is plus or minus three per cent or more. This is particularly so for party identification and housing tenure. For instance, Labour identifiers and local authority tenants tend to be concentrated within certain areas; consequently there is proportionately more variation in a clustered sample than there would be in a simple random sample. But for most variables, especially attitudinal ones, the use of standard statistical tests of significance (based on the assumption of simple random sampling) is unlikely to be misleading. The table below also shows that, when questions were asked of only half the sample, confidence intervals are correspondingly greater.

---

* These estimates do not apply to the data presented in Chapter 6 because these are based on larger samples derived from combining several rounds of *British Social Attitudes* data.

Classification variables		%(p)	Complex standard error of p (%)	95 per cent confidence interval	Weighted n
Q2	**Party identification**				
	Conservative	39.5	1.64	36.28–42.72	1157
	SLD/SDP/'Alliance'	11.3	0.78	9.76–12.84	330
	Labour	33.5	1.62	30.32–36.68	982
A100/B112	**Housing tenure**				
	Owns	70.2	1.88	66.51–73.89	2056
	Rents from local authority	21.3	1.82	17.72–24.88	625
	Rents from housing association	1.7	0.37	0.97– 2.43	50
	Other renting	5.6	0.70	4.22– 6.98	164
Q906	**Age of completing continuous full-time education**				
	16 or under	71.7	1.44	68.87–74.53	2101
	17 or 18	13.9	0.69	12.55–15.25	406
	19 or over	12.2	0.99	10.27–14.13	358
Q82	**Religion**				
	No religion	34.4	1.03	32.39–36.41	1009
	Protestant	48.7	1.13	46.49–50.91	1427
	Catholic	11.1	0.89	9.36–12.84	326
Attitudinal variables					
Q7	**Britain should rid itself of nuclear weapons**	26.1	1.06	24.01–28.19	764
Q11	**Expect inflation to go up**	88.0	0.67	86.69–89.31	2579
Q12	**Expect unemployment to go up**	25.5	1.13	23.28–27.72	746
Q71	**Government should increase taxes and spend more on health, education and social benefits**	56.2	1.11	54.03–58.37	1648
A86a	**Pre-marital sex always or mostly wrong**	22.2	1.74	18.78–25.62	327
A86c	**Homosexual sex always or mostly wrong**	68.2	1.78	64.72–71.68	1002
B100	**Nationalisation/privatisation**				
	Favour more nationalisation	18.4	1.43	15.61–21.19	269
	Favour more privatisation	16.3	1.46	13.44–19.16	238
	Things should be left as now	29.5	1.63	26.31–32.69	865

These calculations are based on the total sample from the 1989 survey (2,930 weighted, 3,029 unweighted), or on A respondents (1,469 weighted, 1,513 unweighted) or B respondents (1,461 weighted, 1,516 unweighted). As the examples above show, sampling errors for proportions based only on the A or B sample, or on subgroups within the sample, are somewhat larger than they would have been, had the questions been asked of everyone.

Notes

1. The population density bands used were as follows:

Region	Density banding (persons per hectare)
North North West }	Under 6; 6–13; over 13
Yorks and Humberside	Under 8; 8–21; over 21
West Midlands	Under 5; 5–34; over 34
East Midlands East Anglia South West }	Under 2; 2–10; over 10
South East	Under 4; 4–8; over 8
Greater London	Under 40; 40–65; over 65
Wales Scotland }	Under 2; 2–10; over 10

2. 'Refusals' comprise refusals before selection of an individual at the address, refusals to the office, refusal by the selected person, 'proxy' refusals (on behalf of the selected respondent) and broken appointments after which the selected person could not be recontacted.
3. 'Non-contacts' comprise households where no-one was contacted, and those where the selected person could not be contacted (never found at home, known to be away on business, on holiday, in hospital and so on).

Northern Ireland Social Attitudes

In 1989, the Nuffield Foundation and the Northern Ireland Office agreed to fund three extensions of the *British Social Attitudes* survey to Northern Ireland. Core questions were asked in both surveys, but in addition there was a special module on community relations in the Northern Ireland questionnaire (Qs. 77–97 and Qs. 915–917). Some of these questions were asked in Britain too,* so allowing us to compare the attitudes of those living in Northern Ireland with the attitudes of people in Britain. The structure of the Northern Ireland questionnaire, and its relationship to the British questionnaire, is shown in Appendix III.

An advisory board consisting of representatives from Social and Community Planning Research, the Policy Planning and Research Unit (PPRU) at Stormont (which also carried out the sampling and the fieldwork), the Policy Research Institute in Belfast (which had responsibility for special analyses), the academic community and the Community Relations Council met several times in the months before fieldwork to plan the survey and design the module on community relations. As with all questionnaire modules, however, final responsibility for its coverage and wording remains with SCPR.

---

* Version B: Qs. 101–109 and Qs. 232–233; both versions: Qs. 915–917.

Sample design

The survey was designed to yield a representative sample of all adults aged 18 or over living in Northern Ireland.

The sample was drawn from the ratings list, the most up-to-date listing of private households, and made available to PPRU for research purposes. People living in institutions (though not in private households in such institutions) were excluded. The ratings list file was first stratified according to region, with addresses in Belfast, East Northern Ireland and West Northern Ireland appearing sequentially on the file.

Because of the small geographical size of Northern Ireland, it was not necessary to cluster addresses within areas. The sample was therefore a simple random sample of all households listed on the ratings list. Selection of addresses was made by taking a random starting point and then, treating the list of addresses as circular, selecting every n th address until the desired number of households had been sampled. The issued sample was 1,398 households.

Selection of individuals

The ratings list provides a good sampling frame of *addresses*, but contains no information about the number of *people* living at an address. So a further selection stage was required to convert the listing of addresses to a listing of individuals.

Interviewers were instructed to call at each address issued in their assignments. They then had to list all people resident at the address who were eligible for inclusion in the sample: that is, all persons currently aged 18 or over living at the address. From this listing of eligible adults, the interviewer selected one respondent by a random selection procedure (using a computerised 'Kish grid').

In Northern Ireland, addresses could not be selected with probability proportionate to the size of the household (as with the electoral register sampling used in *British Social Attitudes*). So before the analysis, the data were weighted to adjust for the fact that individuals living in large households had a lower chance than individuals in small households of being included in the sample. This means that the weights applied to the Northern Ireland sample are, in general, larger than those applied to the British one. All the weights fell within a range between one and seven. The distribution of weights used is shown below.

Weight	No.	%
1	229	26.4
2	448	51.7
3	125	14.4
4	40	4.6
5	16	1.8
6	5	0.6
7	3	0.3

Thus, 26 per cent of households had only one adult present, 52 per cent were two-adult households, 14 per cent were three-adult households, and so on. The average weight applied was 2.06. Because the weighted sample was scaled back to the size of the unweighted sample, both yield 866 interviews.

Fieldwork

Fieldwork was carried out mainly during March and April 1989; only six interviews took place later.

Fieldwork was conducted by 62 interviewers drawn from PPRU's panel. All interviewers attended a one-day briefing conference to familiarise them with the selection procedures and the questionnaires. The interview took on average 75 minutes to administer.

Overall response achieved was:

	No.	%
Addresses issued	1398	
Vacant, derelict, out of scope	94	
In scope	1304	100
Interview achieved	866	66
Interview not achieved	438	34
Refused	264	20
Non-contact	103	8
Other non-response	71	5

A response rate of 65 per cent was achieved in Belfast; it was 70 per cent in East Northern Ireland and 71 per cent in West Northern Ireland.

As in the *British Social Attitudes* survey, respondents were asked to fill in a self-completion questionnaire which was, whenever possible, collected by the interviewer. Otherwise, the respondent was asked to post it direct to a Northern Ireland Post Office box from which it was forwarded to SCPR. If necessary, up to two postal reminders were sent to obtain the self-completion questionnaire from those who had not returned it. In all, 780 respondents returned the self-completion questionnaire, 90 per cent of those interviewed.

Analysis variables

Analysis variables were the same as used in the British survey, though of course the questions about party identification included Northern Irish political parties.

Sampling errors

Because the *Northern Ireland Social Attitudes* survey is drawn as a simple random sample, there are no complex sampling errors to calculate. The sampling error of any percentage, p, can be calculated using the formula:

$$s.e.(p) = \sqrt{\frac{P(100-p)}{n}}$$

Reference

BROOK, L., TAYLOR, B. and PRIOR, G., *British Social Attitudes, 1989 Survey: Technical Report*, SCPR, London (1990).

Appendix II
Notes on the tabulations

1. Figures in the tables are from the 1989 survey unless otherwise indicated.
2. Tables at the end of chapters are percentaged vertically; tables within the text are percentaged as indicated.
3. In tables, '*' indicates less than 0.5 per cent but greater than zero, and '–' indicates zero.
4. When findings based on the responses of fewer than 50 respondents are reported in the text, reference is made to the small base size. Any percentages based on fewer than 50 respondents (unweighted) are bracketed in the end-of-chapter tables, as are the bases.
5. Percentages equal to or greater than 0.5 have been rounded up in all tables (eg. 0.5 per cent = one per cent, 36.5 per cent = 37 per cent).
6. Owing to the effects of rounding weighted data, the weighted bases shown in the tables may not always add up to the expected base.
7. In many tables the proportions of respondents answering "don't know" or not giving an answer are omitted. This, together with the effects of rounding and weighting, means that percentages will not always add to 100 per cent.
8. The self-completion questionnaire was not completed by 14 per cent of respondents in Britain and by 10 per cent of respondents in Northern Ireland (see Appendices I and III). Percentage responses to the self-completion questionnaire are based on all those who completed it.

Appendix III
The questionnaires

As explained in Appendix I, two different versions of the questionnaire were administered in Britain (each with its own self-completion supplement), and a separate questionnaire was administered in Northern Ireland (also with its supplement). The diagram on the next page shows the structure of the personal interview questionnaires and the topics covered (not all of which are reported in this volume).

All six questionnaires (interview and self-completion) are reproduced on the following pages. We have removed the keying codes and inserted instead the percentage distribution of answers to each question. Percentages for the core questions are based on the total sample (2,930 weighted in Britain and 866 weighted and unweighted in Northern Ireland), while those for questions in versions A and B are based on the appropriate subsamples (1,469 and 1,461 weighted). We reproduce first version A of the interview questionnaire in full; then those parts of version B that differ; the two versions of the self-completion questionnaire follow. In the last part of Appendix III we reproduce the interview questionnaire administered in Northern Ireland and its self-completion supplement. Figures do not necessarily add up to 100 because of weighting and rounding, or for one or more of the following reasons:

(i)   We have not always included percentages for those not answering (which are usually very small). They are, of course, included on the datatape.
(ii) Some sub-questions are filtered – that is, they are asked of only a proportion of respondents. In these cases the percentages add up (approximately) to the proportions who were asked them. Where, however, a *series* of questions is filtered (for instance in the last part of Section 2 of the interview questionnaire), we have indicated the weighted base at the beginning of that series, and throughout derived percentages from that base. Medians which could have been derived from unweighted bases of less than 50 have not been given.

(iii) At a few questions, respondents were invited to give more than one answer and so percentages may add to well over 100 per cent. These are clearly marked by interviewer instructions on the questionnaires.

Structure of the questionnaires

Section	Great Britain		All questionnaires	Northern Ireland
1	Politics (short)		Newspaper readership Defence International relations	
2			Economic issues and policies Household income Economic activity Labour market participation	
3			Welfare state National Health Service	
4	Race (short)		Social class Religion	Poverty

Section	Version A only	Version B only		Northern Ireland
5	Moral issues	Race (long) Poverty and state benefits		Moral issues
6	Diet and health (long)	Politics (long)		Diet and health (long)
7	Industry/jobs	Northern Ireland issues		Northern Ireland issues
8	Housing (short)	Housing (long)		Housing (short)
9	AIDS	Diet and health (short)	All questionnaires	AIDS
10			Demographics and other classificatory variables	

As reported in Appendix 1, the *British Social Attitudes* self-completion questionnaire was not completed by 14 per cent of respondents who were successfully interviewed. To allow for comparisons over time, the answers in the supplement have been repercentaged on the base of those respondents who returned it (for version A: 1,274 weighted; for version B: 1,255 weighted). This means that the figures are comparable with those given in all earlier reports in this series except in *The 1984 Report*, where the percentages need to be recalculated if comparisons are to be made.

The *Northern Ireland Social Attitudes* self-completion questionnaire was not completed by 10 per cent of respondents to the main questionnaire. Again the answers in the supplement have been repercentaged on the base of those who returned it (784 weighted).

Two modules developed as part of SCPR's involvement in the *International Social Survey Programme* were fielded on the self-completion supplements: the first, on the subject of women and the family, on version A of the British supplement (Qs.1–19); and the second, on attitudes towards work, on version B of the British supplement and also on the *Northern Ireland Social Attitudes* supplement (Qs.1–21). Some of the findings are presented in Chapter 8 of *British Social Attitudes: special international report (the 6th Report)* and in Chapter 3 of this report.

SCPR

Head Office: 35 NORTHAMPTON SQUARE, LONDON EC1V 0AX
TELEPHONE 01-250 1866

Northern Field Office: CHARAZEL HOUSE, GILSFORD, DARLINGTON,
CO. DURHAM DL2 1EG. TELEPHONE 01325-730888

P.1005

Spring 1989

BRITISH SOCIAL ATTITUDES:

1989 SURVEY

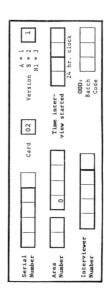

- 1 -

SECTION ONE

N=3029

A

1.a) Do you normally read any daily morning newspaper at least 3 times a week?

			Skip to
	Yes	69.7	b)
	No	30.3	Q.2

IF YES
b) Which one do you normally read?
IF MORE THAN ONE ASK: Which one do you read *most* frequently?

(Scottish) Daily Express	6.5
Daily Mail	7.8
Daily Mirror/Record	17.2
Daily Star	2.5
The Sun	14.9
Today	1.8
Daily Telegraph	5.1
Financial Times	0.4
The Guardian	2.4
The Independent	2.3
The Times	1.4
Morning Star	0.0
Other Irish/Northern Irish/Scottish/regional or local daily morning paper (WRITE IN)	4.7
Others	0.1
More than one	2.2

ASK ALL

2.a) Generally speaking, do you think of yourself as a supporter of any one political party?

			Skip to
	Yes	50.9	d)
	No	49.0	b)

IF NO AT a)
b) Do you think of yourself as a little closer to one political party than to the others?

	Yes	23.6	d)
	No	24.9	c)

IF NO AT b)
c) If there were a general election tomorrow, which political party do you think you would be most likely to support? **CODE ONE ONLY UNDER COL c) & d)**
IF ALLIANCE, PROBE: Social and Liberal Democrat or SDP (Owen)?

	a/d	b/d	c/d
Conservative	24.6	10.2	4.5

IF YES AT a) OR b)
d) Which one? **CODE ONE ONLY UNDER c) & d)**
IF ALLIANCE, PROBE:
Social and Liberal Democrat/Liberal/SLD or SDP (Owen)?

Labour	20.3	7.8	5.3
Social and Liberal Democrat/Liberal/SLD	2.6	2.6	2.3
SDP/Social Democrat	1.1	1.4	1.1
Alliance (AFTER PROBE)		0.1	0.1
Scottish Nationalist	0.9	0.5	7.8
Plaid Cymru	0.1	0.1	0.1
Green Party	0.3	0.3	0.2
Other party/other answer	0.1		1.5
None		3.1	7.0
Refused/unwilling to say	0.8	0.5	1.7

IF ANY PARTY CODED AT c) & d)
e) Would you call yourself very strong ...
(QUOTE PARTY NAMED) ... fairly strong, or not very strong?

Very strong	11.2
Fairly strong	32.9
Not very strong	42.0
Don't know	0.5

- 2 -

A

ASK ALL

3.a) Do you think that local councils ought to be controlled by central government more, less or about the same amount as now?

		Skip to
More	15.5	
Less	37.2	
About the same	37.5	
Don't know	9.7	

b) And do you think the level of local community charges - that is, the poll tax or rates - should be up to the local council to decide, or should central government have the final say? **RECORD IN COL b)**

c) How about the level of council rents? Should that be up to the local council to decide or should central government have the final say? **RECORD IN COL c)**

	b) Local charges	c) Rents
Local council	70.0	79.0
Central government	20.6	12.7
Don't know	8.8	7.9

4.a) Now a few questions about Britain's relationships with other countries.

Do you think Britain should continue to be a member of the EEC - the Common Market - or should it withdraw? **RECORD IN COL a)**

b) And do you think Britain should continue to be a member of NATO - The North Atlantic Treaty Organisation - or should it withdraw? **RECORD IN COL b)**

	(a) EEC	(b) NATO
Continue	67.9	78.6
Withdraw	26.0	10.9
Don't know	5.8	10.0

5. On the whole, do you think that Britain's interests are better served by ... **READ OUT** ...

... closer links with Western Europe,	50.3
or - closer links with America?	17.5
(Both equally)	19.6
(Neither)	2.9
(Don't know)	9.7

6.a) Do you think that the siting of American nuclear missiles in Britain makes Britain a safer or a less safe place to live? **RECORD IN COL a)**

b) And do you think that having its own independent nuclear missiles makes Britain a safer or a less safe place to live? **RECORD IN COL b)**

	(a) American nuclear missiles	(b) Own nuclear missiles
Safer	35.6	54.7
Less safe	51.5	33.8
No difference	1.6	1.2
Don't know	11.2	10.2

- 3 -

	Skip to

A

7. CARD A

Which, if either, of these two statements comes closest to your own opinion on Britain's nuclear policy?

Britain should <u>rid</u> itself of nuclear weapons while persuading others to do the same	26.1
Britain should <u>keep</u> its nuclear weapons until it can persuade others to reduce theirs	71.5
(Neither of these)	1.9
Don't know	0.4

8. Which political party's views on defence would you say comes <u>closest</u> to your own views?

CODE ONE ONLY

ONLY CODE ALLIANCE AFTER PROBE:
Social and Liberal Democrats or
SDP (Owen)?

Conservative	44.0
Labour	22.9
Social and Liberal Democrat/Liberal/SLD	3.5
SDP/Social Democrat	2.2
Alliance (AFTER PROBE)	-
Other (WRITE IN: _____)	1.1
Don't know	21.7
None	4.3

9. CARD B

Which of the phrases on this card is closest to your opinion about threats to world peace?

America is a greater threat to world peace than Russia	13.9
Russia is a greater threat to world peace than America	16.2
Russia and America are equally great threats to world peace	46.9
Neither is a threat to world peace	19.5
(Don't know)	3.5

10.a Do you think the long term policy for Northern Ire-and should be for it ... **READ OUT** ...

... to remain part of the United Kingdom,	30.1
or - to reunify with the rest of Ireland?	54.8
Northern Ireland - independent state	0.3
Northern Ireland should be split in two	0.1
Up to Irish to decide	4.2
Others	1.1
Don't know	8.7

b) Some people think that government policy towards Northern Ireland should include a complete withdrawal of British troops. Would you personally support or <u>oppose</u> such a policy? PROBE: Strongly or a little?

Support strongly	38.0
Support a little	21.1
Oppose strongly	28.6
Oppose a little	15.6
Withdraw in long term	0.4
Let Irish decide	0.9
Other	0.4
Don't know	4.4

- 4 -

	Skip to

A

SECTION TWO

Now I would like to ask you about two of Britain's economic problems - inflation and unemployment.

11. First, inflation: in a year from now, do you expect prices generally to have gone up, to have stayed the same, or to have gone down?

IF GONE UP OR GONE DOWN:
By a lot or a little?

To have gone up by a lot	44.6
To have gone up by a little	43.4
To have stayed the same	7.6
To have gone down by a little	3.1
To have gone down by a lot	0.4
(Don't know)	0.8

12. Second, unemployment: in a year from now, do you expect unemployment to have gone up, to have stayed the same, or to have gone down?

IF GONE UP OR GONE DOWN:
By a lot or a little?

To have gone up by a lot	9.5
To have gone up by a little	15.9
To have stayed the same	37.3
To have gone down by a little	30.0
To have gone down by a lot	4.8
(Don't know)	2.4

13.a) If the government <u>had</u> to choose between keeping down inflation or keeping down unemployment, which do you think it should give highest priority?

keeping down inflation	38.5
keeping down unemployment	56.7
Both equally	2.4
Other	0.2
Don't know	1.5

b) Which do you think is the most concern to <u>you and your family</u> ... **READ OUT** ...

... inflation.	66.5
or - unemployment?	29.8
Both equally	1.5
Neither	0.2
Other	0.1
Don't know	1.2

14. Looking ahead over the next year, do you think Britain's general industrial performance will improve, stay much the same, or decline?

IF IMPROVE OR DECLINE:
By a lot or a little?

Improve a lot	4.9
Improve a little	24.7
Stay much the same	47.0
Decline a little	12.4
Decline a lot	4.3
(Don't know)	6.5

- 5 -

15. Here are a number of policies which might help Britain's economic problems. As I read them out, will you tell me whether you would support such a policy or oppose it?

READ OUT ITEMS i)-x) AND CODE FOR EACH

	Support	Oppose	Don't know	Skip to
i) Control of wages by law	27.7	68.5	3.3	
ii) Control of prices by law	55.5	42.0	2.2	
iii) Reducing the level of government spending on health and education	6.8	92.1	0.8	
iv) Government controls to cut down goods from abroad	67.2	28.3	4.0	
v) Increasing government subsidies for private industry	52.8	39.6	7.1	
vi) Reducing government spending on defence	55.6	40.4	3.8	
vii) a) Government schemes to encourage job sharing	67.3	26.9	5.2	
viii) Government to set up construction projects to create more jobs	86.8	11.1	1.9	
ix) Government action to cut interest rates	83.6	11.6	4.4	
x) Government controls on hire purchase and credit	79.3	17.2	3.3	

16. On the whole, would you like to see <u>more</u> or less state ownership of industry, or about the <u>same</u> amount as now?

More	17.8
Less	24.0
About the same amount	52.7
(Don't know)	5.3

17.a) It is said that many people manage to avoid paying their full income tax. Do you think that they should <u>not</u> be allowed to get away with it - or do you think good luck to them if they can get away with it?

		Skip to
Should not be allowed	75.7	b)
Good luck if they can get away with it	23.8	Q.18
Don't know	0.5	

IF 'SHOULD NOT BE ALLOWED' (CODE 1 AT a)

b) if you knew of somebody who wasn't paying their full income tax, would you be inclined to report him or her?

Yes	10.6
No	60.8
Don't know	1.6
Other answer (WRITE IN:)	2.3
[NOT ASKED]	24.3

- 6 -

ASK ALL

18. Thinking of income levels generally in Britain today, would you say that the <u>gap</u> between those with high incomes and those with low incomes is ... READ OUT ...

		Skip to
... too large,	79.6	
about right,	15.4	
or - too small?	2.6	
Don't know	2.3	

CARD C

19. Generally, how would you describe levels of taxation?

a) Firstly for those with <u>high</u> incomes? Please choose a phrase from this card. RECORD ANSWER IN COL a) BELOW

b) Next for those with <u>middle</u> incomes? Please choose a phrase from this card. RECORD ANSWER IN COL b) BELOW

c) And lastly for those with <u>low</u> incomes? Please choose a phrase from this card. RECORD ANSWER IN COL c) BELOW

Taxes are:	(a) High incomes	(b) Middle incomes	(c) Low incomes
Much too high	2.4	2.1	29.4
Too high	9.2	25.3	50.4
About right	33.4	63.8	15.3
Too low	41.7	6.0	1.7
Much too low	10.0	0.4	0.8
don't know	2.9	2.3	2.2

20.a) Among which group would you place yourself ... READ OUT ...

... high income,	2.6
middle income,	52.1
or - low income?	44.6
Don't know	0.3

CARD D

b) Which of the phrases on this card would you say comes closest to your feelings about your household's income these days?

Living comfortably on present income	27.1
Coping on present income	49.4
Finding it difficult on present income	17.1
Finding it very difficult on present income	6.1
Other (WRITE IN:)	0.1
Don't know	-

- 8 -

N=1462
Qs.24-40

ALL EMPLOYEES (CODE 1 AT Q.23) ASK Qs. 24 - 45

		Skip to

24. How many hours a week do you normally work in your (main) job?

(IF RESPONDENT CANNOT ANSWER, ASK ABOUT LAST WEEK)

MEDIAN: 39 HOURS

AND CODE:
	%
10-15 hours a week	6.0
16-23 hours a week	7.9
24-29 hours a week	5.2
30 or more hours a week	80.9
Don't know	0.0

25.a) How would you describe the wages or salary you are paid for the job you do - on the low side, reasonable, or on the high side? IF LOW: Very low or a bit low?

	%
Very low	11.3
A bit low	28.4
Reasonable	55.7
On the high side	4.5
Don't know	0.1

Other answer (WRITE IN)

b) CARD F
Thinking of the highest and the lowest paid people at your place of work, how would you describe the gap between their pay, as far as you know? Please choose a phrase from this card.

	%
Much too big a gap	14.1
Too big	30.6
About right	43.0
Too small	2.4
Much too small a gap	0.4
Other	0.1
Don't know	9.3

26.a) If you stay in this job would you expect your wages or salary over the coming year to ... READ OUT ...

	%
... rise by more than the cost of living,	15.3
rise by the same as the cost of living,	43.7
rise by less than the cost of living,	29.6
or - not to rise at all?	8.1
(Will not stay in job)	0.9
(Don't know)	2.2

b) Over the coming year do you expect your workplace will be ... READ OUT

	%
... increasing its number of employees,	25.5
reducing its number of employees,	19.6
or - will the number of employees stay about the same?	52.7
Don't know	2.0

Other answer (WRITE IN) | 0.2

- 7 -

		Skip to

21.a) Looking back over the last year or so, would you say your household's income has ... READ OUT ...

	%
... fallen behind prices,	48.6
kept up with prices,	39.5
or - gone up by more than prices?	10.2
(Don't know)	1.6

b) And looking forward to the year ahead, do you expect your household's income will ... READ OUT ..

	%
... fall behind prices,	44.8
keep up with prices,	41.0
or - go up by more than prices?	9.7
(Don't know)	4.1

22. CARD E
Which of these descriptions applies to what you were doing last week, that is, in the seven days ending last Sunday? PROBE: Any others? CODE ALL THAT APPLY IN COLUMN I

IF ONLY ONE CODE AT I, TRANSFER IT TO COLUMN II
IF MORE THAN ONE AT I, TRANSFER HIGHEST ON LIST TO II

	COL I	COL II ECONOMIC POSITION	Skip to
In full-time education (not paid for by employer, including on vacation) A		2.2	Q.67
On government training/employment scheme (e.g. Employment Training, Youth Training Programme, etc) B		0.7	Q.53
In paid work (or away temporarily) for at least 10 hours in the week C		56.4	Q.23
Waiting to take up paid work already accepted D		0.2	Q.53
Unemployed and registered at a benefit office E		2.8	Q.55
Unemployed, not registered, but actively looking for a job F		0.7	Q.55
Unemployed, wanting a job (of at least 10 hrs per week), but not actively looking for a job G		0.5	
Permanently sick or disabled H		3.2	Q.67
Wholly retired from work J		17.5	Q.62
Looking after the home K		15.5	Q.63
Doing something else (WRITE IN:) L		0.2	Q.67

23. IF IN PAID WORK OR AWAY TEMPORARILY (CODE 03 AT Q.21)
N=1689
In your (main) job are you ... READ OUT ...

	%	Skip to
... an employee,	86.7	Q.24
or - self-employed?	13.3	Q.46

- 9 -

A

27.a) Thinking now about your own job. How likely or unlikely is it that you will leave this employer over the next year for any reason? Is it ... **READ OUT** ...

		Skip to
... very likely,	11.1	b)
quite likely,	12.1	b)
not very likely	27.7	
or - not at all likely	48.7	
Don't know	0.2	

IF VERY OR QUITE LIKELY AT a)

CARD G

b) Why do you think you will leave? Please choose a phrase from this card or tell me what other reason there is.

MORE THAN ONE CODE MAY BE RINGED

Firm will close down	1.1
I will be declared redundant	3.0
I will reach normal retirement age	0.9
My contract of employment will expire	1.2
I will take early retirement	0.8
I will decide to leave and work for another employer	13.7
I will decide to leave and work for myself, as self-employed	2.1
I will leave to look after home/children/relative	1.8
Other answer (WRITE IN)	0.9

ASK ALL EMPLOYEES

28.a) Suppose you lost your job for one reason or another - would you start looking for another job, would you wait for several months or longer before you started looking, or would you decide not to look for another job?

Start looking	87.4
Wait several months or longer	5.1
Decide not to look	6.8
Don't know	0.6

IF START LOOKING AT a)

b) How long do you think it would take you to find an acceptable replacement job?

MEDIAN: 1 MONTHS   OR CODE:

		Skip to
Never	2.3	b) Q.29
Don't know	12.3	

IF 3 MONTHS OR MORE, NEVER, OR DK, ASK c)-e). OTHERS GO TO Q.29

c) How willing do you think you would be in these circumstances to retrain for a different job ... **READ OUT** ...

... very willing,	14.4
quite willing,	12.4
or - not very willing?	6.1
(Don't know)	0.7

d) And how willing do you think you would be to move to a different area to find an acceptable job ... **READ OUT** ...

... very willing,	3.4
quite willing,	6.5
or - not very willing?	22.9
(Don't know)	0.7

e) And how willing do you think you would be in these circumstances to take what you now consider to be an unacceptable job ... **READ OUT** ...

... very willing,	3.2
quite willing,	10.6
or - not very willing?	18.6
(Don't know)	1.2

- 10 -

A

29. **ASK ALL EMPLOYEES**

If without having to work, you had what you would regard as a reasonable living income, do you think you would still prefer to have a paid job or wouldn't you bother?

Still prefer paid job	73.7
Wouldn't bother	25.1
Other answer (WRITE IN)	0.7
Don't know	0.3

30.a) During the last five years - that is since March 1984 - have you been unemployed and seeking work for any period?

		Skip to
Yes	20.1	
No	79.8	

IF YES AT a)

b) For how many months in total during the last five years?

MEDIAN: 6 MONTHS

ASK ALL EMPLOYEES

31.a) For any period during the last five years have you worked as a self-employed person as your main job?

Yes	4.5
No	95.5

IF YES AT a)

b) In total, for how many months during the last five years have you been self-employed?

MEDIAN: 24 MONTHS

IF NO AT a)

c) How seriously in the last five years have you considered working as a self-employed person ... **READ OUT** ...

... very seriously,	5.1
quite seriously,	9.2
not very seriously,	11.3
or - not at all seriously?	69.6

ASK ALL EMPLOYEES

32.a) Now for some more general questions about your work.

For some people their job is simply something they do in order to earn a living. For others it means much more than that. On balance, is your present job ... **READ OUT** ...

		Skip to
... just a means of earning a living,	30.8	a)
or - does it mean much more to you than that?	69.1	Q.33

IF 'MEANS OF EARNING A LIVING' (CODE 1 AT a)

b) Is that because ... **READ OUT** ...

... there are no better jobs around here,	7.7
you don't have the right skills to get a better job,	7.5
or - because you would feel the same about any job you had?	12.9
Don't know	0.4

- 11 -

A

33.a) ASK ALL EMPLOYEES
CARD H
Suppose you were looking for another job - which of the things on this card would be most important to you in choosing a new job? Please read through the whole list before deciding.
ONE CODE ONLY IN COL a)

b) And which would be next most important?
ONE CODE ONLY IN COL b)

c) And which would be third most important?
ONE CODE ONLY IN COL c)

	(a) Most imp. in choosing job	(b) Next most imp.	(c) Third most imp.
Convenient working hours	15.2	8.1	7.3
Possibility of promotion	6.0	6.2	8.1
Clean/pleasant working conditions	1.6	3.7	5.8
Strong trade union	0.3	0.7	1.2
Interesting work that makes use of your skills	29.5	14.9	9.1
Work that helps others	4.3	5.1	3.6
Opportunity to get on with your work in your own way	3.8	8.8	10.1
Job security	18.1	11.7	10.9
Outdoor work	1.4	1.3	1.3
Good pay	13.9	22.0	16.6
Friendliness of people you work with	4.0	10.8	14.2
Good fringe benefits (pension, sick pay)	0.9	4.8	8.4
Short working hours	0.4	1.5	2.7
(NONE OF THESE)	0.4	0.3	0.3
(Don't know)	0.1	0.1	0.2

34.a) Apart from overtime are you paid ... READ OUT ...
PAYMENT FOR UNSOCIABLE HOURS COUNTS AS 'BY THE HOUR'
... the same amount per week or month, 68.5
by the hour, so if your hours vary your pay varies, 23.9
or - does your pay include some sort of piecework, payment by performance or commission? 7.4

b) Do you regularly do paid overtime at work? - ... READ OUT ...
by regularly, I mean most weeks.
Yes 28.6
No 68.7

- 12 -

A

35.a) Thinking about the number of hours you work each week including regular overtime, would you prefer a job where you worked ... READ OUT ...
... more hours per week, 4.5 b)
fewer hours per week, 30.0 c)
or - are you happy with the number of hours you work at present? 65.2 Q.36
(Don't know) 0.1

IF WOULD PREFER MORE HOURS PER WEEK (CODE 1 AT a)
b) Is the reason why you don't work more hours because ... READ OUT ...
... your employer can't offer you more hours, 3.8
or - your personal circumstances don't allow it? 0.5
(Both) 0.2 } Q.36

Other reason (WRITE IN)

IF WOULD PREFER FEWER HOURS (CODE 2 AT a)
c) In which of these ways would you like your working hours to be shortened ... READ OUT ...
... shorter hours each day, 10.8
or - fewer days each week? 18.4

Other (WRITE IN) 0.4

d) Would you still like to work fewer hours if it meant earning less money as a result?
Yes 6.8
No 20.6
It depends 1.5
Don't know 0.5

ASK ALL EMPLOYEES
36.a) Suppose there was going to be some decision made at your place of work that changed the way you do your job. Do you think that you personally would have any say in the decision about the change, or not?
Yes 49.7 b)
No 46.8 c)
It depends/Don't know 3.3

IF YES AT a)
b) How much say or chance to influence the decision do you think you would have ... READ OUT ...
... a great deal, 9.6
quite a lot, 20.5
or - just a little? 17.9
(It depends/Don't know) 1.4

ASK ALL EMPLOYEES
c) Do you think you should have more say in decisions affecting your work, or are you satisfied with the way things are?
Should have more say 44.3
Satisfied with way things are 53.8
Don't know 1.0

- 14 -

INTERVIEWER: CHECK Q.37a:

Trade union(s) or staff association recognised at workplace (CODES 1 OR 2 AT Q.37a)

		Skip to
	27.3	b)
Others	44.1	Q.43

41.a)

IF UNION(S) OR STAFF ASSOCIATION RECOGNISED AT a)   N= 862

CARD J

b) Listed on the card are a number of things trade unions or staff associations can do. Which, if any, do you think are the three most important things they should try to do at your workplace?

First, tell me the <u>most</u> important. RECORD IN COL b).

c) Then, tell me the second most important. RECORD IN COL c).

d) And then, the third most important. RECORD IN COL d).

UNIONS OR STAFF ASSOCIATIONS SHOULD TRY TO:	(b) Most important	(c) Second most important	(d) Third most important
Improve working conditions	20.8	22.1	17.0
Improve pay	28.3	23.2	17.0
Protect existing jobs	27.9	19.4	16.6
Have more say over how work is done day-to-day	3.4	6.3	8.7
Have more say over management's long-term plans	6.4	9.5	12.1
Work for equal opportunities for women	2.8	6.2	7.7
Work for equal opportunities for ethnic minorities	0.2	2.0	2.7
Reduce pay differences at the workplace	5.8	5.4	8.5
(NONE OF THESE)	2.0	2.9	5.1
(Don't know)	1.0	1.2	2.4

42.

IF UNION OR STAFF ASSOCIATION RECOGNISED AT Q.41a)   N= 862

CARD K

Do you think that the union(s) or staff association at your workplace has too much or too little power? Please use a phrase from the card.

Far too much power	0.1
Too much power	3.6
About the right amount of power	51.3
Too little power	31.4
Far too little power	5.8
(Don't know/Can't say)	6.2

- 13 -

37.a) At your place of work are there unions, staff associations, or groups of unions recognised by the management for negotiating pay and conditions of employment?   IF YES, PROBE FOR UNION OR STAFF ASSOCIATION

		Skip to
Yes: trade union(s)	3.9	
Yes: staff association	49.2	b)
Both	4.5	
No, none	41.8	
Don't know	0.0	

IF YES (CODES 1 OR 2 AT a)

b) On the whole, do you think these unions or staff associations do their job well or not?

Yes	32.8
No	21.4
Don't know	3.1

c) Is there only one union or staff association recognised by the management or more than one?

Only one	22.9
More than one	33.0
Don't know	1.5

'ONLY ONE' IS 'SINGLE UNION' AGREEMENT

ASK ALL EMPLOYEES

38.a) In general how would you describe relations between management and other employees at your workplace ... READ OUT ...

... very good,	32.0
quite good,	48.6
not very good,	14.2
or - not at all good?	4.3
Don't know	0.3

b) And in general, would you say your workplace was ... READ OUT ...

... very well managed,	25.6
quite well managed,	54.4
or - not well managed?	18.3
Don't know	0.3

39. How would you describe the management's attitude to trade unions at the place where you work? Would you say management ... READ OUT ...

... encourages trade union membership,	10.3
accepts it or would accept it,	32.0
discourages trade union membership,	10.4
or - isn't it really an issue at your workplace?	45.0
Don't know	1.8

CARD I

40. Suppose you left your present job. Which <u>one</u> of these statements would apply to a person who replaced you?

THEY WOULD:

have to be a union member before being considered for the job,	1.9
have to join a union <u>before</u> starting the job,	3.1
have to join a union <u>after</u> starting the job,	10.1
<u>not</u> be required to join a union,	82.5
(Don't know)	2.2

- 15 -

ASK ALL EMPLOYEES

43.a) Are you now a member of a trade union or staff association, either at your workplace or somewhere else?

IF YES: PROBE FOR UNION OR STAFF ASSOCIATION

Yes - trade union member	38.8
Yes - staff association member	4.8
No - not member	56.4
(Refused: won't say)	-

IF UNION OR STAFF ASSOCIATION MEMBER AT a)

CARD L

b) I am going to read some reasons people may have for belonging to a trade union or staff association. For each one, please use the card to say how important it is to you personally.

READ b)-i) BELOW AND CODE FOR EACH

N= 647

	Very important	Fairly important	Not very important	Not at all important	Does not apply to me	Skip to
b) It's a condition of having my job.	21.7	15.9	10.2	13.8	38.3	
c) To get higher pay and better working conditions.	39.3	40.1	9.7	4.0	6.4	
d) To get members' benefits, like financial or health schemes	33.9	36.4	15.0	7.7	6.4	
e) I believe in them in principle	27.4	39.6	19.9	9.3	3.7	
f) Most of my workmates or colleagues are members.	26.1	29.0	21.0	17.6	6.0	
g) To protect me if problems come up.	63.-	29.4	3.7	2.2	0.4	
h) It's a tradition in my family.	7.0	8.2	16.3	34.9	33.2	
i) To help other people I work with.	34.0	42.3	9.6	7.9	5.4	

- 16 -

IF NOT UNION OR STAFF ASSOCIATION MEMBER (CODE 3 AT Q.43a)

N= 815

CARD L

44. I am going to read some reasons people may have for not belonging to a trade union or staff association. For each one, please use the card to say how important it is to you personally.

READ OUT a)-j) BELOW AND CODE FOR EACH

	Very important	Fairly important	Not very important	Not at all important	Does not apply to me	Skip to
a) There is no union at my workplace.	9.0	8.0	16.2	27.6	37.7	
b) No-one has ever asked me to join.	5.3	5.5	16.8	28.7	42.3	
c) I don't approve of the one I could join at my workplace.	1.6	3.5	6.6	11.8	74.9	
d) It costs too much.	1.4	4.7	8.9	23.8	59.4	
e) I disagree with them in principle.	11.3	11.6	15.4	23.7	33.4	
f) It not really appropriate for my kind of work.	10.9	15.5	13.1	33.5	38.2	
g) I can't see any advantage in joining.	13.2	15.1	13.4	15.8	40.8	
h) I feel it would damage my job prospects.	6.3	4.9	9.2	23.6	53.9	
i) Management disapproves of them at my workplace.	6.9	6.6	8.8	21.5	53.0	
j) They would only cause trouble at my workplace.	9.1	7.8	8.5	22.5	49.4	

ASK ALL EMPLOYEES

N= 1462

45.a) Aside from your main job, do you have any other paid job, like a second job or other paid work?

IF YES: Is that regular work or do you only do it sometimes?

Yes - regularly	5.1
Yes - sometimes	3.0
No, no other paid work	91.7

IF YES (CODE 1 OR 2 AT a)

b) How many hours a week do you normally work in these other jobs, not including time spent travelling to work?

DO NOT COUNT MAIN JOB

MEDIAN: [8] HOURS

NOW GO TO SECTION 3 (p.24)

- 17 - N=227 Qs.46-52

ALL SELF-EMPLOYED (CODE 2 AT Q.23): ASK Qs. 46-52

46.a) How many hours a week do you normally work in your (main) job?

MEDIAN: 45 HOURS

(IF RESPONDENT CANNOT ANSWER, ASK ABOUT 'LAST WEEK')

AND CODE:

10-15 hours a week	5.1
16-23 hours a week	8.8
24-29 hours a week	2.0
30 or more hours a week	83.3

b) For about how many years have you been self-employed and doing the same sort of work as now?

PROBE FOR BEST ESTIMATE.
IF LESS THAN SIX MONTHS, CODE '00'.
IF 6 MONTHS OR MORE, ROUND UP TO NEAREST YEAR

MEDIAN: 4 YEARS

c) During the last 5 years - that is since March 1984 - have you been unemployed and seeking work for any period?

Yes	24.9
No	71.1

47. If without having to work, you had what you would regard as a reasonable living income, do you think you would still prefer to do paid work, or wouldn't you bother?

Still prefer paid work	77.6
Wouldn't bother	19.9
Other answer (WRITE IN)	
Don't know	0.0

48.a) Have you, for any period in the last five years, worked as an employee as your main job rather than as self-employed?

Yes	41.9
No	57.8

IF YES, ASK b). IF NO, ASK c)

b) In total for how many months during the last five years have you been

MEDIAN: 24 MONTHS

IF NO AT a)

c) How seriously in the last five years have you considered getting a job as an employee ... READ OUT ...

... very seriously,	1.5
quite seriously,	5.7
not very seriously,	7.4
or - not at all seriously?	42.2
[NOT ASKED]	41.9

- 18 -

ASK ALL SELF-EMPLOYED

49.a) Compared with a year ago, would you say your business is doing ... READ OUT ...

... very well,	14.3
quite well,	20.9
about the same,	40.1
not very well,	8.9
or - not at all well?	0.7
(Business not in existence then)	13.3

b) And over the coming year, do you think your business will do ... READ OUT ...

... better,	41.5
about the same,	42.9
or - worse than this year?	5.9
(Don't know)	2.3
Other (WRITE IN)	5.5

50.a) In your work or business, do you have any partners or other self-employed colleagues?

Yes, have partner(s)	40.1
No	59.0

NOTE: DOES NOT INCLUDE EMPLOYEES

b) And in your work or business do you have any employees, or not?

Yes, has employee(s)	29.9
No	65.7

N.B. FAMILY MEMBERS MAY BE EMPLOYEES ONLY IF THEY RECEIVE A REGULAR WAGE OR SALARY.

51. Now for some more general questions about your work.

a) For some people their job is simply something they do in order to earn a living. For others it means much more than that. On balance, is your present job ... READ OUT ...

... just a means of earning a living,	28.4
or - does it mean much more to you than that?	71.6

IF 'MEANS OF EARNING A LIVING' (CODE 1 At a)

b) Is that because ... READ OUT ...

... there are no better jobs around here,	5.7
you don't have the right skills to get a better job,	7.2
or - because you would feel the same about any job you had?	12.3
[NOT ASKED]	71.6

A

— 20 —

55.a) ALL UNEMPLOYED (CODES 05, 06, 07 AT Q.22): ASK Qs.55-61   N=123   Qs. 55-61

In total how many months in the last five years - that is, since March 1984 - have you been unemployed and seeking work?   **MEDIAN:** 18 MONTHS

b) How long has this present period of unemployment and seeking work lasted so far?   **MEDIAN:** 9 MONTHS

c) How confident are you that you will find a job to match your qualifications ... **READ OUT** ...

... very confident,	18.4
quite confident,	27.6
not very confident,	27.3
or - not at all confident?	25.1

d) Although it may be difficult to judge, how long from now do you think it will be before you find an acceptable job?   **MEDIAN:** 3 MONTHS

Never	13.1
Don't know	30.5

56.a) INTERVIEWER CHECK:

Respondent answered 01-02 months at Q.55d)(above)	26.1
Respondent answered anything else	72.3

IF CODE 2 AT a)

b) How willing do you think you would be in these circumstances to retrain for a different job ... **READ OUT** ...

... very willing,	21.2
quite willing,	23.9
or - not very willing?	19.3
(Don't know)	2.9

c) How willing would you be to move to a different area to find an acceptable job ... **READ OUT** ...

... very willing,	11.2
quite willing,	5.4
or - not very willing?	49.0
(Don't know)	1.7

d) And how willing do you think you would be in these circumstances to take what you now consider to be an **unacceptable** job ... **READ OUT** ...

... very willing,	6.9
quite willing,	18.4
or - not very willing?	39.8
(Don't know)	1.7

57. ASK ALL UNEMPLOYED

If without having to work, you had what you would regard as a reasonable living income, do you think you would still prefer to have a paid job or wouldn't you bother?

Still prefer paid job	75.8
Wouldn't bother	20.2
Other answer (**WRITE IN**)	0.0
Don't know	2.3

A

— 19 —

52.a) ASK ALL SELF-EMPLOYED
CARD H
Suppose you were looking for another job - which of the things on this card would be most important to you in choosing a new job? Please read through the whole list before deciding.
ONE CODE ONLY IN COL a)

b) And which would be next most important?
ONE CODE ONLY IN COL b)

c) And which would be third most important?
ONE CODE ONLY IN COL c)

	(a) Most imp. in choosing job	(b) Next most imp.	(c) Third most imp.
Convenient working hours	14.2	4.6	4.9
Possibility of promotion	3.2	4.7	4.8
Clean/pleasant working conditions	0.5	2.7	5.3
Strong trade union	0.9	0.0	0.9
Interesting work that makes use of your skills	36.5	19.4	9.9
Work that helps others	4.0	7.3	5.3
Opportunity to get on with your work in your own way	8.7	14.7	13.1
Job security	11.9	3.9	7.4
Outdoor work	2.0	2.8	2.3
Good pay	13.7	20.2	18.2
Friendliness of people you work with	2.6	3.0	17.2
Good fringe benefits (pension, sick pay)	0.5	1.4	6.1
Short working hours	0.8	2.3	2.9
(NONE OF THESE)	0.3	0.5	0.5
(Don't know)	0.4	0.4	0.8

Q.67

NOW GO TO SECTION 3 (p.24)

53.a) ALL ON GOVERNMENT SCHEMES OR WAITING TO TAKE UP PAID WORK (CODES 02 OR 04 AT Q.22): ASK Qs.53-54.   N=29

During the last five years (that is since March 1984) have you been unemployed and seeking work for any period?

	(No.)
Yes	(17)
No	(9)

IF YES AT a)

b) For how many months in total during the last five years?   **MEDIAN:** Not calculated

54. If without having to work, you had what you would regard as a reasonable living income, do you think you would still prefer to have a paid job or wouldn't you bother?

	(No.)
Still prefer paid job	(23)
Wouldn't bother	(4)
Other answer (**WRITE IN**)	(-)
Don't know	(-)

NOW GO TO SECTION 3 (p.24)

- 21 -

58.a) Have you ever actually considered moving to a different area - an area other than the one you live in now - to try to find work?

	Skip to
Yes	31.5
No	66.9

IF YES AT a)

b) Why did you not move to a different area? Any other reasons? PROBE FULLY. RECORD VERBATIM.

No jobs anywhere	4.8
Waiting to move	4.5
Housing shortage	9.9
Have already moved in past	4.7
Moving causes too much upheaval	7.9
Other answers	6.0

59. ASK ALL UNEMPLOYED

Do you think that there is a real chance nowadays that you will get a job in this area, or is there no real chance nowadays?

Real chance	62.3
No real chance	35.2

60.a) Would you prefer full or part-time work, if you had the choice?

Full-time	69.7
Part-time	25.2
Not looking for work	2.1
Don't know/Can't say	1.3

IF PART-TIME (CODE 2 AT a)

b) About how many hours per week would you like to work?
PROBE FOR BEST ESTIMATE

	Skip to
MEDIAN: not calculated	(No.) (2)
OR CODE: Don't know	

61.a) ASK ALL UNEMPLOYED

For some people work is simply something they do in order to earn a living. For others it means much more than that. In general, do you think of work as ... READ OUT ...

... just a means of earning a living	35.5
or - does it mean much more to you than that?	62.8

IF MEANS OF EARNING A LIVING (CODE 1 AT a)

b) Is that because ... READ OUT ...

	Skip to
... there are no good jobs around here,	(13)
you don't have the right skills to get a good job,	(14)
or - because you would feel the same about any job you had?	(15)

NOW GO TO SECTION 3 (p.24)

- 22 -

N=539
Qs.62 only

62.a) ALL WHOLLY RETIRED FROM WORK (CODE 09 AT Q.22): ASK Q.62

Do you (or does your husband/wife) receive a pension from any past employer?

	Skip to
Yes	56.8
No	41.9

b) (Can I just check) are you over (MEN:) 65 (WOMEN:) 60?

Yes	91.8
No	8.0

IF YES AT b)

c) On the whole would you say the present state pension is on the low side, reasonable, or on the high side? IF 'ON THE LOW SIDE': Very low or a bit low?

Very low	46.4
A bit low	30.8
Reasonable	13.7
On the high side	0.0

d) Do you expect your state pension in a year's time to purchase more than it does now, less, or about the same?

More	2.6
Less	62.4
About the same	23.1
Don't know	2.9

IF NO AT b)

e) At what age did you retire from work?

YEARS
MEDIAN: 56
OR CODE: Never worked

NOW GO TO SECTION 3 (p.24)

63.a) ALL LOOKING AFTER HOME (CODE 10 AT Q.22): ASK Qs.63-66

N=480
Qs.63-66

Do you currently have a paid job of less than 10 hours a week?

	Skip to
Yes	12.6
No	87.0

INCLUDE THOSE TEMPORARILY AWAY FROM A PAID JOB OF LESS THAN 10 HOURS A WEEK

b) What are the main reasons you do not have a paid job (of more than 10 hours a week) outside the home? PROBE FULLY FOR MAIN REASONS AND RECORD VERBATIM.

Raising children	34.5
Retired/too old	19.2
Prefer looking after home/family	12.6
Unsuitable for available jobs	2.1
No jobs available	1.2
Feel married women shouldn't work	0.9
Husband against working	1.2
Voluntary worker	6.1
Pregnant/ill health	4.7
Dependent relative	1.4
Poverty trap	2.4
Already works less than 10 hours per week	0.7
Childcare costs	0.2
Unpaid work/family business	0.2

- 24 -

SECTION THREE

N=3029
Qs.67-84

67. ASK ALL
CARD M

Here are some items of government spending. Which of them, if any, would be your highest priority for extra spending? And which next? Please read through the whole list before deciding.

ONE CODE ONLY IN EACH COLUMN

	1st Priority	2nd Priority	Skip to
Education	19.1	35.5	
Defence	0.8	2.3	
Health	60.7	22.6	
Housing	6.5	14.8	
Public transport	1.0	1.9	
Roads	1.8	3.1	
Police and prisons	2.2	5.0	
Social security benefits	5.0	8.9	
Help for industry	2.2	4.7	
Overseas aid	0.2	0.4	
(NONE OF THESE)	0.1	0.1	
(Don't know)	0.4	0.6	

68. CARD N

Thinking now only of the government's spending on social benefits like those on the card. Which, if any, of these would be your highest priority for extra spending? And which next?

ONE CODE ONLY IN EACH COLUMN

	1st Priority	2nd Priority
Retirement pensions	43.0	23.7
Child benefits	13.8	15.7
Benefits for the unemployed	11.1	12.7
Benefits for disabled people	25.8	33.8
Benefits for single parents	5.5	11.4
(NONE OF THESE)	0.2	0.8
(Don't know)	0.5	0.7

69. I will read two statements. For each one please say whether you agree or disagree? Strongly or slightly?

	(a) Falsely claim	(b) Fail to claim
a) Large numbers of people these days falsely claim benefits.		
Agree strongly	38.6	50.7
Agree slightly	26.9	33.0
Disagree slightly	13.9	6.3
Disagree strongly	12.3	3.3
(Don't know)	8.4	6.7
b) Large numbers of people who are eligible for benefits these days fail to claim them.		

- 23 -

64.a) Have you, during the last five years, ever had a full or part-time job of 10 hours per week or more?

		Skip to
Yes		32.2
No		67.2

IF YES AT a)

b) How long ago was it that you left that job?

NO. OF MONTHS AGO

MEDIAN: 24

65.a) IF NO AT Q.64a)

How seriously in the past five years have you considered getting a full-time job? ...READ OUT...

PROMPT, IF NECESSARY: FULL-TIME IS 30 HRS+ PER WEEK

... very seriously,	2.3
quite seriously,	2.3
not very seriously,	4.4
or - not at all seriously?	57.5

IF NOT VERY OR NOT AT ALL SERIOUSLY, ASK b)

b) How seriously, in the past five years, have you considered getting a part-time job? ...READ OUT...

... very seriously,	0.9
quite seriously,	5.2
not very seriously,	7.4
or - not at all seriously/	48.3

66. ASK ALL LOOKING AFTER THE HOME

Do you think you are likely to look for a paid job in the next 5 years?

Yes - full-time	5.3
Yes - part-time	31.7
No	54.1

IF YES: Full-time or part-time?

Don't know	0.7
Other (WRITE IN)	5.4

- 25 -

70. Opinions differ about the level of benefits for the unemployed. Which of these two statements comes closest to your own ... READ OUT ...

		Skip to
... benefits for the unemployed are too low and cause hardship,	51.8	
OR - benefits for the unemployed are too high and discourage people from finding jobs?	26.8	
(Neither)	7.9	
Both, because wages are low	0.5	
Both, it varies	4.5	
About right	0.9	
Other answer	0.8	
Don't know	6.7	

71. CARD O
Suppose the government had to choose between the three options on this card. Which do you think it should choose?

Reduce taxes and spend less on health, education and social benefits	2.7
Keep taxes and spending on these services at the same level as now	36.8
Increase taxes and spend more on health, education and social benefits	56.2
(None)	2.4
(Don't know)	1.8

72. CARD P
All in all, how satisfied or dissatisfied would you say you are with the way in which the National Health Service runs nowadays? Choose a phrase from this card.

Very satisfied	6.4
Quite satisfied	30.2
Neither satisfied nor dissatisfied	17.6
Quite dissatisfied	24.5
Very dissatisfied	21.0

73. CARD P AGAIN
From your own experience, or from what you have heard, please say how satisfied or dissatisfied you are with the way in which each of these parts of the National Health Service runs nowadays?
READ OUT i-vi BELOW AND RING ONE CODE FOR EACH

	Very satisfied	Quite satisfied	Neither satisfied nor dissatisfied	Quite dissatisfied	Very dissatisfied	D/K
i) First, local doctors / GPs?	30.0	49.9	7.8	8.2	3.8	0.3
ii) National Health Service dentists?	19.7	50.5	15.7	7.9	3.1	3.0
iii) Health visitors?	12.1	33.4	27.9	6.2	2.2	17.9
iv) District nurses?	16.8	36.6	26.2	3.1	1.1	15.8
v) Being in hospital as an inpatient?	23.9	41.5	13.8	11.1	4.3	5.2
vi) Attending hospital as an outpatient?	15.3	37.2	14.1	18.6	11.0	3.8

- 26 -

74.a) Are you covered by a private health insurance scheme, that is an insurance scheme that allows you to get private medical treatment? FOR EXAMPLE BUPA and PPP

		Skip to
Yes	15.0	
No	84.9	

IF YES AT a)
b) Does your employer (or your husband's/wife's employer) pay the majority of the cost of membership of this scheme?

Yes	8.3
No	6.1
Don't know	0.3

ASK ALL
75.a) Do you think that the existence of private medical treatment in National Health Service hospitals is a good or bad thing for the National Health Service, or doesn't it make any difference to the NHS?

Good thing	24.0
Bad thing	47.0
No difference	24.3
Don't know	4.5

b) And do you think the existence of private medical treatment in private hospitals is a good thing or bad thing for the National Health Service, or doesn't it make any difference to the NHS?

Good thing	38.5
Bad thing	20.9
No difference	36.1
Don't know	4.2

76. CARD Q
Which of the views on this card comes closest to your own views about private medical treatment in hospitals?

Private medical treatment in all hospitals should be abolished	11.8
Private medical treatment should be allowed in private hospitals, but not in National Health Service hospitals	50.2
Private medical treatment should be allowed in both private and National Health Service hospitals	35.3
(Don't know)	2.5

77. Now thinking of GPs and dentists.

	Should	Should not	(Don't know)
a) Do you think that National Health Service GPs should or should not be free to take on private patients?	54.3	41.3	4.0
b) And do you think that National Health Service dentists should or should not be free to give private treatment?	59.1	36.2	4.2

78. It has been suggested that the National Health Service should be available only to those with lower incomes. This would mean that contributions and taxes could be lower and most people would then take out medical insurance or pay for health care. Do you support or oppose this idea?

Support	21.6
Oppose	73.9
(Don't know)	4.3

A   - 27 -

79. Some people think it is best for secondary schoolchildren to be separated into grammar and secondary modern schools according to how well they have done when they leave primary school. Others think it is best for secondary schoolchildren not to be separated in this way, and to attend comprehensive schools.

On balance, which system do you think provides the best all-round education for secondary schoolchildren ... **READ OUT** ...

		Skip to
... a system of grammar and secondary modern schools,	46.9	
or - a system of comprehensive schools?	45.7	
(Don't know)	6.4	
Other: (WRITE IN)	0.8	

SECTION FOUR

80. Now moving on to the subject of social class in Britain.

a) To what extent do you think a person's social class affects his or her opportunities in Britain today ... **READ OUT** ...

... a great deal,	26.8
quite a lot,	41.8
not very much,	24.9
or - not at all?	4.0
Other answer (WRITE IN)	0.1
Don't know	2.2

b) Do you think social class is more or less important now in affecting a person's opportunities than it was 10 years ago, or has there been no real change?

More important now	25.3
Less important now	30.0
No change	42.1
Don't know	2.4

c) Do you think that in 10 years' time social class will be more or less important than it is now in affecting a person's opportunities, or will there be no real change?

More important in 10 years' time	23.6
Less important in 10 years' time	25.9
No change	46.4
Don't know	3.6

CARD R

81a) Most people see themselves as belonging to a particular social class. Please look at this card and tell me which social class you would say **you** belong to? **RECORD ANSWER IN COL a)**

b) And which social class would you say your parents belonged to when you started at primary school? **RECORD ANSWER IN COL b)**

	(a) Self	(b) Parents
Upper middle	1.4	2.3
Middle	28.0	17.0
Upper working	21.4	11.2
Working	44.1	59.4
Poor	2.6	3.5
(Don't know)	1.8	1.0

A   - 28 -

82.a) ASK ALL
Do you regard yourself as belonging to any particular religion? IF YES: Which? **CODE ONE ONLY IN COL a) BELOW - DO NOT PROMPT.**

IF NO RELIGION (CODE 01 AT a)
b) In what religion were you brought up? **PROBE IF NECESSARY:** What was your family's religion? **CODE ONE ONLY IN COL b) BELOW - DO NOT PROMPT.**

	(a) Self	(b) Brought up	Skip to
No religion	34.4 → b)	5.3	
Christian - no denomination	3.2	0.9	
Roman Catholic	11.1	2.8	
Church of England/Anglican	36.7	19.4	
Baptist	1.3	0.6	
Methodist	4.0	1.9	
Presbyterian/Church of Scotland	4.5	2.0	
Free Presbyterian	0.1	0.1	
Brethren	0.1		
United Reform Church (URC)/Congregational	1.0	3.0	
Other Protestant (WRITE IN) _____ (b)	0.9 → c)	0.4	
Other Christian (WRITE IN) _____ (b)	0.7		
Hindu	0.2	0.1	
Jewish	0.4	0.1	
Islam/Muslim	0.4		
Sikh	0.2		
Buddhist	0.1		
Other non-Christian (WRITE IN) _____ (b)	0.3	0.1	
Refused/unwilling to say	0.1 → Q.83	0.7	

IF ANY RELIGION AT a) OR b) ASK c) - OTHERS SKIP TO Q.83
c) Apart from such special occasions as weddings, funerals and baptisms, how often nowadays do you attend services or meetings connected with your religion?
PROBE AS NECESSARY

Once a week or more	13.0
Less often but at least once in two weeks	2.7
Less often but at least once a month	5.3
Less often but at least twice a year	12.0
Less often but at least once a year	6.1
Less often	5.8
Never or practically never	47.6
Varies too much to say	0.6
Refused/unwilling to answer	0.1

- 30A -
SECTION FIVE

N=1513   Qs. A85-A105

A85. IF INTERVIEWING IN ENGLAND OR WALES, ASK ABOUT "BRITAIN"
IF INTERVIEWING IN SCOTLAND, ASK ABOUT "SCOTLAND"

Do you think that divorce in (Britain/Scotland) should be

		Skip to
... easier to obtain than it is now,	12.9	
or - more difficult,	29.7	
or - should things remain as they are?	53.1	
(Don't know)	4.2	

CARD S

A86. Now I would like to ask you some questions about sexual relationships.

a) If a man and a woman have sexual relations before marriage, what would your general opinion be? Please choose a phrase from this card. RECORD IN COL a)

b) What about a married person having sexual relations with someone other than his or her partner? Please choose a phrase from this card. RECORD IN COL b)

c) What about sexual relations between two adults of the same sex? Please choose a phrase from this card. RECORD IN COL c)

	(a) BEFORE MARRIAGE	(b) EXTRA MARITAL	(c) SAME SEX
Always wrong	11.6	55.1	55.5
Mostly wrong	10.7	28.4	12.6
Sometimes wrong	19.5	11.2	9.4
Rarely wrong	11.1	1.2	3.9
Not wrong at all	43.7	1.6	13.7
Depends/varies	2.7	1.7	3.9
Don't know	0.1	0.3	0.4

A87.a) Now I would like you to tell me whether, in your opinion, it is acceptable for a homosexual person ...
READ OUT EACH ITEM AND CODE FOR EACH

	Yes	No	Other answer	Don't know
i) ... to be a teacher in a school?	45.1	46.7	5.0	2.1
ii) ... to be a teacher in a college or university?	55.5	38.0	3.1	1.8
iii) ... to hold a responsible position in public life?	58.1	36.7	2.0	1.4

b) What did you understand the word "homosexual" to mean at this question: ... READ OUT ...

... men only - that is, gays	25.6
Women only - that is, lesbians	0.1
or - either?	73.3
Don't know	0.3

c) Do you think female homosexual couples - that is, lesbians - should be allowed to adopt a baby under the same conditions as other couples?

Yes	17.9
No	77.8
Depends on person	0.8
Other answers	0.7
Don't know	2.8

d) And do you think male homosexual couples - that is, gays - should be allowed to adopt a baby under the same conditions as other couples?

Yes	9.7
No	86.6
Depends on person	0.7
Other answers	0.1
Don't know	2.3

- 29 -

A

83. INTERVIEWER: CODE FROM OBSERVATION FOR ALL RESPONDENTS

		Skip to
White/European	97.1	
Indian/East African Asian/Pakistani/Bangladeshi/Sri Lankan	1.4	
Black/African/West Indian	1.2	
Other (inc. Chinese)	0.3	

ASK ALL

84. Now I would like to ask you some questions about racial prejudice in Britain.

a) First, thinking of Asians - that is, people whose families were originally from India and Pakistan - who now live in Britain. Do you think there is a lot of prejudice against them in Britain nowadays, a little, or hardly any? RECORD IN COL (a) BELOW

b) And black people - that is people whose families were originally from the West Indies or Africa - who now live in Britain. Do you think there is a lot of prejudice against them in Britain nowadays, a little, or hardly any? RECORD IN COL (b) BELOW

	(a) Asians	(b) Blacks
A lot	61.1	52.2
A little	30.6	37.1
Hardly any	5.9	7.8
Don't know	2.2	2.3

c) Do you think there is generally more racial prejudice in Britain now than there was 5 years ago, less, or about the same amount? RECORD IN COL (c) BELOW

More now	31.4
Less now	21.4
About the same	44.3
Don't know	0.2
Other answer (WRITE IN:)	2.1

d) Do you think there will be more, or less or about the same amount of racial prejudice in Britain in 5 years time compared with now?

More in 5 years	32.3
Less	18.6
About the same	45.0
Don't know	0.7
Other answer (WRITE IN:)	3.2

e) How would you describe yourself:
... READ OUT ...

		Skip to
... as very prejudiced against people of other races,	4.2	f)
a little prejudiced,	32.0	
or - not prejudiced at all?	63.0	Q.85
Don't know	0.2	
Other answer (WRITE IN:)	0.3	

IF 'VERY' OR 'A LITTLE' PREJUDICED (CODES 1 OR 2 AT e)

f) Against any race in particular? PROBE FOR RACES AND RECORD. IF 'BLACK' OR 'COLOURED' MENTIONED, PROBE FOR WHETHER WEST INDIAN, ASIAN, GENERAL, ETC. RECORD VERBATIM EVERYTHING MENTIONED.

- 31A -

SECTION SIX

A88. Now some questions on food.

ASK a) to e) ABOUT EACH LISTED FOOD BEFORE GOING TO ASK ABOUT THE NEXT.

> IF NAMED FOOD EATEN AT ALL (CODES 1-5 AT a), SKIP TO c).
> IF NAMED FOOD NEVER EATEN, (CODE 1 AT b), ASK ABOUT NEXT FOOD.

CARD T OR U

a) How often do you eat _____ (FOOD) nowadays?

> IF FOOD CUT OUT AT b) (CODES 2 OR 3 AT b), SKIP TO e).
> ALL OTHERS: ASK c)

b) Have you never eaten _____, or have you cut them out in the last 2 or 3 years or longer ago?

> ALL OTHERS: ASK b)

c) Are you eating about the same amount as you did 2 or 3 years ago, or more _____ less _____?

RECORD UNDER a) BELOW RECORD UNDER b) BELOW RECORD UNDER c) BELOW

CARD T

	(a) EVERY DAY	4-5 DAYS A WEEK	2-3 DAYS A WEEK	ABOUT ONCE A WEEK	LESS OFTEN	NEVER NOWA-DAYS	(b) NEVER EATEN	CUT OUT IN LAST 2 YEARS	CUT OUT 2 OR 3 LONGER YEARS AGO	(c) ABOUT THE SAME AMOUNT	MORE	LESS
PROCESSED MEAT LIKE SAUSAGES, HAM OR TINNED MEAT	4.6	4.8	27.0	37.6	19.3	6.5	25.6	39.1	24.3	61.5	5.7	31.8
BEEF, LAMB OR PORK	3.5	12.4	38.5	31.8	9.4	4.2	17.5	33.2	35.5	66.2	7.0	25.9
EGGS	6.6	8.3	32.2	26.2	15.6	10.8	20.7	53.4	11.0	64.0	7.2	27.3
FISH	0.4	2.0	25.8	43.3	21.7	6.6	44.0	32.4	13.4	72.0	15.9	10.7
CHIPS OR ROAST POTATOES	2.9	8.2	36.0	30.7	15.6	6.4	9.1	54.5	23.6	63.9	5.3	29.7
FRESH FRUIT AND VEGETABLES	56.9	15.9	15.7	4.7	1.8	0.7	36.4	21.8	7.3	66.3	26.8	6.1
BISCUITS, PASTRIES & CAKES	28.6	11.0	23.8	17.2	13.9	5.3	28.5	39.9	17.5	61.3	6.1	31.5

CARD U

	(a) 5 OR MORE SLICES A DAY	3-4 SLICES A DAY	1-2 SLICES A DAY	4-6 SLICES A WEEK	LESS OFTEN	NEVER NOWA-DAYS	(b) NEVER EATEN	CUT OUT IN LAST 2 YEARS	CUT OUT 2 OR 3 LONGER YEARS AGO	(c) ABOUT THE SAME AMOUNT	MORE	LESS
BREAD	18.4	36.8	34.7	6.6	4.2	1.0	13.3	44.5	9.4	69.0	6.9	22.3

N.B. For Qs. A88b-e, responses are percentaged on all those asked each question

- 32A -

> IF EATEN MORE OR LESS (CODES 2 OR 3 AT c), SKIP TO e).

ASK e) ABOUT ANY FOOD CUT OUT (CODE 2 OR 3 AT b) OR EATEN MORE OR LESS (CODE 2 OR 3 AT c)
CARD W

> ALL OTHERS: ASK d)
> THEN GO TO NEXT FOOD

d) Is/(are) _____ good for people, bad for people or neither?

e) You said that you had changed the amount of _____ you eat. Have you changed for any of these reasons? PROBE UNTIL 'NO'. Any other of these reasons?
CARD W

RECORD UNDER d) BELOW RECORD UNDER e) BELOW

CARD W

	(d) GOOD FOR PEOPLE	BAD FOR PEOPLE	NEITHER DON'T KNOW	(e) TO HELP CONTROL MY WEIGHT	I WAS TOLD TO FOR MEDICAL REASONS	IT IS GOOD VALUE FOR MONEY	IT IS POOR VALUE FOR MONEY	I WANTED TO KEEP HEALTHY	I JUST LIKE IT MORE	I JUST DON'T LIKE IT AS MUCH	NONE OF THESE REASONS
PROCESSED MEAT LIKE SAUSAGES, HAM OR TINNED MEAT	21.3	16.7	57.5	15.4	9.7	3.5	4.1	32.0	3.2	18.9	27.6
BEEF, LAMB OR PORK	56.5	5.4	34.0	10.5	9.4	1.2	9.1	25.8	5.3	12.8	32.9
EGGS	65.3	3.0	27.0	4.3	11.1	4.1	0.2	28.6	5.2	14.9	29.3
FISH	86.9	0.5	8.3	8.0	6.1	5.9	6.1	24.4	16.7	11.1	26.0
CHIPS OR ROAST POTATOES	20.5	37.7	37.5	29.0	13.2	1.6	0.2	41.5	5.2	8.5	16.4
FRESH FRUIT AND VEGETABLES	92.4	0.4	3.3	12.9	10.3	5.6	2.6	52.1	17.7	4.8	13.9
BISCUITS, PASTRIES & CAKES	18.7	40.8	36.2	34.9	10.5	0.2	3.3	31.6	9.0	10.0	14.7
BREAD	67.4	2.3	25.0	30.7	6.0	2.5	0.2	20.9	5.2	11.5	28.6

N.B. For Qs.A88 b-e, responses are percentaged on all those asked each question.

- 33A -

ASK ALL

A89.a) Do you ever take sugar in hot drinks nowadays?

		Skip to
Yes	49.1	
No	50.8	b) Q.90

IF YES AT a)

b) Are you taking about the same amount as you did two or three years ago, or more sugar in hot drinks, or less?

About the same amount	30.9
More	1.7
Less	16.3

ASK ALL

A90.a) Do you ever eat sweets or chocolates nowadays?

		Skip to
Yes	84.6	
No	15.3	b) Q.91

IF YES AT a)

b) Are you eating about the same amount as you did two or three years ago, or more sweets and chocolates or less?

About the same amount	40.5
More	7.2
Less	36.5

ASK ALL

A91. Compared with two or three years ago, would you say you are now ...

READ OUT EACH STATEMENT IN TURN

	Yes	No	(Don't know)
a) ... using more low fat spreads or soft margarine instead of butter, or not?	60.0	39.3	0.6
b) ... eating more grilled food instead of fried food, or not?	61.0	38.3	0.6
c) ... eating more fish and poultry instead of red meat, or not?	45.5	53.9	0.5
d) ... drinking or using more semi-skimmed or skimmed milk instead of full cream milk, or not?	42.8	56.8	0.2
e) ... eating more wholemeal bread instead of white bread, or not?	55.6	44.0	0.2
f) ... eating more boiled or baked potatoes instead of chips or roast potatoes, or not?	56.6	42.6	0.7

- 34A -

SECTION SEVEN

ASK ALL

A92. Now I'd like to ask a few questions about industry and jobs.

Suppose you were advising a young person who was looking for his or her first job.

CARD X

Which one of these would you say is the most important, and which next?

ONE CODE ONLY IN EACH COLUMN

	Most Important	Next most important
Good starting pay	4.9	12.6
A secure job for the future	46.0	20.4
Opportunities for promotion	8.9	27.9
Interesting work	35.0	21.6
Good working conditions	4.2	16.2
(Don't know)	0.7	0.9

CARD Y

A93. Suppose this young person could choose between different kinds of jobs anywhere in Britain.

From what you know or have heard, which one of these kinds of jobs is most likely to offer him or her ...

READ OUT AND RECORD UNDER a)-e) BELOW

a) ... good starting pay?

b) ... a secure job for the future? You may choose the same one again or a different one.

c) ... opportunities for promotion?

d) ... interesting work?

e) ... good working conditions?

ONE CODE ONLY IN EACH COLUMN

	(a) Good starting pay	(b) Secure job	(c) Promotion	(d) Interesting work	(e) Good working conditions
A building society	10.0	18.2	12.2	8.0	27.7
A large firm of accountants	16.4	12.8	17.5	9.3	13.7
A large engineering factory	13.2	4.6	8.3	18.9	3.3
A department store	1.4	1.1	5.0	8.6	5.0
The Civil Service	19.2	46.4	31.7	15.0	29.0
A large firm making computers	31.2	14.3	16.9	27.6	13.5
(None of these)	1.1	0.2	0.2	3.7	0.3
(Don't know)	7.1	2.1	7.6	8.3	6.9

- 36A -

CARD AA

A96. Suppose a big British firm made a large profit in a particular year.

a) Which one of these things do you think it would be _most likely_ to do? **RECORD IN COL a) BELOW.**

b) And which one would it be _next most likely_ to do? **RECORD IN COL. b) BELOW.**

c) Now which one do you think _should_ be its _first priority_? **RECORD IN COL c) BELOW.**

d) And which _should_ be its _next priority_? **RECORD IN COL d) BELOW.**

CODE ONE ONLY IN EACH COLUMN

	Likely to do		Should be	
	(a) Most	(b) Next	(c) First priority	(d) Next priority
Increase dividends to the shareholders	32.1	18.5	3.3	3.1
Give the employees a pay rise	4.6	5.1	25.3	13.2
Cut the prices of its products	2.2	2.4	10.7	10.4
Invest in new machinery or new technology	19.9	21.0	27.0	16.4
Improve the employees' working conditions	1.8	4.6	9.5	16.9
Research into new products	9.0	17.9	8.8	17.7
Invest in training for the employees	2.2	5.1	13.1	19.0
Give a bonus to top management	24.1	20.8	0.2	0.7
(None of these)	0.2	0.3	-	0.2
(Don't know)	3.1	3.4	1.2	1.4

A97.a) Do you think that British industry is _more_ efficient than it was five years ago, _less_ efficient, or about the same? **CODE UNDER a) BELOW.**

b) And do you think that, in five years' time, British industry will be _more_ efficient or _less_ efficient compared with now, or about the same? **CODE UNDER b)**

	(a) 5 years ago	(b) 5 years time
More	43.9	42.8
Less	13.5	7.3
About the same	36.4	40.8
(Don't know)	5.7	8.5

- 35A -

CARD Y AGAIN

A94.a) Now taking everything together, which job would you be _most likely_ to advise this young person to choose? **RECORD UNDER a) BELOW**

b) And which _next_? **RECORD UNDER b) BELOW**

c) And which would you be _least likely_ to advise him or her to choose? **RECORD UNDER c) BELOW**

ONE CODE ONLY IN EACH COLUMN

	(a) Most likely	(b) Next	(c) Least likely
A building society	12.7	21.6	4.5
A large firm of accountants	17.6	21.1	3.9
A large engineering factory	9.5	8.9	19.8
A department store	1.5	2.3	49.9
The Civil Service	27.2	17.6	8.9
A large firm making computers	23.7	19.8	4.9
(None of these)	1.9	1.5	1.0
(Don't know)	5.2	6.1	6.0

CARD Z

A95.a) How good do you think Britain is at _selling its goods abroad_, compared with other countries that compete with us? Please choose a phrase from this card. **RECORD IN GRID BELOW.**

b) And in _inventing new products_?
REPEAT FOR EACH STATEMENT c)-i)

	Britain is ...			
	better than most	worse than most	about the same	(Don't know/varies)
a) ... In selling its goods abroad?	10.0	52.5	31.8	5.2
b) ... In inventing new products?	43.4	18.4	32.3	5.4
c) ... In making well-designed products?	41.6	11.7	41.1	4.9
d) ... In investing in new machinery and technology?	12.8	46.3	31.9	8.5
e) ... In attracting the best people to manage its industries?	11.6	36.8	40.1	10.8
f) ... In attracting the best people to work in manufacturing industries?	9.5	31.9	45.8	12.0
g) ... In making goods that people really want to buy?	19.2	25.0	50.6	4.5
h) ... In keeping good relations between management and other employees?	12.0	35.2	44.7	7.5
i) ... In training employees in new skills?	18.9	37.5	35.0	7.9

- 37A -

SECTION EIGHT		Skip to

ASK ALL
CARD BB

98. Now, a few questions on housing. First, in general how satisfied or dissatisfied are you with your own (house/flat)? Choose a phrase from the card.

Very satisfied	41.6
Quite satisfied	45.5
Neither satisfied nor dissatisfied	5.1
Quite dissatisfied	4.8
Very dissatisfied	2.5

99.a) How about the area you live in? Taking everything into account, would you say this area has got better, worse or remained about the same as a place to live during the last two years? RECORD IN COL a) BELOW

b) And what do you think will happen during the next two years: will this area get better, worse or remain about the same as a place to live? RECORD IN COL b)

	(a) Last 2 years	(b) Next 2 years
Better	14.1	14.6
Worse	19.9	16.9
About the same	62.2	65.3
Don't know	3.3	2.4

100. Does your household own or rent this accommodation?
PROBE AS NECESSARY

IF OWN: Outright or on a mortgage?
IF RENTS: From whom?

Owns:	Own (leasehold/freehold) outright	26.3
	Buying (leasehold/freehold) on mortgage	43.9
Rents:	Local authority	21.1
Local authority includes GLC and London Residuary Body		
	New Town Development Corporation	0.2
	Housing Association	1.7
	Property company	0.6
	Employer	0.9
	Other organisation	0.5
	Relative	0.2
	Other individual	3.4
Rent free:	Rent free, squatting, etc.	0.8

101. CODE FROM OBSERVATION AND CHECK WITH RESPONDENT
Would I be right in describing this accommodation as a ...

Detached house or bungalow	22.4
Semi-detached house or bungalow	37.7
Terraced house	23.9
Self-contained, purpose-built flat/maisonette (inc. in tenement block)	11.8
Self-contained converted flat/maisonette	3.3
Room(s) - not self-contained	0.3
Other (WRITE IN:)	0.2

- 38A -

	Skip to

102. And how long have you lived in your present home?
PROBE AS NECESSARY

Less than 1 year	8.3
1 year, less than 2 years	7.1
2 years, less than 5 years	21.4
5 years, less than 10 years	17.9
10 years, less than 20 years	22.7
20 years or more	22.3

SECTION NINE

A103. Now I'd like to ask you about the disease called AIDS. I'm going to read out a list of different kinds of people.

CARD CC

Please choose a phrase from this card to tell me how much at risk you think each of these groups is from AIDS ...

READ OUT AND CODE ITEMS a)-h)

	Greatly at risk	Quite a lot at risk	Not very much at risk	Not at all at risk	(Don't know)
a) ... People who have sex with many different partners of the opposite sex.	69.3	26.7	2.4	0.1	1.1
b) ... Married couples who have sex only with each other.	0.2	0.4	17.2	81.0	0.7
c) ... Married couples who occasionally have sex with someone other than their regular partner.	10.1	50.3	35.6	1.5	1.7
d) ... People who have a blood transfusion.	10.0	27.1	47.2	13.0	2.3
e) ... Doctors and nurses who treat people who have AIDS.	12.7	29.1	43.4	11.0	3.4
f) ... Male homosexuals - that is, gays.	79.4	16.7	1.4	0.1	1.4
g) ... Female homosexuals - that is, lesbians.	42.7	21.9	18.7	9.2	6.7
h) ... People who inject themselves with drugs using shared needles.	93.6	5.2	0.2	0.1	0.6

- 40 -

			Skip to

900a) Can I just check your own marital status? At present are you ... READ OUT ...

CODE FIRST TO APPLY

	Skip to
... married,	65.2
living as married,	4.6
separated or divorced,	5.1
widowed,	8.7
or - not married?	16.3

b) And a few questions about you and your household. Including yourself, how many people live here regularly as members of this household?

CHECK INTERVIEWER MANUAL FOR DEFINITION OF HOUSEHOLD IF NECESSARY.

MEDIAN: [3]

901. Now I'd like to ask for a few details about each person in your household. Starting with yourself, what was your age last birthday?

WORK DOWN COLUMNS OF GRID FOR EACH HOUSEHOLD MEMBER.

	Resp-ondent	2	3	4	5	6	7	8	9	10
a) Sex:										
Male	46.3									
Female	53.7									
b) Age last birthday:										
c) Relationship to respondent:										
Spouse/partner										
Son/daughter										
Parent/parent-in law										
Other relative										
Not related										
d) HOUSEHOLD MEMBERS WITH LEGAL RESPONSIBILITY FOR ACCOMMODATION (INC. JOINT AND SHARED) Yes	81.1									
No	17.2									

* CHECK THAT NUMBER OF PEOPLE IN GRID EQUALS NUMBER GIVEN AT Q.900b)

- 39A -

CARD DD

A104. Please look at this card and tell me whether ...

READ OUT a)-c) BELOW AND CODE FOR EACH

	Definitely should	Probably should	Probably should not	Definitely should not	(Don't know)	Skip to
a) ... employers should or should not have the legal right to dismiss people who have AIDS?	13.2	22.5	30.3	27.7	5.5	
b) ... doctors and nurses should or should not have the legal right to refuse to treat people who have AIDS?	11.0	21.0	27.7	36.9	2.9	
c) ... schools should or should not have the legal right to expel children who have AIDS?	8.8	17.8	28.8	39.1	5.1	

A105. I am going to read out two statements. For each one, please say whether you agree or disagree.

	(a) Sympathy	(b) Research
a) 'People who have AIDS get much less sympathy from society than they ought to get.' Do you agree or disagree? Strongly or a little? CODE ONE IN COL a)		
Strongly agree	27.1	20.4
Agree a little	34.5	22.7
Disagree a little	21.4	24.5
Strongly disagree	11.0	26.3
(Don't know)	5.3	5.3
b) 'More money should be spent trying to find a cure for AIDS, even if it means that research into other serious diseases is delayed.' Do you agree or disagree? Strongly or a little? CODE ONE IN COL b)		

ASK ALL | SECTION TEN | N=3039   Qs.A106,900-902

CARD EE

A106. And now a few questions about yourself.

To which of these groups do you consider you belong?

CODE ONE ONLY

Black: of African or Caribbean or other origin

Asian:

of Indian origin	1.5	
of Pakistani origin	0.8	
of Bangladeshi origin	0.4	
of Chinese origin	-	
of other origin	0.1	

(WRITE IN)

White:

of British origin	92.1	
of Irish origin	2.8	
of other origin	1.9	

(WRITE IN)

Refused/NA   0.2

- 41A -

ASK ALL

902. Apart from people you've just mentioned who live in your household, have you had any (other) children, including stepchildren, who grew up in your household?

NB: INCLUDES CHILDREN NO LONGER LIVING

		Skip to
Yes	37.0	
No	62.8	

A903a) INTERVIEWER TO COMPLETE:

RESPONDENT IS:

Man	44.9	Q.904 b)
Woman	55.1	

IF WOMAN:

b) RESPONDENT IS: (SEE CODE 1, Q.900)

Married	34.2	c)
Not married	20.9	Q.904

IF MARRIED WOMAN:

c) RESPONDENT: Has children (SEE H/H GRID Q.901)   OR Has had children (CODE 1 AT Q.902)   [N=434]

	29.7	d)
Has not	4.5	Q.904

IF MARRIED WOMAN WITH CHILDREN (CODE 1 AT Q.903c)

CARD FF

d) Please use this card to say whether you worked full-time, part-time or not at all ...

READ a)-d) BELOW AND CODE ONE FOR EACH

	Worked full-time	Worked part-time	Stayed at home	Does not apply
a) ... after marrying and before you had children?	70.8	9.4	17.4	1.4
b) ... and what about when a child was under school age?	8.7	28.2	61.4	0.9
c) ... after the youngest child started school?	14.1	42.6	24.0	18.6
d) ... and how about after the children left home?	14.1	17.9	11.3	55.3

- 42A -

ASK ALL

904.a) Have you ever attended a private primary or secondary school in the United Kingdom?

NB: 'PRIVATE' INCLUDES PUBLIC AND DIRECT GRANT SCHOOLS, BUT EXCLUDES NURSERY SCHOOLS AND VOLUNTARY-AIDED SCHOOLS.

		Skip to
Yes	11.9	
No	87.6	
Don't know/Couldn't establish	0.1	

IF MARRIED OR LIVING AS MARRIED (SEE Q.900), ASK b) OTHERS GO TO c)

b) And has your (husband/wife/partner) ever attended a private primary or secondary school in the United Kingdom?

Yes	6.9	
No	62.2	
Don't know/Couldn't establish	0.3	

IF RESPONDENT HAS SON OR DAUGHTER OVER 5 YEARS OLD IN HOUSEHOLD, ASK c). OTHERS GO TO Q.905

c) And (have any of your children/has your child) ever attended a private primary or secondary school in the United Kingdom?

Yes	4.4	
No	34.2	
Don't know/Couldn't establish	0.0	

ASK ALL

905.a) INTERVIEWER: IS THIS A SINGLE PERSON HOUSEHOLD - RESPONDENT ONLY AT Q.901 (p.40)?

YES	11.5	Q.906 b)
NO	88.5	

IF NO AT a)

b) Who is the person mainly responsible for general domestic duties in this household? (WRITE IN RELATIONSHIP TO RESP.)

Respondent mainly	37.3
Someone else mainly (WRITE IN BY WHOM)	36.5
Duties shared equally	13.7

c) INTERVIEWER: IS THERE A CHILD UNDER 16 YEARS IN H.H.? SEE HOUSEHOLD GRID, Q.901 (p.40)

YES	33.4	d)
NO	55.0	Q.906

IF YES AT c)

d) Who is the person mainly responsible for the general care of the children) here? (WRITE IN RELATIONSHIP TO RESP.)

Respondent mainly	14.9
Someone else mainly (WRITE IN BY WHOM)	12.5
Duties shared equally	5.5

- 43 -

ASK ALL

906a) How old were you when you completed your continuous full-time education?

PROBE AS NECESSARY

		Skip to
15 or under	46.4	
16	25.4	
17	7.3	
18	6.6	
19 or over	12.2	
Still at school	0.2	
Still at college, polytechnic, or university	2.0	

Other answer (WRITE IN)

CARD XI

907a) Have you passed any exams or got any of the qualifications on this card?

Yes	57.5	b) Q.908
No	42.3	

IF YES AT a)

b) Which ones? Any others?

CODE ALL THAT APPLY

GSE Grades 2-5 / GCSE - Grades D-G	14.0
GSE Grade 1 / GCE 'O' level / GCE - Grade A-C / School certificate / Scottish (SCE) Ordinary / Scottish School-leaving Certificate lower grade / SUPE Ordinary / Northern Ireland Junior Certificate	38.5
GCE 'A' level/'S' level / Higher school certificate / Matriculation / Scottish SCE/SLC/SUPE at Higher grade / Northern Ireland Senior Certificate	15.6
Overseas School Leaving Exam/Certificate	1.2
Recognised trade apprenticeship completed	6.0
RSA/other clerical, commercial qualification	8.2
City & Guilds Certificate - Craft/Intermediate/Ordinary/Part I	7.4
City & Guilds Certificate - Advanced/Final/Part II or Part III	4.3
City & Guilds Certificate - Full technological	2.3
BEC/TEC General/Ordinary National Certificate (ONC) or Diploma (OND)	4.1
BEC/TEC Higher/Higher National Certificate (HNC) or Diploma (HND)	2.6
Teacher training qualification	3.9
Nursing qualification	3.4
Other technical or business qualification/certificate	6.2
University or CNAA degree or diploma	7.2

Other (WRITE IN)

- 44 -

REFER TO ECONOMIC POSITION OF RESPONDENT (Q.22, page 7)

- If in paid work (CODE 03), ask Q.908 about present (main) job.
- If waiting to take up paid work (CODE 04), ask Q.908 about future job.
- If on govt. scheme (CODE 02), unemployed (CODES 05-07), permanently sick or disabled (CODE 08), retired (CODE 09), looking after the home (CODE 10), or doing something else (CODE 11) ask Q.908 about last job.
- If never had a job, write in at a), then go to Q.909.

Now I want to ask you about your (present/future/last) job. CHANGE TENSES FOR (BRACKETED) WORDS AS APPROPRIATE.

908.a) What (is) your job?   PROBE AS NECESSARY:
What (is) the name or title of the job?

b) What kind of work (do) you do most of the time?   IF RELEVANT: What materials/machinery (do) you use?

c) What training or qualifications (are) needed for that job?

d) (Do) you directly supervise or (are) you directly responsible for the work of any other people?   IF YES: How many?

Yes: WRITE IN NO.:
No: RING: 0000

e) Can I just check: (are) you ... READ OUT ...

		Skip to
... an employee,	85.1	
or - self-employed?	10.1	

IF EMPLOYEE (CODE 1) AT e)

CARD X2

f) Which of the types of organisation on this card (do) you work for?

Private firm or company	54.2	f)
Nationalised industry/public corp.	6.0	
Local Authority/Local Education Authority	11.3	
Health Authority/hospital	5.3	
Central Government/Civil Service	4.8	
Charity or Trust	1.0	
Other (SPECIFY)	2.3	

CODE FIRST TO APPLY

ASK ALL

g) What (is) your employer (IF SELF-EMPLOYED: you) make or do at the place where you usually (work)?   IF FARM, GIVE NO. OF ACRES

h) Including yourself, how many people (are) employed at the place you usually (work) from?
IF SELF-EMPLOYED: (Do) you have any employees?   IF YES: How many?

(No employees)	6.0	g)
Under 10	17.1	
10-24	13.2	
25-99	20.5	
100-499	20.6	
500 or more	16.2	
Don't know	1.0	

Skip to:
O.U.O.
O.C.
E.S.
S.E.G.
SC/NM.M
SIC
H-G

- 45 -

ASK ALL

909a) Can I just check, are you *now* a member
of a trade union or staff association?
PROBE FOR UNION OR STAFF ASSOCIATION
    Yes: trade union   22.7
    Yes: staff association   3.0
    No   74.1

IF NO AT a)

b) Have you *ever* been a member of a
trade union or staff association?
    Yes: trade union   28.4
    Yes: staff association   2.8
    No   42.5

IF NOW OR EVER A MEMBER (CODES 1 OR 2 AT a) OR b)

	YES	NO
c) Have you ever ... **READ OUT AND RING ONE CODE FOR EACH**		
... attended a union or staff association meeting?	38.2	18.7
... voted in a union or staff association election or meeting?	36.4	20.3
... put forward a proposal or motion at a union or staff association meeting?	12.5	44.4
... gone on strike?	18.8	38.2
... stood in a picket line?	9.4	47.5
... served as a lay representative such as a shop steward or branch committee member?	7.7	49.2

IF RESPONDENT IS MARRIED OR LIVING AS MARRIED (AT Q.900a),
ASK Qs. 910-912. OTHERS GO TO Q. 913.
CARD X3

910.a) Which of these descriptions applied to what your (*husband/wife/partner*) was doing last week, that is the seven days ending last Sunday? **PROBE: Any others? CODE ALL THAT APPLY IN COL. I**

IF ONLY ONE CODE AT I, TRANSFER IT TO COL. II
IF MORE THAN ONE AT I, TRANSFER HIGHEST ON LIST TO COL. I

	COL. I	COL. II ECONOMIC POSITION	Skip to
In full-time education (not paid for by employer, including on vacation)	A	0.2	b)
On government training/employment scheme (e.g. Employment Training, Youth Training Programme etc.)	B	0.2	
In paid work (or away temporarily) for at least 10 hours in the week	C	42.6	
Waiting to take up paid work already accepted	D	0.1	Q.911
Unemployed and registered at a benefit office	E	1.7	
Unemployed, *not* registered, but actively looking for a job	F	0.3	
Unemployed, wanting a job (of at least 10 hrs per week), but not actively looking for a job	G	0.5	
Permanently sick or disabled	H	1.7	b)
Wholly retired from work	J	10.5	
Looking after the home	K	12.0	Q.911
Doing something else (SPECIFY)	L	0.1	

IF CODES 01-02, OR 08-11 AT a)

b) How long ago did your (*husband/wife/partner*) last have a paid job (other than the government scheme you mentioned) of at least 10 hours a week?

Within past 12 months	2.0	
Over 1-5 years ago	6.6	
Over 5-10 years ago	6.7	Q.911
Over 10-20 years ago	3.7	
Over 20 years ago	1.3	
Never had a paid job of 10+ hours a week	1.3	Q.912

- 46 -

REFER TO Q. 910 = ACTIVITY OF SPOUSE/PARTNER:

- If spouse is in paid work (CODE 03) - Ask Q.911 about *present* main job.
- If spouse is waiting to take up paid work (CODE 04) - ask Q.911 about *future* job.
- If spouse is unemployed (CODES 05, 06 OR 07), or retired (CODE 09) or looking after home (CODE 10), or doing something else (CODES 01-02, 08, 11), ask Q.911 about *last* job

Now I want to ask you about your (*husband's/wife's/partner's*) job. **CHANGE TENSES FOR [BRACKETED] WORDS AS APPROPRIATE**

911a) What (*is*) the name or title of that job?

b) What kind of work (*does*) he/she do most of the time? What materials/machinery (*does*) he/she use?

c) What training or qualifications (*are*) needed for that job?

d) (*Does*) he/she directly supervise or (*is*) he/she directly responsible for the work of any other people?   IF YES: How many?
    Yes: **WRITE IN NO.:**   0000
    No: **RING:**

e) (*Is*) he/she ... **READ OUT** ...
    ... an employee,   60.0   f)
    or - self-employed?   7.9   g)

IF EMPLOYEE (CODE 1 AT e)
CARD X4

f) Which of the types of organisation on this card (*does*) he/she work for?
    Private firm or company   39.2
    Nationalised industry/public corp.   4.7
    Local Authority/Local Education Authority   7.6
    Health Authority/hospital   3.2
    Central Government/Civil Service   3.4
    Charity or trust   0.5
    Other (SPECIFY)   1.3

ASK ALL

g) What (*does*) the employer (IF SELF-EMPLOYED: he/she) make or do at the place where he/she usually (*works*)? IF FARM GIVE NO. OF ACRES

h) Including him/herself, roughly how many people (*are*) employed at the place where he/she usually (*works*) (from)?
    (No employees)   14.3
    Under 10   8.9
    10-24   14.0
    25-99   13.5
    100-499   11.9
    500 or more   2.4
    Don't know
IF SELF-EMPLOYED: (*Does*) he/she have any employees? IF YES: How many?

i) (*Is*) the job ... **READ OUT** ...
    ... full-time (30 **HOURS+**)   50.9
    or - part-time (10-29 **HOURS**)?   13.0

Skip to / O.U.O. / O.C. / E.S. / S.E.G. / SC/M.NH / SIC / H-G

- 47 -

			Skip to
912.	**IF MARRIED OR LIVING AS MARRIED AT Q.900a)** And what about your spouse/partner: is (he/she) the same religion as you? PROBE AS NECESSARY: That is, Protestant or Catholic or Muslim or Hindu and so on.	Yes 54.9 No 14.4 Refused 0.3	
913.	**ASK ALL** Do you, or does anyone else in your household, own or have the regular use of a car or a van?	Yes 76.2 No 23.7	
914.	**CARD X5** Have you or anyone in this household received any of the benefits on this card during the last five years? IF YES: Which ones? Any others? CODE ALL THAT APPLY		
	Child benefit (family allowance)	44.4	
	Maternity benefit or allowance	9.9	
	One-parent benefit	3.8	
	Family credit (family income supplement)	2.9	
	State retirement or widow's pension	24.9	
	State supplementary pension	1.7	
	Invalidity or disabled pension or benefit	7.3	
	Attendance/Invalid Care/Mobility allowance	3.8	
	State Sickness or injury benefit	9.7	
	Unemployment benefit	16.9	
	Income support (supplementary benefit)	10.7	
	Rate or rent rebate or allowance	13.5	
	Other state benefit(s) volunteered (WRITE IN)	0.1	
	IF NO: CODE	NONE 17.4	

NOW GO TO Q.918 (PAGE 48): Q.915-917 ARE BLANK.

- 48 -

				Skip to
	ASK ALL **CARD X8**			
918a)	Which of the letters on this card represents the total income of your household from all sources before tax? Please just tell me the letter. **NB: INCLUDES INCOME FROM BENEFITS, SAVINGS, ETC.** ONE CODE IN COLUMN a)			
	IF RESPONDENT IS IN PAID WORK (CODE 03 AT Q.22, p.7) ASK b). **OTHERS GO TO Q.919**			
b)	Which of the letters on this card represents your own gross or total earnings, before deduction of income tax and national insurance? **ONE CODE IN COLUMN b)**	(a) House- hold Income	(b) Own Earn- ings	

NB. *On the questionnaire actually used, and on the show card, income bands were identified by a code letter.*

	(a) Household Income	(b) Own Earnings
Less than £2,000	1.2	2.8
£2,000 - £2,999	5.5	2.8
£3,000 - £3,999	5.3	3.2
£4,000 - £4,999	5.9	3.2
£5,000 - £5,999	5.0	3.9
£6,000 - £6,999	4.2	3.7
£7,000 - £7,999	3.4	4.1
£8,000 - £9,999	6.1	6.1
£10,000 - £11,999	8.3	5.8
£12,000 - £14,999	9.6	6.7
£15,000 - £17,999	7.8	3.8
£18,000 - £19,999	5.6	2.0
£20,000 - £22,999	5.2	0.9
£23,000+	14.0	3.5
Don't know	8.4	0.5

			Skip to
919.	**ASK ALL** Do you (or your husband/wife/partner) own any shares quoted on the Stock Exchange, including unit trusts?	Yes 26.0 No 73.3	
920a)	Is there a telephone in (your part of) this accommodation?	Yes 87.7 No 12.2	b) Q.921
	IF YES AT a)		
b)	A few interviews on any survey are checked by a supervisor to make sure that people are satisfied with the way the interview was carried out. In case my supervisor needs to contact you, it would be helpful if we could have your telephone number. WRITE NUMBER IN AT BOX 5 ON CASS FLAP - NOT HERE!	Number given 79.8 Number refused 6.2	

- 49 -

921. ASK ALL

In a year's time we may be doing a similar interview and we may wish to include you again. Would this be all right?

		Skip to
Yes	89.4	
No	9.6	

922. Respondent serial number is:

		Skip to
Even number (0, 2, 4, 6, 8)	49.8	b)
Odd number (1, 3, 5, 7, 9)	50.2	c)

IF SERIAL NUMBER IS EVEN AT a)
SHOW ADVANCE LETTER

b) In early March we sent your household a letter, giving advance notice that an interviewer would be calling to ask for an interview. The letter looked like this (SHOW)

Do you remember receiving this letter?

Yes - remembers letter	32.1	
No - does not	16.8	
Other (WRITE IN)	0.3	

ASK ALL

c) If you were given a choice, would you have preferred ... READ OUT ...

... to have a letter in advance saying an interviewer would call,	50.9	
or - to have an interviewer simply call round,	6.1	
or - wouldn't it really matter?	41.8	
(Don't know)	0.6	

INTERVIEWER: THANK RESPONDENT FOR HIS OR HER HELP, AND COMPLETE Q.923-924.

923.a) The self-completion questionnaire: Was it:

... filled in immediately after interview in your presence	9.6	
or ... left behind to be filled in later	76.7	
or ... refused (WHY?)	13.7	

INTERVIEWER

b) COMPLETE Q.16 ON CASS ABOUT HOW YOU EXPECT SELF-COMPLETION QUESTIONNAIRE TO BE RETURNED

- 50 -

924.a) In addition to respondent, was anybody else aged 16 or older present during part or all of the interview?

		Skip to
Yes	32.1	
No	47.3	
N/A	20.6	

b) TIME INTERVIEW COMPLETED: WRITE IN: 24 hr. clock

c) TOTAL DURATION OF INTERVIEW: MEDIAN: 60 MINUTES

d) INTERVIEWER SIGNATURE AND NUMBER

e) DATE OF INTERVIEW: DAY MONTH YEAR 0 8 9

PLEASE MAKE SURE THAT CASS AND CASS FLAP ARE COMPLETELY FILLED IN. THEN RETURN COMPLETED CASS TO YOUR FIELD OFFICE (LONDON OR DARLINGTON). DO NOT DETACH FLAP.

CHECK MAIN QUESTIONNAIRE AND SELF-COMPLETION (IF POSSIBLE). THEN RETURN BOTH TO THE BRENTWOOD CODING OFFICE AS SOON AS YOU CAN.

B

SCPR

Head Office 35 NORTHAMPTON SQUARE, LONDON EC1V 0AX
TELEPHONE 01-250 1866

Northern Field Office: CHARNLEE HOUSE, GAINFORD, DARLINGTON,
CO. DURHAM DL2 3EG. TELEPHONE 0325-730688

P.1005

Spring 1989

BRITISH SOCIAL ATTITUDES:

1989 SURVEY

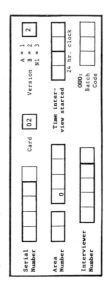

- 30B -

N=1516
Qs. B85-B124

		Skip to

ASK ALL

B85a) On the whole, do you think people of Asian origin in Britain are <u>not</u> given jobs these days because of their race ... **READ OUT** ...

... a lot,	17.8
a little,	38.3
or - hardly at all?	33.7
(Don't know)	10.1

b) And on the whole, do you think people of West Indian origin in Britain are <u>not</u> given jobs these days because of their race ... **READ OUT** ...

... a lot,	24.4
a little,	37.5
or - hardly at all?	28.5
(Don't know)	9.4

B86a) There is a law in Britain <u>against</u> racial discrimination, that is against giving unfair preference to a particular race in housing, jobs and so on. Do you generally <u>support</u> or <u>oppose</u> the idea of a law for this purpose?

Support	68.4
Oppose	27.7
Don't know	2.9

b) Do you think, on the whole, that Britain gives too little or too much help to Asians and West Indians who have settled in this country, or are present arrangements about right?

Too little	10.1
Present arrangements right	45.8
Too much	36.6
Other answer (WRITE IN:) _____	0.7
Don't know	6.1

B87a) INTERVIEWER CHECK:

Respondent is white/European (CODE 1 AT Q.83)	97.3	b)
Other (CODES 2-4 AT Q.83)	2.7	Q.89

IF RESPONDENT IS WHITE/EUROPEAN

b) INTERVIEWER: REFER TO LAST DIGIT OF SERIAL NUMBER:

    IF ODD: Ask Version A of Q.88 AND RING CODE

    IF EVEN OR ZERO: Ask Version B of Q.88 AND RING CODE

- 31B -

	Skip to

VERSION A

B88a) Do you think <u>most</u> white people in Britain would mind or not mind if a suitably qualified person of <u>Asian</u> origin were appointed as their boss? **IF 'WOULD MIND': A lot or a little? RECORD IN COL. a)**

b) And you personally? Would you mind or not mind? **IF 'WOULD MIND': A lot or a little? RECORD IN COL. b)**

c) Do you think that <u>most</u> white people in Britain would mind or not mind if one of their close relatives were to marry a person of <u>Asian</u> origin? **IF 'WOULD MIND': A lot or a little? RECORD IN COL. c)**

d) And you personally? Would you mind or not mind? **IF 'WOULD MIND': A lot or a little? RECORD IN COL. d) THEN GO TO Q.89**

VERSION B

B88a) Do you think <u>most</u> white people in Britain would mind or not mind if a suitably qualified person of <u>black or West Indian</u> origin were appointed as their boss? **IF 'WOULD MIND': A lot or a little? RECORD IN COL. a)**

b) And you personally? Would you mind or not mind? **IF 'WOULD MIND': A lot or a little? RECORD IN COL. b)**

c) Do you think that <u>most</u> white people in Britain would mind or not mind if one of their close relatives were to marry a person of <u>black or West Indian origin</u>? **IF 'WOULD MIND': A lot or a little? RECORD IN COL. c)**

d) And you personally? Would you mind or not mind? **IF 'WOULD MIND': A lot or a little? RECORD IN COL. d)**

	BOSS		MARRIAGE	
	(a) Most people	(b) Self	(c) Most people	(d) Self
Mind a lot	20.9	8.7	41.3	27.8
Mind a little	34.1	11.5	37.6	22.7
Not mind	40.8	77.9	16.7	46.9
Other answer	0.9	0.6	0.6	0.8
Don't know	2.7	0.6	3.3	1.1

WRITE IN: a) _____
            b) _____
            c) _____
            d) _____

- 32B -

ASK ALL

B89a) Some people say there is very little real poverty in Britain today. Others say there is quite a lot. Which comes closest to your view ... READ OUT ...

	Skip to
... that there is very little real poverty in Britain	33.6
or - that there is quite a lot?	62.8
(Don't know)	3.2

b) Over the last ten years, do you think that poverty in Britain has been increasing, decreasing or staying at about the same level?

Increasing	49.5
Decreasing	16.4
Staying at same level	30.9
(Don't know)	2.9

c) And over the next ten years, do you think that poverty in Britain will ... READ OUT ...

... increase,	43.7
decrease,	15.6
or - stay at about the same level?	34.4
(Don't know)	6.0

B90. Would you say someone in Britain was or was not in poverty if ... READ OUT EACH STATEMENT BELOW AND CODE FOR EACH

	Was	Was not	(Don't know)
a) ... they had enough to buy the things they really needed, but not enough to buy the things most people take for granted?	25.3	71.2	3.0
b) ... they had enough to eat and live, but not enough to buy other things they needed?	60.0	38.0	1.5
c) ... they had not got enough to eat and live without getting into debt?	95.1	3.0	1.3

CARD S

B91. Why do you think there are people who live in need? Of the four views on this card, which one comes closest to your own?
CODE ONE ONLY

Because they have been unlucky	10.5
Because of laziness or lack of willpower	19.4
Because of injustice in our society	29.1
It's an inevitable part of modern life	34.3
(None of these)	2.3
Other (WRITE IN)	1.8
(Don't know)	1.8

B92. How often do you and your household feel poor nowadays ... READ OUT ...

... never,	43.1
every now and then,	39.6
often,	9.7
or - almost all the time?	6.8
(Don't know)	0.4

- 33B -

B93a) Think of a married couple without children living only on unemployment benefit. Would you say that they are ... READ OUT ...

	Skip to
... really poor,	12.4
hard up,	49.4
have enough to live on,	26.8
or - have more than enough?	1.6
(Don't know)	9.5

b) Now thinking of a married couple living only on the state pension. Would you say they are ... READ OUT ...

... really poor,	22.1
hard up,	55.2
have enough to live on,	18.7
or - have more than enough?	0.2
(Don't know)	3.4

B94a) Now thinking of a married couple without children living on £53 per week. Would you say they are ... READ OUT ...

... really poor,	42.3
hard up,	48.9
have enough to live on,	6.4
or - have more than enough?	0.1
(Don't know)	1.8

b) And what about a pensioner couple living on £66 per week. Would you say they are ... READ OUT ...

... really poor,	30.3
hard up,	51.5
have enough to live on,	15.9
or - have more than enough?	0.3
(Don't know)	1.5

B95a) Do you think that health care should be the same for everyone, or should people who can afford it be able to pay for better health care?

Same for everyone	49.8
Able to pay for better health	48.9
(Don't know)	0.8

b) Should the quality of education be the same for all children, or should parents who can afford it be able to pay for better education?

Same for everyone	52.3
Able to pay for better	45.8
(Don't know)	1.4

c) And do you think that pensions should be the same for everyone, or should people who can afford it be able to pay for better pensions?

Same for everyone	33.2
Able to pay for better	63.1
(Don't know)	3.1

- 34B -

SECTION SIX

B96. Now I would like to ask some questions about politics.

How much interest do you generally have in
what is going on in politics ... READ OUT ...

		Skip to
... a great deal,	7.3	
quite a lot,	20.2	
some,	30.4	
not very much,	27.9	
or - not at all?	13.7	
(Don't know)	0.2	

CARD T

B97 a) Suppose a law was being considered by Parliament which you thought was really unjust and harmful. Which, if any, of the things on this card do you think you would do? Any others?
RECORD IN COL a) BELOW, THEN ASK b).
MORE THAN ONE CODE MAY BE RINGED.

b) And have you ever done any of the things on this card about a government action which you thought was unjust or harmful? Which ones? Any others?
RECORD IN COL b) BELOW.
MORE THAN ONE CODE MAY BE RINGED.

	(a) Would do	(b) Ever done
Contact my MP	54.2	14.6
Speak to influential person	14.9	3.4
Contact a government department	12.3	3.4
Contact radio, TV or newspaper	14.4	4.1
Sign a petition	70.5	41.2
Raise the issue in an organisation I already belong to	10.9	4.1
Go on a protest or demonstration	14.0	8.4
Form a group of like-minded people	9.6	2.8
(NO - NONE OF THESE)	7.8	48.1
Don't know	0.1	0.1

B98 a) In general would you say that people should obey the law without exception, or are there exceptional occasions on which people should follow their consciences even if it means breaking the law?

Obey law without exception	50.0
Follow conscience on occasions	48.0
Don't know	1.5

b) Are there any circumstances in which you might break a law to which you were very strongly opposed?

Yes	32.8
No	57.8
(Don't know)	8.8

- 35B -

CARD U

B99. Please choose a phrase from this card to say how you feel about
... READ OUT ...

	Very strongly in favour	Strongly in favour	In favour	Neither in favour nor against	Against	Strongly against	Very strongly against	Don't know/ Can't say	Skip to
a) ... the Conservative Party?	4.3	7.3	28.0	20.7	14.2	9.0	14.4	1.6	
b) ... the Labour Party?	5.0	5.6	20.5	26.1	26.4	8.1	5.7	1.8	
c) ... the Social and Liberal Democrat Party? *(Liberal/ Democrats)*	1.3	2.2	14.1	49.2	20.3	4.3	2.7	5.4	
d) ... the Social Democrat Party? *(SDP/Owen)*	0.5	1.3	11.0	51.6	21.0	5.0	3.3	5.9	

IN SCOTLAND ALSO ASK

	Very strongly in favour	Strongly in favour	In favour	Neither in favour nor against	Against	Strongly against	Very strongly against	Don't know/ Can't say	Skip to
e) ... the Scottish Nationalist Party?	0.3	0.9	3.0	3.4	1.2	0.5	0.2	0.5	

IN WALES ALSO ASK

	Very strongly in favour	Strongly in favour	In favour	Neither in favour nor against	Against	Strongly against	Very strongly against	Don't know/ Can't say	Skip to
f) ... Plaid Cymru?	0.1	0.1	0.8	2.0	1.3	0.3	0.5	0.3	

B100a) Are you generally in favour of
... READ OUT ...

		Skip to
... more nationalisation of companies by government,	18.4 ⎫	b)
more privatisation of companies by government,	16.3 ⎬	
or - should things be left as they are now?	59.2	Q.101
(Don't know)	0.7	
Other (WRITE IN:) _____ (Don't know)	4.3	

IF MORE NATIONALISATION OR PRIVATISATION AT a)
b) A lot more/*nationalisation/privatisation/* or a little more?

A lot more	14.3
A little more	20.4
Don't know	4.3

- 36B -

SECTION SEVEN

B101. Now I would like to ask some questions about religion and religious prejudice.
First thinking of Catholics - do you think there is a lot of prejudice against them in Northern Ireland nowadays, a little, or hardly any?

		Skip to
A lot	58.3	
A little	22.1	
Hardly any	5.7	
(Don't know)	13.2	

B102. And now, thinking of Protestants - do you think there is a lot of prejudice against them in Northern Ireland nowadays, a little, or hardly any?

A lot	51.8
A little	24.8
Hardly any	9.3
(Don't know)	13.6

B103. How would you describe yourself:
...as very prejudiced against people of other religions,
a little prejudiced,
or - not prejudiced at all?
...**READ OUT** ...

	0.8
	7.3
	90.6
	0.7
Don't know	0.1

Other answer (**WRITE IN**)

B104a) What about relations between Protestants and Catholics in Northern Ireland? Would you say they are better than they were 5 years ago, worse, or about the same now as then?
IF 'IT DEPENDS', **PROBE BEFORE CODING**

Better	13.7
Worse	26.3
About the same	51.0
	0.1
(Don't know)	8.1

Other answer (**WRITE IN**)

b) And what about in 5 years time? Do you think relations between Protestants and Catholics will be better than now, worse than now, or about the same as now?
IF 'IT DEPENDS', **PROBE BEFORE CODING**

Better than now	13.7
Worse than now	19.4
About the same	55.2
	0.3
(Don't know)	10.7

Other answer (**WRITE IN**)

c) Do you think that religion will always make a difference to the way people feel about each other in Northern Ireland?

Yes	86.2
No	7.3
(Don't know)	1.3
	4.5

Other answer (**WRITE IN**)

- 37B -

B105. Were both your parents of the same religion?
IF NECESSARY: Say, Protestant or Catholic or Muslim or Hindu or Jewish and so on.

		Skip to
Yes	82.1	
No	15.1	
(Refused)	0.1	
(Don't know)	2.0	

B106. If you were deciding where to send your children to school, would you prefer a school with children of only your own religion, or a mixed-religion school?
PROBE IF NECESSARY: Say if you did have school-age children ...

Own religion only	14.9
Mixed-religion school	65.6
(No preference)	17.6
(Don't know)	1.2

B107. When there is an argument between British and the Republic of Ireland, do you generally find yourself on the side of the British or of the Irish government?
IF 'IT DEPENDS', **PROBE BEFORE CODING**

Generally British government	59.2
Generally Irish government	5.2
It depends (**AFTER PROBE**)	11.2
(Neither)	12.9
(Don't know/Can't say)	10.7

B108. At any time in the next 20 years, do you think it is likely or unlikely that there will be a united Ireland? PROBE: Very (likely/unlikely) or quite (likely/unlikely)?

Very likely	3.4
Quite likely	14.9
Quite unlikely	26.9
Very unlikely	41.9
(Even chance)	1.9
(Don't know)	10.3

- 39B -

SECTION EIGHT

ASK ALL
CARD X

110. Now, a few questions on housing. First, in general how satisfied or dissatisfied are you with your own (*house/flat*)? Choose a phrase from the card.

		Skip to
Very satisfied	41.6	
Quite satisfied	45.5	
Neither satisfied nor dissatisfied	5.1	
Quite dissatisfied	4.8	
Very dissatisfied	2.5	

111a) How about the area you live in? Taking everything into account, would you say this area has got better, worse or remained about the same as a place to live during the last two years? **RECORD IN COL a)**

b) And what do you think will happen during the next two years? Will this area get better, worse or remain about the same as a place to live? **RECORD IN COL b)**.

	(a) Last 2 years	(b) Next 2 years
Better	14.1	14.6
Worse	19.9	16.9
About the same	62.2	65.3
Don't know	3.3	2.4

112. Does your <u>household</u> own or rent this accommodation?
PROBE AS NECESSARY
IF OWN: Outright or on a mortgage?
IF RENTS: From whom?

			Skip to
Owns:	Own (leasehold/freehold) outright	26.3	} Q.115
	Buying (leasehold/freehold) on mortgage	43.9	
Rents:	Local authority	21.1	} Q.113
	New Town Development Corporation	0.2	
	Housing Association	1.7	
	Property company	0.6	
	Employer	0.9	} Q.114
	Other organisation	0.5	
	Relative	0.2	
	Other individual	3.4	
	Rent free/squatting, etc.	0.8	Q.118

Local authority includes GLC and London Residuary Body

B113. **IF LOCAL AUTHORITY OR NEW TOWN DEVELOPMENT CORPORATION TENANT (CODES 03 OR 04 AT Q.112)**
Is it <u>likely</u> or <u>unlikely</u> that you - or the person responsible for paying the rent - will buy this accommodation at some time in the future?
IF LIKELY OR UNLIKELY: Very or quite?

Very likely	1.4
Quite likely	2.5
Quite unlikely	1.4
Very unlikely	15.5
Not allowed to buy	0.9
(Don't know)	0.8

B114. **ASK ALL RENTERS (CODES 03-10 AT Q.112)**
How would you describe the rent - not including rates - for this accommodation? Would you say it was ... **READ OUT** ...

		Skip to
... on the high side,	12.1	} Q.116
reasonable,	15.0	
or - on the low side?	1.0	

- 38B -

CARD W

B109a) Under direct rule from Britain, as now, how much do you generally trust British governments of any party to act in the best interests of Northern Ireland? **CODE ONE ONLY UNDER COL a) BELOW.**

b) If there was self-rule, how much do you think you would generally trust a Stormont government in Belfast to act in the best interests of Northern Ireland? **CODE ONE ONLY UNDER COL b) BELOW.**

c) And if there was a united Ireland, how much do you think you would generally trust an Irish government to act in the best interests of Northern Ireland? **CODE ONE ONLY UNDER COL c) BELOW.**

	(a) British govt.	(b) Stormont govt.	(c) Irish govt.
Just about always	5.9	4.8	5.6
Most of the time	33.9	30.1	29.8
Only some of the time	35.9	29.3	30.0
Rarely	9.4	10.9	9.8
Never	3.0	4.5	5.2
(Don't know/Can't say)	11.2	19.6	18.8

- 41B -

B118a) INTERVIEWER CHECK:

Respondent lives in rented accommodation (CODES 03-10 AT Q.112)

	%	Skip to
Respondent lives in rented accommodation	28.6	b)
Others	71.4	Q.121

IF RENTS AT a)

b) If you had a free choice would you choose to rent accommodation, or would you choose to buy?

	%
Would choose to rent	8.4
Would choose to buy	19.4
(Don't know)	0.5

c) And apart from what you would like, do you expect to buy a house or a flat in the next two years, or not?
INCLUDES BUYING PRESENT HOUSE/FLAT

	%	Skip to
Yes - expect to buy	4.4	b)
No - do not expect to buy	22.5	Q.120
(Don't know)	1.1	

ASK ALL RENTERS

B119a) Have you ever owned your own accommodation? That is, lived in a house or flat, which was in your sole or joint name?

	%
Yes	4.2
No	24.2
Don't know	-

IF YES AT a)

b) How long ago was it that you last owned your own accommodation?
PROBE FOR BEST ESTIMATE   MEDIAN: Not calculated

ASK ALL RENTERS

B120. Here are some reasons people might give for not wanting to buy a home. As I read out each one, please tell me whether or not it applies to you, at present.
... READ OUT ...

	Applies	Does not apply	(Don't know)
a) ... I could not afford the deposit	20.4	7.3	0.3
b) ... I would not be able to get a mortgage	19.0	8.2	0.9
c) ... It might be difficult to keep up the repayments	20.9	6.4	0.7
d) ... I can't afford any of the properties I'd want to buy	22.2	5.4	0.4
e) ... I do not have a secure enough job	15.9	11.2	1.0
f) ... I would not want to be in debt	20.5	7.2	0.3
g) ... It would cost too much to repair and maintain	17.1	10.4	0.6
h) ... I might not be able to resell the property when I wanted to	11.1	15.1	1.8
i) ... It is just too much of a responsibility	15.9	11.6	0.5
j) ... At my age, I would not want to change	14.5	13.2	0.4

- 40B -

B115a) IF CURRENTLY OWNS ACCOMMODATION (CODES 01 OR 02 AT Q.112)

Did you, or the person responsible for the mortgage, buy your present home from the local authority as a tenant?

	%	Skip to
Yes	8.2	c)
No	61.8	b)

'LOCAL AUTHORITY' INCLUDES GLC, London Residuary Body and New Town Development Corp.

IF NO AT a)

b) Have you ever lived in rented accommodation?

	%	Skip to
Yes	34.8	c)
No	26.9	Q.116

IF YES AT a) OR b)

c) How long ago was it that you last lived in rented accommodation? INCLUDES PRESENT HOUSE/FLAT.

MEDIAN [14]

d) Were you renting then from a local authority or from someone else?
'LOCAL AUTHORITY' INCLUDES GLC, London Residuary Body and New Town Development Corp.

	%
Local authority	19.9
Private landlord/private co	20.9
Someone else	1.4
Rent free/with job/had accommodation	0.5
Don't know	0.2

ASK ALL

B116a) If you had a free choice, would you choose to stay in your present home, or would you choose to move out?

	%	Skip to
Would choose to stay	62.3	Q.117
Would choose to move out	35.6	b)
(Don't know)	1.5	Q.117

IF MOVE OUT AT a)

b) How keen are you to move out? Are you ... READ OUT ...

	%
... very keen,	13.1
fairly keen,	14.1
or - not that keen?	8.2

ASK ALL

B117a) And apart from what you would like, where do you expect to be living in two years time - do you expect to .. READ OUT ...

	%	Skip to
... stay in this house/flat,	74.0	Q.118
or - move elsewhere?	22.0	b)
(Don't know)	3.5	Q.118

IF MOVE ELSEWHERE AT a)

b) Which do you think is most likely - that you will buy or rent your next home?

	%
Buy	15.3
Rent: from local authority/council	3.0
Rent: from other landlord	2.5
(Don't know)	1.0

IF RENT: PROBE FOR LOCAL AUTHORITY/ COUNCIL OR OTHER LANDLORD

- 43B -

ASK ALL

B124. And just a few questions on food.

Compared with two or three years ago, would you say you are now ...

		Yes	No	(Don't know)	Skip to
READ OUT EACH STATEMENT IN TURN					
a)	... using more butter instead of low fat spreads or soft margarine, or not?	12.7	85.8	1.0	
b)	... eating more fried food instead of grilled food, or not?	8.5	90.5	0.5	
c)	... eating more red meat instead of fish and poultry, or not?	15.9	82.2	1.2	
d)	... drinking or using more full cream milk instead of semi-skimmed or skimmed milk, or not?	15.9	82.7	0.8	
e)	... eating more white bread instead of wholemeal bread, or not?	17.6	81.1	0.6	
f)	... eating more chips or roast potatoes instead of boiled or baked potatoes?	12.7	85.8	0.8	

SECTION NINE

SECTION TEN

N = 3029
Also asked on Version A

CARD Y

125. And now a few questions about yourself.

To which of these groups do you consider you belong?

CODE ONE ONLY

Asian:	**Black:** of African or Caribbean or other origin	1.5	
	of Indian origin	0.8	
	of Pakistani origin	0.4	
	of Bangladeshi origin	-	
	of Chinese origin	0.1	
	of other origin	0.1	
	(WRITE IN)		
White:	of British origin	92.1	
	of Irish origin	2.8	
	of other origin	1.9	
	(WRITE IN)		
	Refused/NA	0.2	

- 42B -

ASK ALL

B121. When you were a child, did your parents own their home, rent it from a local authority, or rent it from someone else?

		Skip to
IF DIFFERENT TYPES OF TENURE, **PROBE FOR ONE RESPONDENT LIVED** **IN LONGEST**	Owned it	37.4	
	Rented from local authority	33.5	
	Rented from someone else	26.0	
Other (**WRITE IN:**)		2.1	
		0.3	

CODE FROM OBSERVATION AND CHECK WITH RESPONDENT

122. Would I be right in describing this accommodation as a ...

Detached house or bungalow	22.4	
Semi-detached house or bungalow	37.7	
Terraced house	23.9	
Self-contained, purpose-built flat/maisonette (inc. in tenement block)	11.8	
Self-contained converted flat/maisonette	3.3	
Room (s) - not self-contained	0.3	
Other (**WRITE IN:**)	0.2	

123. And how long have you lived in your present home?

PROBE AS NECESSARY

Less than 1 year	8.3	
1 year, less than 2 years	7.1	
2 years, less than 5 years	21.4	
5 years, less than 10 years	17.9	
10 years, less than 20 years	22.7	
20 years or more	22.3	

- 51B -   N=1516
                                              Qs. B915-B917

			Skip to
B915a)	Have you ever lived in Northern Ireland for more than one year?	Yes 2.8	
		No 97.1	
b)	And have you ever lived in the Republic of Ireland for more than one year?	Yes 2.5	
		No 96.1	
	CARD X6		
B916a)	In the last 5 years, have you visited Northern Ireland? IF YES: Please tell me from this card how often?	No, never visited 94.2	
		Yes: Once only 3.2	
		A few times 1.8	
		Many times 0.5	
		Lived there 0.1	
	CARD X6 AGAIN		
b)	And in the last 5 years, have you visited the Republic of Ireland? IF YES: Please tell me from this card how often?	No, never visited 92.7	
		Yes: Once only 3.5	
		A few times 2.6	
		Many times 0.9	
		Lived there -	
B917a)	In the last 5 years, have you thought seriously about emigrating from Britain ... that is, leaving permanently? IF YES: How seriously have you thought about it ... READ OUT ...	YES: ... very seriously, 6.2	
		fairly seriously, 6.1	b)
		or - not very seriously? 7.1	
		NO: (Never thought about it) 80.1	
		(Don't know/Can't say) 0.4	Q.918
	IF THOUGHT ABOUT EMIGRATING (CODES 1-3 AT a)		
	CARD X7		
b)	Which of these reasons is the main reason why you have thought about emigrating? Please choose the closest reason on the card	Family reasons 3.3	
		Unemployment 1.1	
	CODE ONE ONLY	Fear of violence or crime 0.6	
		Standard of living 10.6	
		Health reasons 0.5	
	Other (AFTER PROBE) _____	2.3	
		(Don't know/Can't say) 0.3	

A

Head Office: 35 NORTHAMPTON SQUARE, LONDON EC1V 0AX
TELEPHONE 01-250 1866

SCPR

Northern Field Office: CHARGEL HOUSE, GAINFORD, DARLINGTON,
CO. DURHAM DL2 3EG. TELEPHONE 0325-730888

BRITISH SOCIAL ATTITUDES: 1989
SELF-COMPLETION QUESTIONNAIRE

Spring 1989   P.1005

OFFICE USE ONLY:		Area No.
Interviewer		
to enter:		Serial No.
		Interviewer No.
Rec.		

NOTE:
In the self-completion
questionnaires actually used,
boxes were ticked by
respondents to show their
answers to the questions. In
the questionnaires reproduced
here, the boxes have been
removed.

To the selected respondent

We hope very much that you will agree to participate in this important study -
the sixth in this annual series. The results are published in a book each
autumn. The study consists of this self-completion questionnaire and an interview. Some of the questions are also being asked in ten other countries, as
part of an international survey.

Completing the questionnaire

The questions inside cover a wide range of subjects, **but each one can be
answered simply by placing a tick (✓) or a number in one or more of the boxes.**
No special knowledge is required: we are confident that everyone will be able
to offer an opinion on all questions. And we want *everyone* to take part,
not just those with strong views or particular viewpoints. The questionnaire
should not take very long to complete, and we hope you will find it interesting
and enjoyable. It should be filled in by the person selected by the interviewer at your address. The answers you give will be treated as confidential
and anonymous.

Returning the questionnaire

Your interviewer will arrange with you the most convenient way of returning
the questionnaire. If the interviewer has arranged to call back for it, please
complete it and keep it safely until then. If not, please complete it and
post it back in the pre-paid, addressed envelope as soon as you possibly can.

Thank you for your help.

*Social and Community Planning Research is an independent social research
institute registered as a charitable trust. Its projects are funded by
government departments, local authorities, universities and foundations to
provide information on social issues in the UK. This survey series has
been funded mainly by the Sainsbury Family Charitable Trusts, with contributions also from government departments, other charitable foundations,
universities and industry. Please contact us if you require further
information.*

- 1 -

N=1307

Qs.201-30

201. To begin, we have some questions about women.
Do you agree or disagree ...?

PLEASE TICK ONE BOX ON EACH LINE

	Strongly agree	Agree	Neither agree nor disagree	Disagree	Strongly disagree	Can't choose
a. A working mother can establish just as warm and secure a relationship with her children as a mother who does not work.	15.1	42.6	11.6	23.3	5.1	1.7
b. A pre-school child is likely to suffer if his or her mother works.	10.0	36.5	16.6	28.7	6.1	1.8
c. All in all, family life suffers when the woman has a full-time job.	8.0	33.5	16.8	31.5	8.7	0.9
d. A woman and her family will all be happier if she goes out to work.	1.3	17.2	38.3	35.4	3.9	3.7
e. A job is all right, but what most women really want is a home and children.	5.5	25.9	18.9	35.2	11.1	2.5
f. Being a housewife is just as fulfilling as working for pay.	6.6	34.3	20.7	28.8	5.7	2.8
g. Having a job is the best way for a woman to be an independent person.	9.2	52.9	16.0	18.6	1.4	1.3
h. Both the husband and wife should contribute to the household income.	12.8	40.3	24.1	18.6	1.7	2.1
i. A husband's job is to earn money; a wife's job is to look after the home and family.	6.7	21.7	18.0	35.0	17.6	0.8

Do you agree or disagree ...

	Strongly agree	Agree	Neither agree nor disagree	Disagree	Strongly disagree	Can't choose
j. I would enjoy having a job even if I didn't need the money.	8.2	54.0	9.4	21.3	3.5	2.8

Please continue ...

- 2 -

202. Do you think that women should work outside the home full-time, part-time or not at all under these circumstances?

PLEASE TICK ONE BOX ON EACH LINE

	Work full-time	Work part-time	Stay at home	Can't choose
a. After marrying and before there are children?	76.9	13.6	2.3	6.2
b. When there is a child under school age?	2.3	26.2	63.7	6.3
c. After the youngest child starts school?	12.7	67.7	11.3	6.7
d. After the children leave home?	56.9	28.4	2.6	10.5

203. Think of a child under 3 years old whose parents both have full-time jobs.

How suitable do you think each of these childcare arrangements would be for the child?

	Very suitable	Somewhat suitable	Not very suitable	Not at all suitable	Can't choose
a. A state or local authority nursery?	28.8	37.5	16.9	7.7	4.9
b. A private creche or nursery?	29.7	41.6	12.0	6.4	4.7
c. A childminder or baby-sitter?	16.4	38.1	26.8	10.2	3.3
d. A neighbour or friend?	9.6	31.9	35.5	14.3	3.2
e. A relative?	39.3	37.1	12.3	5.8	2.1

204.(a) If you were advising a **young woman**, which of the following ways of life would you recommend?

PLEASE TICK ONE BOX ONLY

To live alone, without a steady partner?	4.1
To live with a steady partner, without marrying?	4.0
To live with a steady partner for a while, and then marry?	42.8
To marry without living together first?	36.8
Can't choose	11.2

Please continue ...

- 3 -

204.b) If you were advising **a young man**, which of the following ways of life would you recommend?

PLEASE TICK ONE BOX ONLY

To live alone, without a steady partner?	4.7
To live with a steady partner, without marrying?	5.2
To live with a steady partner for a while, and then marry?	42.2
To marry without living together first?	35.8
Can't choose	10.6

205. Do you agree or disagree ...?
PLEASE TICK ONE BOX ON EACH LINE

	Strongly agree	Agree	Neither agree nor disagree	Disagree	Disagree strongly	Can't choose
a. Married people are generally happier than unmarried people.	7.6	25.4	39.5	19.4	3.8	3.8
b. Personal freedom is more important than the companionship of marriage.	2.6	9.4	25.3	52.5	6.2	3.3
c. The main advantage of marriage is that it gives financial security.	2.9	14.7	16.9	51.1	12.2	1.6
d. The main purpose of marriage these days is to have children.	3.0	16.8	15.5	54.2	8.2	1.6
e. It is better to have a bad marriage than no marriage at all.	0.9	1.6	3.3	46.9	45.4	1.2
f. People who want children ought to get married.	24.6	45.5	10.2	14.4	3.0	1.1
g. A single mother can bring up her child as well as a married couple.	4.5	25.9	16.9	41.6	9.0	1.4
h. A single father can bring up his child as well as a married couple.	2.9	21.1	17.5	44.4	12.4	1.1
i. Couples don't take marriage seriously enough when divorce is easily available.	14.8	46.0	14.0	20.1	2.7	1.7
j. Homosexual couples should have the right to marry one another.	2.5	10.7	15.1	28.4	37.8	4.8

Please continue ....

- 4 -

A

206. All in all, what do you think is the ideal number of children for a family to have?

PLEASE WRITE THE NUMBER IN THE BOX   **MEDIAN:** 2

207. In general, what do you feel about each of these family sizes?
PLEASE TICK ONE BOX ON EACH LINE

It is ...

A family with:	Very desirable	Desirable	Neither desirable nor undesirable	Undesirable	Very undesirable	Can't choose
a. No children?	1.8	4.9	39.7	31.9	9.8	6.4
b. One child?	2.6	32.9	26.4	23.8	3.1	4.0
c. Two children?	28.7	52.0	11.6	1.6	0.3	2.5
d. Three children?	10.3	36.3	27.2	13.5	3.2	5.2
e. Four children or more?	4.9	16.2	23.2	29.1	16.1	6.4

208. Do you agree or disagree ...?
PLEASE TICK ONE BOX ON EACH LINE

	Strongly agree	Agree	Neither agree nor disagree	Disagree	Strongly disagree	Can't choose
a. Children are more trouble than they are worth.	1.7	1.9	9.3	50.7	35.0	0.8
b. Watching children grow up is life's greatest joy.	29.2	52.3	12.8	3.6	0.5	1.3
c. Having children interferes too much with the freedom of parents.	1.7	7.8	16.8	56.7	15.3	0.9
d. A marriage without children is not fully complete.	10.2	35.0	20.2	26.3	6.0	1.7
e. It is better not to have children because they are such a heavy burden.	1.2	1.4	8.1	58.3	29.2	1.0
f. People who have never had children lead empty lives.	6.7	16.7	21.2	38.6	13.0	3.1

Please continue ....

OFFICE USE ONLY

- 5 -

209. In general, would you say that the law now makes it easy or difficult for people who want to get divorced?

PLEASE TICK ONE BOX ONLY

Very easy	27.1
Fairly easy	48.2
Neither easy nor difficult	14.4
Fairly difficult	5.5
Very difficult	1.3
Impossible	-
Can't choose	3.1

210. And in general, how easy or difficult do you think the law **should** make it for **couples without young children** to get a divorce?

PLEASE TICK ONE BOX ONLY

Very easy	13.0
Fairly easy	31.5
Neither easy nor difficult	28.8
Fairly difficult	16.8
Very difficult	5.5
Impossible	0.5
Can't choose	3.6

211. And what about **couples with young children**? How easy or difficult **should** the law make it for them to get a divorce?

PLEASE TICK ONE BOX ONLY

Very easy	2.4
Fairly easy	14.3
Neither easy nor difficult	30.9
Fairly difficult	29.9
Very difficult	15.8
Impossible	2.2
Can't choose	4.2

Please continue ...

OFFICE USE ONLY

- 6 -

212. When a marriage is troubled and unhappy do you think it is generally better for the **children** if the couple stays together or gets divorced?

PLEASE TICK ONE BOX ONLY

Much better to divorce	14.4
Better to divorce	45.1
Worse to divorce	16.6
Much worse to divorce	3.0
Can't choose	20.3

213. And when a marriage is troubled and unhappy, is it generally better for the **wife** if the couple stays together or gets divorced?

PLEASE TICK ONE BOX ONLY

Much better to divorce	14.6
Better to divorce	51.2
Worse to divorce	9.0
Much worse to divorce	1.6
Can't choose	22.9

214. And when a marriage is troubled and unhappy, is it generally better for the **husband** if the couple stays together or gets divorced?

PLEASE TICK ONE BOX ONLY

Much better to divorce	13.6
Better to divorce	51.9
Worse to divorce	8.7
Much worse to divorce	1.8
Can't choose	23.5

215. Did your mother ever work for pay for as long as **one year** **after** you were born and **before** you were 14?

PLEASE TICK ONE BOX ONLY

Yes, she worked	49.1
No	47.7
Did not live with mother	2.0

Please continue ...

- 7 -

216. Have you ever been divorced?

PLEASE TICK ONE BOX ONLY

Yes 13.0   } **PLEASE ANSWER Q.17 BELOW**
No 71.3   }

Never married 14.8 → **GO TO Q.20, PAGE 8**

217. Are you married or living as married now?

PLEASE TICK ONE BOX ONLY

N=1103

Yes 81.5 → **PLEASE ANSWER Q.18-19 BELOW**

No 18.2 → **GO TO Q.20, PAGE 8**

218.a) Has your husband or wife or partner ever been divorced?

PLEASE TICK ONE BOX ONLY

N=880

Yes 11.7
No 86.7

b) Did you live with your husband or wife or partner before you got married?

PLEASE TICK ONE BOX ONLY

Yes 20.5
No 74.2
Not married 2.7

219.a) Do you and your husband or wife or partner both have paid work at the moment?

PLEASE TICK ONE BOX

N=880

Yes 45.9 → **ANSWER b), BELOW**

No 53.5 → **GO TO Q.20, PAGE 8**

b) Who earns more money?

PLEASE TICK ONE BOX ONLY

N=398

Husband earns **much** more 67.5
Husband earns a **bit** more 18.9
We earn about the **same** amount 5.7
Wife earns a **bit** more 4.5
Wife earns **much** more 2.5

Please continue ...

- 8 -

Qs.220-30   N=1307

220. Now for some questions on different subjects.

Here are a number of circumstances in which a woman might consider an abortion. Please say whether or not you think the law should allow an abortion in each case.

PLEASE TICK ONE BOX ON EACH LINE

	Should abortion be allowed by law?		
	Yes	No	Don't know
The woman decides on her own she does not wish to have the child	49.3	46.1	0.3
The couple agree they do not wish to have the child	59.4	35.4	0.2
The woman is not married and does not wish to marry the man	57.0	37.8	0.4
The couple cannot afford any more children	56.7	38.2	0.2
There is a strong chance of a defect in the baby	87.4	9.5	0.1
The woman's health is seriously endangered by the pregnancy	91.6	5.4	0.1
The woman became pregnant as a result of rape	90.8	6.1	0.1

221. Suppose a married couple want to have their own child, but cannot have one. Should the law allow or not allow them to use each of the methods below? Please assume in each case that it is the only method open to them on medical advice.

PLEASE TICK ONE BOX ON EACH LINE

	It should be		
	Allowed by law	Not allowed by law	Don't know
They try to have a child by artificial insemination, using the husband as donor	90.8	6.6	0.1
They try to have a child by artificial insemination, using an anonymous donor	53.7	42.5	0.2
They try to have a child by having their own 'test-tube' embryo implanted	86.6	9.8	0.3
They find a 'surrogate' mother who agrees, **without payment**, to bear a child for them (by artificial insemination, using the husband as donor)	30.6	65.2	0.2
They find a 'surrogate' mother who is **paid** to bear a child for them (by artificial insemination, using the husband as donor)	18.0	77.9	0.4

A

222. Which of these statements comes closest to your views on the availability of pornographic magazines and films?

PLEASE TICK ONE BOX

They should be banned altogether	39.1
They should be available in special adult shops but not displayed to the public	42.2
They should be available in special adult shops with public display permitted	9.8
They should be available in any shop for sale to adults only	7.3
They should be available in any shop for sale to anyone	0.2

223. a) Suppose a person has a painful incurable disease. Do you think that doctors should be allowed by law to end the patient's life if the patient requests it?

PLEASE TICK ONE BOX

Yes	78.7
No	20.0

b) And if a person is not incurably sick but simply tired of living, should doctors be allowed by law to end that person's life if he or she requests it?

PLEASE TICK ONE BOX

Yes	14.0
No	83.9

224. Are you in favour of or against the death penalty for ...

PLEASE TICK ONE BOX ON EACH LINE

	In favour	Against	Don't know
... murder in the course of a terrorist act?	75.3	19.2	0.4
... murder of a police officer?	71.4	23.4	0.4
... other murders?	72.3	25.8	0.5

Please continue ...

- 9 -

- 10 -

A

225. From what you know or have heard, please tick a box for each of the items below to show whether you think the National Health Service **in your area** is, on the whole, satisfactory or in need of improvement.

PLEASE TICK ONE BOX ON EACH LINE

		In need of a lot of improvement	In need of some improvement	Satis-factory	Very good
a.	GPs' appointment systems	12.4	33.1	43.0	10.6
b.	Amount of time GP gives to each patient	8.3	26.1	53.7	11.2
c.	Being able to choose which GP to see	9.1	20.7	55.6	13.5
d.	Quality of medical treatment by GPs	6.4	20.3	53.8	18.7
e.	Hospital waiting lists for non-emergency operations	45.2	39.5	12.9	0.8
f.	Waiting time before getting appointments with hospital consultants	49.0	37.1	11.0	1.1
g.	General condition of hospital buildings	21.2	39.6	31.3	7.0
h.	Hospital casualty departments	22.4	36.9	31.6	7.8
i.	Staffing level of nurses in hospitals	34.5	40.9	19.5	3.6
j.	Staffing level of doctors in hospitals	35.2	39.8	20.0	3.2
k.	Quality of medical treatment in hospitals	9.2	26.9	46.8	15.9
l.	Quality of nursing care in hospitals	7.9	19.2	41.8	30.0

- 11 -

A.

226. In the last two years, have you or a close family member ...

PLEASE TICK ONE BOX ON EACH LINE

	Yes	No
... visited an NHS GP?	94.2	4.5
... been an out-patient in an NHS hospital?	65.9	31.4
... been an in-patient in an NHS hospital?	46.6	49.8
... visited a patient in an NHS hospital?	73.6	23.8
... had any medical treatment as a private patient?	11.7	85.8

227. Please tick one box for each statement, to show how much you agree or disagree with it.

PLEASE TICK ONE BOX ON EACH LINE

	Agree strongly	Just agree	Neither agree nor dis-agree	Just dis-agree	Disagree strongly
a. Healthy food doesn't usually taste as nice as other food	5.9	20.6	27.5	24.8	20.5
b. Food that is good for you is usually more expensive	17.8	31.0	14.3	24.1	12.1
c. Food that is good for you generally takes too long to prepare	2.8	12.9	26.0	39.8	17.9
d. It is hard to find food that is good for you in supermarkets	2.7	13.9	17.8	43.2	21.7
e. Mothers would eat healthier food if the rest of their families would let them	6.0	20.0	30.8	27.8	14.3
f. As long as you take enough exercise you can eat whatever foods you want	5.1	21.6	17.0	36.2	19.4
g. If heart disease is in your family, there is little you can do to reduce your chances of getting it	3.3	8.3	12.1	36.8	38.6
h. The experts contradict each other over what makes a healthy diet	26.6	43.9	11.0	13.3	3.9
i. People worry too much about their weight	15.6	44.7	17.1	17.7	3.9
j. Good health is just a matter of good luck	4.2	10.1	13.4	35.0	36.4
k. A proper meal should include meat and vegetables	25.3	33.0	14.2	19.2	7.9

- 12 -

A

228. How worried are you about the sorts of food you eat?

PLEASE TICK ONE BOX

Very worried	4.3
Fairly worried	24.1
Not particularly worried	50.4
Not worried at all	20.7

229. Which one of these statements best describes how you feel about the sorts of food you eat nowadays?

PLEASE TICK ONE BOX

I have never felt any need to change what I eat	25.9
I have already changed as much as I am going to	40.7
I ought to change more but probably won't	28.3
I will probably be changing soon	4.4

230. Please tick one box for each statement to show how much you agree or disagree with it.

PLEASE TICK ONE BOX ON EACH LINE

	Agree strongly	Agree	Neither agree nor disagree	Dis-agree	Disagree strongly
A. Social workers should put the child's interests first even if it means taking a child away from its natural parents.	23.2	45.5	17.4	11.5	1.4
B. Social workers have too much power to interfere with people's lives.	9.0	27.2	34.5	25.8	2.6
C. The welfare state makes people nowadays less willing to look after themselves.	8.6	30.2	23.2	31.7	5.4
D. People receiving social security are made to feel like second class citizens.	13.7	39.3	22.5	21.7	2.1
E. The welfare state encourages people to stop helping each other.	4.6	27.1	26.7	35.4	5.3
F. Doctors should be allowed to give contraceptive advice and supplies to young people under 16 without having to inform parents.	6.8	25.7	11.5	35.9	19.5

please continue

- 13 -

A

A & B | N=2604 | Q.231 only

231. Please tick one box for each statement below to show how much you agree or disagree with it.

PLEASE TICK ONE BOX ON EACH LINE

	Agree strongly	Agree	Neither agree nor disagree	Dis-agree	Disagree strongly
a. Government should redistribute income from the better-off to those who are less well off.	18.6	31.5	20.0	22.0	6.6
b. Big business benefits owners at the expense of workers.	14.2	38.6	24.2	18.9	2.6
c. Ordinary working people do not get their fair share of the nation's wealth.	19.9	45.3	17.7	14.4	1.6
d. There is one law for the rich and one for the poor.	29.9	38.7	14.1	13.2	3.2
e. Management will always try to get the better of employees if it gets the chance.	18.4	39.7	21.4	17.5	1.9
f. Young people today don't have enough respect for traditional British values.	18.4	43.2	22.5	13.1	1.9
g. People who break the law should be given stiffer sentences.	33.1	44.3	15.4	5.6	0.7
h. People should be allowed to organise public meetings to protest against the government.	16.7	48.1	25.0	7.9	1.3
i. For some crimes, the death penalty is the most appropriate sentence.	40.1	34.1	7.1	9.9	7.9
j. People should be allowed to publish leaflets to protest against the government.	17.3	45.9	26.0	8.3	1.5

please continue ...

- 14 -

A

PLEASE TICK ONE BOX FOR EACH STATEMENT

231 cont'd

	Agree strongly	Agree	Neither agree nor disagree	Dis-agree	Disagree strongly
k. Schools should teach children to obey authority.	32.5	51.3	10.5	4.4	0.3
l. People should be allowed to organise protest marches and demonstrations.	9.9	40.4	28.4	11.8	2.4
m. The law should always be obeyed, even if a particular law is wrong.	7.9	36.4	25.6	25.8	3.3
n. Censorship of films and magazines is necessary to uphold moral standards.	19.4	49.2	15.2	12.4	2.8
o. The government should spend more money on welfare benefits for the poor, even if it leads to higher taxes.	18.3	42.3	23.0	13.8	1.5
p. Around here, most unemployed people could find a job if they really wanted one.	11.9	40.2	18.8	22.0	6.1
q. Many people who get social security don't really deserve any help.	6.1	21.6	26.6	34.2	10.4
r. Most people on the dole are fiddling in one way of another.	7.2	23.9	30.8	29.1	7.9
s. If welfare benefits weren't so generous people would learn to stand on their own two feet.	7.6	22.6	23.1	33.4	12.3

- 15 -

232. Do you think big businesses or small businesses are generally better at each of these things, or is there no difference?

PLEASE TICK ONE BOX ON EACH LINE

N=1307 Qs.232-41

	Big businesses are better	Small businesses are better	There is no difference
Inventing new products	39.2	22.2	36.5
Making well-designed products	26.7	32.2	39.0
Investing in new machinery and technology	75.9	7.4	14.4
Attracting the best people to work in them	56.8	16.0	24.9
Making goods that people really want to buy	21.8	29.3	46.8
Keeping good relations between management and other employees	7.2	70.4	20.2
Training employees in new skills	44.8	23.6	29.1
Paying their employees a fair wage	34.0	23.2	40.8
Charging fair prices for their products	20.1	34.4	42.9
Caring about their customers	4.9	64.2	28.6

233. Who do you think benefits most from the profits made by British firms?

Please tick one box

Mainly their owners or shareholders	63.6
Mainly their directors and managers	26.7
Mainly their employees	1.6
The public generally	5.4

Please continue ...

- 16 -

234. Please tick one box for each statement to show how much you agree or disagree with it.

PLEASE TICK ONE BOX ON EACH LINE

	Agree Strongly	Agree	Neither agree nor disagree	Disagree	Disagree strongly
a. Consumers are given too little protection by the law	12.5	48.1	22.5	15.0	0.5
b. Too much of industry's profits go abroad	9.0	40.5	37.5	10.7	0.3
c. We would all be better off if British firms made bigger profits	8.5	41.0	25.7	21.0	1.9
d. Britain's economy can prosper without manufacturing industry	1.6	4.2	15.8	59.9	16.4
e. British firms make too much profit	3.3	15.8	33.0	40.2	5.0
f. Britain's schools fail to teach the kind of skills that British industry needs	13.9	51.5	18.3	13.9	0.7
g. Employees who have shares in their companies tend to work harder	13.4	57.9	15.6	10.8	0.5
h. The less profitable British industry is, the less money there is for governments to spend on things like education and health	9.4	51.1	23.0	13.0	1.6
i. British people should try to buy British goods even when they have to pay a bit more for them	13.3	45.7	18.0	19.8	1.9

235. Please tick one box on each line to show your views on government help for industry. Remember that if you say 'definitely' or 'probably', it might require an increase in income tax to pay for it.

Do you think the government should ...

PLEASE TICK ONE BOX ON EACH LINE

	Definitely	Probably	Probably not	Definitely not
... help industry pay for research into new products?	22.2	42.8	25.8	6.4
... help pay for new factories in areas of high unemployment?	39.7	46.9	8.5	2.5
... help industry pay for the cost of replacing out-dated machinery and equipment?	20.4	37.4	31.1	8.5
... help industry pay the wages of people working in declining industries?	13.3	26.9	42.9	13.7
... give people grants to start their own businesses?	39.9	48.0	8.0	1.8
... give firms more help in selling goods abroad?	35.2	43.8	14.8	3.4
... help industry pay for training employees in new skills?	39.3	44.9	10.7	2.4

- 16 -

238. Please tick one box for each statement to show how much you agree or disagree with it.

PLEASE TICK ONE BOX ON EACH LINE

	Agree strongly	Agree	Neither agree nor disagree	Disagree	Disagree strongly
a. Most people with AIDS have only themselves to blame	15.7	39.4	16.6	22.7	4.4
b. The National Health Service should spend more of its resources on giving better care to people dying from AIDS	6.2	33.8	34.4	20.9	3.6
c. Official warnings about AIDS should say that some sexual practices are morally wrong	22.7	38.8	14.7	18.3	4.4
d. Within the next five years doctors will discover a vaccine against AIDS	2.8	30.5	44.9	17.5	2.4
e. AIDS is a way of punishing the world for its decline in moral standards	7.1	19.5	22.4	29.0	20.3

239. As one way of getting to know how AIDS is spreading, it has been suggested that hospitals should be allowed to test any patient's blood (that has been taken for other reasons) to see whether it contains the virus that causes AIDS.

Do you agree or disagree with this suggestion?

PLEASE TICK ONE BOX

Agree strongly 45.6

Agree 41.3

Neither agree nor disagree 5.9

Disagree 5.1

Disagree strongly 1.1

- 17 -

236. 'The City' of London is often called the financial centre of Britain.

Please tick one box on each line to show how much you agree or disagree with each of these statements about 'The City'.

	Agree strongly	Agree	Neither agree nor disagree	Dis- agree	Disagree strongly
a. The success of 'The City' is essential to the success of Britain's economy.	12.7	48.1	24.1	11.1	1.4
b. 'The City' can be relied on to uncover dishonest financial deals without government intervention.	2.5	16.7	34.2	35.5	8.4
c. The government should encourage as many ordinary people as possible to buy shares in British firms.	8.6	47.8	28.4	11.3	1.6
d. Too many 'City' institutions go for quick profits at the expense of long-term investment in British industry.	16.6	48.1	26.7	4.4	1.2

237. Now a few questions about the disease called AIDS.

Please tick one box to show which is closest to your views about the following statement:

Within five years AIDS will cause more deaths in Britain than any other single disease.

PLEASE TICK ONE BOX

It is highly exaggerated 14.2

It is slightly exaggerated 31.4

It is more or less true 52.9

Please continue ...

- 19 -

A

OFFICE
USE
ONLY

240. Thinking of patients whose blood has been tested
for the AIDS virus without their knowledge -
should they ...

PLEASE TICK ONE BOX

<u>Not</u> be told the test has been carried out	5.5
Be told about the test, but <u>not</u> be told the result	1.1
Be told about the test, <u>and</u> have the choice of knowing or not <u>knowing</u> the result	38.0
Be told about the test, <u>and</u> be told the result	54.5

241. As far as you know, have you ever met anyone who was
confirmed as having the virus that causes AIDS?

PLEASE TICK ONE BOX

Yes	5.0
No	94.7

242.a) To help us plan better in future, please tell
us about how long it took you to complete this
questionnaire?

N=2604
A & B

PLEASE TICK ONE BOX

Less than 15 minutes	5.0
Between 15 and 20 minutes	22.2
Between 20 and 30 minutes	31.9
Between 30 and 45 minutes	23.1
Between 45 and 60 minutes	11.0
Over one hour	6.1

b) And on what date did you fill in the questionnaire?

PLEASE WRITE IN

_____ _____ '89
DATE   MONTH   YEAR

THANK YOU VERY MUCH FOR YOUR HELP!

Please keep the completed questionnaire for the interviewer if
he or she has arranged to call for it. Otherwise, please post
it as soon as possible in the pre-paid addressed envelope
provided.

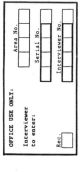

B

SCPR

SOCIAL & COMMUNITY PLANNING RESEARCH

Head Office: 35 NORTHAMPTON SQUARE, LONDON EC1V 0AX
TELEPHONE 01-250 1866

Northern Field Office: CHARLUEL HOUSE, GAINFORD, DARLINGTON,
CO. DURHAM DL2 3EG. TELEPHONE 0325-730888

BRITISH SOCIAL ATTITUDES: 1989
SELF-COMPLETION QUESTIONNAIRE

Spring 1989 P.1005

OFFICE USE ONLY:

Interviewer
to enter:

Rec.

Area No.

Serial No.

Interviewer No.

To the selected respondent

We hope very much that you will agree to participate in this important study -
the sixth in this annual series. The results are published in a book each
autumn. The study consists of this self-completion questionnaire and an interview. Some of the questions are also being asked in ten other countries, as
part of an international survey.

Completing the questionnaire

The questions inside cover a wide range of subjects, but **each one can be
answered simply by placing a tick (/) or a number in one or more of the boxes.**
No special knowledge is required: we are confident that everyone will be able
to offer an opinion on all questions. And we want *everyone* to take part,
not just those with strong views or particular viewpoints. The questionnaire
should not take very long to complete, and we hope you will find it interesting
and enjoyable. It should be filled in by the person selected by the interviewer at your address. The answers you give will be treated as confidential
and anonymous.

Returning the questionnaire

Your interviewer will arrange with you the most convenient way of returning
the questionnaire. If the interviewer has arranged to call back for it, please
complete it and keep it safely until then. If not, please complete it and
post it back in the pre-paid, addressed envelope as soon as you possibly can.

Thank you for your help.

*Social and Community Planning Research is an independent social research
institute registered as a charitable trust. Its projects are funded by
government departments, local authorities, universities and foundations to
provide information on social issues in the UK. This survey series has
been funded mainly by the Sainsbury Family Charitable Trusts, with contributions also from government departments, other charitable foundations,
universities and industry. Please contact us if you require further
information.*

- 1 -

B

N=1297   Qs.201-10

201. Suppose you could change the way you spend your time, spending more time on some things and less time on others.

Which of the things on the following list would you like to spend more time on, which would you like to spend less time on and which would you like to spend the same amount of time on as now?

PLEASE TICK ONE BOX ON EACH LINE

	Much more time	A bit more time	Same time as now	A bit less time	Much less time	Can't choose/ Doesn't apply
a. Time in a paid job?	4.6	7.2	24.3	24.7	5.6	29.3
b. Time doing household work?	2.2	11.6	37.1	19.8	13.8	10.9
c. Time with your family?	25.3	34.1	31.2	1.1	0.5	4.5
d. Time with your friends?	9.1	37.4	44.3	1.4	0.6	2.6
e. Time in leisure activities?	19.0	43.4	27.7	0.9	0.8	4.7
f. Time to relax?	21.8	38.3	31.8	2.0	0.7	1.9

202. Please tick one box for each statement below to show how much you agree or disagree with it, thinking of work in general.

PLEASE TICK ONE BOX ON EACH LINE

	Strongly agree	Agree	Neither Agree nor disagree	Disagree	Strongly Disagree	Can't choose
a. A job is just a way of earning money - no more.	7.0	21.6	12.8	38.9	13.1	2.1
b. I would enjoy having a paid job even if I did not need the money.	6.6	47.0	14.2	18.7	3.9	5.2
c. Work is a person's most important activity.	10.6	25.9	18.5	31.9	8.4	1.7

Please continue ...

- 2 -

B

203. Are you the person responsible for doing the general domestic duties - like cleaning, cooking, washing and so on - in your household?

PLEASE TICK ONE BOX ONLY

Yes, I am mainly responsible   46.5

Yes, I am equally responsible with someone else   18.1

No, someone else is mainly responsible   34.1

204. Think of two people doing the same kind of work. What do you personally think should be important in deciding how much to pay them?

Looking at the things below, please write '1' in the box next to the thing you think should be most important.

Then write '2' next to the thing you think should be next most important. And '3' next to the thing you think should be third most important. Leave the other boxes blank.

In deciding on pay for two people doing the same kind of work how important should be ...

Write 1,2 and 3 in THREE boxes: leave the other boxes blank		
1	2	3
... how long the employee has been with the firm? 6.6	9.5	24.9
... how well the employee does the job? 51.6	19.6	7.6
... the experience of the employee in doing the work? 14.6	40.5	18.4
... the standard rate - giving both employees the same pay? 12.7	5.6	10.1
... the age of the employee? 0.5	2.7	4.1
... the sex of the employee? 0.2	0.5	0.6
... the employee's family responsibilities? 0.4	2.3	3.8
... the employee's education and formal qualifications? 3.0	7.7	18.0

OR TICK:

Can't choose   3.9

Please continue ...

3

B

205. How much do you agree or disagree with these two statements?
PLEASE TICK ONE BOX ON EACH LINE

	Strongly agree	Agree	Neither agree nor disagree	Disagree	Strongly disagree	Can't choose
a. There will always be conflict between management and workers because they are really on opposite sides.	7.7	30.2	18.7	33.2	5.8	3.0
b. Workers need strong trade unions to protect their interests.	12.0	29.1	21.6	26.4	5.9	3.1

206. From the following list, please tick one box for each item to show how important you personally think it is in a job.
PLEASE TICK ONE BOX ON EACH LINE

How important is ...	Very important	Important	Neither important nor unimportant	Not important	Not important at all	Can't choose
a. ... job security?	57.8	37.1	2.8	0.6	0.1	0.6
b. ... high income?	17.7	61.0	13.4	4.3	0.3	0.6
c. ... good opportunities for advancement?	29.6	53.5	9.7	3.5	0.1	1.1
d. ... a job that leaves a lot of leisure time?	7.3	34.7	33.8	17.9	1.4	1.5
e. ... an interesting job?	48.7	45.6	2.8	0.4	0.1	0.3
f. ... a job that allows someone to work independently?	20.2	44.1	23.9	7.5	0.3	1.7
g. ... a job that allows someone to help other people?	17.8	47.3	24.5	6.1	0.6	1.1
h. ... a job that is useful to society?	20.2	42.6	25.2	6.7	1.0	1.7
i. ... a job with flexible working hours?	14.0	31.3	32.1	16.1	2.9	1.6

Please continue ...

4

B

207. Suppose you were unemployed and couldn't find a job. Which of the following problems do you think would be the worst?

Please write '1' in the box next to the worst thing.
Then write '2' beside the next worst thing.
And '3' beside the third worst thing.
Leave the other boxes blank.

Write 1,2 and 3 in THREE boxes: leave the other boxes blank

	1	2	3
Lack of contact with people at work	5.7	9.0	12.4
Not enough money	54.3	18.1	8.5
Loss of self-confidence	17.1	23.4	19.8
Loss of respect from friends and acquaintances	1.0	3.9	5.0
Family tensions	8.4	25.2	19.6
Loss of job experience	2.5	6.6	12.5
Not knowing how to fill one's time	1.4	3.5	10.2

OR TICK:

Can't choose	4.0		

208. Suppose you were working and could choose between different kinds of jobs.
Which of the following would you personally choose?

PLEASE TICK ONE BOX ONLY

a. I would choose ...

... being an employee	47.9
... being self-employed	43.8
Can't choose	7.2

PLEASE TICK ONE BOX ONLY

b. I would choose ...

... working in a small firm	61.1
... working in a large firm	24.2
Can't choose	13.3

Please continue ...

B

208. (cont'd)

And which of the following would you personally choose?

PLEASE TICK ONE BOX ONLY

I would choose ...

c. | ... working in a manufacturing industry | 29.0 |
| ... working in an office, in sales or in service | 51.9 |
| Can't choose | 17.6 |

PLEASE TICK ONE BOX ONLY

I would choose ...

d. | ... working in a private business | 58.4 |
| ... working for the government or civil service | 22.5 |
| Can't choose | 17.4 |

209. On the whole, do you think it should be or should not be the government's responsibility to ...

PLEASE TICK ONE BOX ON EACH LINE

	Definitely should be	Probably should be	Probably should not be	Definitely should not be	Can't choose
a. ... provide a job for everyone who wants one?	36.8	31.1	15.4	10.6	3.8
b. ... provide a decent standard of living for the unemployed?	43.4	38.0	8.6	4.3	3.7

210. Do you usually work 10 hours or more a week for pay in your (main) job?

PLEASE TICK ONE BOX ONLY

Yes, I usually work 10 hours or more a week in my (main) job	56.6 → GO TO Q.13, PAGE 7
No, I usually work less than 10 hours a week in my (main) job	2.4 } PLEASE ANSWER Q.11, PAGE 6
No, I don't work for pay at the moment	40.2

Please continue ...

- 5 -

B

- 6 -

211. Would you like to have a paid job now?

PLEASE TICK ONE BOX ONLY

N=568

Yes, I would like a **full-time** job now (30 hours or more per week)	13.7
Yes, I would like a **part-time** job now (10-29 hours per week)	14.3 } PLEASE ANSWER Q.12 BELOW
Yes, I would like a job with less than 10 hours a week now	11.1
No, I would not like to have a paid job now	56.4 → GO TO Q.22 PAGE 12

212. If you were looking actively, how easy or difficult do you think it would be for you to find an acceptable job?

PLEASE TICK ONE BOX ONLY

N=235

Very easy	4.9
Fairly easy	16.0
Neither easy nor difficult	11.1
Fairly difficult	28.8
Very difficult	30.3
Can't choose	3.5

Please continue ...

OFFICE USE ONLY

B

- 7 -

| PLEASE ANSWER Q.13 - Q.21 |
| ABOUT YOUR MAIN JOB. |

N=738
Qs.213-21

213. Which of the following statements best describes your feelings about your job?

PLEASE TICK ONE BOX ONLY

In my job ...

... I only work as hard as I have to	5.5
.. I work hard, but not so that it interferes with the rest of my life	36.4
... I make a point of doing the best work I can, even if it sometimes does interfere with the rest of my life	55.8
Can't choose	0.4

214. Think of the number of hours you work, and the money you earn in your main job, including any regular overtime.

If you had only one of these three choices which of the following would you prefer?

PLEASE TICK ONE BOX ONLY

Work **longer** hours and earn **more money**	22.1
Work the **same** number of hours and earn the **same money**	61.8
Work **fewer** hours and earn **less money**	7.1
Can't choose	6.1

Please continue ...

OFFICE USE ONLY

B

- 8 -

215. Think of two people doing the same kind of work in your place of work. What do you personally think is important in deciding how much to pay them?

Looking at the things below, please write '1' in the box next to the thing you think is most important at your place of work.

Then write '2' next to the thing you think is next most important. And '3' next to the thing you think is third most important. Leave the other boxes blank.

	Write 1, 2 and 3 in THREE boxes. leave the other boxes blank		
	1	2	3

At your workplace, in deciding on pay for two people doing the **same kind of work**, how important is ....

	1	2	3
... how long the employee has been with the firm?	6.5	10.0	25.3
... how well the employee does the job?	50.8	19.4	10.1
... the experience of the employee in doing the work?	12.8	43.8	17.9
... the standard rate - giving both employees the same pay?	15.3	5.8	11.5
... the age of the employee?	1.1	2.4	4.0
... the sex of the employee?	—	0.3	0.4
... the employee's family responsibilities?	0.3	1.7	2.1
... the employer's education and formal qualifications?	2.8	5.9	16.8

OR TICK:

Can't choose   3.4

Please continue ...

OFFICE USE ONLY

B

- 9 -

216. For each of these statements about your (main) job, please tick one box to show how much you agree or disagree that it applies to your job.

PLEASE TICK ONE BOX ON EACH LINE

	Strongly agree	Agree	Neither agree nor disagree	Disagree	Strongly disagree	Can't choose
a. My job is secure	16.2	38.8	20.5	14.4	4.7	1.3
b. My income is high	2.1	14.5	31.4	36.6	10.5	0.9
c. My opportunities for advancement are high	3.6	18.3	27.5	35.4	9.8	1.3
d. My job leaves a lot of leisure time	3.2	21.9	24.6	37.0	8.5	0.5
e. My job is interesting	19.8	55.0	13.6	6.2	1.7	0.1
f. I can work independently	18.2	58.8	9.2	7.9	1.5	0.4
g. In my job I can help other people	17.6	45.0	19.4	11.7	1.5	0.8
h. My job is useful to society	16.2	37.1	25.2	14.0	1.8	1.2
i. My job has flexible working hours	8.5	26.2	13.2	34.9	11.9	1.4

Please continue ...

B

- 10 -

217. Now some more questions about your working conditions. Please tick one box for each item below to show how often it applies to your work.

PLEASE TICK ONE BOX ON EACH LINE

How often ...	Always	Often	Sometimes	Hardly ever	Never	Can't choose
a. ... do you come home from work exhausted?	6.3	36.2	45.6	7.4	1.5	-
b. ... do you have to do hard physical work?	7.7	14.6	26.7	19.6	28.0	-
c. ... do you find your work stressful?	6.3	22.2	47.8	13.6	5.9	0.3
d. ... are you bored at work?	1.8	3.8	31.0	33.5	26.3	0.1
e. ... do you work in dangerous conditions?	3.3	5.5	20.2	18.5	48.0	1.2
f. ... do you work in unhealthy conditions?	2.9	5.3	22.6	18.8	45.8	1.1
g. ... do you work in physically unpleasant conditions?	2.3	5.2	18.5	18.6	51.1	0.9

218. And which of the following statements about your work is *most* true?

PLEASE TICK ONE BOX ONLY

My job allows me to design or plan *most* of my daily work	37.9
My job allows me to design or plan *parts* of my daily work	37.4
My job *does not really* allow me to design or plan my daily work	22.0

Please continue ...

B

- 12 -

Now for some questions on other subjects.

222.a) Britain controls the numbers of people from abroad that are allowed to settle in this country. Please say, for each of the groups below, whether you think Britain should allow more settlement, less settlement, or about the same amount as now.

PLEASE TICK ONE BOX ON EACH LINE

	More Settlement	Less Settlement	About the same as now
Australians and New Zealanders	9.0	31.8	56.7
Indians and Pakistanis	1.2	66.9	29.5
People from common market countries	8.0	40.5	48.8
West Indians	1.7	61.5	34.1

b) Now thinking about the families (husbands, wives, children, parents) of people who have already settled in Britain, would you say in general that Britain should ...

PLEASE TICK ONE BOX

... be **stricter** in controlling the settlement of close relatives   58.1

or - be **less strict** in controlling the settlement of close relatives   9.2

or - keep the controls about the **same** as now   30.3

223. There has been a lot of debate among teachers about how British schools should cater for children whose parents come from other countries and cultures. Do you think in general that schools with many such children should ...

PLEASE TICK ONE BOX ON EACH LINE

	Yes	No
... Provide them with special classes in English if they require them?	79.9	18.1
Provide them with separate religious instruction if their parents request it?	40.2	57.2
Allow those for whom it is important to wear their traditional dress at school?	43.2	54.6
Allow them to study their mother tongue in school hours?	19.9	77.3
Teach them about the history of their parents' country of origin and its culture?	41.4	55.8
Teach **all** children about the history and culture of these countries?	75.0	22.8

Please continue ....

B

- 11 -

219. If you lost your job for any reason, and were looking actively for another one, how easy or difficult do you think it would be for you to find an acceptable job?

PLEASE TICK ONE BOX ONLY

Very easy	9.1
Fairly easy	35.9
Neither easy nor difficult	18.9
Fairly difficult	21.9
Very difficult	9.8
Can't choose	1.5

220. In general, how would you describe relations at your workplace ...

PLEASE TICK ONE BOX ON EACH LINE

	Very good	Quite good	Neither good nor bad	Quite bad	Very bad	Can't choose
a. ... between management and employees?	21.0	43.9	19.6	7.2	2.2	2.8
b. ... between workmates/ colleagues?	39.8	43.1	9.4	1.2	0.1	2.0

221. How satisfied are you in your (main) job?

PLEASE TICK ONE BOX ONLY

Completely satisfied	11.0
Very satisfied	26.6
Fairly satisfied	44.5
Neither satisfied nor dissatisfied	7.8
Fairly dissatisfied	5.2
Very dissatisfied	1.9
Completely dissatisfied	0.7
Can't choose	0.1

Please continue ...

B

- 13 -

224.a) Central government provides financial support to housing in two main ways.

First, by means of allowances to low income tenants.
Second, by means of tax relief to people with mortgages.

On the whole, which of these three types of family would you say benefits **most** from central government support for housing?

PLEASE TICK ONE BOX

Families with **high** incomes	41.5
Families with **middle** incomes	19.5
Families with **low** incomes	35.4

b) Which of these three views comes closest to your own on the sale of council houses and flats to tenants?

PLEASE TICK
ONE BOX

Council tenants should **not** be allowed to buy their houses or flats	10.5
Council tenants **should** be allowed to buy but **only** in areas with no housing shortage	32.5
Council tenants **should generally** be allowed to buy their houses or flats	55.8

225. Which of the following statements do you think are generally true and which false?

PLEASE TICK ONE BOX
ON EACH LINE

	True	False
Council tenants pay low rents	33.0	60.1
Councils give a poor standard of repairs and maintenance	57.3	36.7
Council estates are generally pleasant places to live	36.0	58.4

B

- 14 -

226.a. Suppose a newly-married young couple, both with steady jobs, asked your advice about whether to buy or rent a home. If they had the choice, what would you advise them to do?

PLEASE TICK ONE BOX

To buy a home as soon as possible	77.9
To wait a bit, then try to buy a home	16.9
Not to plan to buy a home at all	1.4
Can't choose	3.5

b. Still thinking of what you might say to this young couple, please tick one box for **each** statement below to show how much you agree or disagree with it.

PLEASE TICK ONE BOX
ON EACH LINE

	Agree strongly	Just agree	Neither agree nor disagree	Just disagree	Disagree strongly
Owning your home can be a risky investment	6.2	19.7	17.2	27.4	27.2
Over time, buying a home works out less expensive than paying rent	40.8	39.9	10.8	4.9	2.1
Owning your home makes it easier to move when you want to	28.0	37.4	21.1	9.6	2.5
Owning a home ties up money you may need urgently for other things	9.4	25.9	28.5	26.0	8.5
Owning a home gives you the freedom to do what you want to it	35.8	44.9	10.2	5.6	2.3
Owning a home is a big financial burden to repair and maintain	14.3	39.5	24.4	16.1	4.3
Your own home will be something to leave your family	40.5	44.4	10.4	2.2	1.0
Owning a home is just too much of a responsibility	3.9 *	6.9	20.0	34.4	33.2
Owning a home is too much of a risk for couples without secure jobs	23.8	34.2	17.9	17.5	5.3
Couples who buy their own homes would be wise to wait before starting a family	24.6	35.7	24.2	10.1	3.8

Please continue ...

- 18 -

B

231. (pp. 16-17) Same as Q.231 on A version.

232. Some people think that better relations between Protestants and Catholics in Northern Ireland will only come about through more mixing of the two communities. Others think that better relations will only come about through more separation. Which comes closest to your views ...?

PLEASE TICK ONE BOX

Better relations will come about through more mixing	88.3
Better relations will come about through more separation	7.5
Don't know	1.6

233. People feel closer to some groups than to others. For you personally, how close would you say you feel towards ...

PLEASE TICK ONE BOX ON EACH LINE

	Very close	Fairly close	A little close	Not very close	Not at all close
a. People born in the same area as you	9.8	39.5	26.3	14.0	8.8
b. People who have the same social class background as yours	10.2	48.6	27.4	9.1	3.1
c. People who have the same religious background as yours	8.8	26.8	26.2	20.4	15.0
d. People of the same race as you	13.8	42.2	25.9	10.5	5.4
e. People who live in the same area as you do now	8.9	37.2	32.2	14.8	5.3
f. People who have the same political beliefs as you	7.0	27.1	30.8	20.9	11.5

Please continue ...

- 15 -

B

227. Do you think that trade unions in this country have too much power or too little power?

PLEASE TICK ONE BOX

Far too much power	10.8
Too much power	29.0
About the right amount of power	32.7
Too little power	15.6
Far too little power	2.9
Can't choose	8.3

228. How about business and industry? Do they have too much power or too little power?

PLEASE TICK ONE BOX

Far too much power	9.4
Too much power	26.5
About the right amount of power	41.8
Too little power	7.0
Far too little power	0.7
Can't choose	14.0

229. And what about the government, does it have too much power or too little power?

PLEASE TICK ONE BOX

Far too much power	23.8
Too much power	29.9
About the right amount of power	37.1
Too little power	2.9
Far too little power	0.1
Can't choose	5.6

230. What do you think the government's role in each of these industries and services should be?

PLEASE TICK ONE BOX ON EACH LINE

	Own it	Control prices and profits but not own it	Neither own it nor control its prices and profits	Can't choose
a. Electricity	32.1	46.1	14.4	6.5
b. Local public transport	17.6	42.3	30.2	7.4
c. Gas	31.0	46.3	15.2	5.3
d. Banking and insurance	4.4	36.7	46.7	10.2
e. The car industry	3.7	31.1	52.4	10.2
f. The telephone system	23.2	44.7	23.9	6.7
g. The water supply	41.5	36.9	14.2	6.2

OFFICE USE ONLY

B

- 19 -

234. How serious an effect on our environment do you think each of these things has?
PLEASE TICK ONE BOX ON EACH LINE

	Very serious	Quite serious	Not very serious	Not at all serious
Noise from aircraft	9.4	32.7	46.4	9.4
Lead from petrol	45.1	42.9	9.3	1.0
Industrial waste in the rivers and sea	75.0	19.8	2.1	1.5
Waste from nuclear electricity stations	67.1	22.0	6.9	2.2
Industrial fumes in the air	60.0	30.3	6.7	1.4
Noise and dirt from traffic	30.6	50.1	15.2	2.1
Acid rain	57.5	30.9	8.2	1.4
Certain aerosol chemicals in the atmosphere	67.3	24.4	5.6	1.0
Cutting down tropical rainforests	68.2	21.9	6.6	1.7

235.a) Which one of these three possible solutions to Britain's electricity needs would you favour most?
PLEASE TICK ONE BOX

We should make do with the power stations we have already 44.2
We should build more coal-fuelled power stations 36.6
We should build more nuclear power stations 16.1

b) As far as **nuclear** power stations are concerned, which of these statements comes closest to your own feelings?
PLEASE TICK ONE BOX

They create very serious risks for the future 39.7
They create quite serious risks for the future 33.0
They create only slight risks for the future 19.3
They create hardly any risks for the future 5.8

B

- 20 -

236.a) Which one of these two statements comes closest to your own views?
PLEASE TICK ONE BOX

Industry should be prevented from causing damage to the countryside, even if this sometimes leads to higher prices 88.1

OR

Industry should keep prices down, even if this sometimes causes damage to the countryside 9.6
Don't know 0.2

b) And which of these two statements comes closest to your own views?
PLEASE TICK ONE BOX

The countryside should be protected from development, even if this sometimes leads to fewer new jobs 72.1

OR

New jobs should be created, even if this sometimes causes damage to the countryside 23.3

237. Here are some statements about the countryside. Please tick one box for **each** to show whether you agree or disagree with it.
PLEASE TICK ONE BOX ON EACH LINE

	Agree strongly	Agree	Dis- agree	Disagree strongly
a. Modern methods of farming have caused damage to the countryside.	21.1	51.2	24.4	1.0
b. If farmers have to choose between producing more food and looking after the countryside, they should produce more food.	5.2	31.0	52.6	8.7
c. All things considered, farmers do a good job in looking after the country- side.	7.6	64.4	23.0	2.4
d. Government should withhold some sub- sidies from farmers and use them to protect the countryside, even if this leads to higher prices.	9.7	50.5	33.4	3.1

238. Which of these two statements comes closest to your own views?
PLEASE TICK ONE BOX

Looking after the countryside is too important to be left to farmers - government authorities should have more control over what's done and built on farms 46.3

OR

Farmers know how important it is to look after the countryside - there are enough controls and farmers should be left to decide what's done on farms 36.7
Can't choose 15.6

Please continue ...

B

- 21 -

239. Here is a list of predictions. For each one, please say how likely or unlikely you think it is to come true within the next ten years?

PLEASE TICK ONE BOX FOR EACH PREDICTION

	Very likely	Quite likely	Not very likely	Not at all likely
Acts of political terrorism in Britain will be common events	11.9	45.4	37.3	2.8
Riots and civil disturbance in our cities will be common events	9.2	37.5	46.0	4.5
There will be a world war involving Britain and Europe	1.4	7.3	54.6	33.9
There will be a serious accident at a British nuclear power station	11.6	45.8	34.0	5.7
The police in our cities will find it impossible to protect our personal safety on the streets	15.9	47.2	31.2	3.3
The government in Britain will be overthrown by revolution	1.6	5.3	42.2	48.1
A nuclear bomb will be dropped somewhere in the world	3.7	19.9	45.4	28.1

240. Finally some questions about nuclear defence.

a) How likely do you think it is that there will be a nuclear war between Russia and the West before the end of the century - that is, within the next fifteen years? Is it ...

PLEASE TICK ONE BOX

... very likely,	1.7
quite likely,	5.4
not very likely,	44.8
or - not at all likely?	38.2
Can't choose	8.7

b) If there **was** a nuclear war between Russia and the West, which of these statements best describes what you think would happen to Britain?

PLEASE TICK ONE BOX

Battlefield nuclear weapons would be used, but there would be few civilian deaths	3.0
Some British cities would be destroyed, but much of the country would pull through	17.3
Much or all of Britain would be destroyed	62.1
Can't choose	16.2

B

- 22 -

241.a) At the moment, the British government publishes advice on how people should prepare for survival in the event of a nuclear war. Which of the following statements comes closest to your view on what the government **should** do?

PLEASE TICK ONE BOX

It is pointless for the government to do anything, because so few people would survive	29.3
The government should continue only to provide advice on how people can protect themselves	19.4
The government should also provide nuclear shelters to increase people's chances of survival	39.7
Can't choose	9.8

b) Lastly, please tick one box to show which is the **closest** to your views about the following statement:

If there was a major nuclear war, it would result in a worldwide "nuclear winter" with hardly any sunlight and little chance of human survival.

PLEASE TICK ONE BOX

It is highly exaggerated	5.3
It is slightly exaggerated	13.9
It is more or less true	63.3
Can't choose	16.1

242. Same as Q.242 on A version.

SCPR

Head Office: 35 NORTHAMPTON SQUARE, LONDON EC1V 0AX
TELEPHONE 01-250 1866

Northern Field Office: CHAKAZEL HOUSE, GAINFORD, DARLINGTON,
CO. DURHAM DL2 3EG. TELEPHONE 0325-730888

P.1005

March 1989

NORTHERN IRELAND SOCIAL ATTITUDES:

1989 SURVEY

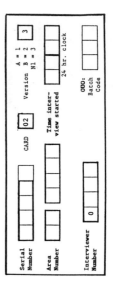

Serial Number

Area Number   CARD 02   Version   A = 1   B = 2   N1 = 3   3

Time inter-
view started   24 hr. clock

Interviewer Number   0   000:
Batch Code

NI

SECTION ONE   — 1 —

N = 866
Qs. 1-20

		Skip to
1.a) Do you normally read any daily morning newspaper at least 3 times a week?	Yes 57.2	b)
	No 42.8	Q. 2

IF YES

b) Which one do you normally read?
IF MORE THAN ONE ASK: Which one do you read most frequently?
ONE CODE ONLY

(Scottish) Daily Express	2.7
Daily Mail	2.7
Daily Mirror/Record	12.9
Daily Star	3.1
The Sun	12.9
Today	1.3
Daily Telegraph	1.6
Financial Times	0.6
The Guardian	1.1
The Independent	1.0
The Times	0.3
Morning Star	0.1
The News Letter	6.1
The Irish News	8.8
The Irish Times	0.2
Other Irish/Northern Irish/Scottish/regional or local daily morning paper (WRITE IN:)	1.9
More than one	—

Other (WRITE IN:) _____

Now a few questions about the UK's relationships with other countries.

	(a) EEC	(b) NATO
2.a) Do you think the UK should continue to be a member of the EEC – the Common Market – or should it withdraw? **RECORD IN COL a)**		
Continue	70.2	65.6
Withdraw	17.4	12.5
Don't know	10.7	19.4
b) And do you think the UK should continue to be a member of NATO – the North Atlantic Treaty Organisation – or should it withdraw? **RECORD IN COL b)**		

3. On the whole, do you think that the UK's interests are better served by ... **READ OUT** ....

... closer links with Western Europe,	36.4
or – closer links with America?	16.6
(Both equally)	31.5
(Neither)	3.0
(Don't know)	12.5

NI   — 2 —

4.a) Do you think that the siting of American nuclear missiles in Britain makes Britain a safer or a less safe place to live? **RECORD IN COL a)**

b) And do you think that having its own independent nuclear missiles makes Britain a safer or a less safe place to live? **RECORD IN COL b)**

	(a) American nuclear missiles	(b) Own nuclear missiles
Safer	25.6	39.7
Less safe	61.0	47.5
No difference	0.8	0.5
Don't know	12.3	11.7

5. CARD A
Which, if either, of these two statements comes closest to your own opinion on UK nuclear policy?

The UK should rid itself of nuclear weapons while persuading others to do the same	37.1
The UK should keep its nuclear weapons until it can persuade others to reduce theirs	58.3
(Neither of these)	2.6
Don't know	1.9

6. Which political party's views on defence would you say comes closest to your own views?
CODE ONE ONLY
ONLY CODE ALLIANCE AFTER PROBE:
Social and Liberal Democrats or SDP (Owen)?
Mainland or Northern Ireland?

Conservative	42.2
Labour	18.6
Social and Liberal Democrat/ Liberal/SLD	2.0
SDP/Social Democrat	0.9
(Mainland – Alliance)	0.3
	0.4
Other (WRITE IN:) _____	
Don't know	26.1
None	9.3

7. CARD B
Which of the phrases on this card is closest to your opinion about threats to world peace?

America is a greater threat to world peace than Russia	9.8
Russia is a greater threat to world peace than America	23.7
Russia and America are equally great threats to world peace	49.3
Neither is a threat to world peace	11.7
(Don't know)	5.4

NI

- 3 -

	Skip to
8.a) Do you think the long term policy for Northern Ireland should be for it ... **READ OUT** ...	
... to remain part of the United Kingdom, — 69.4	
or - to reunify with the rest of Ireland? — 23.7	
NI independent state — 0.6	
NI split into two — -	
Irish to decide — 0.4	
Don't know — 3.7	
b) Some people think that government policy towards Northern Ireland should include a complete withdrawal of British troops. Would you personally support or oppose such a policy? **PROBE:** Strongly support or oppose a little?	
Support strongly — 19.0	
Support a little — 13.5	
Oppose strongly — 46.9	
Oppose a little — 14.1	NOW GO TO Q.9, PAGE 4
Withdraw in long term — 1.5	
Let Irish decide — 0.2	
Others — 0.4	
Don't know — 4.1	

GO TO Q.9, PAGE 4

NI

- 4 -

SECTION TWO

	Skip to
Now I would like to ask you about two economic problems - inflation and unemployment.	
9. First, inflation: in a year from now, do you expect prices generally to have gone up, to have stayed the same, or to have gone down? **IF GONE UP OR GONE DOWN:** By a lot or a little?	
To have gone up by a lot — 42.9	
To have gone up by a little — 43.8	
To have stayed the same — 7.9	
To have gone down by a little — 3.5	
To have gone down by a lot — 0.6	
(Don't know) — 1.2	
10. Second, unemployment: in a year from now, do you expect unemployment to have gone up, to have stayed the same, or to have gone down? **IF GONE UP OR GONE DOWN:** By a lot or a little?	
To have gone up by a lot — 19.7	
To have gone up by a little — 21.8	
To have stayed the same — 33.4	
To have gone down by a little — 20.0	
To have gone down by a lot — 2.3	
(Don't know) — 2.8	
11.a) If the government had to choose between keeping down inflation or keeping down unemployment, to which do you think it should give highest priority?	
Keeping down inflation — 32.9	
Keeping down unemployment — 64.0	
Both equally — 1.6	
Others — -	
Don't know — 0.7	
b) Which do you think is of most concern to you and your family ... **READ OUT** ...	
... inflation, — 55.1	
or - unemployment? — 41.7	
Both equally — 0.8	
Neither — 0.2	
Others — 0.2	
Don't know — 1.3	
12. Looking ahead over the next year, do you think the UK's general industrial performance will improve, stay much the same, or decline? **IF IMPROVE OR DECLINE:** By a lot or a little?	
Improve a lot — 2.9	
Improve a little — 20.9	
Stay much the same — 47.5	
Decline a little — 17.1	
Decline a lot — 3.4	
(Don't know) — 8.1	

- 5 -

NI

13. Here are a number of policies which might help the UK's economic problems. As I read them out, will you tell me whether you would support such a policy or oppose it?

READ OUT ITEMS i)-x) AND CODE FOR EACH

	Support	Oppose	D/K	Skip to
i) Control of wages by law	35.7	60.1	3.9	
ii) Control of prices by law	66.9	30.5	2.6	
iii) Reducing the level of government spending on health and education	7.3	91.2	1.3	
iv) Government controls to cut down goods from abroad	69.8	25.5	4.6	
v) Increasing government subsidies for private industry	65.5	27.0	7.0	
vi) Reducing government spending on defence	56.4	36.6	6.6	
vii) Government schemes to encourage job sharing	76.4	19.4	3.6	
viii) Government to set up construction projects to create more jobs	90.1	7.7	1.9	
ix) Government action to cut interest rates	86.8	8.3	4.7	
x) Government controls on hire purchase and credit	81.9	13.0	4.9	

14. On the whole, would you like to see more or less state ownership of industry, or about the same amount as now?

More	15.1	
Less	22.4	
About the same amount	51.4	
(Don't know)	11.0	

15.a) It is said that many people manage to avoid paying their full income tax. Do you think that they should not be allowed to get away with it - or do you think good luck to them if they can get away with it?

Good luck if they can get away with it	70.7	b)
Should not be allowed	28.6	Q.16
Don't know	0.7	

IF 'SHOULD NOT BE ALLOWED' (CODE 1 AT a)

b) If you knew of somebody who wasn't paying their full income tax, would you be inclined to report him or her?

Yes	7.1	
No	61.6	
Don't know	0.7	
Other answer (WRITE IN:) _____	1.2	

- 6 -

NI

ASK ALL

16. Thinking of income levels generally in Britain today, would you say that the gap between those with high incomes and those with low incomes is ... READ OUT

... too large	86.0	
about right	10.4	
or - too small?	2.0	
Don't know	1.5	

CARD C

17. Generally, how would you describe levels of taxation?

a) Firstly for those with high incomes? Please choose a phrase from this card. RECORD ANSWER IN COL a) BELOW

b) Next for those with middle incomes? Please choose a phrase from this card. RECORD ANSWER IN COL b) BELOW

c) And lastly for those with low incomes? Please choose a phrase from this card. RECORD ANSWER IN COL c) BELOW

	(a) High incomes	(b) Middle incomes	(c) Low incomes
Taxes are: Much too high	4.2	5.4	46.0
Too high	9.4	32.4	37.5
About right	31.5	55.2	12.7
Too low	36.1	4.5	1.6
Much too low	15.9	0.4	0.3

18.a) Among which group would you place yourself ... READ OUT

... high income	2.0	
middle income	47.4	
or - low income?	50.4	
Don't know	0.2	

CARD D

b) Which of the phrases on this card would you say comes closest to your feelings about your household's income these days?

Living comfortably on present income	21.9	
Coping on present income	50.1	
Finding it difficult on present income	19.7	
Finding it very difficult on present income	8.3	
Other (WRITE IN:) _____	-	
Don't know	-	

NI

- 8 -

ALL EMPLOYEES (CODE 1 AT Q.21) ASK Qs.22-33

N = 316
Qs. 22-33

			Skip to

22. How many hours a week do you normally work in your (main) job?

MEDIAN: 39 HOURS

(IF RESPONDENT CANNOT ANSWER, ASK ABOUT LAST WEEK)   AND CODE:

	%
10-15 hours a week	7.3
16-23 hours a week	9.0
24-29 hours a week	3.7
30 or more hours a week	80.0

23.a) How would you describe the wages or salary you are paid for the job you do - on the low side, reasonable, or on the high side? IF LOW: Very low or a bit low?

	%
Very low	12.1
A bit low	27.6
Reasonable	56.8
On the high side	3.4

Other answer (**WRITE IN**)

CARD F

b) Thinking of the highest and the lowest paid people at your place of work, how would you describe the gap between their pay, as far as you know? Please choose a phrase from this card.

	%
Much too big a gap	21.2
Too big	24.4
About right	44.3
Too small	1.1
Much too small a gap	0.6
(Don't know)	7.5

24.a) If you stay in this job would you expect your wages or salary over the coming year to ... **READ OUT** ...

	%
... rise by _more_ than the cost of living,	14.8
rise by the _same_ as the cost of living,	46.8
rise by _less_ than the cost of living,	27.2
or - _not_ to rise at all?	8.9
(Will not stay in job)	0.8
(Don't know)	1.4

b) Over the coming year do you expect your workplace will be ... **READ OUT** ...

	%
... increasing its number of employees,	18.5
reducing its number of employees,	24.3
or - will the number of employees stay about the same?	56.6
Don't know	0.7

Other answer (**WRITE IN**)

NI

- 7 -

			Skip to

19.a) Looking back over the last year or so, would you say your household's income has ... **READ OUT** ...

	%
... fallen behind prices,	52.0
kept up with prices,	39.3
or - gone up by more than prices?	6.4
(Don't know)	2.3

b) And looking forward to the year ahead, do you expect your household's income will ... **READ OUT** ...

	%
... fall behind prices,	51.5
keep up with prices,	37.3
or - go up by more than prices?	5.8
(Don't know)	4.7

CARD E

20. Which of these descriptions applies to what you were doing last week, that is, in the seven days ending last Sunday? PROBE: Any others? **CODE ALL THAT APPLY IN COLUMN I**

IF ONLY ONE CODE AT I, TRANSFER IT TO COLUMN II

IF MORE THAN ONE AT I, TRANSFER HIGHEST ON LIST TO II

	COL I	COL II ECONOMIC POSITION	Skip to
In full-time education (not paid for by employer, including on vacation)	A	2.3	Q.50
On government training/employment scheme (e.g. Employment Training, Youth Training Programme, etc)	B	0.1	Q.39
In paid work (or away temporarily) for at least 10 hours in the week	C	48.0	Q.21
Waiting to take up paid work already accepted	D	0.2	Q.39
Unemployed and registered at a benefit office	E	7.8	Q.40
Unemployed, _not_ registered, but actively looking for a job	F	1.5	Q.40
Unemployed, wanting a job (of at least 10 hrs per week), but _not_ actively looking for a job	G	0.8	Q.40
Permanently sick or disabled	H	4.1	Q.50
Wholly retired from work	J	15.3	Q.45
Looking after the home	K	19.9	Q.46
Doing something else (**WRITE IN:**)	L	—	Q.50

21. **IF IN PAID WORK OR AWAY TEMPORARILY (CODE 03 AT Q.20)**   N=380

In your (main) job are you ... **READ OUT** ...

	%	Skip to
... an employee,	82.5	Q.22
or - self-employed?	17.5	Q.34

- 9 -

NI

25.(a) Thinking now about your own job. How likely or unlikely is it that you will leave this employer over the next year for any reason? Is it ... **READ OUT** ....

		Skip to
... very likely,	12.1	b)
quite likely,	13.1	
not very likely,	29.8	Q.26
or - not at all likely?	44.6	
Don't know	-	

IF VERY OR QUITE LIKELY AT a)

CARD G

(b) Why do you think you will leave? Please choose a phrase from this card or tell me what other reason there is.

MORE THAN ONE CODE MAY BE RINGED

Firm will close down	0.7
I will be declared redundant	4.9
I will reach normal retirement age	0.1
My contract of employment will expire	3.0
I will take early retirement	0.1
I will decide to leave and work for another employer	15.4
I will decide to leave and work for myself, as self-employed	0.8
I will leave to look after home/children/relative	1.7
Other answer (WRITE IN)	-

26.(a) ASK ALL EMPLOYEES

Suppose you lost your job for one reason or another - would you start looking for another job, would you wait for several months or longer before you started looking, or would you decide not to look for another job?

		Skip to
Start looking	87.3	b)
Wait several months or longer	3.7	
Decide not to look	8.2	Q.27
Don't know	0.8	

IF START LOOKING

(b) How long do you think it would take you to find an acceptable replacement job?

MEDIAN: MONTHS [2]

OR CODE:

Never	6.2
Don't know	15.4

27. ASK ALL EMPLOYEES

If without having to work, you had what you would regard as a reasonable living income, do you think you would still prefer to have a paid job or wouldn't you bother?

Still prefer paid job	82.8
Wouldn't bother	16.6
Other answer (WRITE IN)	-
Don't know	0.6

28.(a) During the last five years - that is since March 1984 - have you been unemployed and seeking work for any period?

		Skip to
Yes	23.9	b)
No	76.1	Q.29

IF YES

(b) For how many months in total during the last five years?

MEDIAN: MONTHS [9]

- 10 -

NI

29.(a) ASK ALL EMPLOYEES

For any period during the last five years have you worked as a self-employed person as your main job?

		Skip to
Yes	4.1	b)
No	95.9	c)

IF YES AT a).

(b) In total, for how many months during the last five years have you been self-employed?

WRITE IN: MONTHS [ ] OR YEARS [ ]

Median not calculated → Q.30

IF NO AT a)

(c) How seriously in the last five years have you considered working as a self-employed person ... **READOUT** ...

... very seriously,	7.6
quite seriously,	10.2
not very seriously,	11.1
or - not at all seriously?	66.8

30.(a) ASK ALL EMPLOYEES

As far as you know, does your employer keep any records of your religious background?

Yes	37.7
No	48.4
Don't know	13.7

CARD H

(b) Thinking about the people at your workplace - as far as you know, about how many are the same religion as you - or have you no idea at all? Please choose your answer from this card.

All	15.9
Most	24.5
Half	26.9
Less than half	16.9
None	0.3
(Don't know - no idea)	15.4

31.(a) Aside from your main job, do you have any other paid jobs, like a second job or other paid work?

IF YES: Is that regular work or do you only do it sometimes?

		Skip to
Yes - regularly	4.8	b)
Yes - sometimes	2.3	
No, no other paid work	92.9	Q.32

IF YES (CODE 1 OR 2 AT a)

(b) How many hours a week do you normally work in these other jobs, not including time spent travelling to work?

DO NOT COUNT MAIN JOB

WRITE IN: [ ] Hours per week

Median not calculated

- 11 -

NI

ASK ALL EMPLOYEES

32.a) At your place of work are there unions, staff associations, or groups of unions recognised by the management for negotiating pay and conditions of employment?

		Skip to
Yes	62.8	b)
No	36.7	Q.33
Don't know	0.6	

IF YES

b) On the whole, do you think these unions or staff associations do their job well or not?

Yes	31.0
No	28.6
Don't know	2.8

ASK ALL EMPLOYEES

33.a) In general how would you describe relations between management and other employees at your workplace ... **READ OUT** ...

... very good,	38.2
quite good,	42.6
not very good,	13.1
or - not at all good?	5.5
Don't know	-

b) And in general, would you say your workplace was ... **READ OUT** ...

		Skip to
... very well managed,	34.0	
quite well managed,	48.9	
or - not well managed?	15.7	Q.50
Don't know	-	

NOW GO TO SECTION 3 (p.16)

34.a) ALL SELF-EMPLOYED (CODE 2 AT Q.21): ASK Qs.34-38

N = 64   Qs. 34-38   MEDIAN 45 HOURS

How many hours a week do you normally work in your (main) job?

(IF RESPONDENT CANNOT ANSWER, ASK ABOUT 'LAST WEEK')

AND CODE:

10-15 hours a week	4.6
16-23 hours a week	-
24-29 hours a week	4.0
30 or more hours a week	91.4

b) During the last 5 years - that is since March 1984 - have you been unemployed and seeking work for any period?

Yes	18.5
No	79.5

35. If without having to work, you had what you would regard as a reasonable living income, do you think you would still prefer to do work, or wouldn't you bother?

Still prefer paid work	91.4
Wouldn't bother	8.6
Don't know	-

Other answer (WRITE IN) _____

36. Have you, for any period in the last five years, worked as an employee as your main job rather than as self-employed?

Yes	23.2
No	76.8

- 12 -

NI

37.a) Compared with a year ago, would you say your business is doing ... **READ OUT** ...

... very well,	9.3
quite well,	21.2
about the same,	4b.4
not very well,	15.2
or - not at all well?	1.3
(Business not in existence then)	5.3

b) And over the coming year, do you think your business will do ... **READ OUT** ...

		Skip to
... better,	23.2	
about the same,	57.6	
or - worse than this year?	15.2	Q.50
(Don't know)	2.6	

Other (WRITE IN:) _____

38.a) In your work or business, do you have any partners or other self-employed colleagues?

Yes, have partner(s)	34.4
No	65.6

NOTE: DOES NOT INCLUDE EMPLOYEES

b) And in your work or business do you have any employees, or not?

Yes, has employee(s)	39.1
No	60.9

N.B. FAMILY MEMBERS MAY BE EMPLOYEES ONLY IF THEY RECEIVE A REGULAR WAGE OR SALARY.

NOW GO TO SECTION 3 (p.16)

39.a) ALL ON GOVERNMENT SCHEMES OR WAITING TO TAKE UP PAID WORK (CODES 02 OR 04 AT Q.20): ASK Q.39

During the last five years - that is since March 1984 - have you been unemployed and seeking work for any period?

Yes	No
(3)	(0)

b) If without having to work, you had what you would regard as a reasonable living income, do you think you would still prefer to have a paid job or wouldn't you bother?

		Skip to
Still prefer paid job	(3)	
Wouldn't bother	(0)	Q.50
Don't know	(0)	

Other answer (WRITE IN:) _____

NOW GO TO SECTION 3 (p.16)

- 13 -

NI   N = 85   Qs. 40-44

ALL UNEMPLOYED (CODES 05, 06, 07 AT Q.20): ASK Qs.40-44

40.a) In total how many months in the last five years - that is, since March 1984 - have you been unemployed and seeking work?

MONTHS [30]   MEDIAN: ....

b) How long has this present period of unemployment and seeking work lasted so far?

MONTHS [12]   MEDIAN: ....

c) How confident are you that you will find a job to match your qualifications ... READ OUT ...

		Skip to
... very confident,	6.?	
quite confident,	19.9	
not very confident,	41.4	
or - not at all confident?	32.6	

d) Although it may be difficult to judge, how long from now do you think it will be before you find an acceptable job?

MONTHS [4]   MEDIAN: ....

Never	15.5	
Don't know	47.5	

41.a) **INTERVIEWER CHECK:**

		Skip to
Respondent answered 01-02 months at Q.40d (above)	8.0	Q.42
Respondent answered anything else	92.0	b)

IF CODE 2 AT a)

b) How willing do you think you would be in these circumstances to retrain for a different job ... **READ OUT** ...

... very willing,	30.4	
quite willing,	31.5	
or - not very willing?	19.3	
(Don't know)	7.2	

c) How willing would you be to move to a different area to find an acceptable job ... **READ OUT** ...

... very willing,	15.5	
quite willing,	12.7	
or - not very willing?	59.7	
(Don't know)	0.6	

d) And how willing do you think you would be in these circumstances to take what you now consider to be an unacceptable job. ... **READ OUT** ...

... very willing,	7.7	
quite willing,	19.3	
or - not very willing?	56.4	
(Don't know)	5.0	

ASK ALL UNEMPLOYED

42. If without having to work, you had what you would regard as a reasonable living income, do you think you would still prefer to have a paid job or wouldn't you bother?

Still prefer paid job	85.1	
Wouldn't bother	14.4	
Other answer (**WRITE IN**) _____	-	
Don't know	0.6	

- 14 -

NI

43.a) Have you ever actually considered moving to a different area - an area other than the one you live in now - to try to find work?
IF YES: In Northern Ireland or mainland Britain?

		Skip to
Yes - Northern Ireland	11.0	b)
Yes - Mainland Britain	24.3	
No	64.6	Q.44

IF YES AT a)

b) Why did you not move to a different area? Any other reasons? **PROBE FULLY. RECORD VERBATIM.**

	(No.)
Moved in past	(5)
No housing available	(5)
Too much upheaval	(5)
No jobs anywhere	(2)
Waiting to move	(1)
Other answers	(11)

ASK ALL UNEMPLOYED

44. Do you think that there is a real chance nowadays that you will get a job in this area, or is there no real chance nowadays?

		Skip to
Real chance	38.7	
No real chance	60.2	Q.50

NOW GO TO SECTION 3 (p.16)

ALL WHOLLY RETIRED FROM WORK (CODE 09 AT Q.20): ASK Q.45

45.a) Do you (or does your husband/wife) receive a pension from any past employer?   N = 166

		Skip to
Yes	35.4	c)
No	63.1	e)

b) (Can I just check) are you over (**MEN:**) 65 (**WOMEN:**) 60?

Yes	90.9	
No	9.1	

IF YES AT b)

c) On the whole would you say the present state pension is on the low side, reasonable, or on the high side? IF 'ON THE LOW SIDE': Very low or a bit low?

Very low	47.4	
A bit low	22.6	
Reasonable	19.7	
On the high side	-	

d) Do you expect your state pension in a year's time to purchase more than it does now, less, or about the same?

		Skip to
More	2.2	Q.50
Less	63.9	
About the same	19.7	
Don't know	4.0	

IF NO AT b)

e) At what age did you retire from work?

WRITE IN: [ ] YEARS

Median not calculated

		Skip to
Never worked	-	Q.50

NOW GO TO SECTION 3 (p.16)

- 15 -

NI   N = 184   Qs. 46-49

ALL LOOKING AFTER HOME (CODE 10 AT Q.20): ASK Qs. 46-49

46.a) Do you currently have a paid job of less than 10 hours a week?

		Skip to
Yes	4.8	
No	94.7	

INCLUDE THOSE TEMPORARILY AWAY FROM A PAID JOB OF LESS THAN 10 HOURS A WEEK

b) What are the main reasons you do not have a paid job (of more than 10 hours a week) outside the home? PROBE FULLY FOR MAIN REASONS AND RECORD VERBATIM.

Raising children	14.0
Retired/too old	7.0
Prefer looking after home/family	19.8
No jobs available	5.8
Unsuitable for available jobs	1.2
Pregnant/ill health	2.9
Dependent relative	5.8
Poverty trap	2.9
Already works less than 10 hours per week	1.2
Childcare costs	1.2
Unpaid work/family business	0.6

47.a) Have you, during the last five years, ever had a full or part time job of 10 hours per week or more?

		Skip to
Yes	19.1	b)
No	79.5	Q.48

IF YES AT a)

b) How long ago was it that you left that job?

WRITE IN: NO. OF MONTHS AGO   OR   NO. OF YEARS AGO   → Q.49

Median not calculated

48.a) IF NO AT Q.(47a)

How seriously in the past five years have you considered getting a full-time job? ... READ OUT ...

		Skip to
... very seriously,	1.7	
quite seriously,	3.7	
not very seriously,	6.7	
or - not at all seriously?	67.4	Q.49

PROMPT, IF NECESSARY: FULL-TIME IS 30 HRS+ PER WEEK

IF NOT VERY OR NOT AT ALL SERIOUSLY, ASK b)

b) How seriously, in the past five years, have you considered getting a part-time job? ... READ OUT ...

		Skip to
... very seriously,	2.0	
quite seriously,	6.5	
not very seriously,	8.4	
or - not at all seriously?	56.7	b)

49. ASK ALL LOOKING AFTER THE HOME

Do you think you are likely to look for a paid job in the next 5 years?

		Skip to
Yes - full-time	9.3	
Yes - part-time	27.8	
No	59.3	Q.50
Don't know	0.3	

IF YES: Full-time or part-time?

Other (WRITE IN) _____   2.0

- 16 -

NI

SECTION THREE

ASK ALL

CARD I

50. Here are some items of government spending. Which of them, if any, would be your highest priority for extra spending? And which next? Please read through the whole list before deciding.

N = 866   Qs.50-922

ONE CODE ONLY IN EACH COLUMN

	1st Priority	2nd Priority
Education	15.0	28.5
Defence	1.1	0.8
Health	56.4	22.0
Housing	5.4	13.3
Public transport	0.6	0.9
Roads	2.1	3.9
Police and prisons	1.1	2.8
Social security benefits	12.3	14.9
Help for industry	4.8	9.8
Overseas aid	0.1	1.1
(NONE OF THESE)	0.3	0.4
(Don't know)	0.8	1.3

CARD J

51. Thinking now only of the government's spending on social benefits like those on the card. Which, if any, of these would be your highest priority for extra spending? And which next?

ONE CODE ONLY IN EACH COLUMN

	1st Priority	2nd Priority
Retirement pensions	43.4	16.7
Child benefits	11.8	19.0
Benefits for the unemployed	14.0	18.3
Benefits for disabled people	24.5	33.7
Benefits for single parents	6.1	11.5
(NONE OF THESE)	0.1	0.2
(Don't know)	0.1	0.6

52. I will read two statements. For each one please say whether you agree or disagree? Strongly or slightly?

	(a) Falsely claim	(b) Fail to claim
a) Large numbers of people these days <u>falsely</u> claim benefits.		
Agree strongly	40.8	40.1
Agree slightly	26.5	33.6
Disagree slightly	10.8	11.5
Disagree strongly	13.5	8.1
(Don't know)	8.3	6.4
b) Large numbers of people who are eligible for benefits these days <u>fail</u> to claim them.		

- 17 -

NI

53. Opinions differ about the level of benefits for the unemployed. Which of these two statements comes closest to your own ... **READ OUT** ...

		Skip to
... benefits for the unemployed are too low and cause hardship,	56.3	
OR - benefits for the unemployed are too high and discourage people from finding jobs?	27.2	
(Neither)	6.6	
Both because wages are low	0.7	
Both, it varies	3.3	
About right	0.6	
Other answer	1.1	
Don't know	4.1	

CARD K

54. Suppose the government had to choose between the three options on this card. Which do you think it should choose?

Reduce taxes and spend _less_ on health, education and social benefits	5.0
Keep taxes and spending on these services at the _same_ level as now	37.3
Increase taxes and spend _more_ on health, education and social benefits	50.7
(None)	3.0
(Don't know)	4.0

CARD L

55. All in all, how satisfied or dissatisfied would you say you are with the way in which the National Health Service runs nowadays? Choose a phrase from this card.

Very satisfied	6.1
Quite satisfied	38.8
Neither satisfied nor dissatisfied	17.4
Quite dissatisfied	20.3
Very dissatisfied	17.4
Don't know	0.1

CARD L AGAIN

56. From your own experience, or from what you have heard, please say how satisfied or dissatisfied you are with the way in which each of these parts of the National Health Service runs nowadays? **READ OUT i-vi BELOW AND RING ONE CODE FOR EACH**

	Very satisfied	Quite satisfied	Neither satisfied nor dissatisfied	Quite dissatisfied	Very dissatisfied	D/K
i) First, local doctors/GPs?	30.9	48.9	7.7	7.8	4.7	0.0
ii) National Health Service dentists?	20.0	55.4	12.1	7.9	2.7	1.7
iii) Health visitors?	17.5	39.7	21.9	6.1	2.2	12.2
iv) District nurses?	23.1	42.5	20.5	2.8	0.9	10.0
v) Being in hospital as an inpatient?	33.6	42.0	12.5	5.5	2.5	3.9
vi) Attending hospital as an outpatient?	22.7	42.1	9.9	15.6	7.0	2.6

- 18 -

NI

57.a) Are you covered by a private health insurance scheme, that is an insurance scheme that allows you to get private medical _treatment_? **FOR EXAMPLE** BUPA and PPP

		Skip to
Yes	6.2	b)
No	93.7	Q.58

IF YES AT a)

b) Does your employer _(or your husband's/wife's employer)_ pay the majority of the cost of membership of this scheme?

Yes	2.7
No	3.1
Don't know	0.2

ASK ALL

58.a) Do you think that the existence of private medical treatment in National Health Service hospitals is a good or bad thing for the National Health Service, or doesn't it make any difference to the NHS?

Good thing	21.1
Bad thing	44.5
No difference	28.9
Don't know	5.5

b) And do you think the existence of private medical treatment in private hospitals is a good thing or bad thing for the National Health Service, or doesn't it make any difference to the NHS?

Good thing	33.6
Bad thing	18.9
No difference	39.4
Don't know	7.1

CARD M

59. Which of the views on this card comes _closest_ to your own views about private medical treatment in hospitals?

Private medical treatment in _all_ hospitals should be abolished	13.2
Private medical treatment should be allowed in private hospitals, but _not_ in National Health Service hospitals	45.6
Private medical treatment should be allowed in _both_ private and National Health Service hospitals	37.0
(Don't know)	3.9

Now thinking of GPs and dentists.

	Should	Should not	(Don't know)
60.a) Do you think that National Health Service GPs should or should not be free to take on private patients?	54.7	40.8	4.4
b) And do you think that National Health Service dentists should or should not be free to give _private treatment_?	60.8	33.7	5.4

61. It has been suggested that the National Health Service should be available _only_ to those with lower incomes. This would mean that contributions and taxes could be lower and most people would then take out medical insurance or pay for health care. Do you support or oppose this idea?

Support	26.5
Oppose	66.9
(Don't know)	6.6

- 20 -

		Skip to

NI

65.a) **ASK ALL**
Do you regard yourself as belonging to any particular religion?
IF YES: Which?
CODE ONE ONLY - DO NOT PROMPT

	%	Skip to
No religion	11.8	b)
Christian - no denomination	1.7	
Roman Catholic	35.8	
Church of Ireland/Anglican	17.5	
Baptist	1.6	
Methodist	4.0	
Presbyterian	22.2	c)
Free Presbyterian	0.8	
Brethren	0.4	
Other Protestant (WRITE IN:)	1.5	
Other Christian (WRITE IN:)	0.6	
Hindu	-	
Jewish	-	
Muslim	-	
Sikh	-	
Buddhist	-	
Other non-Christian (WRITE IN:)	0.1	
United Reformed/Congregational	0.7	
Refused/unwilling to say	1.8	Q.66

b) **IF NO RELIGION (CODE 01 AT a)** N = 110
In what religion were you brought up? PROBE IF NECESSARY: What was your family's religion?

	%	Skip to
No religion	4.9	Q.66
Christian - no denomination	2.0	
Roman Catholic	22.5	
Church of Ireland/Anglican	30.4	
Baptist	0.0	
Methodist	7.8	
Presbyterian	30.4	c)
Free Presbyterian	0.0	
Brethren	-	
Other Protestant (WRITE IN:)	-	
Other Christian (WRITE IN:)	-	
Hindu	-	
Jewish	-	
Muslim	-	
Sikh	-	
Buddhist	-	
Other non-Christian (WRITE IN:)	-	
Refused/unwilling to say	1.0	Q.66

c) **IF ANY RELIGION AT a) OR b) ASK c) - OTHERS SKIP TO Q.66**   N = 860
Apart from such special occasions as weddings, funerals and baptisms, how often nowadays do you attend services or meetings connected with your religion?
PROBE AS NECESSARY

	%
Once a week or more	54.2
Less often but at least once in two weeks	6.3
Less often but at least once a month	8.5
Less often but at least twice a year	6.0
Less often but at least once a year	2.1
Less often	3.2
Never or practically never	16.4
Varies too much to say	0.4
Refused/unwilling to answer	2.3

- 19 -

		Skip to

NI

62. Some people think it is best for secondary schoolchildren to be separated into grammar and secondary intermediate schools according to how well they have done when they leave primary school. Others think it is best for secondary schoolchildren not to be separated in this way, and to attend comprehensive schools.

On balance, which system do you think provides the best all-round education for secondary schoolchildren ... **READ OUT** ...

	%
... a system of grammar and secondary intermediate schools,	51.9
or - a system of comprehensive schools?	40.3
Other (**WRITE IN**)	0.7
(Don't know)	7.0

SECTION FOUR

Now moving on to the subject of social class.

63.a) To what extent do you think a person's social class affects his or her opportunities today ... **READ OUT** ...

	%
... a great deal,	29.6
quite a lot,	34.3
not very much,	27.4
or - not at all?	5.9
Other answer (**WRITE IN**)	0.2
Don't know	2.6

b) Do you think social class is more or less important now in affecting a person's opportunities than it was 10 years ago, or has there been no real change?

	%
More important now	28.6
Less important now	30.4
No change	38.0
Don't know	2.9

c) Do you think that in 10 years' time social class will be more or less important than it is now in affecting a person's opportunities, or will there be no real change?

	%
More important in 10 years' time	25.1
Less important in 10 years' time	27.5
No change	44.1
Don't know	3.2

CARD N

64.a) Most people see themselves as belonging to a particular social class. Please look at this card and tell me which social class you would say you belong to? **RECORD ANSWER IN COL a)**

b) And which social class would you say your parents belonged to when you started at primary school? **RECORD ANSWER IN COL b)**

	(a) Self	(b) Parents
Upper middle	1.2	1.6
Middle	23.4	18.7
Upper working	17.3	11.9
Working	51.9	58.4
Poor	4.2	7.9
(Don't know)	1.9	1.2

- 22 -

SECTION FIVE

NI

70. Do you think that divorce in Northern Ireland should be ... READ OUT ...

		Skip to
easier to obtain than it is now,	15.7	
more difficult,	32.5	
or - should things remain as they are?	45.6	
(Don't know)	6.3	

CARD P

71. Now I would like to ask you some questions about sexual relationships.

a) If a man and a woman have sexual relations before marriage, what would your general opinion be? Please choose a phrase from this card. **RECORD IN COL a)**

b) What about a married person having sexual relations with someone other than his or her partner? Please choose a phrase from this card. **RECORD IN COL b)**

c) What about sexual relations between two adults of the same sex? Please choose a phrase from this card. **RECORD IN COL c)**

	(a) BEFORE MARRIAGE	(b) EXTRA MARITAL	(c) SAME SEX
Always wrong	30.0	77.1	76.0
Mostly wrong	13.3	13.3	6.0
Sometimes wrong	15.4	4.6	5.1
Rarely wrong	7.8	0.7	2.0
Not wrong at all	24.4	0.7	5.1
Depends/varies	8.0	2.6	4.7
Don't know	0.2	0.2	0.3

72.a) Now I would like you to tell me whether, in your opinion, it is acceptable for a homosexual person **READ OUT EACH ITEM AND CODE FOR EACH**

	Yes	No	Other answer	Don't know
i) ... to be a teacher in a school?	35.1	54.9	6.3	2.7
ii) ... to be a teacher in a college or university?	44.2	49.0	4.1	2.3
iii) ... to hold a responsible position in public life?	47.8	44.7	2.6	3.7

b) What did you understand the word "homosexual" to mean at this question: ... READ OUT

... men only - that is, gays	30.9
women only - that is, lesbians	0.1
or - either?	67.8
Don't know	0.5

c) Do you think female homosexual couples - that is, lesbians - should be allowed to adopt a baby under the same conditions as other couples?

Yes	11.1
No	85.6
Others	0.6
Don't know	1.9

d) And do you think male homosexual couples - that is, gays - should be allowed to adopt a baby under the same conditions as other couples?

Yes	5.4
No	92.1
Others	0.7
Don't know	1.1

- 21 -

NI

ASK ALL

66.a) Some people say there is very little real poverty in the U.K. today. Others say there is quite a lot. Which comes closest to your view ... READ OUT ...

		Skip to
... that there is very little real poverty in the U.K.	35.5	
or - that there is quite a lot?	62.7	
(Don't know)	1.8	

b) Over the last ten years, do you think that poverty in the U.K. has been increasing, decreasing or staying at about the same level?

Increasing	49.0
Decreasing	19.6
Staying at same level	28.6
(Don't know)	2.3

c) And over the next ten years, do you think that poverty in the U.K. will ... READ OUT ...

... increase,	47.5
decrease,	16.7
or - stay at about the same level?	29.7
(Don't know)	5.6

67. Would you say someone in the U.K. was or was not in poverty ... READ OUT EACH STATEMENT BELOW AND CODE FOR EACH ...

	Was	Was not	(Don't know)
a) ... they had enough to buy the things they really needed, but not enough to buy the things most people take for granted?	27.9	69.3	2.8
b) ... they had enough to eat and live, but not enough to buy other things they needed?	62.1	35.6	2.3
c) ... they had not got enough to eat and live without getting into debt?	92.6	6.0	1.5

CARD O

68. Why do you think there are people who live in need? Of the four views on this card, which one comes closest to your own?

CODE ONE ONLY

Because they have been unlucky	11.9
Because of laziness or lack of willpower	17.7
Because of injustice in our society	24.8
It's an inevitable part of modern life	39.5
(None of these)	1.2
Other (WRITE IN)	2.2
(Don't know)	2.3

69. How often do you and your household feel poor nowadays ... READ OUT ...

... never,	38.0
every now and then,	45.8
often.	8.3
or - almost all the time?	7.2
(Don't know)	0.7

- 23 -

| SECTION SIX |

NI

73. Now some questions on food.

ASK a) to e) ABOUT EACH LISTED FOOD BEFORE GOING TO ASK ABOUT THE NEXT.

> IF NAMED FOOD EATEN AT ALL (CODES 1-5 AT a), SKIP TO c).
>
> IF NAMED FOOD NEVER EATEN, (CODE 1 AT b), ASK ABOUT NEXT FOOD.
>
> IF FOOD CUT OUT AT b) (CODES 2 OR 3 AT b), SKIP TO e).
>
> ALL OTHERS: ASK c)

CARD Q OR R

a) How often do you eat _____ (FOOD) nowadays?

RECORD UNDER a) BELOW

> ALL OTHERS: ASK b)

b) Have you never eaten _____, or have you cut *it/them* out in the last 2 or 3 years or longer ago?

RECORD UNDER b) BELOW

c) Are you eating about the same amount as you did 2 or 3 years ago, or more or less _____?

RECORD UNDER c) BELOW

CARD Q

	(a)						(b)			(c)		
	EVERY DAY	4-6 DAYS A WEEK	2-3 DAYS A WEEK	ABOUT ONCE A WEEK	LESS OFTEN	NEVER NOWA-DAYS	NEVER EATEN	CUT OUT IN LAST 2 OR 3 YEARS	CUT OUT LONGER AGO	ABOUT THE SAME AMOUNT	MORE	LESS
PROCESSED MEAT LIKE SAUSAGES, HAM OR TINNED MEAT	7.5	7.8	33.0	33.3	11.8	6.6	27.7	29.4	39.5	63.4	6.0	30.5
BEEF, LAMB OR PORK	4.5	12.9	44.5	28.3	5.9	3.6	3.7	46.4	27.5	73.1	4.8	21.4
EGGS	10.3	7.8	26.1	20.2	17.5	17.8	25.6	55.6	11.1	66.0	2.9	28.9
FISH	0.7	1.5	15.5	43.2	29.2	9.6	54.2	19.0	18.4	76.5	12.2	10.3
CHIPS OR ROAST POTATOES	3.6	7.3	30.0	31.7	16.3	11.1	33.9	34.8	16.7	71.2	5.5	22.9
FRESH FRUIT AND VEGETABLE	62.6	14.6	13.6	4.7	2.8	1.5	51.7	31.0	6.9	73.2	22.8	3.5
BISCUITS, PASTRIES & CAKES	46.2	8.4	17.6	10.7	9.7	7.4	27.8	39.8	24.8	72.2	5.8	21.2

CARD R

	5 OR MORE SLICES A DAY	3-4 SLICES A DAY	1-2 SLICES A DAY	4-6 SLICES A WEEK	LESS OFTEN	NEVER NOWA-DAYS	NEVER EATEN	CUT OUT IN LAST 2 OR 3 YEARS	CUT OUT LONGER AGO	ABOUT THE SAME AMOUNT	MORE	LESS
BREAD	22.9	31.4	31.2	6.4	2.6	0.8	3.3	3.8	4.4	72.7	4.1	18.7

N.B. For Qs.73 b-e, responses are percentaged on all those asked each question.

- 24 -

NI

> IF EATEN MORE OR LESS (CODES 2 OR 3 AT c), SKIP TO e).
>
> ALL OTHERS: ASK d), THEN GO TO NEXT FOOD

> ASK e) ABOUT ANY FOOD CUT OUT (CODE 2 OR 3 AT b) OR EATEN MORE OR LESS (CODE 2 OR 3 AT c)

CARD S

d) *(Is)/(Are)* _____ good for people, bad for people or neither?

RECORD UNDER d) BELOW

e) You said that you had changed the amount of _____ you eat. Have you changed for any of these reasons? PROBE UNTIL 'NO': Any other of these reasons?

RECORD UNDER e) BELOW

	(d)			(e)							
	GOOD FOR PEOPLE	BAD FOR PEOPLE	NEITHER	TO HELP CONTROL MY WEIGHT	I WAS TOLD TO FOR MEDICAL REASONS	IT IS GOOD VALUE FOR MONEY	IT IS POOR VALUE FOR MONEY	I WANTED TO KEEP HEALTHY	I JUST LIKE IT MORE	I JUST DON'T LIKE IT AS MUCH	NONE OF THESE REASONS
PROCESSED MEAT LIKE SAUSAGES, HAM OR TINNED MEAT	24.7	19.3	52.1	7.7	10.2	2.6	3.0	37.5	6.6	17.0	18.3
BEEF, LAMB OR PORK	55.3	7.1	32.3	5.0	9.2	1.7	11.5	31.7	5.3	12.4	20.2
EGGS	63.0	5.5	23.2	1.5	10.2	1.0	-	34.1	4.8	19.6	18.6
FISH	87.8	0.1	6.9	2.9	9.2	3.7	4.2	27.0	11.9	19.1	19.8
CHIPS OR ROAST POTATOES	17.4	49.2	28.0	14.5	11.8	1.9	-	39.6	6.6	9.9	11.8
FRESH FRUIT AND VEGETABLE	92.9	1.4	5.7	6.8	11.6	1.2	1.0	55.4	8.9	5.8	8.9
BISCUITS, PASTRIES & CAKES	14.5	52.7	27.4	25.7	12.9	0.4	4.0	24.3	12.8	11.2	10.4

	GOOD FOR PEOPLE	BAD FOR PEOPLE	NEITHER	TO HELP CONTROL MY WEIGHT	I WAS TOLD TO FOR MEDICAL REASONS	IT IS GOOD VALUE FOR MONEY	IT IS POOR VALUE FOR MONEY	I WANTED TO KEEP HEALTHY	I JUST LIKE IT MORE	I JUST DON'T LIKE IT AS MUCH	NONE OF THESE REASONS
BREAD	56.8	2.5	27.5	22.5	7.4	0.4	0.4	18.3	6.4	12.1	17.9

N.B. For Qs.A73 b-e responses are percentaged on all those asked each question.

- 25 -

NI

ASK ALL

74.a) Do you ever take sugar in hot drinks nowadays?

		Skip to
Yes	44.8	b)
No	55.2	Q.75

IF YES AT a)

b) Are you taking about the same amount as you did two or three years ago, or more sugar in hot drinks, or less?

About the same amount	30.6
More	1.2
Less	12.7

ASK ALL

75.a) Do you ever eat sweets or chocolates nowadays?

		Skip to
Yes	79.7	b)
No	20.3	Q.76

IF YES AT a)

b) Are you eating about the same amount as you did two or three years ago, or more sweets and chocolates or less?

About the same amount	38.0
More	5.6
Less	35.2

ASK ALL

76. Compared with two or three years ago, would you say you are now ...

READ OUT EACH STATEMENT IN TURN

	Yes	No	(Don't know)
a) .. using more low fat spreads or soft margarine instead of butter, or not?	65.6	34.1	0.0
b) ... eating more grilled food instead of fried food, or not?	68.1	31.4	0.2
c) ... eating more fish and poultry instead of red meat, or not?	44.2	55.6	0.2
d) ... drinking or using more semi-skimmed or skimmed milk instead of full cream milk, or not?	37.8	61.6	0.3
e) ... eating more wholemeal bread instead of white bread, or not?	61.0	38.7	0.1
f) ... eating more boiled or baked potatoes instead of chips or roast potatoes, or not?	66.7	33.2	0.1

- 26 -

NI

SECTION SEVEN

77. Now I would like to ask some questions about religious prejudice against both Catholics and Protestants in Northern Ireland.

a) First thinking of Catholics - do you think there is a lot of prejudice against them in Northern Ireland nowadays, a little, or hardly any?

A lot	32.6
A little	39.7
Hardly any	21.3
(Don't know)	5.8

b) Do you think there is generally more religious prejudice against Catholics now than there was 5 years ago, less, or about the same amount?

More now	20.4
Less now	24.9
About the same	50.0
Other	0.1
Don't know	3.4

c) Do you think there will be more, less or about the same amount of religious prejudice against Catholics in 5 years time compared with now?

More in 5 years	15.0
Less	25.8
About the same	51.8
Other	0.4
Don't know	4.9

78.a) And now, thinking of Protestants - do you think there is a lot of prejudice against them in Northern Ireland nowadays, a little, or hardly any?

A lot	23.0
A little	43.6
Hardly any	26.6
(Don't know)	-

b) Do you think there is generally more religious prejudice against Protestants now than there was 5 years ago, less, or about the same amount?

More now	23.8
Less now	11.1
About the same	59.1
Other	
Don't know	4.0

c) Do you think there will be more, less or about the same amount of religious prejudice against Protestants in 5 years time compared with now?

More in 5 years	17.2
Less	15.9
About the same	59.8
Other	0.8
Don't know	4.8

79. How would you describe yourself:
READ OUT

... as very prejudiced against people of other religions,	1.8
A little prejudiced,	16.0
or - not prejudiced at all?	81.3
Other	0.1
Don't know	0.1

- 27 -

NI

80.a) What about relations between Protestants and Catholics? Would you say they are better than they were 5 years ago, worse, or about the same now as then?

IF 'IT DEPENDS', PROBE BEFORE CODING

		Skip to
Better	21.8	
Worse	27.4	
About the same	47.0	
(Don't know)	1.5	
Other answer (WRITE IN) _____	2.0	

b) And what about in 5 years time? Do you think relations between Protestants and Catholics will be better than now, worse than now, or about the same as now?

IF 'IT DEPENDS', PROBE BEFORE CODING

Better than now	25.9	
Worse than now	16.1	
About the same	52.7	
(Don't know)	0.3	
Other answer (WRITE IN) _____	4.6	

c) Do you think that religion will always make a difference to the way people feel about each other in Northern Ireland?

Yes	86.7	
No	3.4	
(Don't know)	0.6	
Other answer (WRITE IN) _____	3.7	

81.a) Do you think most people in Northern Ireland would mind or not mind if a suitably qualified person of a different religion were appointed as their boss? IF WOULD MIND: A lot or a little?

Would mind a lot	11.5	
Would mind a little	22.8	
Would not mind	57.6	
(Don't know/can't say)	7.7	

b) And you personally? Would you mind or not mind? IF WOULD MIND: A lot or a little?

Would mind a lot	2.7	
Would mind a little	4.0	
Would not mind	91.9	
(Don't know/can't say)	1.0	

- 28 -

NI

82.a) And do you think most people in Northern Ireland would mind or not mind if one of their close relatives were to marry someone of a different religion? IF WOULD MIND: A lot or a little?

		Skip to
Would mind a lot	34.3	
Would mind a little	32.7	
Would not mind	28.3	
(Don't know/can't say)	4.3	

b) And you personally? Would you mind or not mind? IF WOULD MIND: A lot or a little?

Would mind a lot	15.5	
Would mind a little	14.6	
Would not mind	66.8	
(Don't know/can't say)	1.8	

83.a) CARD T

About how many of your friends would you say are the same religion as you - that is, Protestant or Catholic? Please choose an answer from this card.

PROBE AS NECESSARY: As far as you know?

All	16.1	
Most	47.2	
Half	26.0	
Less than half	6.8	
None	0.8	
(Don't know)	0.6	

b) CARD T AGAIN

What about your relatives, including relatives by marriage?

All	42.2	
Most	41.2	
Half	9.3	
Less than half	5.4	
None	1.1	
(Don't know)	0.4	

c) CARD T AGAIN

And what about your neighbours? As far as you know?

PROBE AS NECESSARY: As far as you know?

All	30.8	
Most	31.0	
Half	21.7	
Less than half	7.5	
None	1.2	
(Don't know)	7.3	

84. Were both your parents of the same religion, for instance both Catholic or both Protestant?

Yes	95.0	
No	4.6	
(Refused)	-	
(Don't know)	0.1	

- 30 -

NI

86.a) If you had a choice, would you prefer to live in a neighbourhood with people of only your own religion, or in a mixed-religion neighbourhood?

PROBE IF NECESSARY: Say if you were moving ...

	Skip to
Own religion only ... 22.7	
Mixed religion neighbourhood 71.2	
(Don't know) 5.1	

b) And if you were working and had to change your job, would you prefer a workplace with people of only your own religion, or a mixed-religion workplace?

PROBE IF NECESSARY: Say if you did have a job ...

Own religion only 10.4	
Mixed-religion workplace 84.0	
(Don't know) 4.5	

c) And if you were deciding where to send your children to school, would you prefer a school with children of only your own religion, or a mixed-religion school?

PROBE IF NECESSARY: Say if you did have school-age children ...

Own religion only 36.9	
Mixed-religion school 55.3	
(Don't know) 7.3	

87.a) On the whole, do you think the Protestants and Catholics in Northern Ireland who apply for the same jobs have the same chance of getting a job or are their chances of getting a job different?

IF 'DIFFERENT' OR 'DON'T KNOW' AT a)

	Skip to
Same chance 47.7	
Different chance 41.8	
(Don't know/Can't say) 10.0	Q.88 b)

b) Which group is more likely to get a job - Protestants or Catholics?

IF 'IT DEPENDS': On the whole ...

Protestants 31.3	
Catholics 9.1	
It depends 4.0	
Don't know 4.2	

c) Are they much more likely or just a bit more likely to get a job?

Much more 14.3	
Bit more 25.6	
(Don't know/Can't say) 9.0	

- 29 -

NI

CARD U

For each of the next questions, please use this card to say whether you think Catholics are treated better than Protestants in Northern Ireland, or whether Protestants are treated better than Catholics, or whether both are treated equally.

READ OUT EACH ITEM AND CODE ONE FOR EACH

	Catholics treated much better	Catholics treated a bit better	Both treated equally	Protestants treated a bit better	Protestants treated much better	It depends/ Don't know/ Can't say	Skip to
a) First, the National Health Service in Northern Ireland. How does it treat Catholic and Protestant patients?	2.3	2.?	89.3	1.3	0.1	3.7	
b) What about the Northern Ireland Housing executive - how does it treat Catholics and Protestants who apply for a home?	3.9	7.?	67.0	6.2	1.9	13.0	
c) What about your local district council - how does it treat Catholics and Protestants who apply for jobs?	2.5	5.?	50.0	14.0	6.0	21.5	
d) And what about central government in Stormont - how do they treat Catholics and Protestants who apply for jobs?	2.6	8.?	51.7	14.2	5.1	19.5	
e) What about government schemes for the unemployed - how do they treat Catholics and Protestants who apply for places?	2.8	5.4	74.7	2.3	0.7	13.4	
f) And the RUC - how do they treat Catholic and Protestant members of the public?	0.5	2.3	56.3	19.4	11.7	9.6	
g) What about the army - how do they treat Catholic and Protestant members of the public?	-	0.?	60.7	18.4	8.4	11.2	
h) And the Ulster Defence Regiment - how do they treat Catholic and Protestant members of the public?	0.1	0.?	44.4	25.1	16.8	12.9	
i) And the courts - how do they treat Catholics and Protestants accused of committing non-terrorist offences?	0.2	1.5	82.1	4.5	2.6	8.4	
j) And how do the courts treat Catholics and Protestants accused of committing terrorist offences?	1.3	4.3	71.1	6.7	8.3	7.8	

NI

- 31 -

ASK ALL

Now I'm going to ask separately about employment chances of Protestants and Catholics.

88.a) Some people think that many employers are more likely to give jobs to Protestants than to Catholics. Do you think this happens
... READ OUT ...

		Skip to
... a lot,	14.4	
a little,	47.9	b)
or - hardly at all?	28.9	Q.89
(Don't know)	8.3	

IF 'IT DEPENDS': In general, what would you say?

IF 'A LOT' OR 'A LITTLE' AT a)

b) Why do you think this happens? Do you think it is mainly because employers discriminate against Catholics or mainly because Catholics are not as well qualified as Protestants?

IF 'BOTH', PROBE BEFORE CODING

Mainly because employers discriminate	48.4
Mainly because Catholics aren't qualified	4.7
Both (AFTER PROBE)	3.6
(Don't know/Can't say)	5.5

ASK ALL

89.a) Some people think that many employers are more likely to give jobs to Catholics than to Protestants. Do you think this happens
... READ OUT ...

		Skip to
... a lot,	9.5	
a little,	44.5	b)
or - hardly at all?	35.5	Q.90
(Don't know)	10.1	

IF 'IT DEPENDS': In general, what would you say?

IF 'A LOT' OR 'A LITTLE' AT a)

b) Why do you think this happens? Do you think it is mainly because employers discriminate against Protestants, or mainly because Protestants are not as well qualified as Catholics?

IF 'BOTH', PROBE BEFORE CODING

Mainly because employers discriminate	42.9
Mainly because Protestants aren't qualified	2.6
Both (AFTER PROBE)	3.1
(Don't know/Can't say)	5.1

NI

- 32 -

90.a) Some people say that all employers should keep records on the religion of their employees to make sure there is no discrimination. Other people say this is not necessary. What about you - do you think employers should or should not keep records about their employees' religion?

		Skip to
Should	25.8	b)
Should not	68.6	c)
(Don't know/Can't say)	5.1	c)

IF SHOULD OR SHOULD NOT AT a)

b) Do you feel this way strongly or just a bit?

Strongly	59.7
Just a bit	33.3

ASK ALL

c) Do you generally support or oppose a fair employment law in Northern Ireland, that is a law which requires employers to keep records on the religion of their employees' and make sure there is no discrimination?

		Skip to
Support	50.7	d)
Oppose	39.6	
(Don't know/Can't say)	9.2	

IF SUPPORT OR OPPOSE AT c)

d) Do you (support/oppose) it strongly, or just a bit?

		Skip to
Strongly	56.4	Q.91
Just a bit	31.4	

ASK ALL

91. And thinking about education ...

First, about mixed or integrated schooling - that is, schools with fairly large numbers of both Catholic and Protestant children: do you think the government should encourage mixed schooling, discourage mixed schooling or leave things as they are?

Encourage it	63.5
Discourage it	6.2
Leave things as they are	29.3
Don't know	0.3

- 34 -

NI
ASK ALL

94.a) Generally speaking, do you think of yourself as a supporter of any one political party?

		Skip to
Yes	34.9	d)
No	64.6	b)

IF NO AT a)
b) Do you think of yourself as a little closer to one political party than to the others?

		Skip to
Yes	23.6	d)
No	41.0	c)

IF NO AT b)
c) If there were a general election tomorrow, which political party do you think you would be most likely to support? **CODE ONE ONLY UNDER c & d)** IF MAINLAND ALLIANCE, PROBE: Social and Liberal Democrat <u>or SDP (Owen)</u>?

IF YES AT a) OR b)
d) Which one? **CODE ONE ONLY UNDER c & d)** IF MAINLAND ALLIANCE, PROBE: Social and Liberal Democrat <u>or SDP (Owen)</u>?

IF MAINLAND PARTY NAMED AT c) OR d)
e) If there were a general election in which only Northern Ireland parties were standing, which one do you think you would be most likely to support?
CODE ONE ONLY UNDER e)

	c & d)	e)	Skip to
Conservative	18.6		e)
Labour	6.8		e)
Social and Liberal Democrat/Liberal/SLD	0.7		e)
SDP/Social Democrat	0.6		e)
(Mainland) Alliance (AFTER PROBE)	0.3		e)
Alliance (NI)	4.6	9.3	
DUP/Democratic Unionist Party	7.0	10.8	
OUP/Official Unionist Party	17.5	27.2	
Other Unionist	0.7	1.2	
Sinn Fein	2.7	2.7	
SDLP	14.9	16.8	
Workers Party	2.2	3.1	
Campaign for Equal Citizenship	0.4	0.4	
Other party (WRITE IN)	0.1	0.3	
Other answer (WRITE IN)	0.3	0.3	
None	17.3	19.6	Q-95
D/K	0.5	0.8	

IF ANY NORTHERN IRELAND PARTY CODED AT c) & d) OR e)
f) Would you call yourself very strong ... (QUOTE PARTY NAMED) ... fairly strong, or not very strong?

		Skip to
Very strong	7.9	
Fairly strong	22.2	
Not very strong	41.2	
Don't know	0.3	
Refused/unwilling to say	4.4 / 5.6	Q-95

- 33 -

NI
CARD W

92 Please use this card to say whether you think that <u>Protestants</u> or <u>Catholics</u> in Northern Ireland have a better chance ...

READ OUT EACH ITEM AND CODE FOR EACH

	Catholics have a much better chance	Catholics have a slightly better chance	Both groups have equal chances	Protestants have a slightly better chance	Protestants have a much better chance	(Don't know/can't say)	Skip to
a) ...to go to a good primary school?	0.8	2.7	89.9	3.0	0.3	2.3	
b) ...how about chances to go to a good secondary intermediate school?	0.7	2.7	88.5	4.5	1.1	2.1	
c) ...and chances to go to a good grammar school?	0.8	2.7	85.4	6.9	1.7	2.1	
d) ...and chances to go to university?	1.6	2.8	89.1	2.7	1.1	2.3	

CARD X

93 All pupils in state secondary schools study certain subjects - like English and maths. For each subject I read out, please tell me whether you <u>agree</u> or disagree that <u>all</u> secondary school pupils should <u>have</u> to study it ...

READ a)-g) AND CODE ONE FOR EACH

	Strongly agree	Agree	Neither agree nor disagree	Disagree	Strongly disagree	(Don't know)
a) ...the history of Northern Ireland?	25.9	45.4	9.7	14.5	2.5	1.5
b) ...British history?	18.4	54.8	11.2	12.0	1.6	1.6
c) ...the history of the Republic of Ireland?	14.6	43.3	11.9	21.9	5.8	1.8
d) ...Irish language and culture?	7.8	25.4	15.5	35.6	14.1	3.1
e) ...Protestant religious beliefs?	7.0	34.5	16.9	30.4	6.5	3.2
f) ...Catholic religious beliefs?	7.0	33.8	15.9	31.5	8.3	2.8
g) ...non-denominational religious beliefs - not specifically Catholic or Protestant?	7.4	38.7	19.1	25.8	4.7	3.9

- 35 -

NI
ASK ALL
CARD Y

		Skip to
95.a) Which of these best describes the way you usually think of yourself?	British	44.3
	Irish	25.0
	Ulster	6.9
	Northern Irish	20.0
	(Sometimes British, sometimes Irish)	0.1
	Other)	0.2
	Don't know	C.2
b) When there is an argument between Britain and the Republic of Ireland, do you generally find yourself on the side of the British or of the Irish governments? **IF 'IT DEPENDS', PROBE BEFORE CODING**	Generally British govt.	50.6
	Generally Irish govt.	14.2
	It depends (**AFTER PROBE**)	19.8
	(Neither)	9.6
	(Don't know/Can't say)	5.2
96. At any time in the next 20 years, do you think it is likely or unlikely that there will be a united Ireland? **PROBE:** Very (likely or unlikely) or quite (likely/unlikely)?	Very likely	4.6
	Quite likely	18.4
	Quite unlikely	25.0
	Very unlikely	40.4
	(Even chance)	3.4
	(Don't know)	7.9

CARD Z

97.a) Under direct rule from Britain, as now, how much do you generally trust British Governments of any party to act in the best interests of Northern Ireland? **CODE ONE ONLY UNDER COL a) BELOW**

b) If there was self-rule, how much do you think you would generally trust a Stormont government to act in the best interests of Northern Ireland? **CODE ONE ONLY UNDER COL b) BELOW**

c) And if there was a united Ireland, how much do you think you would generally trust an Irish government to act in the best interests of Northern Ireland? **CODE ONE ONLY UNDER COL c) BELOW**

	(a) British govt.	(b) Stormont govt.	(c) Irish govt.
Just about always	3.9	10.9	2.5
Most of the time	20.9	35.1	16.4
Only some of the time	39.5	26.4	29.1
Rarely	20.3	11.5	19.7
Never	10.6	9.0	22.2
(Don't know/can't say)	4.4	6.5	9.4

- 36 -

SECTION EIGHT

NI
ASK ALL
CARD AA

		Skip to
98. Now, a few questions on housing. First, in general how satisfied or dissatisfied are you with your own (house/flat)? Choose a phrase from the card.	Very satisfied	43.6
	Quite satisfied	44.4
	Neither satisfied nor dissatisfied	3.3
	Quite dissatisfied	5.0
	Very dissatisfied	3.7

		(a) Last 2 years	(b) Next 2 years
99.a) How about the area you live in? Taking everything into account, would you say this area has got better, worse or remained about the same as a place to live during the last two years? **RECORD IN COL a) BELOW**	Better	18.8	17.4
	Worse	17.0	9.5
	About the same	63.5	69.3
	Don't know	0.6	3.1
b) And what do you think will happen during the next two years: will this area get better, worse or remain about the same as a place to live? **RECORD IN COL b)**			

		Skip to
100. Does your household own or rent this accommodation? **PROBE AS NECESSARY** **IF OWN:** Outright or on a mortgage? **IF RENTS:** From whom?	Owns: Own (leasehold/freehold) outright	31.9
	Buying (leasehold/freehold) on mortgage	33.9
	Rents: Housing Executive	27.7
	Housing Association	1.1
	Property company	0.7
	Employer	0.4
	Other organisation	0.2
	Relative	-
	Other individual	2.7
	Rent free: Rent free,squatting, etc.	0.7
101. CODE FROM OBSERVATION AND CHECK WITH RESPONDENT Would I be right in describing this accommodation as a	Detached house or bungalow	34.7
	Semi-detached house or bungalow	24.3
	Terraced house	36.6
	Self-contained, purpose-built flat/maisonette (inc. in tenement block)	2.8
	Self-contained converted flat/maisonette	1.5
	Room(s) - not self-contained	-
	Other (WRITE IN:)	-

- 38 -

NI
CARD CC

104. Please look at this card and tell me whether ...
READ OUT a)-c) BELOW AND CODE FOR EACH

	Definitely should	Probably should	Probably should not	Definitely should not	(Don't know)
a) ... employers should or should not have the legal right to dismiss people who have AIDS?	19.4	22.3	23.4	22.9	6.3
b) ... doctors and nurses should or should not have the legal right to refuse to treat people who have AIDS?	11.8	18.2	26.2	38.7	4.6
c) ... schools should or should not have the legal right to expel children who have AIDS?	9.2	20.4	24.7	38.5	6.7

105. I am going to read out two statements. For each one, please say whether you agree or disagree.

	(a) Sympathy	(b) Research
a) 'People who have AIDS get much less sympathy from society than they ought to get.' Do you agree or disagree? Strongly or a little? CODE ONE IN COL a)		
b) 'More money should be spent trying to find a cure for AIDS, even if it means that research into other serious diseases is delayed.' Do you agree or disagree? Strongly or a little? CODE ONE IN COL b)		
Strongly agree	26.9	22.3
Agree a little	33.1	23.7
Disagree a little	17.3	25.3
Strongly disagree	14.8	24.0
(Don't know)	6.6	4.2

- 37 -

NI

102. And how long have you lived in your present home?
PROBE AS NECESSARY

Less than 1 year	5.5
1 year, less than 2 years	5.2
2 years, less than 5 years	17.0
5 years, less than 10 years	17.5
10 years, less than 20 years	25.2
20 years or more	29.6

SECTION NINE

103. Now I'd like to ask you about the disease called AIDS. I'm going to read out a list of different kinds of people.

CARD BB
Please choose a phrase from this card to tell you how much at risk you think each of these groups is from AIDS ...
READ OUT AND CODE ITEMS a)-h)

	Greatly at risk	Quite a lot at risk	Not very much at risk	Not at all at risk	(Don't know)
a) ... People who have sex with many different partners of the opposite sex.	70.8	24.5	2.1	-	2.0
b) ... Married couples who have sex only with each other.	0.4	0.5	14.9	81.7	1.8
c) ... Married couples who occasionally have sex with someone other than their regular partner.	13.1	49.3	31.7	1.6	3.7
d) ... People who have a blood transfusion	13.3	25.5	42.5	14.1	4.1
e) ... Doctors and nurses who treat people who have AIDS.	9.3	25.1	41.4	19.3	3.9
f) ... Male homosexuals - that is, gays.	82.0	14.3	0.4	-	2.5
g) ... Female homosexuals - that is, lesbians.	55.9	16.7	11.9	5.6	9.2
h) ... People who inject themselves with drugs using shared needles.	90.4	7.5	-	-	1.6

NI

- 39 -

SECTION 10

900a) Can I just check your own marital status?
At present are you ... **READ OUT** ...

	Skip to
... married,	63.7
living as married,	1.0
separated or divorced,	4.4
widowed,	9.7
or - not married?	21.3

CODE FIRST TO APPLY

b) Finally, a few questions about you and your household.
Including yourself, how many people live here regularly
as members of this household?

**CHECK INTERVIEWER MANUAL FOR DEFINITION
OF HOUSEHOLD IF NECESSARY.**

MEDIAN: 3

901. Now I'd like to ask for a few details about each person in
your household. Starting with yourself, what was your *age*
last birthday?

**WORK DOWN COLUMNS OF GRID FOR EACH HOUSEHOLD
MEMBER.**

	Resp-ondent	2	3	4	5	6	7	8	9	10
a) Sex: Male	47.5									
Female	52.5									
b) Age last birthday:										
c) Relationship to respondent:										
Spouse/partner										
Son/daughter										
Parent/parent-in law										
Other relative										
Not related										
d) HOUSEHOLD MEMBERS WITH LEGAL RESPONSIBILITY FOR ACCOMMODATION (INC. JOINT AND SHARED) Yes	74.7									
No	24.1									

* CHECK THAT NUMBER OF PEOPLE IN GRID EQUALS NUMBER GIVEN
AT Q.900b)

NI

- 40 -

ASK ALL

902. Apart from people you've just mentioned who live in your
household, have you had any (other) children, including
stepchildren, who grew up in your household living
At present are you ...

NB: INCLUDES CHILDREN NO LONGER LIVING

		Skip to
Yes	34.5	
No	65.6	

903a) Did you ever attend a mixed or integrated school,
that is, with fairly large numbers of both Catholic
and Protestant children?

IF YES: In Northern Ireland or somewhere else?

Yes - in Northern Ireland	21.1
Yes, somewhere else	2.7
No, did not	75.9
Don't know	0.2

**IF RESPONDENT HAS CHILD(REN) AGED 5 OR OLDER IN HOUSE-
HOLD (SEE GRID) ASK b). OTHERS GO TO Q.904**

b) And have any of your children ever attended a
mixed or integrated school, with fairly large
numbers of both Catholic and Protestants
attending?

IF YES: In Northern Ireland or somewhere else?

Yes - in Northern Ireland	10.2
Yes, somewhere else	0.5
No, have not	35.2
Don't know	-

ASK ALL

**904a) INTERVIEWER: IS THIS A SINGLE PERSON HOUSEHOLD -
RESPONDENT ONLY AT Q.39)?**

		Skip to
YES	9.9	Q.905
NO	90.1	b)

IF NO AT a)

b) Who is the person mainly responsible for
general domestic duties in this household?   Respondent mainly

Respondent mainly	38.8
Someone else mainly (**WRITE IN RELATIONSHIP TO RESP.**)	39.3
Duties shared equally (**WRITE IN BY WHOM**)	10.6

**c) INTERVIEWER: IS THERE A CHILD UNDER 16 YEARS
IN H.H? SEE HOUSEHOLD GRID, Q.901 (p.39)**

		Skip to
YES	43.7	d)
NO	46.4	Q.905

IF YES AT c)

d) Who is the person mainly responsible for
the general care of the child(ren) here?   Respondent mainly

Respondent mainly	20.3
Someone else mainly (**WRITE IN RELATIONSHIP TO RES.**)	17.0
Duties shared equally (**WRITE IN BY WHOM**)	5.6

- 41 -

NI

905. ASK ALL

How old were you when you completed your continuous full-time education?
PROBE AS NECESSARY

		Skip to
15 or under	42.7	
16	26.5	
17	10.3	
18	7.9	
19 or over	10.1	
Still at school	0.5	
Still at college, polytechnic, or university	2.0	
Other answer (WRITE IN)	-	

906a) CARD X1

Have you passed any exams or got any of the qualifications on this card?

		Skip to
Yes	51.4	b)
No	48.6	Q.907

IF YES AT a)

b) Which ones? Any others?
CODE ALL THAT APPLY

CSE Grades 2-5	8.7	32-33
GCSE - Grades D-G		
CSE Grade 1		
GCE 'O' level		
GCSE - Grade A-C		
School certificate	34.4	34-35
Scottish (SCE) Ordinary		
Scottish School-leaving Certificate lower grade		
SUPE Ordinary		
Northern Ireland Junior Certificate		
GCE 'A' level/'S' level		
Higher school certificate		
Matriculation	15.5	36-37
Scottish SCE/SLC/SUPE at Higher grade		
Northern Ireland Senior Certificate		
Overseas School Leaving Exam/Certificate	0.2	38-39
Recognised trade apprenticeship completed	6.9	40-41
RSA/other clerical, commercial qualification	9.2	42-43
City & Guilds Certificate - Craft/Intermediate/Ordinary/Part I	4.5	44-45
City & Guilds Certificate - Advanced/Final/Part II or Part III	2.6	46-47
City & Guilds Certificate - Full technological	0.7	48-49
BEC/TEC General/Ordinary National Certificate (ONC) or Diploma (OND)	1.8	50-51
BEC/TEC Higher/Higher National Certificate (HNC) or Diploma (HND)	1.5	52-53
Teacher training qualification	3.1	54-55
Nursing qualification	3.0	56-57
Other technical or business qualification/certificate	2.7	58-59
University or CNAA degree or diploma	5.6	60-61
Other (WRITE IN)	0.2	

- 42 -

NI

REFER TO ECONOMIC POSITION OF RESPONDENT (Q.20, page 7)

- If in paid work (CODE 03), ask Q.907 about present (main) job.
- If waiting to take up paid work (CODE 04), ask Q.907 about future job.
- If on govt. scheme (CODE 02), unemployed (CODES 05-07), permanently sick or disabled (CODE 08), retired (CODE 09), looking after the home (CODE 10), or doing something else (CODE 11) ask Q.907 about last job.
- If never had a job, write in at a), then go to Q.908.

Now I want to ask you about your (present/future/last) job.
CHANGE TENSES FOR (BRACKETED) WORDS AS APPROPRIATE.

		Skip to
		O.B.O.
		O.C.
		E.S.
		S.E.G.
		SC/NM.M
		SIC
		H-G

907a) What (is) your job? PROBE AS NECESSARY.
What (is) the name or title of the job?

b) What kind of work (do) you do most of the time? IF RELEVANT: What materials/machinery (do) you use?

c) What training or qualifications (are) needed for that job?

d) (Do) you directly supervise or (are) you directly responsible for the work of any other people? IF YES: How many?

Yes: WRITE IN NO.:
No: RING: 0000

e) Can I just check: (are) you ... READ OUT ...

... an employee,	79.6	f)
or - self-employed?	11.3	g)

IF EMPLOYEE (CODE 1) AT e)

CARD X2

f) Which of the types of organisation on this card (do) you work for?
CODE FIRST TO APPLY

Private firm or company	43.6
Nationalised industry/public corp.	5.8
District Authority/Education and Library Board	8.7
Health Board/NHS hospital	10.7
Central Government/Civil Service	7.6
Charity or Trust	1.1
Other (SPECIFY)	2.1

ASK ALL

g) What (does) your employer (IF SELF-EMPLOYED: you) make or do at the place where you usually (work)? IF FARM, GIVE NO. OF ACRES

h) Including yourself, how many people (are) employed at the place you usually (work) from?
IF SELF-EMPLOYED: (Do) you have any employees? IF YES: How many?

(No employees)	7.5
Under 10	18.9
10-24	13.6
25-99	20.5
100-499	20.3
500 or more	9.0
D/K	0.9

- 43 -

NI

ASK ALL

908a) Are you now a member of a trade union or staff association?

Yes: trade union	18.4	c)
Yes: staff association	3.6	b)
No	77.4	

IF NO AT a)

b) Have you ever been a member of a trade union or staff association?

Yes: trade union	27.6	c)
Yes: staff association	1.6	
No	48.2	Q.909

IF NOW OR EVER A MEMBER (CODES 1 AT 2 AT a) OR b)

c) Have you ever ... **READ OUT AND RING ONE CODE FOR EACH**

	YES	NO
... attended a union or staff association meeting?	32.7	18.4
... voted in a union or staff association election or meeting?	27.9	23.2
... put forward a proposal or motion at a union or staff association meeting?	12.5	38.6
... gone on strike?	20.7	30.5
... stood in a picket line?	9.1	42.0
... served as a lay representative such as a shop steward or branch committee member?	6.8	44.2

IF RESPONDENT IS MARRIED OR LIVING AS MARRIED (AT Q.900a), ASK Qs.909-911. OTHERS GO TO Q.912.

CARD X3

909.a) Which of these descriptions applied to what your (husband/wife/partner) was doing last week, that is the seven days ending last Sunday? PROBE: Any others? **CODE ALL THAT APPLY IN COL. I**

IF ONLY ONE CODE AT I, TRANSFER IT TO COL. II
IF MORE THAN ONE AT I, TRANSFER HIGHEST ON LIST TO II

	COL. I	COL. II ECONOMIC POSITION	Skip to
In full-time education (not paid for by employer, including on vacation)	A	0.1	
On government training/employment scheme (e.g. Employment Training, Youth Training Programme etc.)	B	-	
In paid work (or away temporarily) for at least 10 hours in the week	C	35.6	b)
Waiting to take up paid work already accepted	D	0.0	
Unemployed and registered at a benefit office	E	5.2	
Unemployed, not registered, but actively looking for a job	F	0.2	
Unemployed, wanting a job (of at least 10 hrs per week), but not actively looking for a job	G	0.4	
Permanently sick or disabled	H	1.5	
Wholly retired from work	J	6.6	b)
Looking after the home	K	14.8	
Doing something else (SPECIFY)	L	0.2	Q.910

IF CODES 01-02, OR 08-11 AT I

b) How long ago did your (husband/wife/partner) last have a paid job (other than the government scheme you mentioned) of at least 10 hours a week?

Within past 12 months	2.6	
Over 1-5 years ago	6.3	
Over 5-10 years ago	5.2	Q.910
Over 10-20 years ago	3.7	
Over 20 years ago	3.1	
Never had a paid job of 10+ hours a week	2.0	Q.911

- 44 -

NI

REFER TO Q.909 = ACTIVITY OF SPOUSE/PARTNER:

- **If spouse is in paid work (CODE 03) - Ask Q.910 about present main job.**
- **If spouse is waiting to take up paid work (CODE 04) - ask Q.910 about future job.**
- **If spouse is unemployed (CODES 05, 06 OR 07), or retired (CODE 09) or looking after home (CODE 10), or doing something else (CODES 01-02, 08, 11), ask Q.910 about last job**

Now I want to ask you about your (husband's/wife's/partner's) job. **CHANGE TENSES FOR (BRACKETED) WORDS AS APPROPRIATE**

910a) What (is) the name or title of that job?

b) What kind of work (does) he/she do most of the time? IF RELEVANT:
What materials/machinery (does) he/she use?

c) What training or qualifications (are) needed for that job?

d) (Does) he/she directly supervise or (is) he/she directly responsible for the work of any other people? IF YES: How many?

     Yes: WRITE IN NO.:
     No: RING: 0000

e) (Is) he/she ... **READ OUT** ...

... an employee,	52.9
or - self-employed?	9.0

IF EMPLOYEE (CODE 1 AT e)

CARD X4

f) Which of the types of organisation on this card (does) he/she work for?

Private firm or company	26.3	
Nationalised industry/public corporation	6.0	
District Authority/Education and Library Board	7.8	
Health Board/NHS hospital	5.6	
Central Government/Civil Service	5.6	
Charity or trust	0.7	
Other (SPECIFY)	0.8	

ASK ALL

g) What (does) the employer (IF SELF-EMPLOYED: he/she) make or do at the place where he/she usually (works)? IF FARM GIVE NO. OF ACRES

h) Including him/herself, roughly how many people (are) employed at the place where he/she usually (works) (from)?

(No employees) Under 10	6.0	
10-24	13.2	
25-99	8.9	
100-499	12.9	
500 or more	13.3	
IF SELF-EMPLOYED: (Does) he/she have any employees? IF YES: How many?	6.4	

i) (Is) the job ... **READ OUT** ...

... full-time (30 HOURS+)	46.9
or - part-time (10-29 HOURS)?	9.8

Skip to: O.U.O., O.C., E.S., S.E.G., SC/M.NM, SIC, H-G, f), g)

NI   - 46 -

CARD X6

915a) In the last 5 years, have you visited mainland Britain? **IF YES:** Please tell me from this card how often?

	%	Skip to
No, never visited	38.5	
Yes: Once only	17.0	
A few times	34.2	
Many times	9.2	
Lived there	0.8	

b) CARD X6 AGAIN
And in the last 5 years, have you visited the Republic of Ireland? **IF YES:** Please tell me from this card how often?

	%	Skip to
No, never visited	37.4	
Yes: Once only	10.5	
A few times	29.8	
Many times	21.7	
Lived there	0.3	b)

916a) In the last 5 years, have you thought seriously about emigrating from Northern Ireland ... that is, leaving permanently? **IF YES:** How seriously have you thought about it ... **READ OUT** ...

	%	Skip to
YES: ... very seriously,	8.9	
fairly seriously,	10.4	
or - not very seriously?	7.9	
NO: (Never thought about it)	72.0	
(Don't know/Can't say)	0.4	Q.917

IF THOUGHT ABOUT EMIGRATING (CODES 1-3 AT a)
CARD X7
b) Which of these reasons is the <u>main</u> reason why you have thought about emigrating? Please choose the closest reason on the card.
CODE ONE ONLY

	%
Family reasons	3.4
Unemployment	5.3
Fear or violence or crime	8.5
Standard of living	7.3
Health reasons	0.2
Other **(AFTER PROBE)**	1.9

ASK ALL
917a) Generally speaking, do you think of yourself as a unionist, a nationalist or neither?

	%	Skip to
Unionist	38.7	b)
Nationalist	15.4	
Neither	45.6	
(Don't know/Can't say)	0.6	Q.918

IF UNIONIST OR NATIONALIST AT a)
b) Would you call yourself a very strong ... (QUOTE ANSWER AT a) ... fairly strong, or not very strong?

	%
Very strong	9.5
Fairly strong	21.1
Not very strong	23.0
Don't know	0.2

NI   - 45 -

IF MARRIED OR LIVING AS MARRIED AT Q.900a)

911. And what about your spouse or partner: is (he/she) the same religion as you? **PROBE AS NECESSARY:** That is, Protestant or Catholic?

	%	Skip to
Yes	60.2	
No	3.7	
Refused	0.6	

ASK ALL
912. Do you, or does anyone else in your household, own or have the regular use of a car or a van?

	%
Yes	74.4
No	25.2

CARD X5
913. Have you or anyone in this household received any of the benefits on this card during the last five years?
IF YES: Which ones? Any others?
CODE ALL THAT APPLY

	%
Child benefit (family allowance)	51.0
Maternity benefit or allowance	11.1
One-parent benefit	3.9
Family credit (family income supplement)	7.1
State retirement or widow's pension	27.0
State supplementary pension	4.4
Invalidity or disabled pension or benefit	11.8
Attendance/Invalid care/Mobility allowance	4.9
State Sickness or injury benefit	9.2
Unemployment benefit	22.6
Income support (supplementary benefit)	18.9
Rate or rent rebate or allowance	14.2
Other state benefit(s) volunteered (WRITE IN) _____	0.1
NONE	8.3

IF NO: CODE →

914a) Have you ever lived in mainland Britain for more than one year?

	%
Yes	16.0
No	81.8

b) And have you ever lived in the Republic of Ireland for more than one year?

	%
Yes	4.2
No	95.4

- 47 -

NI

ASK ALL

CARD X8

918a) Which of the letters on this card represents the total income of your household from all sources before tax? Please just tell me the letter.

NB: INCLUDES INCOME FROM BENEFITS, SAVINGS, ETC.

ONE CODE IN COLUMN a)

IF RESPONDENT IS IN PAID WORK (CODE 03 AT Q.20, p.7) ASK b). OTHERS GO TO Q.919

b) Which of the letters on this card represents your own gross or total earnings, before deduction of income tax and national insurance? ONE CODE IN COLUMN b)

N.B. On the questionnaire actually used, and on the show card, income bands were identified by a code letter.

	(a) House-hold Income	(b) Own Earn-ings	Skip to
Less than £2,000	1.9	2.0	
£2,000 – £2,999	7.3	2.4	
£3,000 – £3,999	7.0	2.5	
£4,000 – £4,999	9.4	4.8	
£5,000 – £5,999	6.1	5.2	
£6,000 – £6,999	5.0	5.4	
£7,000 – £7,999	7.7	4.5	
£8,000 – £9,999	6.8	5.2	
£10,000 – £11,999	6.9	4.5	
£12,000 – £14,999	6.6	4.5	
£15,000 – £17,999	7.2	1.6	
£18,000 – £19,999	3.5	0.6	
£20,000 – £22,999	4.4	1.1	
£23,000+	8.3	1.3	
Don't know	9.4	0.4	

ASK ALL

919. Do you (or your husband/wife/partner) own any shares quoted on the Stock Exchange, including unit trusts?

Yes	13.9	
No	85.0	

920. Is there a telephone in (your part of) this accommodation?

Yes	82.7	
No	17.1	

INTERVIEWER: THANK RESPONDENT FOR HIS OR HER HELP, AND COMPLETE Q.921-922.

92(a) The self-completion questionnaire: Was it:

... filled in immediately after interview in your presence	50.4	
or ... left behind to be filled in later	40.1	
or ... refused (WHY?) _____	9.5	

b) COMPLETE Q.16 ON CASS ABOUT HOW YOU EXPECT SELF-COMPLETION QUESTIONNAIRE TO BE RETURNED.

- 48 -

NI

922a) In addition to respondent, was anybody else aged 16 or older present during part or all of the interview?

		Skip to
Yes		31.0
No		41.5
N/A		27.4

b) TIME INTERVIEW COMPLETED: WRITE IN: 24 hr. clock [ ]

c) TOTAL DURATION OF INTERVIEW: MEAN: MINUTES [7][5]

d) INTERVIEWER SIGNATURE AND NUMBER

e) DATE OF INTERVIEW:

DAY	MONTH	YEAR
[ ]	[0]	[8][9]

PLEASE MAKE SURE THAT CASS AND CASS FLAP ARE COMPLETELY FILLED IN. DETACH CASS FLAP AND RETURN IN A5 ENVELOPES.

ATTACH REST OF CASS, MAIN QUESTIONNAIRE AND SELF-COMPLETION (IF POSSIBLE) AND RETURN IN A4 ENVELOPE - AS SOON AS POSSIBLE.

Head Office 35 NORTHAMPTON SQUARE, LONDON EC1V 0AX TELEPHONE 01-250 1866 FAX 01-250 1524

Northern Field Office CHIRALZEL HOUSE, GANFORD, DARLINGTON, CO. DURHAM DL1 1EC. TELEPHONE 0235-730888

NORTHERN IRELAND SOCIAL ATTITUDES: 1989
SELF-COMPLETION QUESTIONNAIRE

Spring 1989   P.1005

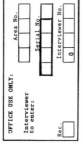

OFFICE USE ONLY:

Interviewer
to enter:

Rec.

Area No.

Serial No.

Interviewer No.

0

To the selected respondent

We hope very much that you will agree to participate in this important study - the sixth in this annual series. The results are published in a book each autumn. The study consists of this self-completion questionnaire and an interview. Some of the questions are also being asked in ten other countries, as part of an international survey.

Completing the questionnaire

The questions inside cover a wide range of subjects, but each one can be answered simply by placing a tick ($\checkmark$) or a number in one or more of the boxes. No special knowledge is required: we are confident that everyone will be able to offer an opinion on all questions. And we want *everyone* to take part, not just those with strong views or particular viewpoints. The questionnaire should not take very long to complete, and we hope you will find it interesting and enjoyable. It should be filled in by the person selected by the interviewer at your address. The answers you give will be treated as confidential and anonymous.

Returning the questionnaire

Your interviewer will arrange with you the most convenient way of returning the questionnaire. If the interviewer has arranged to call back for it, please complete it and keep it safely until then. If not, please complete it and post it back in the pre-paid, addressed envelope *as soon as you possibly can*.

Thank you for your help.

Social and Community Planning Research is an independent social research institute registered as a charitable trust. Its projects are funded by government departments, local authorities, universities and foundations to provide information on social issues in the UK. This survey series has been funded mainly by the Sainsbury Family Charitable Trusts, with contributions also from government departments, other charitable foundations, universities and industry. Please contact us if you require further information.

- 1 -

NI

201. Suppose you could change the way you spend your time, spending more time on some things and less time on others.

Which of the things on the following list would you like to spend more time on, which would you like to spend less time on and which would you like to spend the same amount of time on as now?

PLEASE TICK ONE BOX ON EACH LINE

	Much more time	A bit more time	Same time as now	A bit less time	Much less time	Can't choose/ Doesn't apply
a. Time in a paid job?	10.5	9.3	29.5	12.8	3.9	30.8
b. Time doing household work?	2.7	12.3	37.7	18.2	13.3	12.3
c. Time with your family?	22.0	32.2	39.7	1.4	0.1	2.3
d. Time with your friends?	10.3	39.1	44.1	1.1	0.5	1.8
e. Time in leisure activities?	16.0	39.8	33.3	1.0	0.6	6.0
f. Time to relax?	17.6	34.4	39.4	2.8	1.0	2.1

202. Please tick one box for each statement below to show how much you agree or disagree with it, thinking of work in general.

PLEASE TICK ONE BOX ON EACH LINE

	Strongly agree	Agree	Neither Agree nor disagree	Disagree	Strongly Disagree	Can't choose
a. A job is just a way of earning money - no more.	8.8	24.9	13.0	37.4	10.5	2.5
b. I would enjoy having a paid job even if I did not need the money.	11.1	52.3	9.1	17.4	4.1	3.9
c. Work is a person's most important activity.	16.4	34.0	14.3	25.9	5.3	1.8

Please continue ...

- 2 -

NI

203. Are you the person responsible for doing the general domestic duties - like cleaning, cooking, washing and so on - in your household?

PLEASE TICK ONE BOX ONLY

		OFFICE USE ONLY
Yes, I am **mainly** responsible	46.7	
Yes, I am **equally** responsible with someone else	16.3	
No, someone else is mainly responsible	36.8	

204. Think of two people doing the same kind of work. What do you personally think should be important in deciding how much to pay them?

Looking at the things below, please write '1' in the box next to the thing you think should be most important.

Then write '2' next to the thing you think should be next most important. And '3' next to the thing you think should be third most important. Leave the other boxes blank.

In deciding on pay for two people doing the same kind of work how important should be ...

	Write 1,2 and 3 in THREE boxes: leave the other boxes blank		
	1	2	3
... how long the employee has been with the firm?	7.7	12.7	19.9
... how well the employee does the job?	49.8	17.9	11.3
... the experience of the employee in doing the work?	12.9	38.1	18.1
... the standard rate - giving both employees the same pay?	11.0	5.8	9.9
... the age of the employee?	–	1.2	3.6
... the sex of the employee?	0.4	0.1	1.0
... the employee's family responsibilities?	0.5	0.9	3.5
... the employee's education and formal qualifications?	7.3	9.7	16.4

OR TICK: Can't choose   4.4

NI

- 3 -

205. How much do you agree or disagree with these two statements?

PLEASE TICK ONE BOX ON EACH LINE

	Strongly agree	Agree	Neither agree nor disagree	Disagree	Strongly disagree	Can't choose
a. There will always be conflict between management and workers because they are really on opposite sides.	9.0	35.8	19.8	26.0	3.1	5.1
b. Workers need strong trade unions to protect their interests.	14.4	40.6	18.4	18.8	3.3	3.7

206. From the following list, please tick one box for each item to show how important you personally think it is in a job.

PLEASE TICK ONE BOX ON EACH LINE

How important is ...	Very important	Important	Neither important nor unimportant	Not important	Not important at all	Can't choose
a. ... job security?	67.5	29.6	1.3	0.6	0.1	0.4
b. ... high income?	26.2	57.2	11.0	3.1	0.1	0.8
c. ... good opportunities for advancement?	40.5	49.2	4.9	3.3	0.2	0.9
d. ... a job that leaves a lot of leisure time?	7.0	32.3	28.9	25.8	2.4	1.2
e. ... an interesting job?	46.4	46.6	3.3	1.5	0.1	0.8
f. ... a job that allows someone to work independently?	19.6	44.4	21.7	10.7	0.7	1.5
g. ... a job that allows someone to help other people?	25.0	47.6	19.7	5.3	0.6	0.9
h. ... a job that is useful to society?	28.1	48.1	17.3	3.9	0.6	0.9
i. ... a job with flexible working hours?	15.5	31.3	29.8	18.2	2.6	1.7

OFFICE USE ONLY

Please continue ...

NI

- 4 -

207. Suppose you were unemployed and couldn't find a job. Which of the following problems do you think would be the worst?

Please write '1' in the box next to the worst thing.
Then write '2' beside the next worst thing.
And '3' beside the third worst thing.
Leave the other boxes blank.

Write 1,2 and 3 in THREE boxes: leave the other boxes blank.	1	2	3 (OFFICE USE ONLY)
Lack of contact with people at work	7.6	9.4	13.2
Not enough money	50.6	15.9	7.9
Loss of self-confidence	15.4	21.7	18.0
Loss of respect from friends and acquaintances	1.2	4.9	5.8
Family tensions	5.6	22.5	15.2
Loss of job experience	2.5	5.7	11.4
Not knowing how to fill one's time	3.9	5.5	12.3

OR TICK: Can't choose   6.5

208. Suppose you were working and could choose between different kinds of jobs. Which of the following would you personally choose?

PLEASE TICK ONE BOX ONLY

I would choose ...
... being an employee   44.2
... being self-employed   46.9
Can't choose   8.0

PLEASE TICK ONE BOX ONLY

I would choose ...
... working in a small firm   53.5
... working in a large firm   29.3
Can't choose   16.2

NI

- 5 -

208. (cont'd)

And which of the following would **you personally** choose?

PLEASE TICK ONE BOX ONLY

I would choose ...

... working in a manufacturing industry	28.9
... working in an office, in sales or in service	51.3
Can't choose	18.2

PLEASE TICK ONE BOX ONLY

I would choose ...

... working in a private business	49.7
... working for the government or civil service	33.1
Can't choose	15.5

209. On the whole, do you think it should be or should not be the government's responsibility to ...

PLEASE TICK ONE BOX ON EACH LINE

	Definitely should be	Probably should be	Probably should not be	Definitely should not be	Can't choose
a. ... provide a job for everyone who wants one?	36.1	39.9	12.4	6.2	4.0
b. ... provide a decent standard of living for the unemployed?	48.4	36.0	7.8	2.6	3.5

210. Do you usually work 10 hours or more a week for pay in your (main) job?

PLEASE TICK ONE BOX ONLY

Yes, I usually work 10 hours or more a week in my (main) job	48.3 → GO TO Q.13, PAGE 7
No, I usually work less than 10 hours a week in my (main) job	1.4 ⎫ PLEASE ANSWER Q.11, PAGE 6
No, I don't work for pay at the moment	50.2 ⎭

Please continue ...

NI

- 6 -

N=433

211. Would you like to have a paid job now?

PLEASE TICK ONE BOX ONLY

Yes, I would like a full-time job now (30 hours or more per week)	22.0 ⎫
Yes, I would like a part-time job now (10-29 hours per week)	15.4 ⎬ PLEASE ANSWER Q.12 BELOW
Yes, I would like a job with less than 10 hours a week now	7.4 ⎭
No, I would not like to have a paid job now	52.9 → GO TO Q.22 PAGE 12

212. If you were looking actively, how easy or difficult do you think it would be for you to find an acceptable job?

PLEASE TICK ONE BOX ONLY

N=181

Very easy	1.9
Fairly easy	7.7
Neither easy nor difficult	6.9 ⎫ PLEASE GO TO Q.22 PAGE 12
Fairly difficult	34.1 ⎬
Very difficult	47.4 ⎭
Can't choose	1.3

NI

- 7 -

PLEASE ANSWER Q.13 - Q.21 ABOUT YOUR MAIN JOB.

N=345
Qs.213-21

213. Which of the following statements best describes your feelings about your job?

PLEASE TICK ONE BOX ONLY

In my job ...

... I only work as hard as I have to	7.8
... I work hard, but not so that it interferes with the rest of my life	30.2
... I make a point of doing the best work I can, even if it sometimes does interfere with the rest of my life	58.1
Can't choose	2.0

214. Think of the number of hours you work, and the money you earn in your main job, including any regular overtime.

If you had only one of these three choices which of the following would you prefer?

PLEASE TICK ONE BOX ONLY

Work **longer** hours and earn **more money**	26.7
Work the **same** number of hours and earn the **same money**	61.8
Work **fewer** hours and earn **less money**	5.2
Can't choose	4.7

Please continue ...

NI

- 8 -

215. Think of two people doing the same kind of work in your place of work. What do you personally think is important in deciding how much to pay them?

Looking at the things below, please write '1' in the box next to the thing you think is most important at your place of work.

Then write '2' next to the thing you think is next most important. And '3' next to the thing you think is third most important. Leave the other boxes blank.

Write 1, 2 and 3 in THREE boxes. leave the other boxes blank

At your workplace, in deciding on pay for two people doing the same **kind of work**, how important is ....

	1	2	3
... how long the employee has been with the firm?	10.1	10.2	20.1
... how well the employee does the job?	48.5	23.2	12.6
... the experience of the employee in doing the work?	16.9	38.2	20.9
... the standard rate - giving both employees the same pay?	11.2	5.9	11.7
... the age of the employee?	0.3	2.0	3.4
... the sex of the employee?	-	-	1.3
... the employee's family responsibilities?	0.4	1.0	3.4
... the employee's education and formal qualifications?	4.6	9.8	14.2

OR TICK:

Can't choose   1.5

NI

- 9 -

216. For each of these statements about your (main) job, please tick one box to show how much you agree or disagree that it applies to your job.

PLEASE TICK ONE BOX ON EACH LINE

	Strongly agree	Agree	Neither agree nor disagree	Disagree	Strongly disagree	Can't choose
a. My job is secure	19.7	42.5	12.6	17.7	4.8	1.1
b. My income is high	5.2	12.6	27.7	39.9	12.8	-
c. My opportunities for advancement are high	4.7	16.3	22.0	39.3	14.9	1.0
d. My job leaves a lot of leisure time	2.0	24.0	25.6	35.9	10.2	0.8
e. My job is interesting	21.2	54.1	12.7	7.4	2.9	-
f. I can work independently	21.9	51.4	11.2	11.1	1.5	0.4
g. In my job I can help other people	24.8	50.8	12.1	9.0	1.7	-
h. My job is useful to society	25.8	45.8	16.2	9.0	0.8	0.5
i. My job has flexible working hours	12.6	23.0	12.7	34.2	15.0	0.8

Please continue ...

NI

- 10 -

217. Now some more questions about your working conditions.

Please tick one box for each item below to show how often it applies to your work.

PLEASE TICK ONE BOX ON EACH LINE

How often ...	Always	Often	Sometimes	Hardly ever	Never	Can't choose
a. ... do you come home from work exhausted?	6.7	32.6	44.0	10.8	4.2	0.3
b. ... do you have to do hard physical work?	11.6	17.0	21.0	21.4	27.1	0.3
c. ... do you find your work stressful?	8.7	18.4	47.6	12.1	10.9	0.3
d. ... are you bored at work?	0.9	5.9	26.5	32.1	33.1	0.3
e. ... do you work in dangerous conditions?	4.7	5.5	17.7	17.8	51.7	1.0
f. ... do you work in unhealthy conditions?	4.3	4.3	21.4	20.4	47.7	0.3
g. ... do you work in physically unpleasant conditions?	4.1	7.3	19.0	18.4	49.2	0.5

218. And which of the following statements about your work is most true?

PLEASE TICK ONE BOX ONLY

My job allows me to design or plan *most* of my daily work   36.5

My job allows me to design or plan *parts* of my daily work   35.9

My job *does not really* allow me to design or plan my daily work   26.0

NI

- 11 -

219. If you lost your job for any reason, and were looking actively for another one, how easy or difficult do you think it would be for you to find an acceptable job?

PLEASE TICK ONE BOX ONLY

Very easy	2.9
Fairly easy	25.2
Neither easy nor difficult	13.5
Fairly difficult	33.5
Very difficult	22.1
Can't choose	1.4

220. In general, how would you describe relations at your workplace ...

PLEASE TICK ONE BOX ON EACH LINE

	Very good	Quite good	Neither good nor bad	Quite bad	Very bad	Can't choose
a. ... between management and employees?	23.2	42.5	16.5	8.3	3.8	2.3
b. ... between workmates/ colleagues?	39.5	41.6	7.9	0.9	0.5	2.7

221. How satisfied are you in your (main) job?
PLEASE TICK ONE BOX ONLY

Completely satisfied	15.5
Very satisfied	24.8
Fairly satisfied	46.1
Neither satisfied nor dissatisfied	5.3
Fairly dissatisfied	5.2
Very dissatisfied	1.3
Completely dissatisfied	0.4
Can't choose	0.4

Please continue ...

NI

- 12 -

N=780

Qs.222-40

Now for some questions on different subjects.

222. Here are a number of circumstances in which a woman might consider an abortion. Please say whether or not you think the law should allow an abortion in each case.

PLEASE TICK ONE BOX ON EACH LINE

	Should abortion be allowed by law?		
	Yes	No	Don't know
The woman decides on her own she does not wish to have the child	28.7	67.4	0.8
The couple agree they do not wish to have the child	30.0	65.3	0.6
The woman is not married and does not wish to marry the man	27.9	67.7	0.9
The couple cannot afford any more children	24.4	70.3	0.9
There is a strong chance of a defect in the baby	60.5	34.6	1.5
The woman's health is seriously endangered by the pregnancy	76.0	18.7	1.9
The woman became pregnant as a result of rape	70.2	24.1	2.2

223. Suppose a married couple want to have their own child, but cannot have one. Should the law allow or not allow them to use each of the methods below? Please assume in each case that it is the only method open to them on medical advice.

PLEASE TICK ONE BOX ON EACH LINE

	It should be		
	Allowed by law	Not allowed by law	Don't know
They try to have a child by **artificial insemination**, using the **husband** as donor	77.2	17.2	2.9
They try to have a child by **artificial insemination**, using an **anonymous** donor	37.0	55.2	3.2
They try to have a child by having their own 'test-tube' embryo implanted	71.0	22.4	3.5
They find a 'surrogate' mother who agrees, **without payment**, to bear a child for them (by artificial insemination, using the husband as donor)	25.5	67.6	2.5
They find a 'surrogate' mother who is **paid** to bear a child for them (by artificial insemination, using the husband as donor)	13.6	79.5	2.5

OFFICE USE ONLY

NI

- 13 -

224. Which of these statements comes closest to your views on the availability of pornographic magazines and films?

PLEASE TICK ONE BOX

They should be banned altogether	54.8
They should be available in special adult shops but not displayed to the public	31.8
They should be available in special adult shops with public display permitted	6.7
They should be available in any shop for sale to adults only	4.9
They should be available in any shop for sale to anyone	0.3

225.a) Suppose a person has a painful incurable disease. Do you think that doctors should be allowed by law to end the patient's life if the patient requests it?

PLEASE TICK ONE BOX

Yes	55.4
No	42.6

b) And if a person is not incurably sick but simply tired of living, should doctors be allowed by law to end that person's life if he or she requests it?

PLEASE TICK ONE BOX

Yes	7.5
No	91.1

226. Are you in favour of or against the death penalty for ...

PLEASE TICK ONE BOX ON EACH LINE

	In favour	Against	Don't know
... murder in the course of a terrorist act?	57.4	39.0	1.7
... murder of a police officer?	55.6	39.5	2.1
... other murders?	51.6	43.7	2.2

Please continue ...

NI

- 14 -

227. Please tick one box for each statement, to show how much you agree or disagree with it.

PLEASE TICK ONE BOX ON EACH LINE

	Agree strongly	Just agree	Neither agree nor disagree	Just disagree	Disagree strongly
a. Healthy food doesn't usually taste as nice as other food	10.4	25.1	28.4	21.7	13.0
b. Food that is good for you is usually more expensive	21.3	33.7	16.4	19.9	7.5
c. Food that is good for you generally takes too long to prepare	6.3	17.3	27.7	32.7	14.7
d. It is hard to find food that is good for you in supermarkets	4.3	14.6	24.6	38.2	17.2
e. Mothers would eat healthier food if the rest of their families would let them	8.3	21.0	28.6	27.4	13.0
f. As long as you take enough exercise you can eat whatever foods you want	9.1	23.5	13.9	33.7	18.7
g. If heart disease is in your family, there is little you can do to reduce your chances of getting it	4.5	16.4	13.1	34.1	30.5
h. The experts contradict each other over what makes a healthy diet	26.1	39.8	15.8	13.4	3.0
i. People worry too much about their weight	19.1	43.9	18.0	13.6	4.3
j. Good health is just a matter of good luck	4.4	13.4	15.7	30.2	35.0
k. A proper meal should include meat and vegetables	34.2	31.5	14.8	14.3	4.4

228. How worried are you about the sorts of food you eat?

PLEASE TICK ONE BOX

Very worried	3.8
Fairly worried	24.2
Not particularly worried	48.2
Not worried at all	22.0

OFFICE USE ONLY

15

NI

229. Which one of these statements best describes how you feel about the sorts of food you eat nowadays?

PLEASE TICK ONE BOX

I have **never** felt any need to change what I eat	26.9
I have **already** changed as much as I am going to	33.6
I **ought** to change more but probably **won't**	32.9
I will **probably** be changing soon	5.4

230. Please tick one box for each statement to show how much you agree or disagree with it.

PLEASE TICK ONE BOX
ON EACH LINE

	Agree strongly	Agree	Neither agree nor disagree	Dis- agree	Disagree strongly
A. Social workers should put the child's interests first even if it means taking a child away from its natural parents.	27.8	44.4	15.4	8.5	2.5
B. Social workers have too much power to interfere with people's lives.	7.6	23.9	34.5	29.0	3.3
C. The welfare state makes people nowadays less willing to look after themselves.	8.1	32.9	25.6	27.1	4.7
D. People receiving social security are made to feel like second class citizens.	15.1	39.6	19.1	20.9	3.8
E. The welfare state encourages people to stop helping each other.	6.6	26.7	26.7	32.9	5.8
F. Doctors should be allowed to give contraceptive advice and supplies to young people under 16 without having to inform parents.	7.6	16.3	13.0	33.7	28.3

Please continue ...

OFFICE USE ONLY

16

NI

231. Please tick one box for each statement below to show how much you agree or disagree with it.

PLEASE TICK ONE BOX
ON EACH LINE

	Agree strongly	Agree	Neither agree nor disagree	Dis- agree	Disagree strongly
a. Government should redistribute income from the better-off to those who are less well off.	18.5	37.0	18.8	20.7	3.3
b. Big business benefits owners at the expense of workers.	13.8	42.1	20.0	19.6	2.3
c. Ordinary working people do not get their fair share of the nation's wealth.	20.2	48.3	16.2	12.6	1.4
d. There is one law for the rich and one for the poor.	27.1	38.2	16.3	15.2	1.8
e. Management will always try to get the better of employees if it gets the chance.	17.9	37.7	21.5	20.0	1.2
f. Young people today don't have enough respect for traditional British values.	17.1	43.3	26.9	10.5	0.6
g. People who break the law should be given stiffer sentences.	32.8	44.0	17.0	3.2	1.2
h. People should be allowed to organise public meetings to protest against the government.	13.5	41.5	27.7	13.4	2.3
i. For some crimes, the death penalty is the most appropriate sentence.	32.1	26.9	8.5	16.5	14.6
j. People should be allowed to publish leaflets to protest against the government.	13.8	40.8	30.6	11.5	1.9

OFFICE USE ONLY

- 17 -

NI

OFFICE USE ONLY

PLEASE TICK ONE BOX FOR EACH STATEMENT

	Agree strongly	Agree	Neither agree nor disagree	Disagree	Disagree strongly
k. Schools should teach children to obey authority.	39.0	49.7	6.4	3.7	-
l. People should be allowed to organise protest marches and demonstrations.	8.5	40.3	27.8	18.2	3.6
m. The law should always be obeyed, even if a particular law is wrong.	9.1	30.2	24.3	29.9	4.6
n. Censorship of films and magazines is necessary to uphold moral standards.	29.2	43.9	14.6	9.3	1.7
o. The government should spend more money on welfare benefits for the poor, even if it leads to higher taxes.	23.1	44.1	19.6	11.3	0.7
p. Around here, most unemployed people could find a job if they really wanted one.	7.3	28.0	18.5	31.5	13.6
q. Many people who get social security don't really deserve any help.	5.1	17.3	21.8	39.5	14.6
r. Most people on the dole are fiddling in one way of another.	8.8	24.8	29.0	26.4	9.7
s. If welfare benefits weren't so generous people would learn to stand on their own two feet.	7.0	25.4	21.0	29.4	16.0

- 18 -

NI

OFFICE USE ONLY

232. Some people think that better relations between Protestants and Catholics in Northern Ireland will only come about through more mixing of the two communities. Others think that better relations will only come about through more separation. Which comes closest to your views ...

PLEASE TICK ONE BOX

Better relations will come about through more mixing 90.0

Better relations will come about through more separation 6.4

Don't know 1.4

233. And are you in favour of more mixing or more separation in ...

PLEASE TICK ONE BOX ON EACH LINE

	Much more mixing	Bit more mixing	Keep things as they are	Bit more separation	Much more separation
a. ... primary schools?	39.6	29.4	28.3	0.9	0.6
b. ... secondary and grammar schools?	40.0	33.1	23.9	1.2	0.6
c. ... where people live?	36.2	37.8	22.3	1.2	0.9
d. ... where people work?	41.3	38.2	17.8	1.2	0.2
e. ... people's leisure or sports activities?	47.1	32.5	18.2	0.5	0.4
f. ... people's marriages?	21.3	24.4	42.1	3.0	6.6

NI

- 19 -

234. People feel closer to some groups than to others. For you personally, how close would you say you feel towards ...

PLEASE TICK ONE BOX ON EACH LINE

	Very close	Fairly close	A little close	Not very close	Not at all close
a. People born in the same area as you	14.7	42.9	21.0	13.8	6.4
b. People who have the same social class background as yours	13.2	52.2	22.8	7.5	2.9
c. People who have the same religious background as yours	16.5	47.7	20.2	9.6	4.6
d. People of the same race as you	15.9	48.3	21.0	8.5	4.2
e. People who live in the same area as you do now	14.2	44.3	26.0	10.6	3.6
f. People who have the same political beliefs as you	11.4	38.7	25.3	14.3	8.0

235. Now a few questions about the disease called AIDS.

Please tick one box to show which is closest to your views about the following statement:

Within five years AIDS will cause more deaths in Britain than any other single disease.

PLEASE TICK ONE BOX

It is highly exaggerated	11.8
It is slightly exaggerated	24.1
It is more or less true	61.3

NI

- 20 -

236. Please tick one box for each statement to show how much you agree or disagree with it.

PLEASE TICK ONE BOX ON EACH LINE

	Agree strongly	Agree	Neither agree nor disagree	Disagree	Disagree strongly
a. Most people with AIDS have only themselves to blame	20.7	35.6	17.6	21.3	3.8
b. The National Health Service should spend more of its resources on giving better care to people dying from AIDS	9.2	48.2	26.8	12.7	2.0
c. Official warnings about AIDS should say that some sexual practices are morally wrong	34.4	38.6	13.7	10.1	2.1
d. Within the next five years doctors will discover a vaccine against AIDS	4.4	27.6	46.9	15.9	3.7
e. AIDS is a way of punishing the world for its decline in moral standards	14.5	25.9	23.6	21.3	13.3

237. As one way of getting to know how AIDS is spreading, it has been suggested that hospitals should be allowed to test any patient's blood (that has been taken for other reasons) to see whether it contains the virus that causes AIDS.

Do you agree or disagree with this suggestion?

PLEASE TICK ONE BOX

Agree strongly	40.5
Agree	40.5
Neither agree nor disagree	9.4
Disagree	6.7
Disagree strongly	1.8

OFFICE USE ONLY

- 21 -

             OFFICE
             USE
             ONLY

NI

238. Thinking of patients whose blood has been tested for the AIDS virus without their knowledge - should they ...

PLEASE TICK ONE BOX

Not be told the test has been carried out	5.4
Be told about the test, but __not__ be told the result	2.0
Be told about the test, __and__ have the choice of __knowing__ or not __knowing__ the result	34.9
Be told about the test, __and__ be told the result	55.8

239. As far as you know, have you ever met anyone who was confirmed as having the virus that causes AIDS?

PLEASE TICK ONE BOX

Yes	2.7
No	96.9

240.a) To help us plan better in future, please tell us about how long it took you to complete this questionnaire?

PLEASE TICK ONE BOX

Less than 15 minutes	10.3
Between 15 and 20 minutes	26.4
Between 20 and 30 minutes	35.0
Between 30 and 45 minutes	16.7
Between 45 and 60 minutes	6.6
Over one hour	4.3

b) And on what date did you fill in the questionnaire?

PLEASE WRITE IN

DATE	MONTH	'89
		YEAR

THANK YOU VERY MUCH FOR YOUR HELP!

Please keep the completed questionnaire for the interviewer if he or she has arranged to call for it. Otherwise, please post it as soon as __possible__ in the pre-paid addressed envelope provided.

Subject Index